Constructive Conflicts

Constructive Conflicts

From Escalation to Resolution

Louis Kriesberg

ROWMAN & LITTLEFIELD PUBLISHERS, INC.
Lanham • Boulder • New York • Oxford

ROWMAN & LITTLEFIELD PUBLISHERS, INC.

Published in the United States of America
by Rowman & Littlefield Publishers, Inc.
4720 Boston Way, Lanham, Maryland 20706

12 Hid's Copse Road
Cumnor Hill, Oxford OX2 9JJ, England

British Library Cataloguing in Publication Information Available

Library of Congress Cataloging-in-Publication Data

Kriesberg, Louis.
    Constructive conflicts : from escalation to resolution / Louis
Kriesberg.
        p.   cm.
    Includes bibliographical references and index.
    ISBN 0-8476-8891-7 (cloth : alk. paper). — ISBN 0-8476-8892-5
(pbk. : alk. paper)
    1. Social conflict.   2. Conflict management.   I. Title.
HM136.K757   1998
303.6—dc21   98-14692
                                                                    CIP

ISBN 0–8476–8891–7 (cloth : alk. paper)
ISBN 0–8476–8892–5 (pbk. : alk. paper)

Printed in the United States of America

♾ ™ The paper used in this publication meets the minimum requirements of
American National Standard for Information Sciences—Permanence of Paper for
Printed Library Materials, ANSI Z39.48-1984.

For my grandchildren and their generation

Contents

Figures and Tables

Figures

Tables

Preface and Acknowledgments

L
ike other persons, I look around me with abhorrence and dismay at the brutality of much human conduct, including oppressive domination and destructive conflicts. I am convinced that such conduct is not inherent in the human condition and that with experience, reflection, and creativity we can reduce it. Consequently, two related considerations motivated my writing this book. First, I wanted to develop an empirically grounded understanding of how people prevent or stop destructive conflicts but instead wage relatively constructive conflicts. This consideration arises from observing that many potentially destructive struggles never happen and even when they do, many become transformed and even resolved so that they do not recur. Furthermore, recognizing the inevitability and at times the necessity of struggle if injustices are to be overcome, I believe that more knowledge is needed about how conflicts can be pursued constructively. I want to improve people's understanding so that they can wage their struggles more productively.

Second, I wanted to provide a close linkage between theory/research about social conflicts and the actual practice of problem-solving conflict resolution. This consideration arises from observing the rapid expansion in the practice of problem-solving conflict resolution and in the related fields of theory. Many of these developments are occurring without adequate linkages, persons working in one area often are unfamiliar with what is happening in other domains. In particular, theories about conflict resolution often are congruent neither with actual practice nor with analytic theories about social conflicts. Consequently, I have tried to provide a comprehensive, realistic approach to conflict resolution theory and actual practice.

This book is based on my own studies and my participation in various social conflicts, as well as the work of innumerable other analysts and activists. In this book, I have used elements of the basic framework developed in my *Sociology of Social Conflicts* (1973) and in the revised edition, *Social Conflicts*

(1982), and findings from my research pertaining to the cold war and the conflicts in the Middle East, analyzed in *International Conflict Resolution* (1992). But this is a different kind of book than my earlier writings. I have tried to synthesize a wide range of materials about how conflicts are waged relatively constructively as well as destructively. The presentation provides a coherent perspective, but is not dogmatic; and hopefully, it will stimulate others to reflect on the issues raised.

Several spheres of my life have contributed to developing the ideas and evidence drawn upon in this book, and I note five of them. My engagement in the Program on the Analysis and Resolution of Conflicts (PARC), wonderfully supported by the William and Flora Hewlett Foundation, has been a thought-provoking experience, expanding my understanding of conflict resolution. My experience in training and consulting about conflict resolution and peace studies and my travel and residence in many countries have been sources of much pertinent information and insight. In my teaching, I have learned a great deal from the many graduate students who brought me reports of places and of experiences that enriched my understanding and whose questions and suggestions have made my work more relevant, more current, and clearer than it otherwise would be. Since its founding in 1981, I have been engaged in the Syracuse Area Middle-East Dialogue group (SAMED), consisting, in equal numbers, of members of the Jewish, Palestinian, and "other" communities; our common efforts have given me insights about the bonds of ethnicity, friendship, humanity, and reconciliation. Finally, I have learned much about the role of emotions in conflict and ways of fighting constructively from my many years of participation in re-evaluation counseling, a peer counseling organization.

Necessarily, in writing a book of this scope, based on many years of working on the matters discussed here, I am indebted to numerous people. I wish to acknowledge at least some of them now. First, I want to thank colleagues in the academic worlds of sociology, peace studies, and conflict resolution and in the worlds of partisan struggles and of intervention for their support, encouragement, and prodding. They include Elise Boulding, Raymond Cohen, Irwin Deutscher, William Gamson, Johan Galtung, Juan Gutiérrez, James Laue, John Paul Lederach, Hendrik van der Merwe, Harold Saunders, Gene Sharp, and Charles V. Willie. Second, I appreciate my many associates in the conflict resolution and peace studies communities and in the network of centers supported by the Hewlett Foundation for their encouragement and constructive disagreements. In addition to many persons previously mentioned, they include Ronald Fisher, Herbert Kelman, Deborah Kolb, Jeffrey Z. Rubin, and Carolyn M. Stephenson. Third, I want to express my profound appreciation to my colleagues in the Program on the Analysis and Resolution of Conflicts (PARC) who have helped fashion an exciting and stimulating environment; they include John Agnew, Neil Katz, John D. Nagle, Marjorie L. DeVault, Terrell A. Northrup, Richard E. Ratcliff, and Robert A. Rubinstein.

I owe a special debt of gratitude to those who read the book manuscript and provided editing and substantive help. They include the participants in my graduate seminars who read earlier versions of the book and made helpful comments. My brother Irving Kriesberg, who has been a tireless editor of my writing for decades, again helped greatly. I also appreciate the comments and suggestions of Larry Dunn, Christopher R. Mitchell, Maurice Richter, Marc Ross, and Stuart J.Thorson.

I appreciate Lois Ablin Kriesberg, who not only gave good counsel at several critical points in this book's production, but helped keep me in touch with peoples' everyday realities and their relationship to the book. Finally, I want to thank Dean Birkenkamp and the others who worked on this book at Rowman & Littlefield; Dean gave me the thoughtful collaborative support that I always hoped an editor would provide.

1

Varieties and Stages of Conflicts

Although social conflicts are a necessary part of social life, they need not be waged destructively. This book examines struggles that are waged constructively as well as those that are conducted violently and with great mutual loss. If people understand why some struggles do not deteriorate into mutual destructiveness while others do, they can develop ways to reduce the harm and increase the benefit of social conflicts.

People need to hear the stories of struggles that have avoided extreme contention and violence, had limited destructive episodes, and resulted in considerable mutual benefit. These experiences hold lessons in mitigating the worst hazards of conflicts. The largely nonviolent struggles for India's independence from Great Britain, for American women's suffrage, and for U.S. trade unions' right to organize and bargain collectively demonstrated in their day the effectiveness of protest marches and nonviolent resistance. Those efforts also demonstrated the way such struggles could transform the relations between adversaries so that the outcomes were generally viewed as beneficial and just.[1] They provided models for the people waging the civil rights struggle in the American South in the 1960s. Participants in the people's movements of the 1980s in Eastern Europe, Central America, and the Philippines drew inspiration and lessons from the nonviolent struggles of earlier generations.[2]

This book examines a variety of conflicts, presenting their similarities and differences. The ultimate goal is to provide a tool for developing social conflict theory that can effectively guide policy. Public debate of policy abounds with comparisons among conflicts as people argue for or against a particular course of action. For example, before the U.S. government leaders decided to undertake military action in January 1991 to force the Iraqi army's withdrawal from Kuwait, opponents of intervention framed their arguments in terms of the United States' involvement in the war in Vietnam; advocates of interven-

1

tion invoked the experience of the struggle against Hitler. Too often, however, such simplistic comparisons are misleading and harmful.[3] Thoughtful analysis is thus important to understand struggles and to pursue policies that reduce their harm.

Definitions

The use of the term *social conflicts* in this book presumes that there is such a general phenomenon. The term as defined here encompasses a wide range of situations: *a social conflict exists when two or more persons or groups manifest the belief that they have incompatible objectives.* Nearly every word in that definition needs to be explained. *Social* indicates that we are concerned with conflicts among interacting people. *Two or more* means that the persons involved in a conflict view each other as adversaries in trying to achieve their goals. *Person or group* includes individuals and organizations who claim to represent larger collectivities such as governments, classes, or ethnic communities as well as individuals or organizations not making such claims. *Manifest* means that significant members of at least one of the contending groups exhibits the belief that some of its goals are incompatible with those of another party; this is indicated by attacking the other party, by proclaiming that an adversary must change, or by arousing and mobilizing other members of the group for the struggle. Having *incompatible objectives* means that members of one or more of the parties in a relationship think that the realization of some of their goals is thwarted by another party and therefore requires that party to change in ways it resists.

The word *belief* is used in the definition because how the adversaries view a situation is crucial. The circumstances that some observers might regard as putting people in a competitive or exploitative relationship do not in themselves constitute a conflict. Competition may or may not involve awareness, while conflict does. As Park and Burgess wrote in 1924: "Conflict is always conscious. Indeed it evokes the deepest emotions and strongest passions and enlists the greatest concentration of attention and of effort. Both competition and conflict are forms of struggle. Competition, however, is continuous and impersonal. Conflict is intermittent and personal."[4]

Competing parties strive to attain the same values, whereas conflicting parties may differ about values, as when one group tries to impose its values on another. In addition, competing actors generally strive for what they want, not directly from each other, but from other parties in their environment. Unemployed workers in a city, for example, may be competing for jobs with little attention to each other. But some of the workers, due to their self-identification by gender or ethnicity, may believe that they are in a struggle with persons of other identities.

A relationship that an observer assesses as conflicting, that is not so regarded by the parties involved, does not constitute a conflict by this definition. Some analysts do consider certain relationships as conflicting, even if the partisans are not aware of it. Dahrendorf, for example, asserts that in an imperatively coordinated organization, such as a factory, persons without power are in a conflict relationship with those who have power.[5] If the people involved are not aware of the conflict, some analysts say that they have "false consciousness," using Karl Marx's phrase.[6] Situations that such theorists regard as essentially conflicting may well have a tendency to become manifest social conflicts. In this analysis, those situations are referred to as objective, latent, underlying, or potential conflicts.

Note that this definition does not refer to the means by which the adversaries pursue their objectives. Many observers and partisans include efforts to injure, threaten, or otherwise coerce an opponent as an essential defining characteristic of a conflict.[7] Struggles involving violence and other forms of coercion are given great attention here, but I also want to draw attention to noncoercive means and constructive ways of fighting.

Noncoercive methods include efforts at persuasion and the use of positive sanctions. Using persuasion, one party may try to convince its adversary to agree to its preferences, arguing that to do so would be in the adversary's own best interests or would be consistent with the adversary's values. Using positive sanctions, one party may offer material or symbolic compensation or benefits in exchange for obtaining what it wants. In reality, conflicts are waged using varying combinations of coercion, persuasion, and positive sanctions.

In common speech and in academic analysis, social conflict sometimes means parties having incompatible positions, sometimes it refers to parties thinking they have incompatible goals, sometimes it means parties trying to coerce each other, and other times it means parties using deadly violence against each other. The definition adopted here allows us to consider the great variety of ways struggles are conducted. Although social conflicts have been defined as a kind of situation, we are not concerned with classifying various situations as a conflict or a nonconflict. Rather, we are interested in the course of changes in that situation. We focus on the interaction sequence in which adversaries contend with each other. This may be an hour's quarrel, a month-long confrontation, a year-long war, or decades of feuding. The course of such contentious interactions, often referred to as struggles, provides the organizing structure for this book, as we examine the bases, emergence, escalation, de-escalation, and ending of particular struggles. Furthermore, it is important to recognize that a conflict is typically an aspect of a relationship between parties. While adversaries are fighting, they may also be engaged in noncontentious and even cooperative interactions.

The perspective used in this analysis gives great importance to the way adversaries themselves regard their relationship. People act in accord with their definition of the situation, derived from the customary definitions used by their group. Adversaries develop their own definition of a social conflict as they interact with each other and with other groups.[8] This does not mean that the adversaries wholly agree on the nature of the conflict in which they are engaged. Their disagreements about that are often part of the struggle.

Consider the conflict in and about Palestine when it was under British mandate after the end of the First World War until after the end of the Second. Some Arabs and some Jews living there saw considerable incompatibility and even threat from the other to their vital interests. For some Arabs, considering themselves Palestinians, the increasing number of Jews settling in the area threatened their eventual control of what they regarded as their land. For some Jews, their right to settle in their ancient land was God given and threatened by the opposition of Arabs.

Many Arabs and Jews, however, also saw some benefit, or at least no incompatibility if members of each party pursued their objectives in that land. But in doing so, they sometimes denied the essential claims of the other. Some Jews, in Europe and the United States, regarded the land as sparsely occupied by Arabs and in any case the Arab world was large and could easily accommodate all Arabs. Some Arabs, in Palestine and elsewhere in the Arab world, asserted that they had no quarrel with Jews, who could live anywhere in the world, but objected to Zionists who sought to establish a Jewish state in Palestine.[9] Such disagreements and mutual fears are elements in many conflicts.

This book is primarily about constructive and destructive ways of conducting diverse kinds of conflicts: class-based revolutions, civil rights struggles, community disputes about garbage disposal, border wars, marital fights, communal confrontations, and labor-management struggles. It is necessary to analyze the sources of a specific conflict and its processes of escalation, de-escalation, and settlement in order to consider what alternatives might be pursued to minimize the unwanted aspects of the conflict and to maximize what is desired. Those concerns help frame the questions analysts and partisans seek to answer. Clearly, the study of conflicts cannot be separated from a consideration of what people feel about them and what they want to accomplish.

Questions about Social Conflicts

An infinity of questions might be asked about social conflicts. The mass media generally direct attention at fights and threats of violence. While amicable relations may be good for a human interest story, they are otherwise considered boring. Popular interest, political attention, and scholarly analysis all tend to focus on struggles waged coercively and especially violently. The questions frequently asked, with barely concealed pleasurable excitement, about people engaged in such conflicts include, why are they killing each other? Why are they behaving so brutally?

Many other analytic questions are also posed by scholars, journalists, political leaders, and partisans engaged in struggles. They include, why did a specific conflict erupt when it did? How come it escalated as it did? What brought the adversaries to negotiate an agreement? What enabled one side to win? Why has a terminating agreement endured? Scholars also often try to explain variations in the incidence of different kinds of conflicts, the means used in waging them, or their consequences.

Additional questions arise from policy concerns. What partisans or observers want to know about struggles differs with their values, and with their vested interest in specific fights. Some persons are concerned with the harm done by conflicts. They abhor violence or are concerned about the disruption in relations that a conflict causes. Viewing conflicts negatively, they want to know how they can be prevented, contained, and stopped. Some people regard certain conflicts negatively because they threaten the status quo, the existing conditions, which they like. They ask, what can be done to avert a conflict from erupting, to nip it in the bud, or to suppress it, as can be seen in the literature on counterinsurgency strategies.[10]

Other persons are concerned about injustice, repression, or the denial of the truths they feel to be vital. They view struggles to correct those terrible conditions as moral and desirable. Regarding such struggles positively, they want to know how people can be mobilized to fight the good fight, and to triumph.

Diverse questions are asked about a struggle because the questions arise from different interests and values and not from the inherent nature of a conflict. People who share a set of questions develop a shared way of answering them and of thinking about conflict. Particular conflicts often become models for the way a group thinks about many other conflicts. For example, the U.S. military doctrine until the early 1900s was a kind of frontier or punitive expedition doctrine. Its three basic tenets were first, that war was inevitable, second, that war needed no ideological justification, and third, that war was, as it was for the army's "pacification of the Indians," essentially to facilitate political incorporation or to punish the lawless.[11]

People in similar social and historical settings share certain concerns and assume that these are natural. This is true for analysts of conflicts as well as for partisans in conflicts. Consider the shifting evaluations of community strife. During the 1950s in the United States, many persons concerned about community conflicts felt them to be harmful and often based on unrealistic grounds. The typical conflict seemed to be attacks from the political right upon members of the moderate or liberal establishments who were advocates of innovation in the public schools or were trying to introduce fluoridation into the cities' water systems.[12]

In the 1960s, community conflicts more often arose from attempts of the poor and of Blacks to gain increased influence in decision making.[13] Partisans and observers who were unsympathetic to those making the attacks in the 1950s, were sympathetic to those doing so in the 1960s and believed them to be soundly based on realistic differences in interest.

In the 1970s and 1980s, a backlash to the challenging movements of the 1960s emerged, and new issues affecting the community as a whole, such as environmental degradation, became salient. Sympathy to the interests and views of all the contending parties in such conflicts became more widespread, contributing to and supported by the growth of the conflict resolution movement.

In the 1990s, many conflicts linked to national and transnational movements have become more ideological, intense, and polarized, as in the case of abortion rights in the United States and in the cases of ethnic, religious, and other communal conflicts in many parts of the world. The implications of these developments for the study of conflict analysis and resolution are still not clear. There are signs that one response of observers, intervenors, and analysts is to be more critical of those they regard as extremists, who try to mobilize followers by appealing to feelings of hostility; they also tend to give increased credence to the use of state power, civic institutions, or accommodationist social movements to keep extremists in check.

Evaluations of conflicts often vary with the perspective taken by the observers and analysts. Frequently, those taking the perspective of the larger system within which adversaries interact regard conflicts as disruptive to the system. Those taking the perspective of an adversary tend to view the struggle as desirable to advance justice, or at least necessary, if only to defend themselves against aggression by an opponent.

Even those taking a system perspective need not regard conflicts as harmful.[14] Many persons believe that conflict, if its management is properly institutionalized, is an effective means for discovering truth, for attaining justice, and for contributing to the long-run benefit of a society or an organization. The American judicial system, for example, is based upon the adversary principle. The contest between lawyers for the prosecution and lawyers for the defense, arguing within a court setting, is regarded as the best way of achieving justice. Similarly, for many decades in the United States, both business management and trade unions have generally believed that the struggles between them, conducted through institutionalized collective bargaining, served the long-term interests of the American society as well as their own.

How a person evaluates conflicts depends upon many considerations, including the collectivity with which the person identifies, the issue in contention, and the means used in the struggle. Even analysts of conflicts cannot avoid passing judgment about them. After all, our moral concern about many aspects of conflicts motivates much of our interest in trying to understand them. But, to nonreflectively assume a particular evaluation of struggles does limit and handicap our understanding of them. It can prejudice the analysts' framing of a question and selection of relevant evidence. This is even more true for the partisans in a conflict. Long-term effectiveness of partisans is likely to be enhanced by avoiding self-limiting perspectives.

One safeguard against making handicapping assumptions is to keep in mind the many grounds of evaluation and consequently the alternative judgments of the conflict. We cannot avoid having feelings and making judgments about conflicts, but we can avoid ignoring alternative assessments. Another way to reduce the dangers of thinking about conflicts from too narrow a perspective is to use a comprehensive framework of analysis. This book offers a variety of assessments of conflicts and a comprehensive framework for analyzing them.

Finally, another safeguard against making biasing assumptions is to be explicit about one's own criteria of evaluation. That provides a warning to oneself and to others about what needs to be guarded against. This is an important context for my use here of the terms *destructive* and *constructive struggles*. Their definitions are influenced by my personal values, but also reflect widely shared sentiments. Since the terms refer to the means by which a conflict is waged and also to the benefits of its outcome, I will discuss the meanings of the terms in each of those conflict phases and how certain qualities combine to constitute destructive conflicts.

Varieties of Conflicts

Every fight is unique. Yet each has some qualities in common with others. The commonalities allow us to learn from particular conflicts and apply what has been learned to similar conflicts. A first step in doing this is to discern which conflicts are like and unlike each other in specific ways. Six ways in which conflicts vary warrant consideration: the issues in contention, the characteristics of the contending parties, the relations between the adversaries, the context in which the adversaries contend, the means used to conduct the struggle, and the struggle's outcome.

Issues in Contention

Adversaries wage conflicts over two kinds of issues: interests and values or beliefs. Thus, they may quarrel about interests such as the distribution of material resources that they each want but believe are limited and that each side's share is diminished by what the opposing side gains. Such material resources may include land, money, oil, and water. Other resources are social, involving the relationship between the opponents, such as their relative power or prestige.

Issues in contention may also refer to values or beliefs that each side holds dear. They become matters in contention when one side insists on holding particular values and/or beliefs and acting on them while another party finds them so objectionable that they would forbid the other party from having such ideas or of expressing them in conduct. For example, in the United States, strong disagreements have existed about the right to practice polygamy and currently exist about the right to have abortions. Values or beliefs may also become contested matters when one side feels that the ones it holds are so desirable that it insists that others share them or at least not overtly act in ways that contradict them. This may be seen in struggles about religious and political ideologies.

The characteristics of matters in contention and their bases will be examined in chapter 2. At this time, I stress noncontentious as well as contentious matters in the relations between opponents. Parties in conflict not only have matters in dispute, but also have common and complementary interests. For example, while trade union and management negotiators may be in conflict about the amount of money the workers should be paid, they may also believe that they have common interests in expanding the firm's share of the market and its profits and they have complementary interests in improving the motivation and skill that each party exercises.

These issues can be illuminated using some of the terms and ideas from the field of game theory. This influential field derives from the work of the mathematicians John von Neuman and Oskar Morgenstern.[15] Let us begin with a simple zero-sum game, which requires that what one side wins, the other loses. Suppose two persons, Dan and Joe, play a game of matching nickels; each flips a nickel and if they match (both heads or both tails), Joe gives Dan the nickel; if the coins do not match, Dan gives Joe the nickel. The payoff matrix of the game is shown in figure 1.1. The actor identified on the top of the figure has his payoff written first in each cell. The sum in each cell is constant, zero.

The other major kind of payoff matrix is nonconstant sum; one interesting variety of this is the mixed-motive game. A frequently used example is that of the prisoners' dilemma (PD). The hypothetical story for this game is that two men have been arrested upon suspicion of committing a serious crime. They are guilty, but there is insufficient evidence for conviction of the serious offense but enough for a lesser one. Held in jail, they are not allowed to talk with each other. They have the following possibilities. If they both confess, they will be convicted of the serious offense, but their sentence will be reduced slightly for their cooperation. If one confesses, he gets off without punishment and his confederate gets the maximum sentence of twelve years. If they both hold out and do not confess, they can only be convicted for the lesser offense

Dan

	H	T
H	1, -1	-1, 1
T	-1, 1	1, -1

Joe

Figure 1.1   Zero-sum Payoffs

and be sentenced for one year. The payoff matrix based on years in prison is shown in figure 1.2.

This payoff matrix poses a dilemma for the prisoners. Each would be better off if they both held out and did not confess. Yet, if each considers what he should do, whatever the other man does, he should confess. Thus, if B confesses, A is better off confessing. If B does not confess, A is again better off if he confesses. So if each acts in his individual self-interest, they both will lose. The dilemma can be resolved only if the prisoners could trust each other not to confess.

Many actual conflict situations may be viewed as if they had this PD quality. Consider two countries in an arms race with each other; suppose each has good reason to fear the other. If one government increases its arms expenditures and the other side does not, it believes it will triumph. According to the payoff matrix presented in figure 1.3, one side would gain 12 and the other lose 12. The side that does not increase its arms expenditures when the other side does, would fear that it would be at a military disadvantage and become subject to domination by the other side. If both sides continue to increase

A

	Confess	Not confess
Confess	-9, -9	-12, 0
Not confess	0, -12	-1, -1

B

Figure 1.2   Prisoners' Dilemma Payoffs

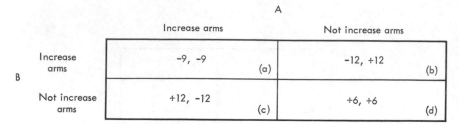

A

	Increase arms	Not increase arms
B **Increase arms**	-9, -9 (a)	-12, +12 (b)
Not increase arms	+12, -12 (c)	+6, +6 (d)

Figure 1.3   Arms Race Payoffs

their arms expenditures, both suffer some loss since they cannot employ the resources used for arms for other purposes, each side losing 9. If both sides would not increase arms spending, they would therefore both be better off, each side gaining 6. Again, if each side pursues its own interest independently, they will both be worse off than if they acted cooperatively.

Of course, actual conflicts do not have such simple payoffs, and the payoffs are not stable or known. But the logic of these simple games is compelling. If the game has a zero-sum payoff matrix, one side must inevitably lose and only one can win. Antagonists in a conflict generally see themselves in such zero-sum situations. In a mixed-motive game, each side can win or lose; but there is also the possibility of a win/win outcome and of a lose/lose outcome. Nevertheless, if each side acts reasonably in its self-interest, both will be worse off than if they acted cooperatively.

In this book we examine how conflicts come to be seen as zero-sum and each side feels terribly threatened. We will also consider how sometimes that does not happen and how, even after it does, a conflict can be transformed in the eyes of the antagonists into one with a possible mutually beneficial outcome. This can occur due to at least two considerations: first, that several issues are in contention in the conflict, and second, that the struggle has more than two parties involved.

As every conflict has more than one matter of contention, it is likely that opponents will have different priorities for these matters. This allows trading off one matter against another. Consider the terms of the 1979 peace treaty between Israel and Egypt. After the 1967 war in which Israel defeated Egypt and its Arab allies, Syria and Jordan, Israel occupied the Sinai, which had been part of Egypt prior to the war. Sovereignty over the Sinai was of paramount importance to the Egyptian government. Security against an Egyptian military attack based in the Sinai was of vital importance to the Israeli government. Among the many provisions of the peace treaty, Egypt gained full sovereignty over the Sinai, and Israel was assured that only limited Egyptian military forces would ever be stationed or moved into the Sinai.

Since many parties are likely to be involved in every conflict and each party is generally involved in several other conflicts, a zero-sum conflict may be transformed into a mixed-motive conflict by changing the salience of the antagonism between any particular set of opponents. Social conflicts generally involve many contending parties. Thus, every adversary has many groups within it, and there are many groups outside who are or might be induced to become allies. In addition, there are entities that crosscut and transcend the adversaries. Thus, in a union-management struggle, the union consists of nationally elected leaders, staff persons, local union officials, and rank-and-file members at varying pay scales; management consists of the labor relations department heads and staff, sales, production, advertising departments, and overall officers. In addition, each group has ties with political parties, government officials, consumers, and stockholders.

Given all these parties, what might seem like a zero-sum conflict can be transformed because it is embedded in a whole set of other conflicts. The dispute can then be seen as a mixed-motive game, in which various benefits can be gained by some adversaries uniting to take them at the expense of other parties. For example, trade union and management leadership may agree in effect to raise wages but cover the costs by raising prices to the consumers.

Adversary Characteristics

Conflicts are often distinguished according to who the adversaries are: nations, persons, ethnic groups, or particular organizations. Large bodies of literature exist about each of these kinds of social conflicts. To facilitate comparisons among various kinds of conflicts, however, we will not only rely on such "natural" designations, but also discuss adversary characteristics in more abstract terms. Adversaries may be distinguished in terms of their culture, size, available means to wage conflicts, and many other ways. But at this point we consider four general features with implications for a struggle's constructive character: the adversaries' self-conception, the significance of constituencies, the clarity of the adversaries' social boundaries, and the degree of internal organization of a conflict party.

Self-Conception

Variations in the way adversaries view themselves help typify conflicts. The degree to which individuals or groups regard themselves as superior beings or as chosen by God or history for a special mission has grave implications for the conduct of a struggle.[16] Religions or political ideologies can be important sources for such self-conceptions. The self-conception as special beings provides justification for destructive militancy against others who are necessarily less valuable.

Constituencies

One critical variation among conflicts is the extent to which the persons directly engaged in a conflict regard themselves as having a constituency they represent. Insofar as such leaders have followers, they must think about mobilizing and maintaining support from their constituencies—or they may find they have no resources or authority to deal with the external adversary. This generates a conflict dynamic that tends to be quite different from cases where the disputants believe they are acting only for and by themselves.[17]

In this book, I give particular attention to large-scale conflicts in which constituency concerns are important. But it should be recognized that we are not dealing with two sharply distinguished kinds of conflicts. Even in an argument between a husband and a wife, differences in gender, kinship, or ethnicity may be the basis for each to think she or he stands for a larger group than the person alone. On the other hand, even in a conflict between two national governments, the government heads may focus on the interpersonal dynamics between them and become concerned with personal honor, to some extent independent of their role as heads of governments. Clearly, any particular conflict may incorporate or be incorporated in other conflicts.

Boundary Clarity

The social boundaries of each participant in a conflict may be more or less clear, recognized, and maintained by the members of the antagonistic parties and the other members of the social system to which they belong. For example, the boundaries between particular ethnic groups may be sharp and sustained by law and custom controlling communication and movement across the social boundaries, and controlling nearly all aspects of life. This was the case in southern United States during the years of Jim Crow laws and in South Africa during the years of apartheid. In other times and places, the boundaries between some ethnic groups have been vague and permeable, and the realms of life governed by ethnic designation have been limited.

The clarity of social boundaries have important implications for the possible emergence of social conflicts from underlying social differences and for the course and resolution of a conflict once it emerges. The clarity of the boundaries often depends upon social markers; they are not inherent in the physical features of the members of the socially defined categories. Insofar as the distinctions are generally recognized, members of any of the distinguished categories are available to be mobilized to claim more resources for themselves.

The differences between men and women are interesting in these regards. Many differences are relatively visible and generally recognized. The boundary is not permeable in the sense that persons readily change membership from one category to another, but it is permeable in the sense that there is considerable interaction across the boundary. The boundary does mark off differences that are relatively comprehensive in that many aspects of life are shaped by belonging to one gender rather than another.

The clarity of the boundaries of contentious social movements and social movement organizations is only partly affected by the clarity of the boundaries of the categories of people from whom membership is drawn. For example, within the movement for women's rights renewed in the 1960s in the United States, many organizations are loosely and informally bounded while others are tightly bounded; some have only women members and others include male as well as female feminists.

Clear and strong boundaries between potential and actualized adversaries ease the mobilization of each for waging a conflict and hamper the communication and shared interests that might limit the escalation and hasten the resolution of a conflict. The clarity and strength of borders are matters of degree and vary among kinds of adversaries and over time. Thus, in the contemporary world, countries are relatively clearly bounded; every person is expected to belong to a state. National and international rules and institutions define citizenship and channel exchanges among citizens of different states.

Nevertheless, countries vary in the degree to which their citizens are controlled in these regards and the legitimacy government officials have in mobilizing their constituents for a conflict.

In general, contending parties in a community or societal conflict are less clearly bounded. Sometimes it is difficult to distinguish the social categories that serve as recruiting grounds for the active participants in the contending groups. It is true there may be some established, tightly knit organizations engaged in a struggle; but they almost always need a broader and more loosely bounded body of supporters.

Conflicts between adversaries with varying degrees of boundedness tend to be studied differently. In the case of relatively unbounded conflict units, as in community disputes, particular attention is given to how potential participants in a conflict come to feel they have grievances and how they are mobilized and organized to engage in conflict behavior. In the case of fights between relatively clearly bounded units, as in international or industrial conflicts, the mobilization of members is often less problematic, and analysts focus on leaders' decision making or the means used in pursuit of the disputed goals. One benefit from studying many kinds of conflicts and developing a framework for analysts is that it encourages considering something as problematic that would otherwise mistakenly be taken for granted. Thus, it is worthwhile to examine how governments try to mobilize and maintain popular support for a struggle against a purported external adversary. The U.S. government's involvement in the long war in Vietnam and the short war in the Persian Gulf illustrate that point.[18]

Degree of Differentiation

Related to the boundedness of the parties in a conflict is the degree of internal differentiation. In highly differentiated parties, such as states, various persons or groups within them play specialized roles. What concerns us here is the degree and character of the specialization for external relations. Some groups are essentially combat organizations and a large proportion of their members and resources are devoted to external conflicts. Other organizations have relatively few differentiated roles specializing in conducting conflicts with adversaries. For example, compare national governments and city governments or compare ethnic separatist organizations and traditional religious denominational organizations.

Consider some of the variations among national governments and between them and other kinds of adversaries. National governments often devote immense proportions of their societies' resources to external relations, particularly conflicting ones relying on coercive means. For example, in 1987, as the cold war was ending, Iraq devoted 30.2 percent of its gross national product (GNP) to military expenditures; Saudi Arabia devoted 22.0 percent, and Iran, 20.7 percent.[19] The United States, with its huge GNP, supported the world's most powerful military force with 6.5 percent of its GNP. Other countries devoted only a small fraction of their GNPs to the military; one, Costa Rica, boasts that it has no army and spent 0.6 percent of its GNP for military functions.

The subgroups within an adversary that are assigned to prepare for and to conduct external conflict are likely to scan the environment searching for external enemies. The existence of external threats justifies their activities and the allocation of resources to them. They may exaggerate, even unwittingly, the threat from outside and garner prestige, power, and economic benefits for fending off an alleged enemy.

Relationship of the Adversaries

The nature of the relationship between adversaries is another fundamental way of distinguishing among kinds of conflicts. For example, the adversaries may differ in the kind of history they have had with each other—of being allies, of each having been victims of atrocities committed by the other, or of living together amicably. At this time, we consider three other significant ways relationships vary: (1) the number of adversaries engaged in a struggle, (2) the degree to which the adversaries are integrated with each other, and (3) the degree to which one party dominates the other.

Number

Commonly, the number of adversaries in a conflict is assumed to be two; indeed, some analysts argue that even if many conflict parties are engaged in a struggle, ultimately they form two sides. But the number of parties on each side has significant consequences for the course of a struggle, and we will distinguish between dyadic and various-sized, multiparty conflicts.

The adversaries may be two clearly bounded entities: persons, governments, or organizations. They also may be several independent parties, each seeking its own goals in a free-for-all fight. Typically, as the struggle goes on, many of the parties tend to coalesce into camps. Sometimes, conflicts are undertaken by two opposing sets of parties, each constituted as a coalition or alliance. If not at the outset, then as the conflict escalates in scope, other parties with links to those already engaged join the fight.

In multiparty conflicts, even when two sides are formed, defections and shifts in allegiance often occur. The possibility of such shifts affects how members of each side wage the conflict against the presumed common enemy.

Integration

Integration refers to the mutual involvement the parties have with each other. At one extreme, the parties may be so interdependent that neither could survive without the other. Or, in order for each to achieve what it wants, cooperation with the other is desirable or even necessary. Their conflict with each other is about how to cooperate and work together. At the other extreme, the adversaries may be almost wholly independent of each other. Each party can and does function with little exchange or other kind of interaction with the other.

Domination

Dominance refers to the control one party exercises over the other; asymmetrical interdependence is a kind of domination. Thus, party B may be dependent on party A for goods or services that it needs while lacking alternative sources. Party A may be able to use force to deny alternative sources, as when slaveholders impose an asymmetrical dependency relationship on slaves. A relationship of domination, then, depends on the alternatives available to each party—on the permeability of the system they constitute.

One basis for a person or group's domination is its ability to threaten or impose negative sanctions; these may include physical coercion and the denial of needed resources. This ability may be recognized as legitimate by the dominated party or accepted because of the greater physical force the dominant party possesses and its greater control over needed resources.

But domination may also rest on the ability to manipulate and to use positive sanctions to ensure compliance by the subordinated party, creating dependency on the superordinant party. Domination may also be exercised by control over the ways of interpreting what is happening in the relationship.

The control may be carried out in the way ideas are expressed and communicated. When all these forms of domination are combined and strongly employed, the dominant party may be regarded as exercising hegemony.[20] For example, a society may be dominated that way by an ethnic group, ruling class, or ideological party that controls the organs of the state.

Domination, then, does not necessarily entail intentionality by the preeminent party. The inequality in resources and authority may be so great that both those dominating and those dominated accommodate to it with little self-awareness. This also means that dominance is not always directed to bring about specific actions desired by the dominating party.

Control is rarely total. Some resistance is always possible and the dominating party may take that into account in the extent to which it imposes sanctions or takes advantage of its superior position. It may constrain itself from being overly exploitative, fearing a rise in resistance.

This discussion has not used the word *power,* and yet power relations obviously have great relevance for analyzing social conflicts. One problem is that the word is understood in so many different senses that using it easily leads to misunderstandings. How it is used in this study is best explained in the context of a few general observations.

The term *power* sometimes refers to a social system's capacity to accomplish an agreed-upon task, but often it refers to the relationship between groups within a system in which one group directs the other.[21] Given the attention in this book to conflicts, the latter meaning is more pertinent. Power refers here to a person or group's ability to induce another party to act as the power wielder wishes, even (but not necessarily) against the resistance of those others. That ability may rest on actual or threatened negative sanctions (coercion). But it may also rest on the use of positive sanctions (the provision of benefits). Power may also rest on the sense of identity that the subordinates share with those exercising power, finding their persuasion convincing.[22]

People may follow directives of the power wielders because they believe those with power have the authority to issue the directives and employ coercion; this is legitimate power. The legitimacy rests on the subordinates' acceptance of the right of the power wielders to employ sanctions and the subordinates believe the persuasive arguments used by the power holders.

The critical matter about social conflicts is that no side is in full control. Efforts to exercise power are contested—the essence of a conflict. The term *power* will generally refer, here, to having resources that can be used as inducements, particularly coercion, but also positive sanctions and persuasion.

Recognition should also be given to the way partisans themselves use these terms, since they may not make the distinctions made here. But they are cognizant of inequalities in resources and what that means for domination and resistance. They often speak of power differences in terms of one side imposing its will on another.

Contexts

Conflicts vary in their social context, which is usefully viewed as the social system of which they are a part. The adversaries themselves constitute a social system and are also part of larger social systems. Often conflicts are distinguished in terms of their context, as in references to family, community, national, and regional conflicts. Simply enumerating those systems indicates that adversaries may contend with each other in many systems at the same time. Furthermore, various members of each adversary party may disagree about which system or systems are appropriate and which are wrong fits. For example, when Great Britain was at war against Germany from 1939 to 1945, some class, ethnic, and national liberation struggles within England or within the British Empire were subordinated; but some groups, for example in India, saw this as an opportune time to increase their challenge, with support from the enemies of Great Britain.

As the earlier discussion about interdependency and domination between two parties indicated, the degree of asymmetry or of domination depends on the extent to which the parties are a closed system. The kind of relations either party has with other parties, inside and outside of the system, provides alternatives that make one or another party believe it is strong or weak. The parties in a conflict quarrel about what their relevant boundaries are. This is evident in communal conflicts. The Tamils in Sri Lanka may see themselves as a vulnerable minority relative to the Sinhalese; while the Sinhalese may feel threatened by the Tamils in Sri Lanka because of the many Tamils living in southern India. The Catholics of Northern Ireland may see themselves as an oppressed minority dominated by the Protestants in Northern Ireland and the rest of the United Kingdom; while the Protestants may feel threatened as a minority within the island of Ireland encompassing Northern Ireland and the Republic of Ireland.

Sometimes one of the adversaries views itself as representing the social system in which its adversary is a constituent part. Governments often so regard themselves in conflicts with groups or organizations within the polity they claim to oversee and coordinate. Often, but not always, this claim is accepted by the adversary that regards itself as a part of the political order that is legitimately coordinated by the government. This often creates a dilemma for an ethnic minority in a society ruled by a dominant ethnicity.

When parties do not agree about the nature of the system they constitute, the conflicts are particularly contentious and difficult to settle. Thus, a government claiming jurisdiction over the society as a whole may be attacked by one segment as being the agent of an opposing segment and not representative of the entire society. For example, trade union officials may charge that the city government is a tool of the firm they are striking against and that the police are aiding the firm's management.

Sometimes the contention is even more direct, as when a superordinate unit claims to represent all subordinate units, including one that challenges it. For example, university administrators may argue that they represent all the interests of the university community, but student leaders may view them as serving the narrow interests of the corporations.[23]

A social system generally includes more components than the adversaries. There are many parties with some stake in a conflict and its course of development. They may become engaged in the conflict, sometimes to assist one or another opponent. They sometimes intervene to limit the conflict or to help resolve it. The norms they hold regarding appropriate means of struggle consequently influence the choices the antagonists make about how to wage their fight.

Means

Conflicts are often distinguished by the way they are conducted. For example, they may be conducted through a variety of generally understood conflict modes, such as negotiations or war; or they may be viewed as short antagonistic episodes or as prolonged struggles, using many modes of conflict sequentially. Two dimensions of the means used in conflict are especially important here: the degree of regulation and the level of severity. Regulation entails rules about how a conflict may be pursued and procedures for reaching decisions to settle a dispute. Such rules may be more or less institutionalized; regulations are institutionalized insofar as they (1) have been internalized by the participants; (2) are expressed in tradition, formal writing, or some other embodiment external to the participants; and (3) are enforced by sanctions.[24] These rules may be quite effective in governing conduct. They are effective insofar as the participants engaged in a conflict agree about the rules and believe the rules are legitimate enough that violating them would make the antagonists feel guilty. In addition, if the participants experience the rules as external to them, they are less free to interpret them as they would like. Furthermore, certainty of punishment if violations are committed also increases the likelihood of compliance.[25]

When disputes are highly institutionalized, they are often not regarded as conflicts. For example, in long-established democratic societies, the issue of which political party will control the government may be discussed using the metaphors of military campaigns, but they also are spoken of as sporting contests. On the whole, they are conducted according to generally accepted rules, and analysts and participants think of them as contests rather than as conflicts.

A major dimension of the level of severity of a conflict is the degree of injury suffered by those engaged in the conflict. The injuries may be equally shared, or, more likely, greater harm is endured by one of the parties than another. The injuries may result from violent or nonviolent coercion, such as firing guns, burning buildings, or imposing economic sanctions.

Much harm done in the course of a struggle is unintentional and is often self-inflicted. Preparing for struggle exacts costs in forgoing using resources for consumption or investment. The harm can also be more direct, as when military preparations result in accidental deaths or injuries. In waging the cold war, for example, the development of nuclear weapons and their testing and production caused great environmental damage resulting in extensive illness in the former Soviet Union and to a lesser degree in the United States.

Severity of injury also includes harm done to those not engaged in the conflict. That may refer to noncombatants, such as the innocent civilians in a city suffering "collateral damage," and those who flee to avoid being killed. Such injuries result from military fighting, riots, and revolutionary struggles. Sometimes the harm done to noncombatants is intentional, meant to dry up support for the combatants, to drive people of the other side away, or to commit genocide.

In addition to the physical injuries inflicted by coercive behavior, whether violent or nonviolent, conflicts vary in the severity of the psychic trauma and other long-lasting psychological damage people suffer. These injuries affect persons directly and indirectly involved in the struggle as well as those who regard themselves as not involved.

Another dimension of severity that should be noted pertains to subjective, rather than behavioral, aspects of how a struggle is waged. Conflict parties vary in how strongly their members feel hostility and hatred toward their adversary, and how many of them have such feelings. Conflict parties also vary in their beliefs about their adversary. Sometimes many of their members think that their opponents are inferior humans or not fully human, with destructive consequences.

That subjective and behavioral intensity vary together might also seem likely; thus, feeling angry at an enemy would be expected to fuel attempts to hurt the enemy. However, there are reasons why the feelings and behavior do not coincide. Feelings of hatred and resentment may be stifled when their expression might appear to be ineffective or counterproductive. On the other hand, great injury may be inflicted upon an adversary with little or no hostile feeling accompanying the violence. This is most likely when large collectivities are fighting, using complex technologies of violence with a high division of labor. Researchers studying the American soldiers of the Second World War concluded that even among combat infantrymen "hatred of the enemy, personal and impersonal, was not a major element in combat motivation."[26]

How antagonistically partisans feel and how hostilely they act vary greatly in struggles. Each varies somewhat independently in relation to the other, as when soldiers use weapons that kill people they do not know or even see, explaining that "we are doing our job." But people's actions and feelings do affect each other, and people expect them to be associated, so that high levels of one justify high levels of the other. Moreover, they both are affected by similar conditions and so are likely to vary along similar trajectories.

This study focuses on relatively nonregulated conflicts and on those that also entail great violence or the potentiality of becoming very destructive. Comparisons will also be made with relatively regulated conflicts to provide insights regarding the prevention and limitation of destructive conflicts.

The severity with which a conflict is waged is affected by the degree of regulation, but is not determined by it. The content of the rules governing conflict may allow for the use of various degrees of coercion, including violence. Severity also varies somewhat independently in relation to conflict regulation because there is more than one dimension of severity and they do not vary in the same way. Generally, nevertheless, regulated conflicts tend to be less severe than unregulated ones.

Outcome

Finally, some conflicts are characterized by their outcome. For example, part of the definition of a revolution is that it entails a fundamental change in social relations within a society, resulting from a popularly based struggle often using violence. In this analysis, three general qualities of outcomes are particularly important.

One set of qualities pertains to the question, who wins the struggle? For partisans in a fight, that is generally what matters: each side tries to defeat the adversary and gain what it sought to win. Certainly, the outcome of a struggle can be examined in terms of the degree to which one side triumphs and the other loses. But, of course, both sides may lose a great deal, and sometimes adversaries can discover solutions that provide them both with much of what they sought.

Second, an important dimension of outcomes is the degree to which adversaries have become more integrated rather than more separated. Some conflicts are waged with one side seeking greater separation from its adversary, for example in wars of secession or wars of national liberation. Other conflicts are waged to gain more integration, for example in the form of reduced segregation and free participation in governance. Even if not an intentional goal, the outcome may entail movement toward increased integration or increased separation.

The third relevant dimension of outcomes is the degree to which an outcome is the basis for a renewed severe struggle rather than a resolution of the conflict with little prospect of a major conflict. Some outcomes are imposed by one side and are experienced as a humiliation that must be revenged or as a harsh, costly burden that must be overthrown. Other outcomes are regarded as acceptable or perhaps beneficial to the principal adversaries, although perhaps in varying degrees.

Combinations Constituting Destructiveness

Many other distinctions can be and are made about conflicts, combining two or more of the characteristics already discussed. One additional distinction of particular relevance for this analysis is between destructive and constructive struggles.[27] Although no conflict is wholly constructive or wholly destructive, struggles vary in several ways between those absolutes. Therefore, we will examine varying degrees of destructiveness and constructiveness, assessing both the means by which a conflict is waged as well as its outcome.

Conflicts are waged destructively insofar as the means are severe and many participants suffer great harm. The harm may result from various forms of coercion and violence, and from expressions of hostility based upon values and beliefs about the enemy. Furthermore, destructiveness increases as the scale of the conflict expands, with increased numbers of adversaries participating. In addition, destructiveness is greater insofar as the issues at stake involve threats to the very survival of the members of the adversary groups, or of one of the groups as a collective entity. Finally, destructive conflicts tend to have characteristics that contribute to the struggle's self-perpetuation. These components of destructiveness tend to covary together.

Generally, I will discuss the destructiveness of a conflict as a whole, incorporating the various adversaries' injuries. But often the destructiveness is asymmetrical, with one side waging a destructive campaign and the other suffering immense injury. This is especially true of genocidal attacks against a whole people.[28]

The constructive waging of a struggle is not simply the absence of destructive elements. Such conflict is often pursued using persuasive efforts and promises of benefits, rather than relying wholly or largely on coercive threats or actions. The adversaries recognize each other as legitimate entities and do not threaten the other's existence. They interact to solve the problem they face together: their conflict; but they seek to construct a mutually acceptable outcome. Such problem-solving approaches may be taken by each side's representatives and/or significant groups within one or more sides in the struggle. Again, these qualities may characterize conduct of members of one side more than another.

Conflict outcomes are destructive insofar as they are imposed unilaterally, with little or no regard to the interests and needs of the party imposed upon. The outcome is regarded by one or more parties as oppressive and requiring redress, or as humiliating and requiring revenge. The interpretations of the interests and needs of the imposed-upon party, however, are not always those of its proclaimed leaders, particularly if they are not legitimate or would not reciprocate such regard. Unless a fundamental transformation of one or more of the adversaries occurs, destructive outcomes tend to be the basis for a renewed and destructive struggle.

Conflict outcomes are constructive insofar as the parties regard them as mutually acceptable. Moreover, they are constructive insofar as they provide a basis for an ongoing relationship in which future conflicts will tend to be waged constructively.

These assertions of definitions undoubtedly raise many questions and provoke disagreements. As the analyses in this book proceed, many of the possible objections will be addressed. Meanwhile, they provide the starting place for a serious consideration of the morally and empirically complex subject of waging constructive struggles.

Struggles generally consist of a sequence of conflict modes, with varying degrees of constructiveness and destructiveness. Figure 1.4 schematically illus-

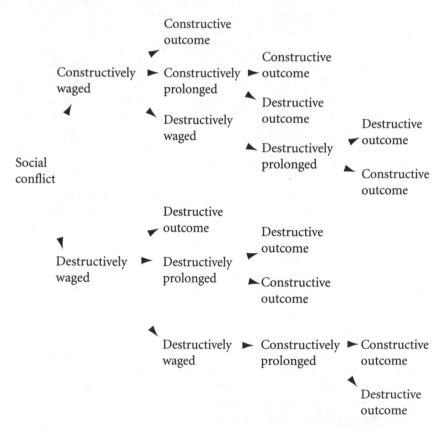

Figure 1.4   Alternative Sequences of Destructiveness and Constructiveness

trates some alternative sequences. It suggests that a relatively constructively waged struggle may soon yield a constructive outcome; in many ways, this fits the struggle to end legal segregation in the American South in the 1950s and 1960s and the struggle for Catalan autonomy in Spain after 1975. It also suggests how a destructively waged struggle may result in a prolongation of destructiveness and finally result in a destructive outcome; in many ways, struggles for various forms of Kurdish separatism in Turkey and in Iraq fit here. Figure 1.4 suggests many other possible sequences, including how a relatively destructively waged struggle may ultimately yield a relatively constructive outcome. In at least some regards, this fits the East-West cold war, the struggle for Indian independence from Great Britain, and the struggle against apartheid in South Africa. Obviously, the terms *constructive* and *destructive* usually refer to extremely complex matters that cannot be captured wholly in a word. Furthermore, as long as adversary parties survive, no outcome is final. Nevertheless, using the constructs of destructive and constructive conflicts can provide guidance in choosing what deserves particular attention.

Stages of Conflicts

This book is primarily organized in accord with the course of a conflict, as it emerges, escalates, de-escalates, and is settled. This assumes that a conflict is isolatable from the never-ending relations among people. Many conflicts clearly have a beginning, a middle, and an end; the adversaries often construct a conflict this way. They may even recognize that a series of short-term fights, of a day or a month, are embedded in a long-term conflict. How the adversaries define the course of a conflict obviously has profound implications, as when the parties perceive a transition from one stage to another that permits new sets of behavior.

Analysts and observers may accept the parameters of a conflict, as the partisans themselves have constructed them. But they can and often do make up their own stages, perhaps arguing that the partisans will come to recognize the appropriateness of their theoretically based stages. They may also argue that if the partisans persist in an incorrect perception, they will be damaged in unanticipated ways as the conflict progresses. These issues are analyzed in subsequent chapters; in this section, only the bare outlines of a series of stages is presented.

The existence of a potential conflict stage, of underlying conditions that are likely to result in an overt conflict, is assumed or hypothesized by many adversaries, intermediaries, observers, and theoreticians of conflict. They are likely, however, to disagree about what those underlying conditions are. We will examine the variety of possible bases for social conflicts in chapter 2.

Many circumstances that could result in a conflict do not. An important stage of a conflict is reached when potential adversaries come to believe that they in fact are adversaries, desiring incompatible goals. This may include a period during which one or more parties probe and explore the reality of that belief. The processes of conflict emergence are examined in chapter 3.

A third stage is when the adversaries begin to pursue their incompatible goals. This stage of escalation is expressed in increasing intensity of the means of conflict, often entailing coercion. The variety of ways a conflict may be pursued is discussed in chapters 4 and 5, and the processes of escalation are examined in chapter 6. A conflict in which adversaries threaten and try to damage each other, it turns out, is only one possible stage in the larger set of relations potentially adversarial parties may have. Figure 1.5 indicates that from all the relations between a set of parties, only a subset of those are potentially conflicting; and only a subset of those actually emerges as social conflicts; and of these, only some are pursued contentiously. Even in that subset, only some exhibit coercive acts; finally, only a subset of those conflicts becomes destructively waged. A particular struggle, however, may go through various sequences of becoming more or less destructively conducted, as diagrammed in figure 1.4.

Conflicts not only escalate; they also de-escalate after a brief or extended transition. A protracted conflict may have many escalating and de-escalating episodes, and only in retrospect can we discern a long-term transformation from intractable antagonism to de-escalation leading to a resolution of a conflict. In chapter 7, transitions toward reduced antagonism and the processes of de-escalation are examined. In chapter 8, the roles of intermediaries in settling disputes constructively are discussed. In chapter 9, possible outcomes are described and the process of negotiating a settlement is examined.

Whatever the outcome of a conflict, social life continues and the conflict has consequences. There are consequences for every party to the conflict, to their relationships, and to the larger social systems of which they are a part. Those covarying consequences are analyzed in chapter 10.

Figure 1.5   Conflict Funnel

Finally, in chapter 11, the various elements developed in this study are applied to each conflict stage and the possibilities of resolution and reconciliation are examined. In addition, the approach taken is specified for different kinds of conflicts. We also consider the implications of the interpretations made here for policies that are conducive to waging conflicts constructively.

Although all conflicts do not go unilinearly through all the stages identified here, it will prove helpful to consider these stages and why some conflicts move from one stage to the next more or less destructively. A diagram of the potential sequence of stages is shown in figure 1.6. The series of arrows forming the circle indicates that a conflict emerges, escalates, de-escalates, terminates, and results in an outcome that becomes the basis for another conflict. How the previous stage is enacted heavily influences the next stage. The short arrows entering from outside and inside the circle indicate that factors internal to each adversary as well as social environmental factors also affect each stage. This simple model will be further developed in the course of the discussion, and a more elaborate diagram is discussed in the concluding chapter.

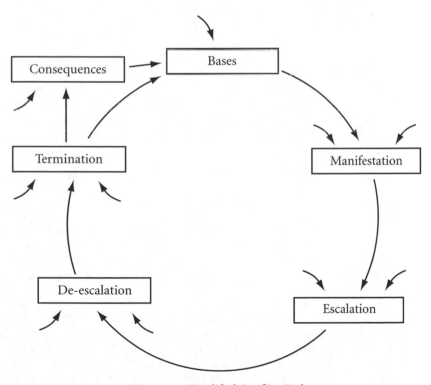

Figure 1.6   Simplified Conflict Cycle

Conclusions

The many ways social conflicts vary have been discussed in order to facilitate systematic comparisons and to provide guidelines for generalizing and for policy making. Social conflicts vary in the issues in contention, characteristics of the adversaries, the relations between the adversaries, the social context of the conflict, and the modes used in the struggle. These variations have implications for the propensity for conflicts to be waged constructively.

This book focuses on conflicts among relatively large, differentiated adversaries and conflicts that are relatively unregulated with the potential of violence. Despite the great variety of conflicts, this study will consider possible commonalities among various kinds of conflicts. One commonality is the movement conflicts undergo in their course from one stage to the next. Given the focus on constructive conflicts, I will consider how constructive aspects of a conflict, throughout its course, are fostered and how destructive ones are prevented or limited.

Throughout, I will give considerable attention to how the partisans of conflicts and the potentially involved bystanders view their struggle. Conflicts necessarily involve intentionality, perceptions, and other subjective phenomena. They are social constructs, but the antagonists often disagree about the way they see a conflict, so no party can construct the conflict as it wills.

Adversaries struggle in the context of an external world. There are many aspects of the social and physical world that are external to a conflict party and cannot be viewed in whatever way its members wish without adverse repercussions. A discussion of the complex interplay between conditions that shape perceptions and perceptions that become conditions begins in the next chapter.

Notes

1. As considered in later chapters, such transformations are never total nor necessarily everlasting. Many persons within the camp that seems to have gained much often accept less than they had hoped to achieve; and many persons in the camp that has seemed to have failed struggle on and under new circumstances undertake another version of the old struggle.

2. A considerable literature is developing about learning from past experience, particularly in the field of international relations. See, for example, Jack S. Levy, "Learning and Foreign Policy: Sweeping a Conceptual Mine Field," *International Organization* 48 (Spring 1994): 279–312. Studies of social movement organizations seeking to advance justice document how ideas and practices applied by one social movement organization are transmitted to and transformed by other organizations at a later time. See, for example, Ron Pagnucco and John D. McCarthy, "The Proliferation of Non-Violent Direct Action under Repressive Regimes: The Emergence, Struc-

ture and Strategy of SERPAJ," in *Religion and Politics in Comparative Perspective*, ed. Bronislaw Misztal and Anson Shupe (Westport, Conn.: Praeger, 1992).

3. This issue is increasingly examined in the field of international relations. See, for example, Ernest R. May, *"Lessons" of the Past* (New York: Oxford University Press, 1973); Robert Jervis, *Perception and Misperception in International Politics* (Princeton, N.J.: Princeton University Press, 1976); Yuen Foong Khong, *Analogies at War: Korea, Munich, Dien Bien Phu, and the Vietnam Decisions of 1965* (Princeton, N.J.: Princeton University Press, 1992); and Levy, "Learning and Foreign Policy."

4. Robert E. Park and Ernest W. Burgess, *Introduction to the Science of Sociology* (Chicago: University of Chicago Press, 1924), 574. Similarly, Kenneth Boulding defines conflict as a form of competition in which the competing parties recognize that they have mutually incompatible goals; see his *Conflict and Defense* (New York: Harper & Row, 1962).

5. Ralf Dahrendorf, *Class and Class Conflict in Industrial Society* (Stanford, Calif.: Stanford University Press, 1959).

6. Karl Marx, *The Poverty of Philosophy* (New York: International Publishers, 1963); originally published in 1847.

7. Lewis A. Coser, for the purpose of his study of the functions of social conflict, provisionally took the term to mean "a struggle over values and claims to scarce status, power and resources in which the aims of the opponents are to neutralize, injure or eliminate their rivals." See *The Functions of Social Conflict* (New York: The Free Press, 1956), 8. Hubert M. Blalock, Jr., defines conflict as "the intentional mutual exchange of negative sanctions, or punitive behaviors, by two or more parties" (*Power and Conflict: Toward a General Theory* [Newbury Park, Calif.: Sage, 1989], 7).

8. The significance of the way people define the situation in which they are acting for the way they act has long been recognized. The observations of William I. Thomas are frequently cited in this regard. See *The Unadjusted Girl* (Boston: Little Brown and Company, 1923), 41–44; and William I. Thomas and Florian Znaniecki, *The Polish Peasant in Europe and America* (New York: Knopf, 1927), 1847–49. The idea has been developed from many sources and elaborated to stress the collective nature of the social definitions, for example, Peter L. Berger and Thomas Luckman, *The Social Construction of Reality* (New York: Doubleday, 1966).

9. Zionism refers to the social and political movement to establish a home in Palestine for the Jewish people. The initial formulation of this Jewish national independence movement is usually credited to Theodor Herzel and the publication in 1896 of his book *The Jewish State: An Attempt at a Modern Solution to the Jewish Question*. Zionism had its initial base of support among Jews in Eastern Europe, where their persecution was severe. Important differences among Zionists existed from the beginning and persist, including cleavages between religious and secular Zionists, and among the latter between the democratic socialist Labor Zionists and the more militant nationalist Revisionists.

For accounts of the Jewish-Palestinian relations, see Baruch Kimmerling and Joel S. Migdal, *Palestinians: The Making of a People* (New York: The Free Press, 1993); Amos Elon, *The Israelis: Founders and Sons* (New York: Holt, Rinehart and Winston, 1971); Edward W. Said, *The Question of Palestine* (New York: Vintage Books, 1979); and Fred J. Khouri, *The Arab-Israeli Dilemma*, 3d ed. (Syracuse, N.Y.: Syracuse University Press, 1985).

10. There is an extensive literature on low-intensity warfare and counterinsurgency; for example, see Michael T. Klare and Peter Kornbluh, eds., *Low Intensive Warfare* (New York: Pantheon Books, 1987).

11. Morris Janowitz, *The Professional Soldier* (Glencoe, Ill.: The Free Press, 1960), 261.

12. Adding fluorides to the drinking water, where the water was not already high in fluorides, strengthened teeth and retarded tooth decay. Generally viewed as a public health measure, some opponents regarded it as an unwarranted and dangerous governmental intrusion. For an analysis of the many kinds of community conflicts of that period, see James Coleman, *Community Conflict* (New York: Free Press, 1957).

13. For example, see Warren C. Haggstrom, "The Power of the Poor," 205–23, in F. Riesman, J. Cohen, and A. Pearl, eds., *Mental Health of the Poor* (New York: Free Press, 1964).

14. See, for example, Lewis Coser, *The Functions of Social Conflict* (New York: Free Press, 1956); Georg Simmel, *Conflict and the Web of Intergroup Affiliations* (New York: Free Press, 1955), originally published in 1908 and 1902; and William Graham Sumner, *What Social Classes Owe Each Other* (Caldwell, Idaho: Caxton Printers, 1952), originally published in 1883.

15. John von Neumann and Oskar Morgenstern, *Theory of Games and Economic Behavior* (Princeton, N.J.: Princeton University Press, 1944); current research about the prisoners' dilemma, largely experimental, is published regularly in the *Journal of Conflict Resolution.*

16. For example, see Johan Galtung, "Global Projections of Deep-Rooted U.S. Pathologies," Occasional Paper 11, Institute for Conflict Analysis and Resolution, Fairfax, Va.: George Mason University, 1996.

17. Peter B. Evans, Harold K. Jacobson, and Robert D. Putnam, eds., *Double-Edged Diplomacy: International Bargaining and Domestic Politics* (Berkeley: University of California Press, 1993).

18. The increasing popular resistance to America's involvement in the Vietnam War demonstrated that a government, particularly a democratic one, cannot assume that there will be support by the citizens. U.S. government and military leaders took that into account in waging the war against Iraq: plan for a very intense, short war and few casualties.

19. The figures are taken from Ruth Leger Sivard, *World Military and Social Expenditures, 1991* (Washington, D.C.: World Priorities, 1991).

20. Antonio Gramsci, *Selections from the Prison Notebooks* (New York: International Publishers, 1971).

21. In addition to the power *over* others and the power *with* others to accomplish collective tasks, the power *from* others (autonomy) is an important kind of power; see Louis Kriesberg, *Social Inequality* (Englewood Cliffs, N.J.: Prentice-Hall, 1979), 24–25. Power over others presumes a zero-sum relationship and has been a traditional as well as radical meaning given to the term (For discussions, see Blalock, *Power and Conflict* and C. Wright Mills, *The Power Elite* [New York: Oxford University Press, 1956].). Power with others has been a meaning of power used by some structural functionalists in the past, for example, Talcott Parsons, *Politics and Social Structure* (New York: Free Press, 1969). Interestingly, a related meaning is found in feminist approaches to social

theory. See Lynne M. Woerhle, "Social Constructions of Power and Empowerment: Thoughts from Feminist Approaches to Peace Research and Peace-Making," in *Social Theory and Nonviolent Revolutions: Rethinking Domination and Rebellion*, eds. Nancy Bell and Lester R. Kurtz (Austin: University of Texas at Austin Press, 1992).

22. Kenneth E. Boulding, *Three Faces of Power* (Newbury Park, Calif.: Sage, 1989); Carolyn M. Stephenson, *Common Sense and the Common Defense* (Syracuse, N.Y.: Syracuse University Press, forthcoming).

23. For example, this was evident in the development of the student protests of the 1960s, as at the University of California at Berkeley; see Max Heirach, *The Spiral of Conflict: Berkeley 1964* (New York: Columbia University Press, 1968).

24. Peter M. Blau, *Exchange and Power in Social Life* (New York: John Wiley, 1964), 273–76.

25. For example, Charles R. Tittle found that crime rates are lower when the certainty of punishment is higher, see his "Crime Rates and Legal Sanctions," *Social Problems* 16 (Spring 1969): 409–23.

26. Samuel A. Stouffer, Arthur A. Lumsdaine, Marion Harpur Lumsdaine, Robin M. Williams, Jr., M. Brewster Smith, Irving L. Janis, Shirley A. Star, and Leonard S. Cottrell, Jr., *The American Soldier: Combat and Its Aftermath*, vol. 2 (Princeton, N.J.: Princeton University Press, 1949), 166.

27. For discussions of the distinction between constructive and destructive conflicts, see Morton Deutsch, *The Resolution of Conflict: Constructive and Destructive Processes* (New Haven, Conn.: Yale University Press, 1973).

28. The accounts of the horrors of genocide deserve to be experienced to appreciate how destructive conflicts can become. Even in those contexts, however, there are social and personal variations that warrant attention. See Helen Fein, *Accounting for Genocide* (New York: The Free Press, 1979).

2

Bases of Social Conflicts

Each side in a conflict usually blames the other's aggressive behavior for the fight. An observer, however, might conclude that the adversaries are mistaken: each is actually seeking to defend what it has and its defensive efforts are incorrectly perceived by the other as threatening.[1] Or the observer may believe that the basis of the conflict is a natural consequence of the imbalance of power among the adversaries and the lack of agreed-upon procedures for managing issues in dispute between them.

Certainly, the explanations for the cold war given by the Soviet and U.S. leaders during that period were quite different, one side asserting that communist ideology was inherently expansionist and the other arguing that capitalism's inherent drive for markets underlay the conflict. Analysts and observers offered many other "real" reasons. These included that the conflict was an example of traditional international great power rivalry and that the conflict was based on mutual fear that was not well grounded and incorporated important elements of misunderstanding. Obviously, which explanation one accepts has implications for how one believes the conflict will and should be pursued and resolved.

Participants as well as observers of struggles interpret the conflicts in which they are engaged or that they are observing. Those interpretations are based on theory, although the theory may be unrecognized, elementary, or inconsistent. Making the theory more explicit and coherent tends to improve the understanding of partisans and observers alike. This task is facilitated by considering alternative theoretical explanations and consiering which alternatives do not fit our experience and evidence. We cannot prove any explanation to be true, but it is possible to disprove some assertions. Refuting some explanations strengthens our confidence in the explanations that remain consistent with our information. In this chapter and throughout the book, alternative

30

ideas will be considered in this light. Before examining various theoretical bases for conflicts, I will discuss the nature of any theoretical explanation.

Theoretical Explanations

The partisans in conflicts offer explanations for their conduct and that of their enemies. The explanations they use are important in mobilizing support, in deciding which means will be effective, and in ultimately agreeing to settle the conflict. Therefore, those explanations cannot be ignored. But neither can they be accepted as the full truth.

Would-be intermediaries, academic analysts, and many other observers try to discover what actual conditions generate the partisans' belief that they are in conflict. Knowing those conditions, they think, would provide a powerful instrument in predicting the outbreak and course of a conflict and would be of inestimable value in mitigating the destructiveness of a conflict and also in attaining a just resolution. One of the great appeals of Marxism for many people around the world was that it purported to assert the true grounds of conflict; consequently, those who acted in accord with those conditions were acting on the side of history. With that certainty, one could judge other people's ideas about the basis of a conflict as correct or as false.

Yet, how can we possibly know which conditions underlie a conflict without reference to the attitudes and injuries nurtured by people engaged in the conflict? Or, if the conflict is not yet manifest, how can one know what conditions are simmering unseen below the surface? Such judgments depend upon having a general theory about the sources of conflicts and the conditions that turn potential conflicts into active ones.

There is no consensus in the field of conflict studies about the validity of any such theory. Furthermore, even if there were a widely accepted general theory of social conflicts, it could not explain why one fight erupts and another lies dormant, how one escalates and another subsides. We can never have enough detailed information about a specific conflict to predict when and how it will escalate and de-escalate.

Theoretical propositions relating to social conflicts are often expressed in terms of tendencies and likelihoods. Some matters can be stated with more certainty than others, as when general parameters are recognized comparable to the establishment of climatic zones in weather prediction. Statements about certain conditions such as income inequality can be made with greater certainty because they refer to phenomena that are relatively stable and open to measurement; phenomena not highly susceptible to the vagaries of human perception and opinion such as relative population size can also be more readily predicted.

For this analysis, we need to assume neither a "subjectivist" nor an "objectivist" view of truth. We need not decide whether the mind "makes up" the world or "copies" the world. The perspective of the philosopher, Hilary Putnam, is useful in overcoming the seeming contradiction of that duality. He suggests that "the mind and the world jointly make up the mind and the world."[2]

Our minds interact with the world in complex ways. One aspect of that complexity warrants noting at this point. We cannot know objects in the world directly; rather, we use our senses, augmented by many kinds of instruments to perceive them. Furthermore, objects have dispositions or tendencies rather than fixed qualities. That is, our perception of objects or situations depends on their context, the conditions in which they function. This is obvious in the case of an object's color. For example, an object that appears red can be seen as differently colored depending on the light cast on it; furthermore, different objects that appear red may do so for quite different reasons. Even the property of a cube of sugar to dissolve in water is not intrinsic to it, but depends on the condition of the water and many other conditions.[3]

Finally, a distinction should be made in regard to theorizing *about* conflicts and acting *in* them. Theory generalizes about a set of conflicts and what they have in common. Action, on the other hand, is carried out in a specific fight, which always has unique qualities. This distinction is familiar to physicians who distinguish between knowing the general processes of physiology and pharmacology and knowing the background and circumstances of an individual patient. Good clinical practice utilizes both kinds of knowledge and does not rely on one alone.

These observations provide the context for reviewing different theoretical claims about the bases of social conflicts. Among the innumerable theories about the bases of conflicts, many stress conditions and processes that exist independent of the adversaries' subjective awareness. These are constructs of the theoretician. Other theories emphasize the subjective processes of actual and potential conflict adversaries. In either case, the theories, to be assessed, should provide the links between conditions posited by the analysts and the beliefs about the conflict held by the adversaries.

In discussing the major social scientific approaches in this chapter, I distinguish among those that emphasize factors internal to one or more potential adversaries, factors relating to the system of which the potential antagonists are a part, and factors pertaining to the relationship between the possible adversaries.

Internal Factors

Many theoretical approaches stress features of the potential adversaries as the source of conflicts. Of course, these are not the explanations usually noted by the adversaries about themselves, but they often do attribute the cause of the conflict to the other side's internal characteristics. Some theoretical approaches also point to conflict-generating features of specific individuals, groups, or societies, but many emphasize characteristics shared by all persons, groups, or societies.

Since social conflicts are ubiquitous, it might seem reasonable to look for the underlying bases of conflicts in universal characteristics of humans or their societies. This view may be seen in certain theories about human nature and human needs, theories about widely shared processes of social interaction, and also theories about inherent features of human societies.

Human Nature

Popular thought frequently attributes the struggles among humans to be due to "human nature," suggesting our helplessness in stopping or controlling these antagonisms. If human nature is understood to mean what is intrinsic to humans, independent of their socialization, it is difficult to imagine discovering what that might be. Humans cannot survive without being nurtured and socialized in a social environment. Positing human nature without socialization is really impossible; it cannot be conclusive and must be quite general.

The search for what might be regarded as underlying human nature, nevertheless, persists. It takes three major paths. One is the biological and evolutionary way, including the study of other animals, particularly those that are genetically close to humans. Another path is to research psychological and social-psychological processes, ideally in a wide variety of societies. The third path is to study many different human societies, seeking commonalities among them.

Focusing on the biological nature of humans has recurrent attractiveness. Some of this work selects specific patterns of behavior found in several animal species, regards them as instinctive, and then attributes apparent similarities among humans to such instincts. For example, territoriality is to be found in a variety of animal species and thus a "territorial imperative" may be attributed to humans.[4] But this ignores the absence of territoriality in many species and, even among those exhibiting it, research reveals that its occurrence depends on specific ecological conditions.[5] Furthermore, humans' sense of land is symbolically understood and socially constructed; recognition of that undermines the predictability and innateness of a biological instinct of territoriality. Finally, it is important to remember that territory is an issue in many conflicts, including gang "turf" battles, disputes between government officials and citizens in religious communities, and particular international wars in a period of sovereign states. But this is partly because space, like power, can be used in many ways and permeates most relationships; consequently, a variety of issues may be framed as territorial.

Some research about sociobiological factors affecting social behavior restricts itself to phenomena within similar social organizational domains, for example, face-to-face groups. Comparisons among species should also take into account the degree of genetic similarity with humans. For example, Allan Mazur examined status ranking in small established groups among chickens and many primate species.[6] Ranking was found in all the groups, but this was expressed by overt threats and physical attacks among the species most distant from humans. Among humans and the genetically closest primates, expressions of deference are exhibited subtly and the dominant animals quietly perform control and service functions. This evolutionary evidence can be interpreted as indicating that humans establish dominant relationships not by threats and physical violence but by contributions to the group, for which they receive deference.

In addition to seeking human nature in biological and evolutionary evidence, studies of human psychology and social psychology may indicate fundamental human processes. The studies would have to demonstrate universality among humans, at least within specified social conditions. Although we lack such demonstrations, several processes have been presented by analysts as likely to be universally possible under certain conditions. I discuss one of those processes here, and others will be discussed in relationship to various phases of social conflicts.

In the work of Freud, and as developed by many psychoanalysts, unconscious emotional processes affect much of human conduct. For example, a person may have impulses or thoughts that are unacceptable to him or her; these may then be projected onto other persons or groups. Thus, some people may resolve their feelings of guilt about being ambivalent toward their parents by idealizing authority figures and directing their hostile feelings toward outgroups.[7] This is the basis for the large body of research about the authoritarian personality.

More generally, in human societies, infantile, primitive drives need to be controlled. This occurs through the internalization of a superego and the functioning of a strong ego. The emotion or affect that arises from frustrations of those primitive drives may be displaced onto a wide variety of objects. This is the case when the ego is inadequately functioning. For example, there is evidence that prejudice and animosity against members of a minority group are exacerbated by such displacement; this is scapegoating.[8] The human capability of displacement, however, does not mean that it always occurs; people vary greatly in exhibiting this pattern, and social conditions greatly affect its appearance and target.

Anthropological and historical evidence reveals widespread violence perpetrated by humans against each other. But clearly, violence is not constant and universal, and much cooperation is also to be found among humans. Societies vary greatly in the levels of violence among their members and against non-members.

In 1989, a distinguished international group of geneticists, anthropologists, psychologists, biochemists, and other researchers summarized the state of scientific knowledge about the bases of violence and war in the Seville Statement. The statement was endorsed by the United Nations Educational, Scientific, and Cultural Organization (UNESCO) and was subsequently endorsed by many scientific and professional associations. The statement concludes that "it is not scientifically correct to say that war or any other violent behavior is genetically programmed into our human nature," or "that in the course of human evolution there has been a selection for aggressive behavior more than for other kinds of behavior."[9] A sociological statement on war and peace, endorsed by the Section on Peace and War of the American Sociological Association in 1992, stresses the evidence that social conditions account for the great variations in degrees and varieties of violence.

Social Interaction

Conflict and violence may arise from forces internal to one of the parties in a conflict, without those sources being attributed to human nature or to universal features of humans. A great variety of social processes may generate conflicts, depending on particular social conditions.

Consider the idea that when people feel frustrated, they will act aggressively, trying to harm those who are frustrating them.[10] If frustration always resulted in aggression and aggression were always caused by frustration, we would have a fundamental premise for a theory of conflicts. It is not, however, so simple.

Research on frustration and aggression makes it clear that the feeling of frustration depends on the goals and intentions of those who regard themselves to be blocked. The goals and intentions, however, may not be evident to the outside analyst. Research also indicates that the manifestation of aggression depends upon the availability of a target that seems appropriate. Frustration may result in attacking behavior against a primary source of the frustration; but the attack may also be directed elsewhere; that is, it may be displaced against a vulnerable scapegoat. The frustration may even be turned inward in self-blame. Consequently, while there may often be a relationship between frustration and aggression, just how frustration is experienced and aggression is manifested depends upon a great many social conditions that need to be specified.

In addition to processes relating to human emotions, cognitive processes play important roles in the emergence and course of conflicts. Thus, people tend to exaggerate the differences between themselves (however that is defined) and others. This occurs through several processes, including *categorization*, the tendency to simplify social reality and to impose dichotomies upon continuous dimensions, and *assimilation*, the tendency to fit new information into prior understandings.[11]

Furthermore, members of a group tend to evaluate their own attributes more positively than those of the other group, even when the attributes are the same. Thus, the same behavior viewed as steadfast or principled by one side will be regarded as pigheaded or stiff-necked when exhibited by the adversary.

In addition to such specific theories or hypotheses about sources of conflicts, a large body of theory and research indicates that socialization may make persons and groups prone to conflict. Socialization occurs primarily through an infant's and child's experience with his or her mother and father, but also with siblings and other kin, with peers, and with institutions such as schools and the mass media. What is learned in socialization varies by groups, but in some ways it is also unique to each person. Depending on the nature of past experience and the current social context, the socialization processes have conflict-relevant effects.

Considerable research supports the idea that harsh socialization of the young produces aggressive adults who are prone to engage in overt conflict.[12] Harsh socialization includes severe physical punishment and also emotional deprivation. The connection between such experiences and later tendencies for aggression and violence may be explained by learning theory, encompassing imitation, modeling, and reinforcement. It may also be explained by the processes previously noted, such as projection of unwanted feelings and frustration-generated aggression.

Research also supports the generalization that males in many societies tend to be conflict and violent prone as a result of male identity confusion.[13] This pattern can occur through several mechanisms. For example, males growing up in a male-dominated society with fathers who are distant develop very strong bonds with their mothers and then must break those bonds to meet expectations of proper male behavior. To sever those ties may be frustrating, and furthermore the way to do so may require behavior that is regarded as "masculine": tough, strong, and prideful.

These patterns of interaction that tend to generate hostility, aggression, and overt conflict do not fully account for even the internal factors that underlie social conflicts. Everyone also feels empathy, love, and solidarity with some other people and views them as friends, allies, and partners.[14] Those feelings and views may counter or constrain the workings of the mechanisms generating conflict.

There is evidence that youngsters who had warm, affectionate, and loving child-rearing experiences are well prepared for cooperative relations later in life.[15] Open expression of affection toward children and close father-child relations foster the development of skills that are needed to nonviolently resolve conflicts.

Social System

A society, an organization, or a family may have characteristics that impel its members to act in ways that generate conflicts with other social units. These characteristics include conditions that foster emotions and cognitions driving members of social systems to externally directed attacking behavior. The characteristics include cultural values and norms that foster antagonistic behavior toward members of other social systems; and they include institutions and social structures that engender external conflict.

These psychological and social-psychological processes, if they are to be relevant for the conduct of a social system, must be experienced by a significant proportion of the members of those systems. For example, a society undergoing disorienting rapid change or a deterioration of living standards may produce feelings of frustration in many society members.[16] The feelings of frustration may be expressed in great animosity against a vulnerable external social target, or a segment of the society who are redefined as nonmembers. This process helps account for the rise of Nazism in Germany, as high inflation and the worldwide depression worsened socioeconomic conditions and reduced many people's status and living conditions. But such channeling is not inevitable; it depends on the repertoire of possible responses and the alternatives presented by leaders. After all, the economic depression did not result in a fascist regime in the United States or in most other countries.

Some observers have argued that the patterns of child rearing and other experiences of socialization when shared by society members tend to produce a people with a national character, which may include traits of aggressiveness.[17] For example, during the Second World War, some American and British analysts reasoned that the German national character was authoritarian, obedient to those above and arrogant to those below themselves. After the war, however, the profoundly changed German policies and relations with the U.S. and allied governments contributed to the turning away from such interpretations.

A culture is increasingly recognized as varying among persons who share it and, although transmitted by socialization by others, is acquired and formed by each person sharing it.[18] Consequently, subcultures within each culture are likely to exist. This view avoids reification of culture, so that it is not regarded as uniform and rigid. Keeping these understandings in mind, we will not reiterate them every time we discuss a culture and cultural differences.

The values and norms incorporated by people growing up with a given culture may promote external conflict or they may restrain it. Feminist analysts, for example, point out that most societies are patriarchal in values and structure.[19] They are dominated by men who are socialized to value competitiveness, dominance, honor, and toughness. The Mexican term *macho* is widely used to refer to this particular sense of masculinity, which stresses bravery and sensitivity to challenges to honor.

Groups, organizations, and societies are differentiated, with their members playing specialized roles. In many social systems, this includes roles for defending the systems' members from external attack. Their status and resources depend in part on the size of the threat and their success in defeating it. Consequently, they have an interest in proclaiming a great external threat, and perhaps even in provoking it to enhance their status, power, and control over resources.

This reasoning underlies the warnings about the dangers of the military-industrial complex, as expressed by President Dwight D. Eisenhower in his 1961 farewell address.[20] There is a large literature on the way the military establishments, defense industries, political leaders, and other groups on both sides advanced their interests by helping to sustain and even intensify the cold war. In many ethnic and other intercommunal conflicts, persons seeking political or other forms of power may try to mobilize feelings of fear and distress, attributing responsibility to outside enemies.

Implications

The theoretical ideas we have considered indicate how forces internal to a person, group, or country may foster behavior that brings about conflict. But that is not a necessary outcome; after all, many internal factors and processes also foster cooperation with people who might be regarded as outsiders. The outcome of those diverse social and psychological factors and processes depends on the social context and the relations with possible adversaries.

Nevertheless, there is enough evidence to recognize that conflicts can be primarily the result of one party's internally driven actions. If not the sole source, such internal factors often contribute to the bases of conflicts and their exacerbation. Insofar as analysts consider this to be true for a particular conflict, they would regard the conflict as *unrealistic* in its origins, if not in its manifestation.

Internal factors, however, are generally mixed with other kinds of factors: those pertaining to the system context and those pertaining to the relations among the potential adversaries. The internal factors may provide some of the motive for antagonistic behavior, and at the same time other factors help channel that behavior. Even for a person or group whose antagonism is largely internally driven, justifications must be given in terms that resonate and appear plausible to supporters.

System Context

Many theories about wars, revolutions, and even fights between husbands and wives stress the importance of the social system within which the potential antagonists function. Among the many features of the system, theoretical approaches varyingly emphasize certain ones: the significance of its culture and institutions, the degree to which the system is characterized by scarcity of resources, the power distribution among the system members, and the consistency and stability of the system.

Culture and Institutions

Everything else being equal, insofar as people share values and norms, they tend not to come into conflict with each other. In addition, of course, the content of the cultural values and beliefs greatly affects the likelihood of conflicts erupting. Cultures provide people with standards by which they judge what is fair and just. As examined in chapter 3, the feeling among group members that they are suffering unfairly is an essential component for the emergence of a conflict.

Cultures also provide norms and values about recognizing conflicts and how to conduct them. Cultures vary in the degree to which direct confrontations are regarded as acceptable and in the rules for their expression and management. Among peoples or among particular segments of the society, expression or even acknowledgment of particular kinds of conflicts may be considered improper. For example, in many cultures women are socialized to believe that it is proper that they subordinate their interests to those of their husbands and hence do not recognize many issues as conflictful.

Social systems have institutionalized ways of handling conflicts. The legal institutions in each society are the major instrument for managing conflicts among its members as well as conflicts between the government and those it governs. Furthermore, the political institutions provide ways of managing conflicts over the allocation of resources and about making policy for the collectivity. In addition, formal and informal procedures serving the same functions exist within many organizations and communities.

Insofar as these institutions are regarded as legitimate by society members, matters that might otherwise become the subject of violent conflict do not. If such institutions are lacking or are not seen as legitimate for segments of the social system, differences are likely to become contentious. This contributes significantly to the occurrence of international conflicts.

Scarcity

Conflicts arise when potential adversaries come to view themselves as being in a zero-sum relationship. That is likely insofar as the potential adversaries exist in a social system where what they seek is scarce and the system is small and closed. The extent to which a system has little of what is desired and is small and closed are related. When the system includes many parties in addition to the possible adversaries and when system members interact readily with nonmembers, much of what the adversaries want may be obtained from others within the system or from people outside it.

Consider even a desired resource such as the income of two groups, one of which is employed by the other. The two sides certainly would seem to be in a zero-sum relationship, if they constituted the entire system. But if they are producing a product or service for sale to customers, they might cooperate to pass on costs to the customer or produce a more attractive product and win additional customers, thus increasing the amount of income they have to distribute between themselves.

Moreover, income may be regarded not only as an amount of money used to purchase goods, but also as a symbol of relative status. In the latter case, the income relative to some other group's income is what is significant. If potential adversaries compare their incomes to each other and to no one else, then the more one has relative to the other, the less the other has. This is inherently zero-sum. But obviously, many other possibilities are imaginable, depending upon which group is used as the standard of reference.

Power Distribution

Not only the power relationship between potential adversaries, but also the relative power of all the parties in the system to which they belong affects the likelihood of conflicts occurring. In a system dominated by one actor, weak potential adversaries tend not to become contentious. Evidence for this may be seen in the stability and absence of overt conflict among states in a region dominated by a great power, as in the former Soviet Union. When the authority of that central power receded, ethnic conflicts among different nationalities became more salient.

In a system of many actors with relatively equal power, conflicts are more likely to occur than when there is a dominant actor. The potential adversaries see possibilities of advancing their relative position, and in trying to do so bring about a conflict.

These generalizations should be understood as tendencies that hold, everything else being equal. Great inequalities in power distributions, however, not only affect the prospects of any actor being able to change them, but also may be the source of the oppression and exploitation regarded as illegitimate. The inequalities themselves then become grievances and components of an emerging conflict.

Consistency and Stability

No social system is wholly consistent and stable. Inconsistencies are often found among the values that are shared by people in a social system. For example, a policy promoting school busing or narrowly based school taxes may seem to be more consistent with different shared values: equality of opportunity or the right of parents to use their resources to advantage their children. Although people may hold both values, they are likely to rank them differently in choosing which policy to support.

Social systems also are marked often by inconsistencies between the values held and the practices followed by their members. Such inconsistencies certainly are the bases of many social conflicts. For example, in 1944, Gunnar Myrdal concluded from the wide-ranging study he led about the conditions of American Negroes that America faced a profound dilemma.[21] He found a widely and deeply held American creed upholding the ideals of equality of opportunity and the rights of freedom and justice. But the Negroes were denied elemental civil and political rights and a fair opportunity to make a living. This discrepancy constituted a problem for Whites and for Negroes.

Rapid change of any social system places strains on its members. The change is never at the same rate for all components of the system; consequently, some elements lag behind others. For example, particular attitudes may not keep up with new circumstances, or at times various segments of the system generate differences in interests and values that bring people into conflict. This is true in communities where swift changes in population due to the entry of people from another part of the metropolitan area, country, or region of the world generate conflicts.[22] Some analysts also argue that social change that moves a society out of equilibrium is a necessary condition for revolution. As Chalmers Johnson wrote, "So long as a society's values and the realities with which it must deal in order to exist are in harmony with each other, the society is immune from revolution."[23]

Finally, abrupt changes in the international system tends to produce interstate conflicts. For example, a revolutionary regime generally alters the international system as it tries to create a social and political space for itself. The probability of conflicts increases as other regimes see threats or opportunities to settle old scores arising from the changes. This is supported by a study of interstate conflicts between 1816 and 1976.[24] Militarized interstate disputes tend to follow revolutionary changes in regimes; thus, in a system that does not change in size, the mean number of disputes that begin when revolutionary change is low amounts to 3.41, but rises to 8.86 when the change is medium, and to 11.50 when it is high.

Implications

It should be apparent that many systemic conditions are likely to foster the manifestation of conflicts among that system's members. These conditions are more likely to be noted by outside analysts than by the parties engaged in struggle. Nevertheless, the boundaries and many other features of any social system are generally socially constructed by its members, affected to some extent by contentious as well as harmonious interactions with nonmembers.

Insofar as systemic factors are important components of the bases of conflicts, controlling or preventing conflicts is not wholly within the capability of any one of the potential adversaries. The systemic factors change over a longer time period than is usually true for the adversaries' patterns of relations with each other.

Relations between Adversaries

The third set of factors that generate conflicts pertains to the relations between potential adversaries in a conflict. These factors are frequently cited by the adversaries themselves, each side attributing the conflict's existence to the treatment it received from the other side. Analysts also frequently point to the relationship between possible adversaries as the crucial component of a conflict's origin. Conflicts explained in terms of adversarial relations are often regarded as *realistic*. Even where internal and contextual factors are long-term or partial contributors to a conflict, they will not be sufficient to generate a conflict unless the adversaries' relations are sufficiently antagonistic.

Who will become adversaries in a conflict should not be taken for granted. People may be divided in infinite ways. Almost any division of people into two or more sets can be the basis for collective identity and therefore organized into conflict groups.[25] To understand the emergence of conflicts, we need to consider the many cleavages among people that form the categories from which antagonists arise.

Some divisions are well established, preexisting the emergence of a particular conflict. They may have been formed in the course of a long-past fight or they may have arisen wholly in another context. This is the case for organizations such as churches, trade unions, and governments. Such organizations have leaders who generally have authority to commit the organization or an even wider constituency to act in opposition to other organizations.

People may also be divided into groupings that are less clearly bounded and articulated. People make socially recognized distinctions, although agreement about them may be incomplete and no generally accepted organizations exist to represent them in conflicts. These distinctions involve collective self-definitions and also efforts by some people to define and separate themselves from others. Such distinctions exist throughout the world, based on characteristics such as lifestyles, location in the labor market, religion, ethnicity, language, gender, age, and ideology.

Finally, potential adversaries may arise from analytically conceived categories. That is, a theorist constructs analytic distinctions that bound quasi groups. These may become the recruiting grounds from which social groups are mobilized. For example, Ralf Dahrendorf argues that within imperatively coordinated systems such as industrial corporations, there is a dividing line between those with authority and those without; the two categories are quasi groups from which under certain conditions social groups form and engage in conflict.[26]

Many aspects of the relations between potential adversaries may be the source of conflicts, and various theoretical approaches select different aspects as being particularly important. I will discuss three important dimensions of the potentially adversarial relationship: inequality, differences, and integration.

Inequality

Domination as discussed in chapter 1 refers to the control one party exercises over another. Inequality refers to a wider range of phenomena than domination. The unequal distribution of power, status, or access to goods and services or whatever else is considered desirable by possible adversaries is widely regarded as the basis of conflict. This has been emphasized notably by Marxists and even by those elaborating and arguing against Marxism.[27] Thus, Marxists generally have stressed the preeminence of class differences in social conflicts. Class has been defined by Marxists in terms of the ownership of the means of production. The owners are the capitalists who expropriate the product of the labor of those they employ, the proletariat. Max Weber, writing in the early part of the twentieth century, emphasized other forms of market inequalities and also power and status inequalities.

Presumably, every person or group wants more of what they regard as good, and that brings them into competition and conflict with each other. Inequality exacerbates the problem because those with less want more when they see that others have more and they tend to hold those others responsible for denying them an equal amount. Inequality may also generate conflicts because those with more may believe they have a claim to even more, and furthermore they usually have the resources to try to enhance their position. The idea that inequality produces conflict may rest on assumptions about human nature. One assumption is that people are not so pliable at birth that they can be socialized to accept as proper that they have less than other humans. In other words, people will generally object to having less and not regard such a situation as legitimate. Another assumption may be that people want more than others because of an innate competitive tendency; to have more confers status and power. The desire is to have more *relative* to others regardless of any intrinsic worth of the items.

Another assumption may be that individuals have a set of basic human needs, and if those are not satisfied, people will seek to get them satisfied. The inequality in itself is not the issue, it is claimed, but rather the attainment of minimal standards so that those basic needs are met. Theorists or activists who assert they know what conditions underlie a conflict, whether or not the adversaries recognize them, often make such assumptions.

For example, the American Declaration of Independence, adopted on 4 July 1776, asserted "that all men are created equal, that they are endowed by their Creator with certain unalienable Rights, that among these are Life, Liberty, and the pursuit of Happiness." The denial of those rights would bring about an effort to gain them.

Among contemporary writers, John Burton has particularly emphasized the necessity to satisfy basic human needs if a conflict is to be resolved.[28] Drawing on the work of Paul Sites, he posits eight needs in the individual: a need for response, a need for security, a need for recognition, a need for stimulation, a need for distributive justice, a need for meaning, a need for rationality and to be seen as rational, and a need for control.

The idea that there exists basic human needs or rights generally appears to rest on the belief that these are ordained by God or are inherent in human nature. To claim that they exist in particular manifestations and ranking and are independent of culture and social conditions, subjects the assertions to the same criticisms as those leveled against assuming that there are human instincts or drives for aggression. In this work, human needs and rights will be regarded as dispositions, varying in intensity, preciseness, and independence from social conditions. For example, the human need to live in personal physical security, without threat of physical harm, is probably widely shared and less subject to cultural variations and interpretations than is the need to freely and openly express thoughts and feelings.

Inequality can be viewed as a source of conflicts without making any of these assumptions about human nature or about God. Rather, a conflict arises when people agree about what is desirable and then have different amounts of what they desire. This is a consensually based source of conflict.[29] What people want, how they are to obtain what is desired, and what claims they make for what is desired depend on social conditions. Often, people must share a cultural upbringing to agree about what is desirable.

Consensus about what is desirable, however, may be the basis for cooperation as well as conflict. When two actors want the same thing and each can attain it only insofar as the other does, they have reason to cooperate. This may occur because they identify with each other and share a common identity. Two parties may also have reason to cooperate because what they want can only be achieved by cooperative action. Thus, they each may control part of what is needed to do the desired task. For example, to produce irrigation or hydroelectric power, parties controlling opposite banks of a river need to cooperate.

Furthermore, variations in socialization among societies, ethnicities, genders, and social classes tend to make at least certain amounts of inequality seem appropriate and be widely accepted; that possibility, too, must be considered. In short, inequality often does make for conflicts; but inequality alone generally does not suffice to activate a latent conflict.

Differences

Lack of consensus about what is desirable can also be the basis of conflict. If there is dissensus about what is desirable and one party insists that the other agree with its preferences, the basis for a dissensual conflict exists. This is in the realm of conflicts about differences in religion, culture, values, and lifestyles.

These ideas derive from the work of many contemporary analysts who emphasize that reality is socially constructed. That is, people use language and other symbolic systems to define and give meaning to their experience.[30] They do this together, and their resultant beliefs then become the reality to which each of them must relate. Furthermore, these beliefs are transmitted across generations and through social space, giving them an even stronger appearance of external reality. Having somewhat varying perspectives or backgrounds can engender greatly different visions of reality and of right.

One source of such diversity is the varying experiences that different generational cohorts have in their formative years.[31] For example, persons politically maturing in a period of a great depression or a great war develop enduring orientations from that historical experience, setting off their generation from others. They develop a common set of concerns, beliefs, values, and sometimes even identity. These ways of thinking need not be identical; within the same age cohort, subgroups may form conflicting interpretations of the same experience. In any case, intergenerational differences in collective mentalities are a source of youth movements challenging those in authority and other dissensual conflicts.

Differences among people about their views of who they are and of the nature of the social world are the source of conflict only if certain other beliefs are also held. Thus, if members of a group think that the religious convictions of another group are a matter of indifference to them, or think the convictions are simply quaint or even convenient for them, no conflict will arise. If, however, one or more sets of people feel that the other's religious views are morally outrageous, then an underlying conflict exists. The outraged persons are likely to want to change the views and/or behavior of those holding such improper convictions. Or, suppose that a group of people is so convinced of the virtue and validity of its views that it considers it urgent that others accept its views and learn the truth and so gain salvation. Certainly, political and religious revolutionary movements, upon gaining power in one country, have often set out to proselytize and spread the good news. This has been true of advocates for example, of the American, the Cuban, and the Iranian revolutions.

Dissensus about values, beliefs, and other aspects of life abound; they need not be as broadly encompassing as a religion or political ideology to be the basis of a conflict. For example, in the United States in the 1960s, men wearing their hair long and those wearing it short often saw each other as members of antagonistic cultures. Even what appear to be small differences to outside observers can be given great symbolic meaning by the partisans involved in a conflict.

Both consensual and dissensual factors are intertwined as sources of conflicts. Consider the renewed struggle of women for greater equality, arising in the 1960s in the United States. For many women and men, the struggle was and is not only about equal work opportunities and equal pay for equal work. Disputants in the struggle for greater equality frequently also differ in their evaluation of characteristics associated with masculinity and femininity. Thus, some people feel that in business at least, it is good to be aggressive, dominating, competitive, stoic, risk-taking, and physically tough. They label such characteristics masculine and assume they are possessed by men. They further assume that feminine characteristics must be the opposite of masculine and that women are or should be feminine; it then follows that women are less highly regarded in the workplace than men.

Feminists in the women's liberation movement do not concur with these values and beliefs.[32] Some argue that such stereotypical characterizations of male and female roles constrain and limit both men and women, forcing them to be less than they might otherwise be. The liberation of women from the restricted social role they learn and must play would also liberate men from their circumscribed masculine role. Other feminists agree that there are differences in the way men and women tend to think, feel, and act, but they invert the masculine evaluations. The feminine emphasis on human relationships, openness to emotional expressiveness, and aversion to hierarchy are esteemed.

A great variety of differences in lifestyle, physical features, and values held can be the basis of differences in evaluation and ranking. People may be socialized to agree with the ranking, even if they themselves possess a characteristic that is accorded low status. This may result in low self-esteem or even self-hatred among people with those characteristics. For example, many African Americans in the recent past sought to lighten their skin color and straighten their hair; the assertion that black is beautiful is an effort to counter the feelings of self-denigration that underlay such acts.

Differences in values and beliefs and the evaluations of characteristics possessed by a person or group often are the basis of dissensual conflicts. People tend to think that their way of life and their characteristics are good and indeed better than those held by other people. This widespread phenomenon among different peoples is recognized in the term *ethnocentrism*, the tendency for people to regard themselves as the standard by which others should be evaluated.[33]

Integration

In addition to inequality and differences between possible adversaries, the degree to which they are integrated might be expected to increase their likelihood of competing and fighting. After all, parties who have nothing to do with each other will not contend with each other; conflict is a way of relating. Indeed, the more parties interact with each other, the more matters they have to quarrel about. On the other hand, it is also true that as parties are more involved with each other, each tends to derive benefits from the relationship, making conflict avoidance likely. The degree and nature of the integration must be considered.

The previous discussions suggest that integration between parties who are relatively equal and whose differences are small tends to make conflicts unlikely. On the other hand, integration between parties who are relatively unequal and who are markedly different tends to generate grievances.

The ease with which parties can withdraw from their relationship also has implications for the possible occurrence of conflict between them. Insofar as one or more parties can easily leave the relationship, the chances of conflict are reduced. The would-be antagonists have options other than fighting. In some circumstances, everyone in each adversary unit may be able to leave and establish new relationships; this is typically the case in competitive market relations. Often, while individuals may leave, the units cannot survive without continuing their relationship; this is the case, for example, in labor-management relations in a corporation. And sometimes, the individuals constituting the unit find it almost impossible to leave; this is the case, for example, with prison inmates and sometimes for members of ethnic groups living alongside each other.

Finally, groups in any long-term relationship have a history. That past experience helps provide a context and a way of interpreting current inequalities and differences. If a group of people believes that in the past it has been exploited or humiliated by another, the group is likely to interpret current undesirable circumstances as a continuation of old injustices, be less willing to accommodate, and seek retribution.

Synthesis

The multitude of theoretical approaches to explaining the sources of conflicts raises four questions. First, how may the explanations be combined? Second, do the many explanations indicate that there are a multitude of potential conflicts? Third, how are these possible conflicts related to each other? Finally, how come conflicts arise so infrequently when so many are possible?

Combining Approaches

The various approaches we have been discussing are best considered as complementary rather than as competing. One or another approach may be more helpful about some issues than others, for example, about the source of conflicts generally or about the emergence of a particular conflict, about the predisposing conditions or the proximate cause of a conflict, and about one kind of conflict rather than another.

Many approaches stress factors and processes *within* a potential adversary. These include psychological, cultural, and social structural conditions. But they in themselves are not sufficient to account for engaging in a struggle with any particular antagonist at any given time. The social context and the relationship with particular potential adversaries make necessary contributions. Whether or not these general factors result in a conflict at a particular time and place, nevertheless, depends on the specific actions taken by the potential antagonists.

The relative contribution of these components to explaining the sources of conflicts varies with the kind of conflict. For conflicts among large-scale, clearly bounded adversaries with enduring relationships, and functioning within the context of shared rules for conflicts, diffuse social-psychological factors are likely to be less significant than in interpersonal or intragroup conflicts. Thus, the relative explanatory power of the approaches we have been discussing will differ whether we seek to account for variations in labor-management conflicts in an industry with collective bargaining or for variations in staff-line conflicts among managers in industrial corporations.

Since social conflicts must involve conscious formulations of adversaries and issues, we need to give particular weight to how those formulations are constructed by the partisans themselves. But such formulations cannot just be made up by any of the partisans. These constructions are built up and negotiated by the contending parties, and they are constrained by social and nonsocial aspects of their world that have more or less strict dispositions.

The factors examined in this chapter are largely preparatory conditions. They provide the fuel for conflicts; but it takes a spark or sometimes considerable tinder to get the fire started. Once ignited, the availability of fuel to sustain the conflict is important for its persistence.

Multiplicity of Possible Conflicts

Clearly, there are many reasons for people to fight with each other. Thus, antagonisms often arise from internal forces. For example, within every society, some people are inadequately socialized or suffer experiences that make them prone to see others as threatening. Some of these ill-adjusted persons even play leadership roles in protecting or advancing the interests and desires of groups they claim to represent.

Such internal conditions sometimes disrupt a whole system and may result in greater justice for many members of the system. No social system functions with total harmony and stable equilibrium. Internal inconsistencies or rapid change within a social system may provide an impetus to be aggressive against external actors. Or, particular factions may come to believe that their relative position within their own society or organization will be enhanced by conflict with a competing one. This may seem obviously true for the warriors within such social systems, but often it is also true for leaders beset by internal challengers or for ideologues seeking a special niche.

In addition, the overarching social context within which potential adversaries function is often a contributing and even a primary source of conflict among competing parties. Thus, the encompassing system may not provide adequate ways of reconciling the inequalities and differences among persons and groups. International conflicts are often attributed to the anarchic nature of the world; it is full of inequities and lacks an authoritative way to allocate resources or to legitimately adjudicate disputes.

The relations among possible adversaries are the most proximate factors in the sequence of conflict emergence. They also are particularly relevant for the way the actors themselves construct a conflict and are most amenable to short-term conflict resolution. There are innumerable individual and collective identities and unlimited opportunities for groups to see themselves as an "us" being oppressed or threatened by a "them."

In short, the bases for possible conflicts are infinite. Just as clearly, many underlying conflicts remain unrecognized and do not become overt, sometimes because they are overshadowed by more salient struggles.

Interlocking Conflicts

The vast number of conflicts in which every person or group may be engaged are not independent of each other: they are interlocked in many ways.[34] Some emerge and become salient, blocking the eruption of others. As new conflicts become salient, they may reduce the significance of the previously primary conflict, allowing the old one to de-escalate and even become resolved.

Analyzing the variety of conflicts in which a set of adversaries is engaged and analyzing how those struggles are linked can help explain the shifts in the conduct of each conflict. I will discuss three dimensions of linkages: (1) the degree of connection over time, (2) the degree of connection through overlapping entities and issues, and (3) the degree of connection through the concurrence of conflicts.

Connection over Time

Each conflict can be viewed as one fight in a large ongoing struggle or as a discrete episode. An analyst may note that a conflict, essentially between the same adversaries about the same issues, has a history and an anticipated future. Thus, the conflict may be regarded as one in a linked series of episodes between adversaries with generations of enmity. Therefore, some observers regard the cold war of 1945 to 1989 as only one episode in the more enduring rivalry between Russia and America.

The adversaries have their own views and they often disagree with each other about when their conflict began and for how long it has been waged. For example, in the United States what was called the Cuban Missile Crisis is generally thought to have started with the October 1962 discovery by a U.S. reconnaissance plane that Soviet missile bases were under construction in Cuba. In the Soviet Union, the episode was referred to as the Caribbean Crisis and began in 1961 with the U.S. efforts to forcefully overthrow the Castro-led government of Cuba.[35]

Whether an episode is regarded as discrete or as connected with others and therefore as a battle in an ongoing war has important implications for the handling of possible contentions. Viewed as an incident in a protracted struggle, a contention is likely to be regarded as momentous, but little noted if regarded as an isolated matter in an otherwise pacific environment. Thus, a labor-management difference can be regarded as more or less serious, depending on its context. For some analysts and partisans, it might be seen as a part of a long-enduring class struggle. As Marx and Engels wrote in the Communist Manifesto, "The history of all hitherto existing society is the history of class struggles."[36]

Connection through Overlapping Entities and Issues

People have many characteristics that individually may be the basis for identity and for opposition to people with different characteristics. The characteristics may tend to coincide, as when members of an ethnic community not only reside in a particular region, but also generally have relatively high incomes, share the same religion, and speak the same language (not spoken by others). Then, if they live in a country where members of another ethnic community reside in a particular region, have relatively low incomes, share a different religion, and use a different language, the lines of cleavage are considered to be superimposed.

Often, however, the lines of cleavage do not coincide, but crosscut each other. For example, members of two ethnic communities may share the same language and not live in different localities and they are similarly diverse in their incomes. In that case, the class difference does not coincide but crosscuts their ethnic difference. It is then possible for people to be mobilized into opposing ethnic *or* class groupings, but in either case, some members of each camp will have ties with some members of the opposing side.

These two kinds of structural conditions have different dispositions for conflicts. Crosscutting lines of cleavage are expected to inhibit conflicts from emerging and to moderate them if they do. Superimposed lines of cleavage, on the other hand, are expected to generate conflicts and intensify them when they arise.[37]

In addition to these possibly overlapping bases of identity and organization, people have characteristics that tend to be nested within each other, like wooden Russian dolls. For example, Anwar Sadat was president of Egypt, a member of the Arab nation, and of the broader Islamic community. He could think of himself as advancing the interests of his person, his government, his country, the Arab nation, or the Islamic community. He could regard his adversary to be the head of the Israeli government, the State of Israel, world Jewry, or Western imperialism.

A single conflict may engage many different sets of adversaries. The antagonists themselves often disagree about which adversary is the significant one. Frequently, the leaders of one side say they are in conflict only with the leaders of the other side, not with their followers or the people they claim to represent. For example, when the U.S. President George Bush mobilized the U.S. public and an international alliance against the Iraqi invasion of Kuwait, he insisted the struggle was against President Saddam Hussein, not the Iraqi people.

It follows that conflicts themselves are often overlapping and embedded in each other. For example, the cold war was superimposed upon the Arab-Israeli conflict between the mid-1950s and mid-1980s, exacerbating each of them.[38]

Connection through Concurrence

Each party in a conflict has its own set of possible adversaries. It could be involved in many simultaneous fights, or it may subordinate or even deny all but one of them. Thus, leaders of almost any organized conflict party face threats from some of their constituents or from internal rivals.

Each party in a general conflict, then, emphasizes one or more subconflicts but tends to ignore others. The adversaries in any given conflict may accord different priorities to that confrontation relative to others each faces. One adversary may even regard an enemy as a friend if it is confronted by an even worse enemy; following the dictum, "the enemy of my enemy is my friend."

This coexistence of concurrent potential conflicts helps account for the eruption and the termination of one rather than another fight as the salience of one changes. For example, consider the changing primary adversaries with whom Saddam Hussein, president of Iraq, has been in conflict: Syria, Iran, Kuwait, the United States, Iraqi Kurds, and so on. The eruption of one conflict, then, may exacerbate others or inhibit them from becoming manifest.

Absence of Overt Conflict

Most possible conflicts do not become manifest, and of those that do, most are managed using means regarded by the participants as legitimate. This needs to be recognized if we are to understand why conflicts do erupt and are waged destructively.

For example, considering the many possible conflicts between husbands and wives in their daily living together, the relative infrequency of fights can be understood in most societies by the wife's typical deference to her husband's preferences. This occurs even in the domain of preparing meals. As Marjorie DeVault has observed, "The invisibility of the work that produces 'family,' the flexibility underlying perceptions of 'choice' about the work, and the association between caring work and the supposedly 'natural' emotions of a loving wife and mother all tend to suppress conflict over housework."[39]

Beginning in the early 1960s and continuing into the early 1970s, students in universities in South Korea, the United States, Mexico, France, Poland, and many other countries believed they were in conflict with the university administrators, the dominant elites of their countries, or with other authoritative groups. Students demonstrated in the streets, seized control of university buildings, and otherwise acted to change the policies they opposed. But most of the time in nearly all countries, students do not see themselves in conflict with university or government authorities. This acquiescence can be explained by the dominance of the authorities that is so pervasive as to be unrecognized. The argument is that prevailing ways of thinking are often components of hegemonic domination.[40] In such cases, according legitimacy to power inequality can effectively deny that underlying conflicts exist.

Often a conflict does not emerge simply because individuals find other means of coping with the inequalities and differences that they find unsatisfactory. Seeking to escape from the relationship they find punishing, they emigrate, they divorce, or they quit their jobs. People also resist, using barely conscious ways to express their discontent; as, for example, in employment relations they dislike, they may come in late, be absent, work slowly, or act ineptly.

Individuals also frequently try to escape the conditions they find unsatisfactory by seeking personal advancement. Some try by currying favor with those with authority who can give them what they want. Others work hard, acting as they think their superiors want them to act.

In some situations, alternatively, people may deny that anyone else is responsible for their unsatisfactory conditions but see no way out. They think it is a matter of fate, luck, or God's will. Or they may believe their condition is the result of their own failings as a person, and they may seek solace in drunkenness. Others, seeing no exit and no way to change the reality, withdraw and passively accept what they deem immutable.

Finally, people may even engage in violent and hurting behavior against others and only marginally be engaged in a conflict as defined here. For example, a person may lash out against someone else to hurt that person, but the action is largely expressive and is not directed to get that other person to do or give anything. This may occur in interpersonal relations and be driven by inner psychological processes.

Some of us may regard one or more of these alternatives as better than conflict, and others of us regard them as worse, depending on the groups involved and their circumstances. That is why we sometimes favor stirring up a conflict while at other times we try to prevent one from arising.

Notes

1. Misunderstandings can be discerned in conflict episodes more easily than in a conflict viewed as a whole. For example, consider the dangerous events in October 1961 when Soviet and U.S. tanks confronted each other at Checkpoint Charlie at the newly constructed Berlin Wall. For a discussion of the incident, see Raymond L. Garthoff, "Berlin 1961: The Record Corrected," *Foreign Policy* 84 (Fall 1991): 142–56.

From the U.S. perspective, the confrontation began with the insistence that East German police check the diplomatic passport of a senior U.S. diplomat driving into East Berlin. Not recognizing East German authority, the diplomat insisted that only a Soviet officer could do so. This was followed by assertive U.S. probes and moving ten M-48 tanks to Checkpoint Charlie.

Access to new information provides an understanding of the confrontation from the Soviet perspective. Immediately prior to the episode, the Soviets had learned that U.S. combat engineers had replicated a section of the Berlin Wall in a secluded area so that tanks with bulldozer attachments could experiment with ways to break down the wall. Sending U.S. tanks to the wall was readily seen as a provocation and was countered by sending an equal number of Soviet tanks to the wall.

Apparently erroneously, each side saw the other as intentionally provocative and threatening. Each countered that threat by bringing up its tanks, and each was convinced afterward that its show of force was effective in forcing the other side to back down.

2. Hilary Putnam, *Reason, Truth, and History* (New York: Cambridge University Press, 1981), xi; the discussion here draws from Hilary Putnam, *The Many Faces of Realism* (LaSalle, Ill.: Open Court, 1987).

3. Some dispositions are more *strict* than others; for example, bodies with non–zero-sum rest mass cannot travel at the speed of light is a strict disposition. See Putnam, *The Many Faces of Realism*, 10.

4. For example, Robert Ardrey has written in *The Territorial Imperative* (New York: Dell, 1966), 5, "We act as we do for reasons of our evolutionary past, not our cultural present, and our behavior is as much a mark of our species as is the shape of a human thigh bone. . . . If we defend the title to our land or the sovereignty of our country, we do it for reasons no different, no less innate, no less ineradicable, than do lower animals."

5. Vasquez reviews this literature and also the research reporting the high frequency of territorial issues in international wars. He concludes that humans are not "hard-wired" with an instinct for territoriality, but, quoting Somit, may be " 'soft-wired' to favor certain behaviors and cultural options." See John A. Vasquez, *The War Puzzle* (Cambridge: Cambridge University Press, 1993), 139–52, and Albert Somit, "Humans, Chimps, and Bobnobos: The Biological Bases of Aggression, War, and Peacemaking," *Journal of Conflict Resolution* 34 (September 1990): 553–82.

6. Allan Mazur, "A Cross-Species Comparison of Status in Small Established Groups," *American Sociological Review* 38 (October 1973): 513–30.

7. See Myron Rothbart and Scott Lewis, "Cognitive Processes and Intergroup Relations: A Historical Perspective," in *Social Cognition: Impact on Social Psychology*, eds. P. G. Devine, D. L. Hamilton, and T. M. Ostrom (San Diego: Academic Press, 1994). The major work that generated much subsequent research is Theodor W. Adorno, Else Frenkel-Brunswik, D. J. Levinson, and R. N. Sanford, in collaboration with Betty Aron, Maria H. Levinson, and W. Morrow, *The Authoritarian Personality* (New York: Harper Brothers, 1950).

8. Bruno Bettleheim and Morris Janowitz, *Dynamics of Prejudice* (New York: Harper, 1950).

9. The Seville Statement has been reproduced widely. The source for the quotations here and for the Sociological Statement on War and Violence, drafted by Louis Kriesberg, is Robert Elias and Jennifer Turpin, eds., *Re-Thinking Peace* (Boulder, Colo.: Lynne Rienner, 1994), 66.

10. This idea has been the subject of considerable research. An early formulation of the idea is to be found in John Dollard, Leonard W. Doob, Neal E. Miller, O. H. Mowrer, and Robert R. Sears, *Frustration and Aggression* (New Haven, Conn.: Yale University Press, 1939). A review of research may be found in Leonard Berkowitz, ed., *Roots of Aggression* (New York: Lieber-Atherton, 1969).

11. For reviews of related literature, see Patricia G. Devine, David L. Hamilton, and Thomas M. Ostrom, eds., *Social Cognition: Impact on Social Psychology* (San Diego: Academic Press, 1994).

12. This work is reviewed and developed in Marc Howard Ross, *The Culture of Conflict* (New Haven, Conn.: Yale University Press, 1993). Also, see Vamik Volkan, *The Need to Have Enemies and Allies: From Clinical Practice to International Relationships* (New York: Jason Aronson, 1988).

13. See Ross, *The Culture of Conflict*; also Beatrice B. Whiting and John W. M. Whiting, *Children of Six Cultures: A Psycho-Cultural Analysis* (Cambridge, Mass.: Harvard University Press, 1975).

14. Research and theorizing is relatively less developed on these matters than on the processes making for antagonistic feelings and conduct. Feminist writers have noted this neglect and directed attention to social relationships and caring for others. See, for example, Carol Gilligan, *In a Different Voice: Psychological Theory and Women's Development* (Cambridge, Mass.: Harvard University Press, 1982); Joan Tronto, "Beyond Gender Difference to a Theory of Care," *Signs: Journal of Women in Culture and Society* 12 (April 1987): 644–63; and Margaret M. Riordan, "Keeping the Candle Lit: The Ethic of Just Care in the Context of Catholic Peace and Justice Activism," unpublished doctoral dissertation, Syracuse University, 1997; also see Arnold P. Goldstein and Gerald Y. Michaels, *Empathy: Development, Training, and Consequences* (Hillsdale, N.J.: Lawrence Erlbaum Associates, 1985).

15. Ross, *The Culture of Conflict*, 61–62; and Ashley Montagu, ed., *Learning Non-Aggression* (New York: Oxford University Press, 1978).

16. This effect is emphasized by analysts of mass societies, in which many people are isolated and alienated. See, William Kornhauser, *The Politics of Mass Society* (New York: Free Press, 1959).

17. Alex Inkeles and Daniel Levinson, "National Character: The Study of Modal Personality and Sociocultural Systems," 977–1020, in Gardner Lindzey, ed., *Handbook of Social Psychology*, vol. 2 (Reading, Mass.: Addison-Wesley, 1954).

18. Theodore Schwartz, for example, writes, "Culture consists of the derivatives of experience, more or less organized learned or created by the individuals of a population, including those images or encodements and their interpretations (meanings) transmitted from past generations, from contemporaries, or formed by individuals themselves" ("Anthropology and Psychology: An Unrequited Relationship," in *New Directions in Psychological Anthropology*, eds. T. Schwartz, G. White, and G. Lutz [Cambridge: Cambridge University Press, 1992], p. 324).

19. Betty A. Reardon, *Sexism and the War System* (Syracuse, N.Y.: Syracuse University Press, 1996).

20. President Eisenhower said, "In our councils of government we must guard against the acquisition of unwarranted influence, whether sought or unsought, by the military-industrial complex. The potential for the disastrous rise of misplaced power exists and will persist" (cited in Charles W. Kegley, Jr., and Eugene R. Wittkopf, *American Foreign Policy Pattern and Process* 2d ed. [New York: St. Martin's Press, 1982], 255). For other analyses of the military-industrial complex and the workings of a power elite, see C. Wright Mills, *The Power Elite* (New York: Oxford University Press, 1956), and Steven J. Rosen, ed., *Testing the Theory of the Military-Industrial Complex* (Lexington, Mass.: Heath, 1973). Also see Dale R. Herspring and Ivan Volgyes, eds., *Civil-Military Relations in Communist Systems* (Boulder, Colo.: Westview, 1978).

21. Beginning in 1938, with funds from the Carnegie Corporation, the Swedish social scientist Gunnar Myrdal led a large number of social scientists to examine all aspects of the Negroes' conditions and of the attitudes of Whites in the United States. The major book culminating this massive study is Gunnar Myrdal, with the assistance of Richard Sterner and Arnold Rose, *An American Dilemma: The Negro Problem and American Democracy* (New York and London: Harper & Brothers, 1944).

22. James S. Coleman, *Community Conflict* (Glencoe, Ill.: The Free Press, 1957). Also see theories about strain generating social movements, Neil Smelser, *The Theory of Collective Behavior* (New York: The Free Press, 1963).

23. Chalmers Johnson, *Revolutionary Change* (Boston: Little, Brown, 1966), 60.

24. Zeev Maoz, "Joining the Club of Nations: Political Development and International Conflict, 1816–1976," *International Studies Quarterly* 33 (June 1989): 199–231.

25. Many characteristics can be selected to serve as a basis for coordination, as a way for people to group themselves for their mutual benefit. See Russell Hardin, "Self-Interest, Group Identity," 15–45, in John L. Comaroff and Paul C. Stern, eds., *Perspectives on Nationalism and War* (Luxembourg: Gordon and Breach, 1995).

26. See the influential book by Ralf Dahrendorf, *Class and Class Conflict in Industrial Society* (Stanford, Calif.: Stanford University Press, 1959).

27. See Karl Marx and Friedrich Engels, *The Communist Manifesto* (Chicago: H. Regnery, 1954); Max Weber, *The Theory of Social and Economic Organization*, translated by A. M. Henderson and Talcott Parsons (New York: Oxford University Press, 1947); and Dahrendorf, *Class and Class Conflict in Industrial Society*. Also see studies of revolutions and domestic struggles.

28. John Burton, *Conflict: Resolution and Provention* (New York: St. Martin's, 1990).

29. The distinction between consensual and dissensual conflicts is based on the work of Vihelm Aubert, "Competition and Dissensus: Two Types of Conflict and Conflict Resolution," *Journal of Conflict Resolution* 7 (March 1963): 26–42.

30. Peter L. Berger and Thomas Luckmann, *The Social Construction of Reality* (New York: Doubleday, 1966); Erving Goffman, *Frame Analysis* (New York: Harper Colophon, 1974), and Michael J. Shapiro and Hayward R. Alker, eds., *Challenging Boundaries* (Minneapolis: University of Minnesota Press, 1996).

31. This idea has been developed particularly by Karl Manheim. See his *Essays on the Sociology of Knowledge* (London: Routledge and Kegan Paul, 1952). Also see Rudolf Heberle, *Social Movements* (New York: Appleton-Century-Crofts, 1951), and Richard G. Braungart and Margaret M. Braungart, "Political Generations" in *Research in Political Sociology*, vol. 4, ed. R. G. Braungart and M. M. Braungart (Greenwich, Conn.: JAI Press, 1989), 281–319.

32. Gilligan, *In a Different Voice*; and Andrea Nye, *Feminist Theory and the Philosophies of Man* (New York: Croom Helm, 1988).

33. A comprehensive assessment of the literature on ethnocentrism is available in Robert A. LeVine and Donald T. Campbell, *Ethnocentrism* (New York: John Wiley, 1972).

34. For an earlier formulation of the concept, see Louis Kriesberg, "Interlocking Conflicts in the Middle East," in *Research in Social Movements, Conflicts, and Change*, vol. 3, ed. Louis Kriesberg (Greenwich, Conn.: JAI Press, 1980).

35. Raymond L. Gartoff, *Reflections on the Cuban Missile Crisis*, rev. ed. (Washington, D.C.: The Brookings Institution, 1989), and Richard Ned Lebow and Janice Gross Stein, *We All Lost the Cold War* (Princeton, N.J.: Princeton University Press, 1994), 19–145.

36. The manifesto was drawn up and published in 1848. Engels noted later that all history referred to all written history, believing that preliterate societies had primitive communism. See Max Eastman, ed., *Capital, The Communist Manifesto and Other Writings by Karl Marx* (New York: The Modern Library, 1932), 321.

37. Thus, when ethnic groups in a society are ranked in a superordinate and subordinate fashion, conflicts are likely to be more intense than in societies in which the

ethnic groups are not ranked. See discussion by Donald L. Horowitz, *Ethnic Groups in Conflict* (Berkeley: University of California Press, 1985), 21–36.

38. Louis Kriesberg, *International Conflict Resolution: The U.S.-USSR and Middle East Cases* (New Haven, Conn.: Yale University Press, 1992).

39. Marjorie L. DeVault, "Conflict over Housework: A Problem that (Still) Has No Name," in *Research in Social Movements, Conflict and Change*, vol. 12, ed. Louis Kriesberg (Greenwich, Conn.: JAI Press, 1990).

40. Antonio Gramsci, *Letters from Prison* (New York: Harper & Row, 1973), and Martin Carnoy, *Education as Cultural Imperialism* (New York: David McKay, 1974).

3

Emerging Conflicts

Although all potential conflicts do not erupt into overt struggle, many do. The outbreak of a fight often seems sudden, but it usually is the result of many gradual changes. The circumstances that produce a social conflict may have persisted for a long time; yet, some necessary condition, in retrospect, was missing. To illustrate, members of two ethnic communities may have interacted with widespread individual acts of discrimination and resistance for many years, but they did not act collectively to change the relationship. Then, an event may indicate that effective collective resistance is possible and many members enduring discrimination coalesce and act on their demands to end discrimination, igniting a struggle.

Social conflicts emerge when four conditions become minimally satisfied. Innumerable combinations of the four conditions may generate a social conflict, a high level of one compensating for a low level of another.[1] The first condition is that the parties to the conflict think of themselves as entities separate from each other. Second, one or more of the parties must have a grievance. Third, one or more of the parties must formulate goals to change another person or group so that the grievance will be reduced. Fourth, members of the aggrieved party must believe that they can bring about the desired change in the antagonist.

The conditions require elaboration before we can explain how they arise. First, we consider self-awareness. For an individual, developing a sense of self is an essential part of becoming a person. Each person's self-conception is a unique combination of identifications used to describe who the person is. Those self-identifications include terms as broad as *woman* or *man, Catholic* or *Muslim,* or as narrow as being a member of one particular family. Therefore, although a self-identity may be thought to coincide with a particular living human being, the boundaries may be wider. Identities sometimes extend to families or ethnic communities, so that people sacrifice their individual lives to preserve their larger selves.

In interpersonal conflicts, individuals can be regarded as the parties to a conflict. For most of the struggles discussed here, however, the adversaries are larger and a collective identity is necessary. People who share the same identity think of themselves as having a common interest and a common fate.

Some parties, such as trade unions, national governments, and political parties, preexist a particular conflict and their members take their readiness to fight for granted. However, even such identities are neither fixed nor unitary, often being modified as a conflict develops. Thus, union leaders or government leaders must mobilize their constituents for a particular fight and in doing so may define that constituency more narrowly or broadly, by emphasizing membership or shared ideology or the character of the opposition.

The second condition is that members of a possible adversary group feel aggrieved. They think they have less of what they want of a consensually valued resource or feel that their values are not adequately respected or supported. Moreover, they believe that these inadequacies are unjustified, that they are entitled to have what they lack.

The third condition for a social conflict to arise is that members of the aggrieved conflict party develop goals opposing an adversary. The goals are not necessarily fully and clearly articulated. What is essential is that one group believes that another collectivity is responsible for its grievances. The aggrieved party believes that if the other party would change, its dissatisfaction would be lessened. Its leaders may formulate specific demands of the other group; but whether clearly formulated or not, the other group rejects the demands.

The fourth condition is that members of the aggrieved party believe their actions can induce the other party to change. They may not have a clearly articulated strategy, but they think that their actions can improve their circumstances.

These four conditions are highly interdependent. Thus, who we are, what we have to complain about, who is responsible, and what we can do about it all help shape each other. Still, it is useful to distinguish among these conditions and examine how each comes into play and together account for the eruption of a conflict. These conditions provide the tinder and the spark that ignite a struggle, that is, fueled by the underlying conditions discussed in the previous chapter. Characteristics of potential adversaries, of their social contexts, and of their relationships with each other influence the maturation of each of the four conditions.

Identity

As already suggested, identities vary from individuals to vast collectivities and they may be long-enduring or relatively ephemeral. To understand how struggles erupt, escalate, de-escalate, and become resolved, we must know how identities are formed and re-formed, and how they shift in salience. For example, in the 1950s and 1960s many people living in what was then Yugoslavia felt pride in having stood up to the Soviet Union in 1948 and in creating a new economic system that seemed promising.[2] Although the practice was not widespread, some citizens of Yugoslavia regarded themselves as Yugoslav, and this identity was growing in the 1960s and 1970s.[3] Yet in the 1990s, most people in Yugoslavia felt that their identities as Serbs, Croats, Slovenes, Muslims, or Bosnians were much more salient than their identity as Yugoslavs.

In this analysis, I assume that identities are socially constructed on the bases of various traits and experiences that people have. The characteristics are open to varying interpretations; but they are not all equally susceptible to every interpretation. Furthermore, some characteristics are treated seriously by the principals, while other characteristics are regarded as trivial.

The debates about the nature of ethnicity are illuminating in these regards. Some analysts speak of ethnicity as a primordial phenomenon, relatively permanent and unchanging.[4] Others stress that it is socially constructed, with people choosing a history and common ancestry and creating, as much as discovering, differences from others. In the perspective taken here, most aspects of ethnicity are considered socially constructed, but some traits of ethnicity are not easily modifiable by social processes.

Some traits seem to be fixed at birth or soon thereafter, such as parental descent, religious origin, place of birth, and skin color. Other traits may be acquired or modified later, such as political ideology, language spoken, costume worn, or food eaten. Insofar as the traits chosen to define membership in an ethnicity are of the former variety, ethnic status is ascribed; and insofar as they are modified or acquired in later life, ethnic status is achieved.[5]

Thus, skin color is an important marker of identity in some societies but not in others. In the United States, relatively great attention is given to skin color, especially of Blacks. There is even a tendency to dichotomize color into black and white, claiming that having any Black parentage makes a person Black. But in some countries ethnicity is defined in terms of traits that may be acquired later in life; for example, in Mexico, "Indians" can become "Mestizos" by wearing Western clothing and speaking Spanish.[6]

Some societies rely even more than does the United States on ascribed traits to define membership. Thus, in the United States, citizenship is open to anyone who swears to support the Constitution and meets certain residence requirements. In a sense, even being an American is defined in terms of the values that a person holds. On the other hand, in Kuwait, Japan, Israel, Germany, and Saudi Arabia, citizenship is easier to obtain for those who by descent are Kuwaitis, Japanese, Jews, Germans, or Saudis, respectively.

Identities largely defined in terms of ascribed traits are difficult to discard or escape. They are likely to be the basis of intergroup conflict, since individual solutions are less available. Qualifications to this tendency are enlightening. Sex and age are set at birth, but they are not a universal and constant basis for the formation of conflict groups engaged frequently in destructive struggles. This is true for sex differences, partly because individual men and women live in great intimacy and complement each other in socially prescribed ways. Age differences are also peculiar in that every one was young once and nearly all young people want and expect to be older; besides there are intimate intergenerational bonds. Nevertheless, in many societies and institutions, men dominate women and women often resist and struggle to modify the domination. Political and economic struggles along generational lines also do arise in particular circumstances.

Ethnic as well as other identities often serve as a basis for mobilization and organization.[7] They are symbols around which people can rally for their individual and common benefit. The choice of one or another identity, with varying content, may be explained by reference to possible group members' characteristics, to their social context, and to their relations with others.

Membership Characteristics

Certain human characteristics are especially likely to become the bases for organizing a collectivity for a struggle. Moreover, the combination of traits and their distribution within a population are important determinants of the emergence of adversaries. Four interrelated characteristics foster forming a self-identified collectivity: homogeneity, ease of communication, clear boundaries, and organizational potential.

Homogeneity of Members

Insofar as members of a social category are perceived by themselves to be similar in traits, the likelihood they will form a shared identity is increased. Their homogeneity tends to facilitate communication and to foster a sense of solidarity and shared fate. To illustrate, the French speakers of Quebec tended to share religion and class position, which facilitated mobilizing support for Quebec autonomy or independence. On the other hand, the ethnic heterogeneity of American workers has been one of the frequently observed difficulties in the United States to build worker solidarity for trade union membership or for class-conscious political parties.[8] The high degree of occupational differentiation also hinders working-class solidarity.[9] Such heterogeneity becomes the basis for conflicts within the social category, weakening the sense of identity for members of the category as a whole.[10]

Women's solidarity as a conflict group opposing men is also handicapped by their heterogeneity. Not only do they have the diversity of men in terms of ethnicity, region, and occupation, but in many societies their marital status and their husbands' occupational positions have great importance for them as well. These kinds of heterogeneity generate dissensual as well as consensual issues of contention among women, weakening their shared identity.[11]

Ease of Communication

A prerequisite for a sense of common identity is communication among the members of the population that may become the conflict group. Insofar as communication is easy, the members are likely to develop a shared identity. Many factors affect the ease of communication, including the members' number, proximity, and density, their social and technical skills, their sharing of a common language, and the social and nonsocial links among them.

Increased opportunities for effective communication among members of potential conflict groups tend to increase their sense of identity; they may also increase the feeling of dissatisfaction and the belief that a grievance can be reduced. Changes in such opportunities are often slow and gradual but then suddenly become evident.

To illustrate, prior to the October 1917 Russian Revolution, the increasing concentration of workers in very large factories supported the growth of proletarian solidarity. Although the industrial proletariat was small, Theda Skocpol notes, "it was disproportionately concentrated both in large-scale industrial enterprises and in major industrial centers."[12] This facilitated communication, mobilization, and organization and so contributed to the emergence of opposition to the czar, and ultimately to the October Revolution.

The reduction of constraints upon communication can suddenly liberate people to mobilize as a conflict group. This is the basis of fear by authoritarian or totalitarian governments that allowing a little freedom will undermine their rule. Nevertheless, to placate some dissenters or to use pressure from below against bureaucratic rigidity, government leaders or a faction of them may encourage the open expression of opinion. For example, Mao Zedong, believing the Chinese Communist Party needed "rectification," encouraged constructive criticism of the party bureaucracy in the 1956–57 Hundred Flowers movement. The resulting vehement criticism was soon suppressed by those who felt attacked and the hard-liners' position was reestablished. The development in the former Soviet Union was different following Mikhail Gorbachev's *glasnost* policy encouraging open discussion. Gradually, the expression of dissent and opposition to the previous policies of the Communist Party and the government it controlled built a momentum that became impossible to reverse.

Populations vary greatly in possessing the social and technological resources facilitating communication. Insofar as persons in a population can readily communicate with each other, they will tend to develop collective self-consciousness and express this in organizational form. Thus, one of the factors that accounts for the order in which trade unions have been established is the ability of the workers to communicate and organize. Printers, for example, were among the first of the craftsmen to form trade unions. Dominant groups have often sought to deny or restrict the development of skills that are helpful for communication. Consider how in the United States, education had been forbidden for slaves and even after slavery, African Americans did not have equal access to education. For generations, too, women did not have equal educational opportunities.[13]

Clear and Stable Boundaries

Insofar as the social boundaries of population categories are clear and unchanging, their members tend to develop a sense of solidarity and common fate. Thus, members of a caste are more likely to think of themselves as having a shared identity and fate than are members of a social class, whose boundaries are diffuse with members entering and leaving.

The combination and distribution of those characteristics we are discussing, homogeneity, ease of communication, and organization, always must be considered within some boundaries. Thus, whether a social category is highly homogenous or not depends on the boundaries used by an analyst or by the members themselves. The distribution of these characteristics may radically shift when the boundaries change.

The salience of one identity rather than another is likely to change when the boundaries of a social category or group move. Changes in international political boundaries are particularly visible, for example, when states sign treaties recognizing new territorial borders after a war. Boundaries between religious, class, or ethnic groups tend to move less abruptly, but they too shift over time.

Organizational Potential

The degree and nature of a quasi group's organizational potential greatly affect the likelihood that the group will become mobilized as a collectivity. The more highly integrated and interdependent are the members of a group, the more likely are they to see themselves as a collectivity with common interests. Variations in such self-conceptions can be noted among members of different occupations.[14] Miners, for example, are vitally interdependent in their work activities and historically have had a high sense of solidarity compared with other occupational groups.[15] Of course, the solidarity of miners is often reinforced by other factors, such as isolation and concentration.

Networks, linking persons and small groups, are crucial in the development of collective identity in potential conflict groups. These preexisting groups and links facilitate communication and the creation of shared identities, giving certain issues salience. They are also crucial in mobilizing people, in developing a feeling of dissatisfaction, and in creating the belief that their dissatisfaction can be alleviated by their efforts.[16] This is illustrated by the rise of the American civil rights movement against segregation in the American South. The movement rested on the local churches and other already-existing organizations and the interpersonal channels linking them.[17]

Finally, it is necessary to note the important role that leaders and persons of authority play in choosing which identity should be given salience. Leaders articulate and use the resources they control to put forward identities that include some people while excluding others. Their resources include the symbols of authority they are able to claim, the patronage they can offer, and the coercion they can threaten.

Social Context

The social setting within which conflict groups may emerge greatly affects their sense of identity. I note, here, only a few ways this occurs. The prevailing ways of thinking in every period of history profoundly affect how people characterize themselves. Identifications in terms of religious beliefs, class relations, ethnicity, or lifestyles are more or less salient in different times and places. For example, class consciousness has been more prevalent in European societies than in the United States.

Prevailing ways of thought have significance beyond how parties think of themselves. Those ways of thinking provide the concepts by which other people define them, and the shared understandings support some claims more than others. Thus, in an age sympathetic to nationalism, ethnic group members tend to claim the right of collective self-determination, and they find support for such claims from nonmembers.[18]

The social context provides a repertoire of possible identities to assume. Ones that have been taken by others and used to advance their interests serve as models, and similar or parallel identities then become salient. Thus, in the United States, African Americans in the 1960s' civil rights struggle stressed their identity as Blacks and served as models for other disadvantaged people. Many groups formed, using their disadvantaged position as a basis for identity and claim making. As women, gays, Hispanics, the deaf, and many other categories of people developed pride in that aspect of who they were, still other people felt free to find their identity in comparable experiences of discrimination and oppression.

Adversary Relations

In defining themselves, groups also define others; and in defining their opponents, they also define themselves. Each self-conscious collectivity defines nonmembers; indeed, identity is in good measure established in contrast to others.[19] We know who we are by emphasizing how we are not like others. Thus, many former colonial peoples, Arabs, Africans, and Latinos define themselves by affirming their separation from Western ideals and values. Thus, too, during the cold war, being an American was defined by many people partly as being anticommunist.

Absence of a clear contrast group hampers the formation of a collective identity. At the turn of the nineteenth century, workers in a locally owned mine or mill knew who the adversary was and that helped define them. But since the turn of the twentieth century, when the mine or mill is owned by a vast conglomerate and the managers, too, are hired hands, the adversary is less clear.

The inclination of people to evaluate their own group as superior to others is widely noted. This tendency toward ethnocentrism contributes to the sense of people living in a world in which it is "us" against "them."[20] But it is important to note that this is not true for every collective identification all the time. Often members of one people find members of another interestingly different and enjoy their music or food or other traditional products.[21] Social psychological research indicates that attachment to one's country— patriotism—is a factor separate from feelings of national superiority— nationalism.[22]

Self-identifications become salient in relationship to other persons, and therefore are partly situational. For example, a person's identity as an American is less salient when she is in the United States than when she is visiting another country. There is evidence that persons living in ethnically heterogenous neighborhoods take their ethnicity more seriously than do those in ethnically homogenous neighborhoods.[23] The derogatory content of stereotypes and the feelings of antagonism, however, can be greater and more resistant to change when people are isolated from each other and those views are inculcated without contradictions.

The content of a collective identity, as well as awareness of it, is shaped by interaction. Such interaction is never wholly symmetrical. If a group is relatively powerful, it will try to impose its definitions upon other groups. The Nazis' violent imposition of their characterization of who and what Jews were stands as a grotesque example of that tendency. In most instances, the imposition of a definition and characterization is less organized and violent; but some degree of imposition is discernable in many relationships.

For example, "race," in the United States as in many societies, is socially constructed.[24] In the United States, anyone with any African ancestry has generally been classified as Black, and often cultural patterns are regarded as associated with that social race. That classification and those characterizations were originally constructed and imposed by the largely self-defined Whites.

In cases with illegitimate power inequalities, the subordinate group will try to reject the definitions and characterizations imposed by superordinates. What ensues is a struggle over who has the right to define membership and the qualities of each group. But, interestingly, under long-term domination, many members of the dominated group internalize the evaluations of those who dominate them. The result may be self-hatred and self-denigration, which inhibits challenging the system of domination. Some members of the subordinated group, however, may overcome those views and begin to challenge an adversary, and in the ensuing struggle others in the group develop pride in their self-assertion.

Particular forms of identification are forged by particular kinds of domination. Thus, nationalist identification often emerges in the face of coercive treatment by foreign armies. For example, when Japanese troops invaded China in 1937, they took ruthless action against the entire rural population, arousing intense anti-Japanese feelings among the peasants.[25] That invasion and subsequent occupation raised the Chinese peasants' sense of citizenship and their interest in strengthening the Chinese state.

Changing Identities

A shift in identities frequently plays a significant role in the outbreak of a conflict. Thus, broad identities may dissipate and the organizations that sustain them weaken so that other identities become more salient. This happened in the late 1980s for many people in Yugoslavia. Their identifications as communists and as Yugoslavs were undermined, and old ethnic and religious identities became more prominent.

Identities may also broaden, generating new lines of social cleavages, as old ones become subordinate. This is illustrated in the argument that the world is entering a period of civilizational conflicts, for example, between adherents of Western civilization and adherents of the Islamic civilization.[26] Such interpretations and predictions, if widely accepted, can become partly self-fulfilling.

A sudden high rate of migration can bring populations with different identities into closer relations and require higher levels of coordination. Shifts in political borders also can produce changes in the proportions of people with varying identities, making old solutions less applicable. Such changes often contribute to the emergence of conflicts.

Even with little change in identities, conflicts erupt when grievances increase, contentious goals to redress the grievance are formulated, or confidence in being able to reduce the grievance increases. I discuss changes in each of those conditions in turn.

Grievance

The condition that receives most analytic and popular attention as the origin of a conflict is the grievance felt by one or more adversaries. This is understandable, since contending groups usually account for their entering a conflict by reference to the injustice of their circumstances.[27] Undoubtedly, an increase in feeling aggrieved contributes to the emergence of a conflict. Three sources of increasing grievance are especially noteworthy: changes in membership characteristics, in the social context, and in relations with the adversary.

Membership Characteristics

Explanations of grievance often stress the deprivations experienced by members of the challenging group. Most easily considered for consensual conflicts, deprivation can also apply to dissensual conflicts. One body of theory stresses the magnitude of absolute or objective deprivation, and another stresses relative or subjective deprivation. Evidence relating to each view will be examined before considering how they fit together.

Magnitude of Deprivation

According to the approach emphasizing absolute deprivation, the more deprived people are, the worse they feel.[28] People do not need great insight to know that they are deprived. An important corollary of this idea is that people who are low ranking in several dimensions are more deprived and tend to feel more dissatisfied than do people who rank low in one or two dimensions, but not in others.

Survey data from many societies indicate that persons with low occupational status or at low economic levels tend to be generally dissatisfied as measured by responses to several kinds of questions.[29] Similarly, occupational studies generally find that the lower the prestige, income, or work autonomy of an occupation, the more likely are its incumbents to be dissatisfied and want to leave it.[30] Furthermore, low rank in different dimensions, like education and income, have a cumulative negative effect on individuals.[31]

Dissatisfaction, however, is not always translated directly into a source of conflict eruption, or even necessarily to a sense of grievance. Other conditions must be met, but in several ways deprivation interferes with meeting them. First, people who rank low on a consensually valued dimension tend to think poorly of themselves and wish to avoid identifying themselves in terms of that dimension; consequently, they are disposed to avoid interacting with others similarly placed. The resulting weak solidarity interferes with collective recognition of dissatisfaction.

Furthermore, severely deprived persons tend to be preoccupied with day-to-day efforts at coping rather than developing a shared sense of grievance. Even moderate deprivation can be mentally restricting. For example, a public opinion study in nine countries found that workers, compared with middle-class respondents, were less likely to identify with persons of their own nation not of their own class and also less likely to identify with members of their own class in other countries.[32]

Accommodation to severe deprivation can even take the form of suppression and denial of hostile feelings and lead to placating and ingratiating behavior.[33] And severe deprivation disposes people to despair of changing their circumstances. These reactions also hamper the development of a collective sense of grievance.

A final difficulty with the magnitude of deprivation as an explanation of grievance must be noted. In many struggles, the party that initiates the pursuit of a contentious goal is relatively advantaged. It is often the stronger, the richer, or the higher status groups that seek more of what they already have from less-capable opponents.[34] Perhaps they do so because they can; but it may be that by their standards, they feel deprived. For that reason, among others, we must examine subjective factors.

Relative Deprivation

For people to have a grievance, they must judge their circumstances as inadequate by a standard that they deem legitimate. A considerable body of theory and research attempts to explain how those standards are set. A good starting point for examining those attempts is the work on reference groups.[35] The term includes *normative* groups (or individuals), providing a source of norms and values, and *comparison* groups, providing standards for evaluation of one's self. In the 1950s, relative deprivation was widely used to interpret survey data but came to be criticized because analysts either simply asked people to identify the reference group they used or retrospectively posited one.[36]

One way to approach predicting which of many possible reference groups actually will be chosen grew from the work on rank disequilibrium, status inconsistency, or rank incongruence. The idea is that persons who are high along some dimensions and low along others will be especially dissatisfied. One reason is that people within a social system tend to have similar ranks in different hierarchies; therefore, a person with inconsistent rankings is odd, is treated as odd, and feels odd. In other words, rank disequilibrium is experienced as a strain.[37]

This strain is compounded by the tendency of others to relate to persons in disequilibrium in terms of those persons' low ranks while they try to relate to others in terms of their high ranks.[38] The results of this kind of interaction may be seen for example in a work setting where supervisors are rarely women; a male worker may try to "put down" a woman supervisor as just a woman and the supervisor may treat the male worker as just a subordinate.[39] The resulting anger may be displaced toward vulnerable social targets, generating a conflict that is resistant to resolution by the conduct of the ostensible antagonists.[40]

The third reason status inconsistency may be a source of grievance is that it tends to make people feel their low rank is particularly objectionable. This is because they tend to use their high rank as a reference level; that rank becomes the basis of claims to be of high rank in all dimensions.

There is a possible problem with this reasoning, however, as with other aspects of reference-group theory. Perhaps some people take their low ranking as a reference level and feel good that they are high ranking on another dimension. Without having an independent basis for deciding which kind of inconsistency is likely to have a particular effect, plausible explanations can be made after the fact, for whatever feeling people report.

Some efforts have been made to specify which kinds of rank incongruencies have particular effects. Thus, persons ranked high on ascribed dimensions (for example, ethnicity) or dimensions that are considered investments (such as education) but low on achieved or reward dimensions (for example, income or occupational status) may be called underrewarded. They tend to experience failure and feel disappointment and anger.[41] On the other hand, persons ranked low on ascribed or investment dimensions and high on achieved or reward dimensions would tend to feel successful and contented, but some may feel guilt.

The results of a study among male manual workers is consistent with this reasoning. Geschwender found that workers with inconsistent ranks who were underrewarded tended to exhibit symptoms of individual unrest, indicated by responses to questions about job and neighborhood dissatisfaction and about participation in various activities.[42]

According to another line of reasoning, certain statuses have great importance in each society or group and each is a "master" status.[43] For example, in American society occupation is often used to locate people socially. Consequently, people would be expected to use their occupation as their standard of reference. The manual/nonmanual distinction has been a fundamental one, marking a boundary behind which each group conducts most of its social relations. Therefore, high-income manual workers would be expected to think that they are doing well compared with others with whom they identify and socialize. Evidence supports this reasoning.[44] By the same reasoning, low-income white-collar workers would be expected to be particularly dissatisfied, but the evidence from the same studies does not indicate that effect.

Although the reasoning and evidence about status inconsistency seem plausible, substantive considerations have limited its utility in explaining the emergence of social conflicts.[45] We noted why status inconsistency would not uniformly contribute to feeling dissatisfied, beyond what would be expected by an additive model. Thus, under some circumstances, persons may use their low rank as a standard of reference. Furthermore, for some people at least, being high in certain hierarchies would compensate for being low in others.

On the whole, the simpler and probably more valid strategy is to assume that the additive model provides a basic accounting for a person's degree of dissatisfaction.[46] That is, the lower a person's ranking and the greater the number of low rankings, the greater will be the person's dissatisfaction. Certain kinds of status inconsistencies, under specific conditions, may also affect the sense of grievance. Thus, rank disequilibrium may be a source of disturbance in a small group where it affects face-to-face interaction, but in a larger social system, such as a society, the resulting crosscutting ties may be integrative.[47]

So questions about deprivation accounting for a sense of grievance remain. In order to feel aggrieved, people must believe that the deprivation is not right. Another influential approach offers a solution: people feel aggrieved insofar as they experience a discrepancy between what they have and what they *expect* to have.[48]

The discrepancy may arise in three ways, as shown in figure 3.1. In type A, members of a society or a segment of the society, or an organization's members experience a decline in what they have had for a long time and therefore had come to expect would continue. The decline may be due to a poor harvest and rising food prices or it may be due to a decline in a group's autonomy, territorial control, or respect and deference from others.

Type B has been stressed in explanations for the outbreak of the French Revolution and many others.[49] Revolutions are thought to follow not a long period of consistently bad times, but a deterioration after a period of improving conditions. The argument is that when people's attainments have been rising, they expect them to continue to rise. Therefore, when attainments do not keep rising or even decline, people are disappointed and feel aggrieved.

The third source of discrepancy between expectations and attainments, type C, is rising expectations. People's expectations about what they should have may increase for several reasons. One reason is that people learn, for example from the mass media, that others have much more of what they would like to have. Shortly after World War II, the idea was widely discussed that traditional societies would undergo modernization; in part that expectation was based on people in underdeveloped countries discovering what was available in economically advanced countries.[50] The result would be a breakdown in the traditional order, rising expectations, and revolutionary demands if the expectations were not fulfilled.

Another reason expectations rise is that leaders promise future benefits and achievements. They may even take actions and institute programs that are presented as the means to attain those gains. The failure to achieve the promises would result in a discrepancy between the raised expectations and the reality. That discrepancy can be the source of conflict, between the aggrieved

TYPES OF CHANGES

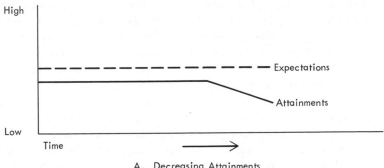

A. Decreasing Attainments

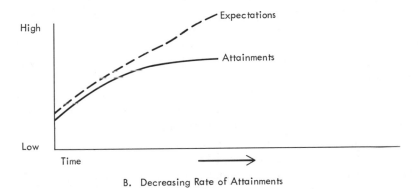

B. Decreasing Rate of Attainments

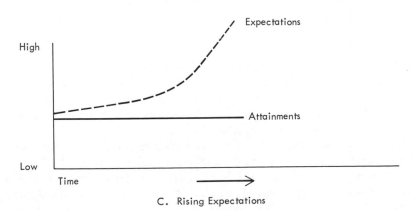

C. Rising Expectations

Figure 3.1   Types of Changes in Expectations and Attainments

and those they think are culpable for the failure. Perhaps the high expectations of many social movement activists in the early 1960s in the United States contributed later to more severe conflicts as the promised gains were not fulfilled.

Evidence that declining attainments after a long period of improvement generates outbreaks of revolutions, riots, or protest generally has been indirect. Studies have related revolutionary efforts or domestic turmoil to changes in previous conditions; but the feeling of grievance has only been inferred.[51] We have noted, however, that dissatisfaction has many possible sources and furthermore it may or may not be expressed in contentious behavior.

Changes in expectations relative to attainments have several limits as an explanation of discontent resulting in conflict behavior. Poor conditions may be made endurable by promises of improvements in the future. The raised expectations of a glorious future have often made people willing to accept current sacrifices for a long time. It is also plausible that if conditions have been improving, people are able to absorb a setback with less bitterness. Under other circumstances, a new deprivation may be experienced as a personal failure that induces guilt or self-hate so that no outwardly directed efforts at redressing the grievance are taken. This is often the case with unemployment. In some cases, the deprivation may lessen positive feelings without increasing negative ones.[52] Consequently, deprivation itself may not appreciably raise the level of conflict-generating discontent. Finally, the partial improvement of conditions may be sufficient to satisfy rather than arouse appetites. For example, many European immigrants found American industrial conditions much better than their previous conditions and were, therefore, less dissatisfied than American-born workers.[53]

The existing level of deprivation and degree of equilibrium affect how *changes* in attainments and expectations impact upon conflict-relevant grievances. Thus, a fall in economic well-being from an already low level may impose such severe burdens that expectations quickly fall as well. If high levels in other rank systems had been sustained, however, the reaction to a fall in economic well-being might be greater.

The various explanations for an increased sense of grievance can also be expected to have varying pertinence for different segments within a large-scale adversary. Leaders and would-be leaders of a conflict party are a particularly important segment, often acting to arouse a sense of grievance among the rank and file. The sources and nature of their discontent may indeed be different from the grievances of their followers.

There is evidence that in status systems within clearly marked boundaries, those toward the top of a low-ranking stratum tend to be satisfied.[54] Yet it is usually from these levels that the leaders of the discontented emerge.[55] This is partly because the higher ranking persons within each stratum have the social status and skills that make them likely to be leaders of others in their stratum.

Furthermore, such persons are in some ways marginal; they do not fit clearly in the low-ranking or the high-ranking strata. Marginality can be a source of insight and understanding of different groups, which is useful for leaders.[56]

Leaders and would-be leaders play critical roles in arousing discontent. Indeed, opponents of movements to redress grievances often argue that the movements are the result of "outside agitators." And those who would mobilize people to struggle against their oppression stress the need to scratch the wounds inflicted by the oppressors and so increase the awareness of their pain.[57] However, analysts using a structural approach emphasize the forces directly affecting the constituency for a possible struggle and the relatively small role that leaders can play in raising consciousness. These two views should be seen as complementary, providing depth of vision.

Interaction between leaders and followers is inevitable. Followers choose their leaders and leaders use a variety of inducements to gain and hold followers. Leaders must present views that make sense to their followers, given their experiences. Experiences have dispositions to be interpreted in particular ways, but some experiences have stricter or more limited dispositions than others. For example, a study of Black neighborhoods found that popular discontent with the police could be accounted for without recourse to the role of Black community leaders, but feelings of economic exploitation by the local businesses were more dependent upon leaders' interpretation.[58]

Social Context

The social context within which potential adversaries confront each other often changes and helps arouse the partisans' sense of grievance. Changing social context not only is a possible source of actual deprivation, but also helps provide the criteria for judging conditions to be unsatisfactory.

Sources of Deprivation

It should be stressed that the social conditions discussed in chapter 2, which could be the source of dissatisfaction, are not static and certain changes often result in groups feeling aggrieved. Thus, increased immigration tends to alter the demographic balance among ethnic, cultural, religious, and class categories. People previously in a relatively advantaged category may regard these immigrants as threatening their superior economic position or political power.

Changes in the global economy and a society's place in it can be a source of strains within and among societies. Shifts in investments, trade patterns, and labor flows often exacerbate inequalities within and among countries, often providing the bases for feelings of grievance.

Evaluation of Conditions

Prevailing ways of thinking and communicating provide the language in which deprivations are articulated and evaluated. In various historical periods and within different civilizations and cultures, the *Zeitgeist,* or spirit of the times, provides widely shared sentiments, social norms, and ways of thinking. These conventions may be the discourses of religion and spirituality, of class struggle, of ethnic and other communal differences, of individualistic psychology, or of innumerable other discourses. They include various standards about what is valuable, whether personal freedom, social equality, collective self-determination, or stable order.

In the 1960s and 1970s, in the United States and in many other parts of the world, social equality was highly valued and groups that had been relatively disadvantaged were widely perceived to deserve remedial social action. This standard was generally recognized as legitimate even by those who were not the disadvantaged. In the 1980s and 1990s, however, there were signs of backlashes and of renewed importance given to individual rights. The view that individuals should maximize and retain their gains from the marketplace became more prevalent and legitimate.

Each claim of unjustified deprivation that is effectively voiced provides impetus for other groups to make comparable claims. Inequities and discrimination accepted as "natural" come to be questioned when others challenge the propriety of their deprivations. This was evident in the United States in the 1960s and 1970s, with the demand for greater equity by Blacks, women, the poor, and many other communities.

Finally, standards may be raised by the actions and words of those who have authority in the social system encompassing the immediate partisans in a conflict. For example, the 1954 U.S. Supreme Court decision (*Brown v. Board of Education*) declaring segregated schools unconstitutional was made unanimously by the most authoritative interpreters of the fundamental law of the country. That decision raised the expectations of Blacks throughout the United States.[59]

Structural characteristics of the social system in which possible adversaries are embedded may affect the rate of conflicts within the system. Studies of international conflicts, for example, examine the incidence of wars as related to different alliance structures and economic relations in the world system. Thus, too, status inconsistency can be regarded as a system characteristic, assessing the degree to which the countries in the world are inconsistent in military expenditures, economic strength, and prestige.[60] High rank disequilibrium might be conducive to international conflict since national leaders would seek to alter that status quo. On the other hand, high disequilibrium might contribute to crosscutting ties, while high consistency would reinforce lines of cleavage and make international conflict more likely.

Empirical studies for the years 1946–1964 found that the incidence of wars correlated moderately with the degree of status inconsistency.[61] But a replication, covering the years 1950–1980, did not find this relationship.[62] Perhaps this is explained by the greater global dominance of the United States in the earlier period and a greater dispersal of power during the later years. Thus, during the earlier period, the strong hegemonic capabilities of the United States and the deep political cleavage of the cold war meant that status inconsistency tended to be related to the struggle between the hegemon's group and the challenging group. In the later period, status consistency would be more indicative of fundamental cleavages in the international order.

Adversary Relations

The changing relations between potential adversaries are often the precipitating source of one or more parties feeling dissatisfied. To understand the emergence of a conflict we must take into account changes in positive bonds and interests, as well as changes in negative ones.

Positive aspects of relations between potential adversaries include cooperative, complementary, and shared interests. A deterioration of those positive bonds and activities, as well as an increase in negative ones, contributes to the outbreak of a conflict. Changes in the relative balance between cooperative and antagonistic aspects of the relationship are crucial to the emergence of a social conflict.

Positive Bonds

Possible adversaries also are integrated and share positive bonds, interests, and identities in many ways. The salience of such positive ties tends to inhibit a sense of grievance while their deterioration may contribute to feeling aggrieved.

One important positive aspect of the relationship between potential adversaries is the extent to which their members hold common identities. For example, most Blacks and Whites in the United States feel that they all are Americans. The loss of a common identity creates the space for secondary antagonisms to become primary ones, as happened to many peoples in the former Soviet Union with the loss of shared identity as mutual supporters of communism and also as Soviet citizens.

An important positive aspect of a relationship is the extent to which the potential adversaries share a common goal and work together cooperatively to attain it. This typically is a major cohesive force in social life. Within industrial organizations, for example, workers and managers collaborate to produce products that will be marketed to earn money for the organization and that they share with owners and others, to varying degrees. Shared goals are based on consensus, on the similarities in values and beliefs that people have. Cooperative activities may also be aided by dissensus, as people complement each other, differing in what they enjoy doing.

Shared goals and cooperative activities do not necessarily ensure harmony or the avoidance of overt conflict. When failure to attain a common goal creates disappointment, each group may blame the other for the failure. If leaders of a society or an organization clearly fail to attain the shared goals, they are likely to be challenged by rivals and face rejection by significant constituencies.

Even if the goals are being achieved, the particular allocation of gains from the cooperative effort is likely to be a source of dissatisfaction. One group may feel it is controlled and exploited by another. Where the allocation can be attributed to market forces, however, the dissatisfaction is often deflected, perhaps to persons viewed as competitors.

Another positive aspect of relations is the degree to which members of potential adversary groups have ties that crosscut their lines of cleavage. These include interpersonal bonds or alliances against third parties. Thus, persons with friendships across possible conflict-group boundaries are less likely to construe potentially contentious issues between the groups antagonistically. For example, in one local election in the United States, allegations were raised by one party against Jews. Jews who had ties with gentiles tended not to respond with ethnocentrism, especially if they spoke about the issue with their gentile friends.[63]

Still another positive aspect of a relationship is the degree of affection potential antagonists have toward each other. As Lewis Coser writes, "The closer the relationship, the greater the affective investment, the greater also the tendency to suppress rather than express hostile feelings."[64] This was discussed in the previous chapter, in regard to the frequent denial by wives of conflicts with their husbands.

A paradox arises in the interplay among these positive aspects of relationships. Thus, at high levels of involvement, parties may make high demands of responsiveness from each other and then find that these are not met. This evokes disappointment and sometimes anger and resentment. A related process is particularly relevant for dissensual conflicts. People tend to feel particularly outraged about disagreements with others who are supposed to be close. This is one reason for the vehemence in conflicts about doctrinal differences that outsiders may consider trivial. The intensity of struggles when one faction disagrees with the views of their religious or ideological cobelievers is illustrative.

Negative Bonds

One or more parties in a relationship are likely to feel aggrieved in response to damaging actions taken by others. Those negatively viewed actions derive from the three dimensions of relationships discussed in chapter 2: inequality, differences, and integration between possible adversaries.

1. *Inequalities.* Increasing inequalities between potential adversaries tend to arouse a sense of grievance among the relatively disadvantaged. Many of the processes generating a feeling of grievance within a potential adversary have been discussed earlier. What is particularly pertinent here is the way one party appears to be increasing its gains at the expense of another. Often it is the relatively advantaged that makes use of its advantages to gain even more, arousing hostility among the relatively disadvantaged.

Those with superior power, particularly in large and self-sustaining social systems like a society, often successfully convince those with less power that they are not deprived and have no grounds for grievance. Formal and informal means of education or indoctrination convince the weaker that the existing allocation of what is consensually valued conforms with shared standards of equity and legitimacy.[65] Interestingly, arguments in terms of such standards also may become restraints upon the superordinates. Suppose, for example, that subordinates are to be convinced that they owe obedience because of the benefits granted to them by superordinates. Then the superordinates are constrained to honor the terms of exchange in order to maintain their claims against the subordinates. The failure to deliver the expected benefits becomes the source of grievance.

2. *Differences.* The existence of different values and beliefs becomes a grievance when one side tries to impose its views on another. This may occur as a result of several possible developments. The parties with different values and beliefs may be brought into close social proximity, for example by migration. The conduct of one group may seem increasingly objectionable to another group as the conduct becomes more prominent; and the objecting group may try to stop the conduct or to remove the other people. This is sometimes mixed with concerns about competition, as when people immigrate into new areas.

Another development contributing to the emergence of dissensually derived grievances is an increase in the salience of religious or ideological views among adherents, and their efforts to win converts to their views. This zealotry can result in proselytizing efforts that are rejected and resisted, constituting a social conflict.

3. *Integration.* Although a high level of integration between potential adversaries generally inhibits the emergence of a grievance, in particular circumstances it can contribute to developing a sense of grievance. Thus, when mutual dependence is not equal one side may find itself subject to threats based on its dependence. The dependence one party has for the goods or services provided by another party makes it vulnerable to a reduction or withdrawal of those goods or services.

Decreases in the anticipated goods or services one party receives from the other can readily become a grievance. The denial of previously granted rights can be the trigger to arouse anger and mobilize resistance. For example, the 1964 student uprising at the Berkeley campus of the University of California was ignited by the university administration's move to enforce restrictions on political activity on a section of university property that had been used for a wide variety of political action.[66]

Closing Observations

If antagonism is denied and divisive issues are unrecognized, the gravity of the contradictions are likely to grow. When the grievance is finally acknowledged, it may break out in greater intensity than if it had been expressed earlier. For example, repressive governments may be ignorant of and unresponsive to popular wishes and be overwhelmed when the grievances do emerge and are openly expressed. The relatively sudden collapse of the communist-controlled regimes of Eastern Europe at the end of the 1980s is illustrative.

A sense of grievance arises from many sources within each possible adversary, in the relations between them, and in their social context. Although factors from all these sources combine to account for the content and the strength of the grievance, the relative significance varies for different kinds of grievances. The contradictory effects of various bases for feeling aggrieved explain why such feelings in themselves will not ignite a struggle.

Forming Contentious Goals

For a conflict to emerge, the cause of the grievance must be attributed to the conduct of other persons. The members of an aggrieved party must formulate a goal directed at those others that if achieved they believe would reduce their grievance. The aggrieved may seek more money, control over land, more autonomy, or other matters from another party.

Contentious goals are infinitely various. Nevertheless, it is useful to consider two major dimensions of goals. One is the direction of the change sought: toward greater integration or toward greater separation. The other dimension pertains to the magnitude of the changes being sought in the relationship between the adversaries, ranging from small reforms to fundamental restructuring.

Along the dimension of integration-separation, goals to achieve greater integration include attaining equal opportunities for educational and occupational positions, becoming assimilated, or converting the other side. At the opposite extreme, goals to achieve greater separation include autonomy, independence, or the expulsion or destruction of the adversary. In between are goals that seek not to alter the existing state of integration, but seek rather to modify the adversary relationship.

The magnitude of the changes sought range greatly. At one extreme, the goals aspire to only small changes, such as modifications in allocating the resources to be shared or modifications in the policies being implemented by the adversary. These goals are often of an aggregate rather than a collective character. That is, the goals pertain to opportunities for members of the quasi group as individuals, rather than as a unitary group.

At the other extreme, a revolutionary change in who has the authority to make allocations may be the objective. These goals often have a relatively collective character, as when a transformation is sought so that new groups or classes dominate. In between the extremes, are goals to reform relationships, alter policies, or oust leaders. Leaders of an ethnic minority, for example, may seek increased representation by its members in policy making. Even a coup by a military junta taking over the highest government offices from another junta, regarded as a palace revolution, often does not entail a radical change in the society.

In a sense, the magnitude of the change sought is a function of the discrepancy between the goals of the adversary camps. The greater the difference between their goals, the more radical each side's goals will be regarded by their opponent. As we observe in chapter 4, greater discrepancy also tends to result in using relatively destructive means of struggle.

Finally, we note a frequently used designation of variations in goals: the left-right dimension. This designation is used by many partisans, often contesting its meanings. Therefore, we should consider this dimension, even if the more general variations previously discussed better meet our analytic needs. Seeking to restructure the relationship or change the policy between social strata is generally considered "left" insofar as the objective is to increase equality in class, status, or power differences.[67] Another characterization of this dimension stresses who is making claims on whom. Thus, when the disadvantaged make claims against those who have relative advantage, their objectives are considered leftist. When members of the dominant group seek to maintain or enhance their position, their objectives are regarded as rightist or even reactionary.[68]

Certainly, the nature of the goals being pursued has implications for the course of a conflict. For example, conflicts about the allocation of resources are relatively amenable to compromise, since the resources are generally divisible. This is typically the case in consensual disputes. Some consensual conflicts, however, involve radical restructuring of the adversary relationship and are not easily settled. This is the case when a revolutionary group seeks to end private ownership of large agricultural estates; such goals are unitary and not easily divisible.[69]

Dissensual conflicts are often about issues that are viewed as involving significant changes in the adversary and are relatively difficult to settle via compromise. This is typically the case when one party tries to convert the other to its way of believing. However, a group's goal, for example, to attain greater autonomy for its members to practice their religion, is often amenable to negotiation.

Goals incorporate mental constructs of future desired conditions and usually are embedded in a set of ideas about the partisans' plight and what can be done about it. These goals and ideas may be more or less shared and deeply held by group members. They also are varyingly well articulated, they may only be implicit and inferred from indirect verbal expressions and from conduct. Thus, Hobsbawm has observed that although the classical city mobs, acting before they had access to formal political processes, manifested ideas in their actions.[70] Mob participants expected to achieve something, assumed that the authorities would be responsive to their actions, and directed their activities selectively against the rich and powerful. We are especially interested, here, in sustained intergroup struggles and those parties who usually hold explicit goals, often formulated by leaders.

The question of what shapes contentious goals can now be addressed. It is answered by consideration of the characteristics of the members of possible adversary groups, their social context, and the relations between them.

Membership Characteristics

Among the many aspects of the quasi group's membership that affect the formation of goals, three are particularly significant: leadership, culture and social system, and the members' grievances.

Leadership

Leaders of a possible conflict group play a primary role in formulating contentious goals. Discontent may be widespread among the members of a quasi group but be dormant and festering. Leaders, to mobilize the followers for a struggle, must convince them that their grievances are attributable to the actions of other people. The leaders explain that view and help formulate the specific demands whose satisfaction would reduce or even end their grievance.

The analysis made by leaders about the source of the grievance is often contested, particularly by those accused.

Indeed, it is possible that feelings arising from internal sources are displaced upon outsiders. This may be the case with attributions of conspiracies conducted by elite groups or by particular ethnic groups.

The leaders' analysis must persuade a significant proportion of the quasi group that they can alter those people they believe to be responsible for their grievance. Leaders holding offices of authority generally have advantages in making persuasive arguments. Thus, government or church officials tend to be accorded credence by those recognizing their legitimacy to explain what is happening and why.

Government officials who attribute responsibility for a problem to a foreign power can usually count on the loyalty of their constituency in accepting the attribution. As Barry B. Hughes concludes, after reviewing studies of the American public's response to foreign policy crises, "It appears that, almost regardless of prior attitudes of the public, regardless of the popularity of the president and regardless of how well the president handles the crisis, a large proportion of the population will support him."[71]

The task for would-be leaders of opposition groups is greater. They must rely more on charisma or use their legitimate authority based in a subunit of the social system whose leadership they would challenge. For example, Dr. Martin Luther King, Jr., drew on his authority as the minister of the Dexter Avenue Baptist Church in Montgomery, Alabama, in helping to arouse and mobilize the Blacks of Montgomery to carry out the bus boycott initiated in 1955; he drew on his broader charisma to arouse the widening general support.[72]

Culture and Social System

Which goals seem convincing depend in part on the experiences and belief systems of the adversary group's members. Thus, members who believe that they previously improved their condition by formulating goals that blamed particular others for their unsatisfactory conditions and changed the others' conduct are likely to replicate that formulation. Thus, trade union members who have improved their working conditions by making claims to do so through collective bargaining with managers are likely to try that again.

Conversely, having formulated and pursued goals that were unsuccessful in the past discredits those goals from being pursued in the future. This is not a simple matter, however; the argument may be made that the goal was simply not pursued with sufficient vigor and persistence.

Sociocultural and psychocultural qualities within a quasi group help shape the emergence of contentious goals, as noted in chapter 2. These are usually relatively stable features of a group. Therefore, the emergence of a contentious goal requires some new development, combining with the prevailing sociocultural and psychocultural tendencies.

Grievance

The emergence and character of a contentious goal is greatly affected by the grievance to be redressed. By considering how different grievances affect the formulation of goals, we can resolve some of the apparent contradictions about the importance of different sources of discontent.

People who feel they are generally deprived, or who suffer further deterioration of their condition, tend to support more radical goals than do people with status inconsistency or whose improving conditions were halted. During the Great Depression of the 1930s, voices calling for radical change emerged within the U.S. labor movement. But when economic conditions later improved, trade union members advocating more reformist goals regained influence.[73] African Americans in the United States during the 1960s provide another example. Blacks with higher education and income usually agitated for integration, while those who were less educated or more disadvantaged tended to support Black separatist objectives.[74]

Among persons who are not greatly deprived, however, status inconsistency may be associated with utopian goals. Thus, in the 1960s, college students with status inconsistency tended to belong to organizations with utopian goals, while those with more consistent backgrounds tended to belong to more conventional political groups.[75]

The direction of goals, whether to the left or right, toward increasing or decreasing inequalities, also depends on the nature of the discontent. Even moderately deteriorating conditions for those who had been well off dispose them to favor goals that restore previous inequalities. Reactionary political movements have drawn disproportional support from such persons. Status inconsistencies with ascribed or investment statuses that are higher than achieved or reward statuses, such as persons with high ethnic ranking and low incomes, tend to support conservative or reactionary goals; while persons with overrewarded kinds of inconsistencies, such as persons with low ethnic standing but high incomes, tend to support more egalitarian aims.[76]

The pattern of status inconsistency affects the content of contentious goals in other ways. People are inclined to raise themselves along the dimensions in which they have relatively low status and therefore, tend to challenge those who are above them on those dimensions. This challenge helps shape their goal. Thus, persons with low ethnic and high occupational and income levels would try to raise the status of their ethnicity by campaigns against prejudice directed at their ethnic group.

In short, the content of the grievance profoundly affects the emergence and character of a contentious goal. Thus, if economic conditions deteriorate for group members, they will seek to improve the conditions by aiming to change those they hold responsible. But the emergence and character of a goal is affected not only by attributes of the quasi group's members but also by their social context and their relations with their presumed adversaries.

Social Context

The prevailing ways of thinking in the social environment help channel the group members' formulation of goals, suggesting who is to blame and what they must do to rectify the injustice. Thus, in some eras and civilizations, economic forces and class struggles are widely thought to be the predominant forces shaping social relations. Consider that in many parts of the world during much of the twentieth century, Marxist analyses of domestic and international relations were widely used to account for the injustices people experienced, and to point to solutions. With the evident failures, immense social costs, and final collapse of the Soviet Union, Marxist analysis was widely discredited. The capitalist class was less often seen as the oppressor and a strong government less often regarded as a necessary counterforce.

Since the mid-1970s, the take-home pay of many American workers has declined; and increasingly, families have two earners to compensate for this decline.[77] Responsibility for declining disposable income has been variously attributed. One set of explanations points to decreased worker productivity due to worker incompetence and laziness, or to managerial short-sightedness and greed, or to diversion of research and development investment into military projects. Other explanations point to the government for increasing taxes to support government bureaucrats, unnecessary military expenditures, give-aways to those who will not work, or corruption and waste. Some explanations emphasize the increasing globalization of the economy, pitting American workers against the lower-paid workers in most parts of the world; this can be framed as the necessary working of impersonal market forces or the machinations of international corporations. Finally, some people point to increasing competition within the American economy by the growth of women's participation in the labor force and new waves of immigration.

Clearly, the nature of the goals formulated by members of an adversary group will be quite different depending on which combination of explanations they choose. Some of the variations in goals are presented and argued within the context of the institutionalized political system. Others fall outside of politics, erupting into the social conflicts of particular concern here.

In much of the world, for many decades, more issues and grievances have become politicized and attributed to power and authority rather than to private or moral responsibility.[78] Kate Millett's influential 1970 book, *Sexual Politics*, was one of many examples that explained women's oppression in terms of power relations.[79]

Politicization has often been combined with ideologies of a universalistic nature, such as Marxism, liberalism, and conservatism. They are universalistic in their applicability and in their openness; believers try to convince everyone to share their beliefs. Recent decades have seen a renewed attraction of more particularistic ideologies. This may have been partly a response to the impersonality of universal ideologies and to their failures to satisfy felt needs relating to communal and moral concerns. The collapse of the Soviet Union and the evident failure of communist ideology as manifested there enhanced the credibility of alternative worldviews, particularly in parts of the world where it had been influential.

The attraction of particularistic ways of thinking is evident in the emphasis on ethnicity and some kinds of religious fundamentalism. Ethnic and religious communities celebrate their own ways, and some of them have significant restrictions on admitting persons who do not have a family background as a member of the community.

Nationalism in some ways combines ethnic and other communal identities with political claims, including having an independent state. Nationalism has long been an important influence in the formulation of contentious goals. Revolutionary challenges to a government can be aided by robing them in nationalistic claims. For example, a government may be charged with being the instrument of foreign powers; this has been the message of many revolutionary movements in Third World countries. This charge contributed to the mobilization of Iranian resistance to Shah Mohammad Reza Pahlavi, his government's collapse, and the coming to power of Ayatollah Ruhollah Khomeini in 1979.[80]

The social environment helps each conflict group determine who its adversary is, and so influences its goals. The visibility and the vulnerability of different groups in a society make them more or less likely adversaries. Some groups, like governments, are likely targets since they presume to be responsible for a wide range of social and economic as well as political conditions. Other groups, such as ethnic minorities, may be vulnerable to attack and available to be blamed for grievances, arising from many sources. Thus, traditions of anti-Semitism have made Jews such targets at various times in history.[81]

Another aspect of the social context is important; insofar as a social system appears to be closed and contracting, potential adversaries within it regard themselves to be in a zero-sum situation and will formulate goals to redress their grievances in those terms. There may be predispositions, based on experience, for some groups of people to view their world as a limited one. This is evident in studies in the late 1950s and early 1960s in Latin America indicating that citizens there believed societal limits were inflexible and that what one group gained another lost.[82] Experiencing expanding opportunities, conversely, tends to dampen the belief that contending parties are in a zero-sum relationship. This tendency is exemplified by the reduced incidence of wars among European states when their colonial empires were expanding elsewhere.[83] In the nineteenth century, the United States' expanding economy and open frontier offers another example. Those conditions probably reduced the sense that people were living in a zero-sum society.

Third parties and their possible evaluations also significantly influence the goals adversaries formulate. Contending groups often consider the reactions of such third parties in order to gain their support or lessen their opposition.

This sometimes is a reason to moderate the goals in order to rally wider support.[84]

Finally, the degree and form of institutionalized conflict regulation affects the formulation of goals, particularly their radicalism. Units that are part of a larger system with legitimate institutionalized means of reaching collective decisions tend to formulate reformist goals.

Adversary Relations

Similar to the formation of identity, adversaries help shape each other's contentious goals. A potential conflict group may formulate objectives that in some ways mimic those of its opponent or develop ones that magnify the differences. An illustration of the former process may be seen in the formation of Zionist goals in response to the intensified persecution of Jews in Russia toward the end of the nineteenth century. Zionists aimed to establish a national home and have a social and economic life like the Russians and others among whom they lived, emphasizing doing productive labor, especially on the land. This was one kind of response to persecution and the denial of the right to own land and to farm it. If they could not be accepted as Russians or Germans because they were Jews, then as Jews they would have their own country. Palestinian nationalism, in turn, was strongly affected by Palestinians' experience with Zionism and the establishment of Israel.[85]

Differences in the goals sought and the very identity of each adversary may be stressed, as each compares itself to the other. Thus, one party in a dissensual conflict may emphasize particular qualities and goals of the adversary in order to help shape its own goals. During the cold war, some Americans stressed the antireligious goals of the Soviet leadership, which implied that American goals were at least in part to advance religious beliefs, and specifically Christian ones. This was an important component of the Christian Right ideology in the 1960s, as articulated by Dr. Fred Schwarz and Billy James Hargis.[86]

The demands one party makes on another are also affected by the structure of their relations with each other. Ethnic groups, for example, may be in competition with each other or one may be able to discriminate against the other in the allocation of opportunities or benefits. The goals sought in each circumstance tend to differ. Or, consider how the goals of different economic classes are based on the nature of the class relationship. An analysis of agrarian revolutions demonstrates how certain agricultural relations generate particular revolutionary or reform goals. For example, in one structural relationship, the noncultivators derive their income from the ownership of the land and the cultivators earn their income in the form of wages, as migratory workers. Revolutionary nationalist movements are likely to erupt in such migratory estate systems in colonial areas. Certain other conditions must exist for such movements to emerge. Although migratory workers may generally feel aggrieved, they usually lack the resources for organizing to fight. But if the migratory workers must revert to village subsistence holdings when the harvest ends, traditional tribal or peasant leadership could provide the resources needed for organization. The traditional village authorities will join the migratory laborers in the revolutionary nationalist movements, Paige concludes, "only when their own economic base of support is being ended by the same estate system that is exploiting the poor laborers."[87] This resulted in the rise of revolutionary movements in Vietnam and in Angola during the 1950s and 1960s.

The leaders and intellectuals who seek to formulate a goal for their group often do so taking into account its impact not only on mobilizing their group but also on influencing the adversary. If members of the adversary side can be induced to question the morality and justice of their position, then the chances of arousing feelings of guilt or shame, acts of defection, and readiness to yield will increase. That will give further evidence to the group members that they can get what they seek from the adversary. Consequently, aims are often formulated in terms of shared values such as justice, freedom, or equality, as when leaders of national independence movements lay claim to the rights of a people to rule themselves.

This reasoning also suggests that immediate aims may be chosen from among the array of possible goals in terms of those that are most likely to be yielded by the adversary. Consider European-American opposition to possible integration aims of African Americans in the 1960s. According to a 1963 national survey, about 80 percent of the Whites conceded that Negroes ought to have as good a chance as the White people to get any kind of job; about 75 percent favored equal access to public facilities, about 60 percent said that White and Negro students should go to the same schools; but fewer than 50 percent disagreed with the statement that White people had a right to keep Negroes out of their neighborhoods if they wanted to.[88] Legal and political equality was probably even more generally supported by Whites than those matters.[89] There is some, but not a perfect correspondence between Whites' preferences and the Blacks' goal priorities. In addition, the vulnerability of those who controlled these different spheres of life, the kinds of tactics available to Blacks, and considerations of the Blacks' dissatisfactions and organizational needs influenced the choice of goals.

Finally, the attractiveness of pursuing a particular goal is affected by the group's feelings toward the other side.[90] If one group hates another, it will derive extra pleasure by pursuing an aim that humiliates its adversary. Vengeance can be sweet. Lacking such feelings, advocates may choose a less extreme goal. On the other hand, if positive feelings abound, a goal may be chosen that minimizes the harm to the opponent, even if it fails to maximize the group's own benefits aside from the vicarious utility of the other side's satisfaction. The gratification of retribution and humiliation may sometimes lead a group to pursue goals that would otherwise seem to be self-defeating or would inflict self-losses greater than what might be won.

Believing Redress Is Possible

The fourth condition to be satisfied for a conflict to emerge is for at least one party to believe that it can do something to change an adversary and/or the adversary's conduct, thereby attaining more of what it wants. The importance of satisfying this condition is increasingly recognized by analysts of social conflicts. One indication of this is the change in emphasis in theories about the emergence of social movements. For many decades, the strain, alienation, or dissatisfaction experienced by some population groups were used to explain the rise of a social movement. Beginning in the 1960s, such theories drawing from general ideas about collective behavior, were superseded by theories stressing how groups mobilized resources to seek redress for their grievances.[91] Discontent is taken for granted, but the ability to change conditions that are unsatisfactory explains the rise of challenging social movements. Even terrible conditions may be endured without contention if those who suffer them believe that they cannot correct the behavior of those they regard as responsible or that the attempt will result in repression and even worse conditions.

The availability of legitimate and credible means of seeking redress may provide an alternative to coercive contention. Within many societies, electoral politics or a judicial system may seem effective and make less necessary the kinds of struggles that are examined here.

People may come to believe that they can improve their unsatisfactory conditions, if necessary by contentious methods, because they believe that their capabilities have increased or that the capabilities of those they would correct have decreased. Such new beliefs follow changes within one or more of the adversaries, changes in their social context, or changes in the relations among the adversaries.

Membership Characteristics

Many features of the quasi-group members contribute to their sense that they can act to reduce their grievances. Two are particularly noteworthy: capabilities and leadership.

Increased Capabilities

As members of a potential adversary group improve their conditions, their dissatisfaction may be expected to decline. But their improved conditions also tend to give them resources that prompt them to believe that their conditions can be improved much more.

The earlier discussions of status inconsistency in accounting for a sense of grievance are relevant here. If people have high ranks along some dimensions, they are likely to have resources that give them reason to believe that they might improve their rank along other dimensions, at least compared with those who are uniformly low.

On the other hand, research findings also indicate that some responses to status inconsistency interfere with trying to reduce dissatisfaction. Thus, having incongruent statuses subjects people to inconsistent claims and directives. A frequent reaction to such cross pressures is to reduce attention and withdraw interest from the issues in contention among the status groups.[92] This would diminish the belief that unsatisfactory conditions could be corrected, and that may dampen recognizing dissatisfaction. Furthermore, the discomfort of some kinds of rank inconsistencies may be expressed in anxiety that also interferes with believing that unsatisfactory conditions can be improved.[93]

Leadership

Leaders play a major role not only in shaping an identity, developing a sense of grievance, and formulating a conflict goal, but also in helping their constituents believe that they can achieve the goals they seek. This in part depends on offering an analysis of the opposing sides' relative weakness, of the historical trends, of the sympathy of those not yet engaged in the struggle, and of their own significant resources.

Goals differ in the time that appears needed to attain them. Leaders can help develop a long-term strategy with a sequence of subgoals, starting with relatively immediate and attainable ones that then provide the basis for reaching larger goals. For a conflict organization to mobilize support and sustain itself, the succession of goals must be closely related to the group's capacities relative to its opposition.

Particularly for emerging conflict organizations, the formulation of short-term attainable goals is important in building confidence and gaining support.[94] The immediate goals should be feasible and if reached should not end the sense of grievance if the organization is to persevere and win its larger goals. Thus, organizers of the poor in American community action programs during the 1960s found that building a conflict organization was relatively successful when initial demands were first met with resistance and then with acquiescence. Resistance was important because it seemed to confirm the necessity for struggle. Acquiescence then further supported the effectiveness of struggle.

Leaders also play an important role in forming coalitions of diverse interests. Those coalitions enable a conflict to be undertaken with a prospect of victory, and they also shape the goals of the conflict. For example, after the Iraqi invasion of Kuwait in August 1990, U.S. President George Bush was able to quickly construct a coalition including nearly all Arab governments and the permanent members of the UN Security Council. This gave international legitimacy and the capability of threatening and waging a land war from Saudi Arabia. It also constrained the conflict; the coalition probably could not be held together for long without decisive action, and the goal would best be limited to driving the Iraqi forces from Kuwait.[95]

The history of the U.S. labor movement illustrates the search for goals attainable with the resources that were likely to be available. During the nineteenth century, many national trade unions with comprehensive goals arose but did not survive: the Knights of Labor, the National Labor Union, and the Industrial Workers of the World.[96] The "pure and simple trade unionism" of the American Federation of Labor provided a set of immediate and long-term goals that were at least partially attainable.

Leaders often try to convince their followers that they have the capability to wage a successful struggle by pointing to the past when they possessed what they now propose to achieve. For example, a feminist leader may argue that in early human history, women were socially superior to men and were worshipped by them.[97] An ethnic leader may argue that in the past, members of his ethnicity were much more advanced than the barbarian peoples around them. In addition, leaders often argue that the opposition is weak and getting weaker while their side is strong and getting stronger.

Leaders agitate, then, not only by trying to increase their followers' discontent, but also by raising the hope that this can be changed, and by their own efforts. That seems paradoxical. To depict how exploited and victimized people are seems to contradict the possibility of such people bettering themselves against the wishes of the exploiters. One solution to the paradox is to use the power of weakness. Desperation can engender determination and recklessness; having little, there is little that can be withheld from those who appear weak. Thus, Marx and Engels, in the *Communist Manifesto*, exhorted the workers of the world to unite in struggle, since "you have nothing to lose but your chains."

The task is often easier for leaders of a group with considerable resources in some arenas but disatisfied in certain other arenas. An economically advantaged community may believe it can use its resources to gain more political autonomy and so not be required to share its resources with the disadvantaged of the larger society. Thus, in Spain, the two regions with particularly strong movements for autonomy have long been the Catalan and Basque regions; they both have been relatively advanced economically.[98]

Social Context

The social context affects a potential conflict party's belief that it can better its condition in several ways. For one, other groups making improvements against opposition provide models of what might be accomplished by struggle. They also may contribute to reinforcing beliefs about the efficacy of particular means of struggle, such as nonviolent resistance.

The social context includes people who are not clearly members of the adversary parties. They are an audience that the partisans address, pointing to the injustice they suffer in order to win support. Some members of that audience may be drawn into the struggle, and as they are, the conflict expands. An aggrieved party may seek redress, therefore, if its members believe their cause can be made visible and will win sympathy and support from persons not engaged in the struggle.

Outsiders sometimes take the initiative in entering a potentially conflictful situation. They tend to enter to help those with whom they feel linked by class, ethnicity, ideology, or other interests or identities. Such "outside agitators" or would-be exporters of revolution will be unable to ignite a flame if there is no dry tinder.

Adversary Relations

For a potential conflict group with a grievance and a contentious goal, the perceived weakness of the adversary opens up the opportunity to initiate a conflict. An opponent may indicate such weakness in several ways. It may act inconsistently, hesitantly, and incompetently, and reveal disunion and lack of conviction in its own positions. That may give credence to the view that a deterioration of conditions is due not only to that party's erroneous policies, but also to its vulnerability to pressure. Thus, analysts of revolutions generally agree that one of the immediate causes of revolts is the appearance of uncertainty and of self-doubt among the authorities. This may be signaled by verbal signs of panic and by defections. Such signals invite more radical goals; they may indicate that fundamental restructuring of authority relations rather than reforms are needed and are possible.

Changes in the relative power of potential antagonists is often the prelude to conflict emergence. Revolutionary situations, therefore, typically arise when the governmental power has been eroded, often as a result of external wars that have strained the government's capacity and made its weaknesses apparent. Skocpol's analysis of the great revolutions of France, Russia, and China reveals that the state in each case had been strained beyond its capacity by its international ventures.[99] Laqueur summarizes many of the reasons that war has been decisive in the emergence of revolutionary situations in modern times. He observes:

> Most modern revolutions, both successful and abortive, have followed in the wake of war. . . . These have occurred not only in the countries that suffered defeat. The general dislocation caused by war, the material losses and human

sacrifices, create a climate conducive to radical change. A large section of the population has been armed; human life seems considerably less valuable than in peacetime. In a defeated country authority tends to disintegrate and acute social dissatisfactions receive additional impetus from a sense of wounded national prestige. . . . The old leadership is discredited by defeat, and the appeal for radical social change and national reassertion thus falls on fertile ground.[100]

Finally, it should be noted too that a group believing that it has overwhelming dominance may tend to exploit that dominance and so provoke resistance from the exploited, subordinated, or vulnerable party. Furthermore, extreme acts of repression may fail to be effective, but rather convince groups previously unengaged in a struggle that they have no alternative but to resist or face extreme sanctions in any case.

Conclusions

A conflict emerges when members of one or more potential conflict parties develop a shared identity, generate a sense of grievance, form a goal that another party, being responsible for the grievance, be changed, and come to believe that they can bring about that change. These four components are highly interdependent, affecting each other as a struggle becomes manifest.[101] Each component is necessary, but none is sufficient by itself; furthermore, various combinations of different levels of each can result in the initiation of a conflict. Together, they provide the impetus for at least one side to move against another, igniting a struggle.

Just as conflicts may be considered to occur for varying time periods, a day, a few years, or even several decades, the conflict's emergence can be considered to be quite short or very extended. We generally consider large-scale conflicts to occur over an extended period and the emergence to also require many years for the antagonists to develop the necessary level of readiness. This is the case when we analyze social revolutions as compared with community disputes.

The analysis indicates the significance of three components in addition to feeling aggrieved. A sense of identity for each party in the conflict is necessary, although sometimes taken for granted by analysts. Furthermore, formulating a goal to bring about a change in a particular other person or group in order to redress the grievance is a critical element in the emergence of a conflict. Finally, the belief among members of the aggrieved party that by their efforts they can attain what they want, even against the wishes of the other side, is necessary.

It is important to recognize the significance of a party considering its ability to gain what it seeks in deciding to engage in a conflict. But that does not mean that a conflict results simply from a rational calculation by each party to get as much as it thinks it can get. An overwhelming sense of grievance may also engender a conflict as an aggrieved party acts from desperation.

Three sets of sources for each component have been mapped out. One set is internal to each potential conflict party. These internal sources may result in beliefs among members of a potential conflict party about who is responsible for their troubles, and that may target scapegoats so that the resulting conflict is regarded by observers and analysts as unrealistic.

The internal features and the social context of potential adversaries affect each of the components necessary for the emergence of a conflict. In this analysis, however, the ways adversaries affect each other's conduct is emphasized. This is important because it means that no one party is totally in charge of a struggle's outbreak or course. It also means that each party can influence how its possible adversary behaves in the emergence and development of a conflict.

This analysis has wide-ranging implications for conflict prevention and resolution. It suggests several strategies for preventing the eruption of social conflicts: inhibiting the development of salient oppositional identities, ameliorating the grounds for a sense of grievance, diverting the formulation of goals attributing responsibility for the grievance to others, or inhibiting the development of the belief that those feeling a sense of grievance can redress it by acting against another person or group. Merely listing such possibilities should suggest that often we do not want to prevent a conflict from emerging. We may think that justice would be served if a conflict were waged, constructively if possible.

Notes

1. In earlier writing, I cited three conditions, grouping together the belief in the ability to make a desired change and the feeling of dissatisfaction to constitute having a grievance. See Louis Kriesberg, *The Sociology of Social Conflicts* (Englewood Cliffs, N.J.: Prentice-Hall, 1973) and the revised edition, *Social Conflicts* 1982. I now believe that it is useful to emphasize the importance of the belief that the desired change is possible and therefore distinguish it from feeling dissatisfied.

2. In 1948, the COMINFORM (the Communist Information Bureau) led by the Communist Party of the Soviet Union, accused Josip Broz Tito, the leader of the Yugoslav Communist Party and government, of deviating from the communist line. Tito defied the Soviets and relations between the parties and governments were ruptured. Yugoslavia developed its own form of market socialism, with factories comanaged by the workers and managers.

3. Thus, the percentage of the adult population of Yugoslavia identifying themselves as Yugoslavs increased from 1.7 percent in 1961 to 5.4 percent in 1981. The percentage varied greatly among the republics and provinces of Yugoslavia; in 1981 it

varied from 8.2 percent in Croatia and in Vojvodina, to 7.9 percent in Bosnia/Herzegovina, to 1.4 percent in Slovenia, to 0.7 percent in Macedonia, and to only 0.1 percent in Kosovo. See Dusko Sekulic, Garth Massey, and Randy Hodson, "Who Were the Yugoslavs? Failed Sources of a Common Identity in the Former Yugoslavia," *American Sociological Review* 59 (February 1994): 85.

4. For discussions of primordialism and constructionism, see Richard H. Thompson, *Theories of Ethnicity: A Critical Appraisal* (New York: Greenwood Press, 1989); for constructionist approaches see Benedict Anderson, *Imagined Communities: Reflections on the Origin and Spread of Nationalism*, rev. ed. (London: Verso, 1991), and Paul R. Brass, *Ethnicity and Nationalism: Theory and Comparison* (Newbury Park, Calif.: Sage, 1991). A hybrid approach, viewing ethnic consciousness as a potentiality that is realized only under certain conditions has been articulated by John L. Comaroff, "Humanity, Ethnicity, Nationality: Conceptual and Comparative Perspectives on the U.S.S.R.," *Theory and Society* 20 (1991): 661–87.

5. The distinction between ascribed and achieved statuses has been elaborated by Talcott Parsons, *The Social System* (Glencoe, Ill.: The Free Press, 1951), 63–65.

6. Pierre L. van den Berghe, *Race and Racism: A Comparative Perspective*, 2d ed. (New York: Wiley, 1978).

7. Russell Hardin, "Self Interest, Group Identity," in *Perspectives on Nationalism and War*, ed. John L. Comaroff and Paul C. Stern (Luxembourg: Gordon and Breach, 1995).

8. Selig Perlman, *A Theory of the Labor Movement* (New York: Augustus M. Kelley, 1920), 162–69, and Derek C. Bok and John T. Dunlop, *Labor and the American Community* (New York: Simon & Schuster, 1970), 30.

9. William H. Form, "Conflict within the Working Class: The Skilled as a Special-Interest Group," in *The Uses of Controversy in Sociology*, ed. Otto N. Larsen (New York: Free Press, 1976).

10. For example, faculty heterogeneity was found to be correlated with disputes among high-school teachers and administrators. See Ronald G. Corwin, "Patterns of Organizational Conflict," *Administrative Science Quarterly* 14 (December 1969): 507–20.

11. There is evidence from several countries that the husband's class location is a major determinant of the wife's subjective class identity. See Janeen Baxter, "Is Husband's Class Enough? Class Location and Class Identity in the United States, Sweden, and Australia," *American Sociological Review* 59 (April 1994): 220–35. That tendency would weaken solidarity based on women's own occupational positions. The importance of marital status and marital roles for women and hence the varying significance of the homemaker role for women can be the source of other differences that reduce women's solidarity. This is a factor in the struggle about the right to have an abortion, between women favoring choice and women favoring the right to life.

12. Theda Skocpol, *States and Social Revolutions: A Comparative Analysis of France, Russia, and China* (Cambridge: Cambridge University Press, 1979), 92.

13. Eleanor Flexner, *Century of Struggle* (Cambridge, Mass.: Harvard University Press, 1959), 23–40.

14. Joel Seidman, Jack London, Bernard Karsh, and Daisy L. Tagliacozzo, *The Worker Views His Union* (Chicago: The University of Chicago Press, 1958); and Louis

Kriesberg, "Customer Versus Colleague Ties among Retail Furriers," *Journal of Retailing* 29 (Winter 1953–54): 173–76.

15. Alvin W. Gouldner, *Patterns of Industrial Bureaucracy* (New York: Free Press, 1954).

16. See the literature on resource mobilization and social movements; for example: Anthony Oberschall, *Social Conflict and Social Movements* (Englewood Cliffs, N.J.: Prentice-Hall, 1973); and Charles Tilly, *From Mobilization to Revolution* (Reading, Mass.: Addison-Wesley, 1978); Doug McAdam, John D. McCarthy, and Mayer Zald, eds., *Comparative Perspectives on Social Movements* (New York: Cambridge University Press, 1996); and the annual, *Research in Social Movements, Conflicts and Change*, published by JAI Press.

17. Aldon D. Morris, *The Origins of the Civil Rights Movement* (New York: Free Press, 1984).

18. For example, in the 1950s and 1960s, colonial rule was losing its legitimacy and European empires were dissolving. The incidence of ethnonationalist struggles rose. See Ted R. Gurr, *Minorities at Risk* (Washington, D.C.: United States Institute of Peace Press, 1993).

19. Fredrik Barth, ed. *Ethnic Groups and Boundaries* (Boston: Little, Brown and Company, 1969). Also see Eric Voegelin, "The Growth of Race Idea," *Review of Politics* 2 (1940): 283–317, and Tomatsu Shibutani and Kian M. Kwan, *Ethnic Stratification* (New York: Macmillan, 1965).

20. Robert A. LeVine and Donald T. Campbell, *Ethnocentrism: Theories of Conflict, Ethnic Attitudes, and Group Behavior* (New York: John Wiley & Sons, 1972), and W. A. Elliott, *Us and Them: A Study of Group Consciousness* (Aberdeen: Aberdeen University Press, 1986).

21. Louis Kriesberg, "Ethnicity, Nationalism, and Violent Conflict in the 1990s," *Peace Studies Bulletin* 2 (Winter 1992–93): 24–28.

22. Daniel Druckman, "Social Psychological Aspects of Nationalism," 56–59, in Comaroff and Stern, *Perspectives on Nationalism and War*.

23. See J. T. Borhek, "Ethnic-Group Cohesion," *American Journal of Sociology* 76 (July 1970): 33–46.

24. Race is generally understood to refer to genetically determined differences among major groupings of humans. But, biologically, humans are a single species. The only biological meaning to "race" is to broad, overlapping genetic pools, lacking clear boundaries. On the basis of selecting some traits, people in many societies construct "social races." These are often clearly bounded, allowing for the classification of individuals.

25. Chalmers A. Johnson, *Peasant Nationalism and Communist Power* (Stanford, Calif.: Stanford University Press, 1962).

26. This argument was made in an article that drew great attention when published, by Samuel P. Huntington, "The Clash of Civilizations?" *Foreign Affairs* 72 (Summer 1993): 22–49.

27. Bert Klandermans, "The Social Construction of Protests and Multiorganizational Fields," in *Frontiers in Social Movement Theory*, ed. Aldon Morris and Carol Mueller (New Haven, Conn.: Yale University Press, 1992).

28. This does not necessarily mean that the less dissatisfied people are, the happier they are. Research indicates that self-assessed happiness or well-being is based upon

the balance of positive and negative feelings. A person may have a lot of both, a lot of one and a little of the other, or a little of both. See Norman M. Bradburn, *The Structure of Psychological Well Being* (Chicago: Aldine, 1969).

29. Alex Inkeles, "Industrial Man: The Relation of Status to Experience, Perception, and Value," *American Journal of Sociology* 66 (July 1960): 1–31.

30. Robert Blauner, *Alienation and Freedom: The Factory Worker and His Industry* (Chicago: The University of Chicago Press, 1964).

31. Bradburn, *The Structure of Psychological Well Being*, 95, and Norman M. Bradburn and David Caplovitz, *Reports on Happiness* (Chicago: Aldine, 1965), 10–11.

32. William Buchanan and Hadley Cantril, *How Nations See Each Other* (Urbana: University of Illinois Press, 1953).

33. Bertram P. Karon, *The Negro Personality* (New York: Springer Publishing Co., 1958), and Seymour Parker and Robert J. Kleiner, "The Culture of Poverty," *American Anthropologist* 72 (June 1970): 516–27.

34. An analysis of interstate wars between 1820 and 1964 found that national capability correlated 0.64 with war initiation. See Stuart A. Bremer, "National Capabilities and War Proneness," in *The Correlates of War: II*, ed. J. David Singer (New York: The Free Press, 1980).

35. Herbert H. Hyman, "The Psychology of Status," *Archives of Psychology*, no. 269 (1942); Robert K. Merton and Alice S. Kitt, "Contributions to the Theory of Reference Group Behavior," in R. K. Merton and P. F. Lazarsfeld, eds., *Studies in the Scope and Method of "The American Soldier"* (New York: Free Press, 1950); and W. G. Runciman, *Relative Deprivation and Social Justice* (Berkeley: University of California Press, 1966).

36. Manford H. Kuhn, "The Reference Group Reconsidered," in *Symbolic Interaction: A Reader in Social Psychology*, ed. J. Manis and B. Meltzer (Boston: Allyn and Bacon, 1967).

37. Everett C. Hughes, "Dilemmas and Contradictions of Status," *American Journal of Sociology* 50 (March 1944): 353–59, and Gerhard E. Lenski, "Status Crystalization: A Nonvertical Dimension of Social Status," *American Sociological Review* 19 (August 1954): 405–13.

38. Johan Galtung, "A Structural Theory of Aggression," *Journal of Peace Research* 2 (1964): 95–119.

39. Even the appearance of a woman giving direction to a man doing his work may be a source of strain. To minimize this, for example, waitresses in restaurants generally place the customer's orders on a spindle from which the male cook can take the order. See William F. Whyte, *Human Relations in the Restaurant Industry* (New York: McGraw-Hill, 1948); also see Rosabeth Moss Kanter, *Men and Women of the Corporation* (New York: Basic Books, 1977).

40. Seymour Martin Lipset and Earl Raab, *The Politics of Unreason: Right Wing Extremism in America, 1790–1970* (New York: Harper & Row, 1970).

41. James A. Geschwender, "Continuities in Theories of Status Consistency and Cognitive Dissonance," *Social Forces* 46 (December 1967): 160–71, and Elton Jackson, "Status Consistency and Symptoms of Stress," *American Sociological Review* 27 (August 1962): 469–80.

42. James A. Geschwender, "Status Inconsistency, Social Isolation, and Individual Unrest," *Social Forces* 46 (June 1968): 477–83. Similarly, studies of happiness found that older persons with high education but low income are less likely to be happy than

one would expect by simply adding together the effects of the ranks along those two dimensions. Presumably, younger persons tend to believe they can still raise their incomes to a level appropriate for their education. See Bradburn, *The Structure of Psychological Well Being*, 69, and Bradburn and Caplovitz, *Reports on Happiness*, 10–11.

43. Hughes, "Dilemmas and Contradictions of Status."

44. Runciman, *Relative Deprivation and Social Justice*, 188–208, and Bradburn, *The Structure of Psychological Well Being*, 196.

45. In addition to the substantive issues, a methodological issue, the identification problem, arises from the difficulty in distinguishing an additive effect from an interactive effect of two or more variables. In an additive model, each explanatory variable affects the dependent variable independently in relation to the other; hence the effects can be added together. In an interaction model, the effects of each variable depend upon the other. The identification problem occurs because several different combinations of additive and interactive effects could produce the same results. Consequently, without additional information, allocation of the effects to a simple deprivation or to a relative deprivation (based on status inconsistency) is indeterminate. See H. M. Blalock, Jr., "Status Inconsistency and Interaction: Some Alternative Models," *American Journal of Sociology* 73 (November 1967): 305–15.

46. Using surveys conducted in fourteen countries, analysis revealed a high rank correlation between the socioeconomic level of the country and the average level of current satisfaction. See Hadley Cantril, *The Pattern of Human Concerns* (New Brunswick, N.J.: Rutgers University Press, 1965). For a related study, see Philip J. Stone, "Expectations of a Better Personal Future," *Public Opinion Quarterly* 34 (Fall 1970): 346–59. Also see Donald J. Treiman, "Status Discrepancy and Prejudice, *American Journal of Sociology* 71 (May 1966): 651–64.

47. Werner Landecker, "Status Congruence, Class Crystallization, and Class Consciousness," Sociology and Social Research 54 (April 1970): 343–55.

48. Ted Robert Gurr, *Why Men Rebel* (Princeton, N.J.: Princeton University Press, 1970).

49. Crane Brinton, *The Anatomy of Revolution* (New York: Vintage, 1955), originally published in 1938; and James C. Davies, "Toward a Theory of Revolution," *American Sociological Review* 27 (February 1962): 5–19.

50. See the detailed analyses in Daniel Lerner, with the collaboration of Lucille W. Pevsner, *The Passing of Traditional Society: Modernizing the Middle East* (Glencoe, Ill.: The Free Press, 1958).

51. David Snyder, "Collective Violence Processes: Implications for Disaggregated Theory and Research," in *Research in Social Movements, Conflicts and Change*, vol. 2, ed. Louis Kriesberg (Greenwich, Conn.: JAI Press, 1979).

52. Bradburn, *The Structure of Psychological Well Being*.

53. J. S. Ellsworth, Jr., *Factory Folkways* (New Haven, Conn.: Yale University Press, 1952).

54. Runciman, *Relative Deprivation and Social Justice*.

55. For example, Seymour Martin Lipset, *Agrarian Socialism* (Berkeley: University of California Press, 1950), 179–98.

56. Shibutani and Kwan, *Ethnic Stratification*, 351–61.

57. Saul Alinsky, *Reveille for Radicals* (New York: Vintage, 1946); Donald C. Reitzes

and Dietrich C. Reitzes, *The Alinsky Legacy: Alive and Kicking* (Greenwich, Conn.: JAI Press, 1987); and Warren C. Haggstrom, "Can the Poor Transform the World?" in *Among the People*, ed. Irwin Deutscher and Elizabeth J. Thompson (New York: Basic Books, 1968).

58. Peter H. Rossi and Richard A. Berk, "Local Political Leadership and Popular Discontent," *The Annals*, September 1970, 111–27.

59. Inge Powell Bell, *CORE and the Strategy of Non-Violence* (New York: Random House, 1968), and National Advisory Commission on Civil Disorders (Kerner Commission), *Report of the National Commission on Civil Disorders* (New York: Bantam, 1968).

60. Edward Azar and N. Farah, "The Structure of Inequalities and Protracted Social Conflict: A Theoretical Framework," *International Interactions* 4 (1981): 317–35.

61. M. A. East, "Status Discrepancy and Violence in the International System: An Empirical Analysis," in *The Analysis of International Politics*, ed. J. N. Rosenau, V. Davis, and M. A. East (New York: Free Press, 1971).

62. Thomas J. Volgy and Stacey Mayhall, "Status Inconsistency and International War: Exploring the Effects of Systemic Change," *International Studies Quarterly* 39 (March 1995): 67–84.

63. Martin S. Weinberg and Colin J. Williams, "Disruption, Social Location and Interpretative Practices: The Case of Wayne, New Jersey," *American Sociological Review* 34 (April 1969): 170–82.

64. Lewis A. Coser, *The Functions of Social Conflict* (New York: Free Press, 1956), 62.

65. Michael Mann, "The Cohesion of Liberal Democracy," *American Sociological Review* 35 (June 1970): 423–39.

66. Max Heirich, *The Spiral of Conflict* (New York: Columbia University Press, 1971).

67. Of course, the terms *left* and *right* are used with different meanings in different historical contexts. For example, in the initial post-Soviet period in Russia, left sometimes meant those favoring radical change and increased freedom and sometimes those favoring maintaining a great deal of socioeconomic equality and much of the old state apparatus. In the United States of the 1980s and 1990s, left and right were also related to issues of morality, with the right often advocating the use of state power to ensure adherence to what were claimed to be traditional values. Also see Seymour Martin Lipset, "Fascism—Left, Right, and Center," *Political Man*, ed. S. M. Lipset (New York: Doubleday, 1960).

68. Tilly, *From Mobilization to Revolution*, 203.

69. Paige makes this distinction between divisible and unitary goals, pointing out that demanding the abolition of private ownership of large agricultural estates is proclaiming a unitary goal, while demands for a 10 percent increase in wages is a divisible goal. See Jeffrey M. Paige, *Agrarian Revolution: Social Movements and Export Agriculture in the Underdeveloped World* (New York: The Free Press, 1975).

70. E. J. Hobsbawm. *Primitive Rebels* (New York: W.W. Norton, 1965), 108–16. Originally published in 1959.

71. Barry B. Hughes, *The Democratic Context of American Foreign Policy* (San Francisco: W.W. Freeman, 1978), 38. Also see John E. Mueller, *War, Presidents, and Public*

Opinion (New York: John Wiley and Sons, 1973), and John Mueller, "American Public Opinion and the Gulf War," in *The Political Psychology of the Gulf War*, ed. Stanley A. Renshon (Pittsburgh: University of Pittsburgh Press, 1993).

72. Taylor Branch, *Parting the Waters: America in the King Years, 1954–63* (New York: Simon and Schuster, 1988), 105–205.

73. John T. Dunlop, "The Development of Labor Organizations," in *Labor Economic and Industrial Relations*, ed. Joseph Shister (Philadelphia: Lippincott, 1951).

74. Gary T. Marx, *Protest and Prejudice* (New York: Harper & Row, 1969), 57, 117.

75. Richard G. Braungart, "The Utopian and Ideological Styles of Student Political Activists," paper presented at the 2d Annual Meeting of the International Society of Political Psychology, Washington, D.C., 1979.

76. David R. Schmitt, "An Attitudinal Correlate of the Status Incongruency of Married Women," *Social Forces* 44 (December 1965): 190–261; and Leonard Broom and F. Lancaster Jones, "Status Consistency and Political Preference: The Australian Case," *American Sociological Review* 35 (December 1970): 989–1001.

77. For analyses of the extent and explanations for the decline in take-home earnings from wages and the growing income inequality in the United States, see Denny Braun, *The Rich Get Richer* (Chicago: Nelson-Hall, 1991); Paul Blumberg, *Inequality in an Age of Decline* (New York: Oxford University Press, 1980); and Timothy Smeeding, "America's Income Inequality: Where Do We Stand?" *Challenge* (September-October 1996): 45–53.

78. Gurr, *Why Men Rebel*, 179.

79. Kate Millett, *Sexual Politics* (New York: Doubleday, 1970), 125–27.

80. Many other economic and cultural factors contributed to the Iranian revolution and to the appeal of anti-Westernism. See Farrokh Moshiri, "Iran: Islamic Revolution against Westernization," in *Revolutions of the Late Twentieth Century*, ed. J. A. Goldstone, T. R. Gurr, and F. Moshiri (Boulder, Colo.: Westview Press, 1991); and Misagh Parsa, *Social Origins of the Iranian Revolution* (New Brunswick: Rutgers University Press, 1989).

81. Robert S. Wistrich, *Antisemitism: The Longest Hatred* (New York: Pantheon, 1991).

82. Gurr, *Why Men Rebel*, 125–26.

83. Richard N. Rosecrance, *Action and Reaction in World Politics* (Boston: Little, Brown, 1963).

84. Such considerations affect changes in goals as well. For example, the relatively radical Palestinian organization, the Popular Democratic Front for the Liberation of Palestine (PDFLP), published a circular in 1969 arguing that its goal of "throwing the Jews into the sea" had done "grave damage" to the Arab position and argued for a goal of creating a "democratic Palestinian state" in which Arabs and Jews would live in peace. See Yehoshafat Harkabi, "Liberation or Genocide?" *Transaction* 7 (July–August 1970): 63.

85. See note 9 in chapter 1.

86. David H. Bennett, *The Party of Fear: From Nativist Movements to the New Right in American History*, 2d ed. (New York: Vintage, 1995), 328–31.

87. Paige, *Agrarian Revolution*, 36.

88. Paul B. Sheatsley, "White Attitudes toward the Negro," *Daedalus* 95 (Winter 1966): 224.

89. J. Allen Williams and Paul L. Wienir, "A Reexamination of Myrdal's Rank Order of Discrimination," *Social Problems* 14 (Spring 1967): 443–54.

90. In the language of economists, this is called vicarious utility. See Stefan Valavanis, "The Resolution of Conflict When Utilities Interact," *Journal of Conflict Resolution* 2 (June 1958): 156–69.

91. For discussions of the resource mobilization approach to the study of social movements, see Mayer N. Zald and John D. McCarthy, *The Dynamics of Social Movements* (Cambridge, Mass.: Winthrop, 1979); Doug McAdam and David A. Snow, *Social Movements: Readings on Their Emergence, Mobilization, and Dynamics* (Los Angeles: Roxbury, 1997); and the annual series *Research in Social Movements, Conflict and Change*, published by JAI Press.

92. Paul F. Lazarsfeld, Bernard Berelson, and Hazel Gaudet, *The People's Choice* (New York: Columbia University Press, 1944), and Martin Kriesberg, "Cross-Pressures and Attitudes," *Public Opinion Quarterly* 13 (Spring 1949): 5–16.

93. Elton F. Jackson in "Status Consistency and Symptoms of Stress" reports that "persons whose inconsistency is due to high racial-ethnic status and low occupational and educational status tend to respond to their stress" with high levels of psychophysiological symptoms (476).

94. Alinsky, *Reveille for Radicals*; Reitzes and Reitzes, *The Alinsky Legacy*; and Haggstrom, "Can the Poor Transform the World?"

95. Louis Kriesberg, *International Conflict Resolution* (New Haven, Conn.: Yale University Press, 1992).

96. Selig Perlman, *A Theory of the Labor Movement* (New York: Augustus M. Kelley, 1928).

97. Gloria Steinem, "A New Egalitarian Life Style," *New York Times*, 26 August 1971, 37.

98. Juan Diez Medrano, *Divided Nations: Class, Politics, and Nationalism in the Basque Country and Catalonia* (Ithaca, N.Y.: Cornell University Press, 1995).

99. Theda Skocpol, *States and Social Revolutions: A Comparative Analysis of France, Russia, and China* (Cambridge: Cambridge University Press, 1979).

100. Walter Laqueur, "Revolution," *International Encyclopedia of the Social Sciences*, vol. 13 (New York: Macmillan, 1968), 501.

101. Some conflict analysts combine particular components in order to distinguish different kinds of conflicts. For example, identity and interest conflicts are sometimes differentiated. Identity conflicts refer to struggles about dissensual issues such as core values and values held by one or more parties to a fight, while interest conflicts are based on what would be regarded here as consensual issues. See Jay Rothman, *Resolving Identity-Based Conflict in Nations, Organizations, and Communities* (San Francisco: Jossey-Bass, 1997).

4

Alternative Conflict Strategies

The conventional understanding among partisans and observers of conflicts is that coercion is needed to induce an adversary to yield. Often, violence is regarded as the ultimate recourse to be used in settling a conflict. In actuality, conflicts are often waged in many noncoercive ways; and when coercion is applied, it can be done in diverse nonviolent ways. An adversary may promise future benefits to an opponent, if the opponent agrees to yield some of what the adversary seeks. Or, the adversary may try to convince its opponent that to provide what it requests would be in the opponent's own true interests. Such noncoercive inducements are likely to be combined with some coercion; but often, the coercion is limited and not necessarily destructive of positive relationships between the adversaries.

Each contending party adopts a strategy, or more likely a set of strategies, to attain its goals. The strategies combine a variety of inducements in a series of short-term tactical actions. This does not require that alternatives be consciously reviewed, their likely effectiveness assessed, and their costs weighed before one is selected. At times, a tactic may be used because it appears to be the only reasonable one available and no reflection seems required. But even in those circumstances, alternatives were conceivable and an analyst should consider what they might be and why the parties did not consider them. An examination of the constraints on choice of tactics is a crucial part of any conflict analysis.

Usually, however, in conflicts between large-scale adversaries, alternative strategies are seriously considered, often briefly and in a small circle but sometimes at length and with extensive participation. After all, a conflict strategy is a means toward a desired goal; it is not simply expressive behavior. Just because one opponent or analyst judges that behavior to be ineffective, counterproductive, or merely expressive does not mean that it is so regarded by those doing it. For example, Blacks, but not Whites, generally viewed the 1960s riots in urban American ghettos as protest actions that would affect public policies.[1] But conflict behavior usually also has expressive components; some members of a conflict party getting intrinsic pleasure from the behavior, even in hurting the enemy. Insofar as expressiveness is significant, the strategy is not well calculated and the conflict tends to be self-perpetuating and destructive.

Each adversary selects a strategy to pursue its goals, but the way that struggle is conducted is not wholly determined by one side. The adversaries jointly shape the mode of struggle actually employed. Some conflict modes are highly institutionalized and ritualized and the adversaries mutually agree to employ one of those modes; this occurs in cultures with norms about duels, feuds, strikes, judicial proceedings, and so on. Some conflict modes may not be so clearly guided by rules, but the adversaries recognize that they are conducting a struggle in an agreed-upon mode, such as, waging a war. In some struggles, however, the parties disagree about what mode is being used; one side may proclaim it is engaging in respectful petition or protest, while the other regards the conduct as an unlawful threat to authority and violently represses it, as occurred at Tiananmen Square in Beijing in June 1989.

The strategies and modes used in a conflict usually undergo changes in the course of a struggle, as we will see in the subsequent chapters on conflict escalation and de-escalation. This and the next chapter focus on the variety of ways conflicts are conducted and the many factors and processes affecting the choice of means. This analysis will help account for conflict escalation and de-escalation.

Types of Inducements

Conflicts are often differentiated in terms of the strategies and modes employed: for example, wars, mediated collective bargaining, nonviolent resistance, palace coups, and riots are often considered different kinds of conflicts. The comparison of different conflict modes will be facilitated by referring to their basic elements: the inducements each side combines to conduct a struggle. Three basic inducements are generally recognized: coercion, reward, and persuasion.[2] Distinguishing among the inducements requires reliance on a common standard. Several standards might be used, including the actors' intentions, the recipients' perceptions, the analysts' characterization of effects, or the way the actions are presented by those performing them. The way actions are presented is relatively ascertainable and usually will be the standard used here; its use does not preclude consideration of the other ways of distinguishing inducements.

Coercive Inducements

Coercion is a major element of the struggles examined here. Coercion refers to actions, including symbolic ones, that injure or threaten injury to the adversary; they are presented as efforts to intimidate and deter or otherwise to force the opponent to comply with the demands made by the coercer. The cessation of coercion, then, is conditional on the opponent's compliance and is not simply carried out for its intrinsic pleasure.

Coercive inducements have many forms and degrees. One significant distinction is between coercion that is threatened and coercion that is actualized. Coercion is generally threatened before being applied, in the hope that the threat will suffice. Another important distinction lies between violent and nonviolent coercion. The term *violent coercive inducements* refers to threatened or actual direct physical damage to people or their possessions. This is a conventional definition and useful for the present analysis, but other conceptions should be recognized. Johan Galtung has argued for broadening the concept of violence to include actions or inactions by some people such that "human beings are being influenced so that their actual somatic and mental realizations are below their potential realizations."[3] Galtung has reasoned with great influence that, "if people are starving when that is objectively avoidable, then violence is committed."[4] On the other hand, for many people, even killings may not be regarded as violent when they are done by legitimate authorities.[5] For some members of the public, the use of force is regarded as necessary to maintain law and order and consequently is not considered to be violent. In this analysis, the use or threatened use of force to injure others is violence, whoever does it.

The magnitude of coercive inducements varies greatly, but not along a single dimension. A high level of coercion is evident when force is used to change the conditions of the target group, most extremely by extensive killing of group members, as in cases of genocide. Actions directly changing conditions also include forced removal of people from a territory and resettling others in their place. More typically, coercion is used against members of the opposing sides, thus weakening and intimidating members of the other side so that they comply. It includes attacks against the other side's defensive forces but also against leading figures of the opposing side. This may take the form of police repression of individuals that includes torture and "disappearances" of alleged dissenters. Nonviolent coercion, such as boycotts or economic sanctions, are generally presented as of lower magnitude than violent coercion.[6] At a lower level of coercion, a threat may be made to withhold payment or services upon which the other party depends. For example, where employees have few options, even an unrealized threat by an employer can be quite effective. In close personal relations, the mere expression of disapproval or anger is also coercive.

Coercive inducements also vary in their cost to their user. Threats may seem cheap, but to be credible the threatener must appear capable of carrying them out. That means, that a government threatening warfare must have a military capability that seems strong relative to the country being threatened. That can be very expensive and be a great burden on a society's economy. Actually carrying out a threat can be even more costly, in terms of both exercising the coercion and suffering the consequences of underestimated retribution. The cost of a strategy imposes constraints on escalating and prolonging a conflict.

Furthermore, coercion varies in the precision with which it can be employed. It is often a very blunt and imprecise means of inducing an adversary to change. Typically, in large-scale conflicts, inducing the leaders of the adversary to change involves subjecting their constituents to coercion. Such coercion may turn counterproductive as the wavering constituency may rally to support their leadership against the outsider. The broad use of coercion, then, tends to widen the conflict, add to its destructiveness, and sometimes prolong it.

Rewards as Inducements

Rewards are obvious inducements, but they are relatively neglected in the analysis of social conflicts. An extensive body of theory and research indicates the value of rewards rather than punishments in such areas as child rearing and learning generally.[7] Offering a reward for compliance can be more effective and precise than punishing for noncompliance. For example, in the early 1990s, the U.S. government had become deeply concerned about North Korea's nuclear program and sought United Nations approval for strong economic sanctions. By June 1994, plans to attack North Korea's nuclear facilities were prepared. The danger of a war was averted when former President Jimmy Carter went to North Korea and persuaded Kim Il Sung, North Korea's leader, to freeze the nuclear program. The U.S. and North Korean governments then conducted negotiations leading to the October 1994 Agreed Framework, according to which North Korea would roll back its nuclear arms program and the United States would gradually normalize political and economic relations, help replace nuclear reactors, and supply heavy fuel oil.[8]

Positive sanctions are more likely to be used and to be effective in the closing stages of a conflict than during a period of escalation or of intense antagonism. Offers of benefits while a conflict is being waged with great coerciveness would tend to be regarded with suspicion by the recipient.[9] An exchange of benefits, such as of prisoners on each side, however, may be a way of signaling the possibility of eventually normalizing relations.

Rewards or positive sanctions take a variety of forms in a social conflict. A conflict party may offer or provide material benefits as an inducement to obtain what it seeks. Benefits may include money, land, or promises of access to occupational positions. In addition, positive sanctions include nontangible benefits such as approbation or status recognition. This means that the conflict party with greater resources or of higher status is relatively more capable of using positive sanctions.

As in the use of negative sanctions, the recipients of positive sanctions vary, particularly in large-scale conflicts. Certain individuals or factions within the recipient party are more likely to obtain the benefits than are others. More extremely, the benefits may be covertly offered to the leaders of the opposing side; in which case in many cultures it would be regarded as corruption. Sometimes collective bargaining agreements are considered "sweetheart contracts," when the contract terms offer little to the workers, but the union negotiator has received side payments from the management.

David A. Baldwin has noted several intriguingly different properties of negative and positive sanctions.[10] If a conflict party seeks to influence an opponent by a promise, the opponent's compliance obligates the conflict party to give a reward, while the failure to comply does not require any action. On the other hand, a conflict party using threats must act when there is no compliance. Consequently, promises tend to be more costly when they succeed, and threats more costly when they fail.

Persuasive Inducements

Persuasive inducements are couched as efforts to influence an opponent by communicating arguments, information, or appeals to alter the other side's perception of the conflict.[11] If effective, the process of persuasion involves the receiver becoming convinced of the correctness of the sender's goal and voluntarily accepting it. Persuasive inducements are frequently used in conflict, but often they are accompanied by some degree of coercion.

Although persuasive inducements are readily observed in social conflicts, the analysis of their role in conflicts has been neglected, perhaps because antagonists rarely acknowledge that the enemy has convinced them of anything. Yet, since conflicts arise and persist only because adversaries *believe* they have incompatible goals, persuasion might be expected to play a significant role in the emergence, escalation, and transformation of conflicts. Persuasive efforts are likely to be relatively greater at the initial stages of conflict emergence, before mutual mistrust has intensified. Then, as a conflict enters a de-escalating phase, they may be renewed as one or both sides try to convince the other that its belief in the incompatibility of their goals is misguided or that their common interests should be given higher priority.

Persuasive inducements vary in content, depending upon who is trying to influence whom, what the issues in contention are, and the stage the struggle has reached. Persuasive efforts may be couched in appeals to shared values about justice, fairness, or freedom. The other side, sharing those values, is urged to be true to them and give what is being sought. Persuasive arguments may also stress that the adversaries have common or complementary interests, or at least not conflicting ones. The argument is presented that those interests would be well served by the adversary agreeing to what the would-be persuader asks. An example of such arguments stressing complementary interests may be seen in the Austrian leaders' efforts to end the occupation of their country by the Soviet, U.S., British, and French military forces following World War II. The Austrian leaders convinced the Soviet leaders that Austria would not join the Western military alliance and would be neutral and that such a position served their interests and those of the Soviet Union as well. Together with changes in Soviet thinking and actions taken by the Western allies, this resulted in Soviet agreement to end the occupation in 1955.[12]

Arguments that the adversaries have a common interest can be enhanced by emphasizing that they have a common antagonist. For example, in the negotiations in Moscow to reach the 1963 partial nuclear test ban, U.S. officials noted the advantages of restraining countries with nuclear weapons and increasing pressure on China to inhibit development of its nuclear weapons capability.[13]

Another kind of argument used by a contending party seeks to reassure the adversary that what it wants constitutes no danger to the adversary. For example, a conflict party may argue that it wants self-determination or autonomy regarding some aspect of its members' lives or access to resources and that this would not adversely affect the other party. This might be argued in terms of shared values or norms of fairness, pointing out that in similar circumstances, the adversary would make the same claims. The contending party's leaders may ask the adversary to consider what its claim looks like from its perspective.

Finally, persuasive inducements may provide information to convince the opponent that agreement would be advantageous.[14] The information is likely to be expressed as predictions of future losses or forgone gains if the other side does not change as desired. Predictions of future losses, generally called warnings, foretell terrible consequences, but only if those matters are not under the persuader's control. If they were, the predictions would be regarded as threats. For example, leaders of a protesting organization may point out that if they fail to get what they seek, another leadership or a rival organization will take over and be more hostile than they are. Information may also come in the form of forecasting future benefits if the opponent changes and agrees to give what the would-be persuader asks; for example, other parties would praise them. If what is predicted were under the control of the party making the predictions, it would be a promise; when it is not, it has been called a mendation.[15]

These persuasive inducements have been discussed as symbolic communications, using a verbal or written language. The appeals, arguments, and information, however, also can be conveyed in other formats. Cultural products such as paintings, songs, photographs, films, and videos can be used persuasively with great effectiveness, especially in efforts by leaders to mobilize their own constituency. In relations between adversaries, it may be that members of one contending party will try to convince the rank and file of the other side that their goals are just.

In conflict relations, partisans often say that actions speak louder than words. Indeed, appeals, arguments, and information may be more convincingly conveyed by the contending party's behavior than by what it says. The gestures, policies, and a thousand other kinds of actions by members of a contending party are observed and interpreted by the other side and provide credibility to the words uttered. Thus, we cannot fully separate persuasive inducements from other kinds of inducements. In any particular mode of waging a conflict, positive and negative sanctions tend to be combined with persuasive efforts.

These three kinds of inducements, coercion, reward, and persuasion, have been discussed as direct and explicit ways of trying to affect an opponent. But the efforts may also be indirect, in which case we might be speaking of covert actions and of efforts to manipulate the opposing side. For example, one side may try to subvert or reduce an adversary leaders' constituency support by covertly buying off supposed supporters. Or, one side may try to influence a third party to reduce its support for the opposing side.

Strategies and Modes of Struggle

Coercive and noncoercive inducements are combined in many ways to construct particular tactics, strategies, and modes of conflict. They may be short-term tactics, such as a protest march, or long-term strategies, such as a guerrilla war. The long-term strategy incorporates many tactics, generally conducted in sequence. Each adversary adopts particular strategies, sometimes without reflection, and as the adversaries interact in struggle, they fashion a specific mode of conflict. Many modes have generally recognized characteristics. Adversaries may agree, for example, that a particular action is part of "collective bargaining." They then share certain expectations about what the other side will do, and feel constrained not to act outside the mutually understood rules. Sometimes adversaries disagree about what mode of struggle is being used; one side may say it is engaged in a struggle for national liberation, and the other asserts that the legitimate authorities are being challenged by a small terrorist band. When there are such disagreements, the adversaries obviously are less constrained by shared rules.

Modes of conflict, as social constructions, are a kind of social invention.

Think of legal systems, which are collectively enacted to provide procedures by which many disputes and conflicts are conducted and settled within a society. Even wars may be considered social constructs; Margaret Mead has argued that war is an institution that was invented.[16]

The various ways by which struggles are conducted are presented here in terms of a fundamental dimension: the degree to which the means of conflict are regulated and institutionalized. But, I will also note how they vary in combining different inducements. These variations affect how destructive or constructive a struggle is.

Institutionalized Conflict Regulation

Since social conflicts are omnipresent, every social system has contrived ways to manage them.[17] In all societies there are norms and rules for conducting and settling conflicts, and they tend to be institutionalized. The judicial system in most countries is an example of a highly institutionalized set of regulations for conducting and settling disputes between individuals and/or corporate entities. The decision makers in these systems tend not to be the disputants themselves, but, directly or indirectly, authorities such as judges, juries, or heads of religious or political organizations. Adversaries generally pursue and resolve conflicts by their own actions within the confines of institutionalized regulations, as when management-union contentions, are conducted by the parties within a set of laws about fair labor practices and collective bargaining.

Struggles about how the social system as a whole should act are generally conducted within agreed-upon structures of governance. Most societies, have governmental organizations whose officers have the authority to make decisions regarding collective actions. In many democratic societies and organizations, the incumbents have competed for those offices in an electoral process, having taken different positions about such decisions. Such electoral politics may be so routine and so well regulated that contesting political parties are not regarded as being in a social conflict, except metaphorically. By the definition used in this book, however, they are in conflict.

Struggles that are *not* conducted according to highly institutionalized regulations are of most interest in the present analysis. It is useful, to examine even relatively regulated conflicts because fights often break out of regulated bounds, and it is important to understand how that happens and how the conflict sometimes comes to be destructively waged. It is also useful to understand how previously destructive conflicts become fairly and legitimately regulated. Such understanding will be furthered by examining the major variations in conflict regulations and their institutionalization and the factors affecting those variations.

Degree of Regulation

As previously noted, rules often govern in great detail many aspects of adversarial conduct, which can be true even for conflicts waged with deadly violence. Thus, in many societies, quarreling men have fought duels in which careful protocol was followed and one of the men was badly hurt or killed by the other. Wars in some historical periods have been waged with considerable restrictions, compared with the relatively unlimited wars of the last two centuries. For example, in European wars between about 1640 and 1740, fighting was halted to gather the harvest, and the fighting did not involve the populace at large.[18] Furthermore, during that period, some restraints against exploiting technological innovations for war making were exercised.

Even in recent interstate wars, certain restraints can be noted. Bacteriological weapons, for example, have not been employed in warfare. Chemical weapons have generally not been used since the First World War. One exception was their employment as a defoliating agent by U.S. military forces in Vietnam. Their employment by Iraqi military forces was feared by the U.S. and allied forces during the 1991 war to restore Kuwait's independence, but they were not used. Such restraints, however, may reflect fear of retaliation or doubts about their effectiveness more than any normative constraints or institutionalized regulations. This conclusion is suggested by the use of chemical weapons against civilians within Iraqi jurisdiction in 1988.[19] The grotesque brutality of genocidal attacks in Rwanda in 1994 and in parts of the former Yugoslavia in 1993–1995 illustrate the absence of elemental overarching regulations in some conflicts, but highlights their expected presence in most conflicts.[20]

The brutality in civil wars and revolutions does not necessarily bespeak the absence of a legitimate authority imposing adherence to regulations. Many of the worst atrocities in modern human experience have been conducted by government agents claiming the mantel of legitimate authority: the destruction of millions of civilians by the Nazis, the "ethnic cleansing," by rape, torture, and killings in Croatia and Bosnia, and the torture and killings by the Argentinean military junta in its "dirty war" against critics of the government are illustrative of atrocities carried out by agents of "legal authorities."[21]

The *content* of regulations as well as their existence, then, is crucial. The rules may greatly limit any challenges regarding the privileges of the dominant political party, class, ethnicity, or other group. The dominants, after all, generally make the rules. This is illustrated by the history of the American labor movement. American trade unions were considered illegal conspiracies until the middle of the nineteenth century. Even at the end the nineteenth century, courts generally issued labor injunctions forbidding workers from striking. When the Sherman Antitrust Act was enacted in 1890, the provision against corporations colluding to control a market was implemented against workers acting collectively in trade unions.[22] In totalitarian societies, conflict regulations were used to suppress certain conflicts in order to sustain the ruling party in power. Thus, in the former Soviet Union, the existence of class or nationality conflicts were denied by the Communist Party leadership. They were supposed to have been overcome in the new system the Communist Party had established.

The term *conflict regulation* refers to the rules that govern the contending parties' conduct in a social conflict. But rules that are unilaterally imposed should not be regarded as regulations; rather, policies that allow one party to violently suppress another are more accurately viewed as a mask for partisan struggle than as regulations. This suggests that the label "conflict regulation" may sometimes be contested. Authentic regulation exists insofar as the contending parties recognize each other's legitimacy and regard the rules governing their conflict as legitimate.

Degree of Institutionalization

Institutionalized regulations are sanctioned by legitimate authority, appear to exist external to those in conflict, and are internalized by the partisans in the conflict.[23] The existence of legitimate sanctions to reward compliance and punish violations are crucial elements of the institutionalization of the regulations and their maintenance. Sanctions may be threatened, or promised, by elected officials, religious leaders, charismatic leaders, or friends and associates. They include fines, incarceration, condemnations, prizes, and the promise of everlasting life in heaven.

The effectiveness of the sanctions depends not only on their magnitude but also on the certainty of their implementation. That likelihood of enforcement is increased insofar as it is in the interest and capability of particular persons to enforce them. Consequently, not only do the rules themselves tend to serve the interests of those who are dominant in the social system, but those rules that particularly favor the dominants are the ones most likely to be enforced.

Regulations are more highly institutionalized insofar as they appear to be long standing and external to the people in contention. Rules embodied in written form or orally transmitted beyond one generation take on an independent quality that helps maintain and foster adherence to them. These rules may be codified by persons accorded the authority to do so, and that makes the rules less vulnerable to differing interpretations by contending parties.

Finally, institutionalization is greater insofar as the regulations are internalized by the members of each of the adversary parties and the other members of their social system.[24] People are taught the legitimacy of rules governing conflicts and the agents who interpret and enforce them. When the rules are internalized through socialization and other social learning, people police themselves and anticipate feeling guilty or ashamed if they violate the rules.

Bases of Regulation and Institutionalization

The fundamental factor underlying the content of the rules governing conflict behavior and the institutionalization of the rules is the prior recurrent practices. Repeated actions come to be expected and after a while deviations become not only violations of these expectations but also illegitimate.[25] The social logic is compelling: the way things are done is the way they should be done because that is the way they have been done.

The adversaries' anticipation of continuing relations fosters conflict regulation. Furthermore, insofar as the contending parties expect that they will have recurrent conflicts, they tend to develop shared understandings about how they should each pursue their goals.[26] Certain ways of waging a conflict may come to be regarded as out of bounds. It follows that patterns of conflict behavior that are stable and expected to be stable are more likely to become institutionalized than those that are rapidly changing.

Several aspects of the relationship between the contending parties particularly affect the development of rules regarding their conflict behavior. Insofar as the parties are integrated with each other and have a shared culture, their conflict behavior will be regulated. Their greater separation and autonomy hampers conflict regulation. The level of inequalities between the adversaries also affects the regulation of their conflict behavior, but in contradictory ways. On the one hand, insofar as the parties are equal, rules governing their conflict behavior will be more equitable and adherence to them will be more acceptable to all parties. (It was the increased power of the American trade unions, aided by political influence in the 1930s, that resulted in the widespread institutionalization of rules governing collective bargaining.) On the other hand, if power inequalities are great, the dominant party may largely impose rules governing conflict behavior.

The characteristics of the contending parties also affect the development of conflict rules and their institutionalization. Thus, the culture of a party affects the likelihood that some procedures and not others will be considered legitimate and amenable to institutionalization. Many of the Catalan people in Spain, for example, think of themselves as "deal-makers" who have always tended to negotiate about issues in dispute. They offer that as an explanation for their successful negotiated achievement of regional autonomy.[27] More generally, in Western societies there is a tendency for disputants in a controversy to have internalized expectations that there will be a winner and a loser, and their contentious behavior is guided by that expectation. In many traditional societies and often in Asian cultures, the goal is to restore harmonious relations between the contending parties, and participants and intermediaries have internalized those expectations so that conflict becomes a search for resolutions that will enable the parties to resume coexistence in reasonable tranquillity. These expectations are often embodied in laws and informal rules.

The social system in which the contending parties belong profoundly affects the content and institutionalization of conflict rules. Legitimate agents of an overarching social system foster and may even impose rules governing conflict between constituent contending parties. This is an asset of governments. Political philosophers have long pointed to this vital role of governments in solving one of the inherent problems of social life: the threat of unbridled conflict.[28]

Finally, the kind of issues in contention affects the degree to which conflict behavior is controlled by institutionalized regulations. For example, conflicts in which the contending parties do not think their vital interests or fundamental identities are at stake tend to be relatively susceptible to institutionalized regulation. This is also the case insofar as the disputes require speedy and definitive settlement. This is illustrated in the findings of an analysis of American commodity exchanges, such as fabric makers selling to clothing manufacturers.[29] One factor was found to be highly related to the use of commercial arbitration rather than the usual legal process of bringing a law suit. That factor was the perishability of the product. Presumably, for goods that quickly lose their value, such as fresh vegetables and fish, it is important to reach a speedy decision.

Illustrative Modes

To illustrate how coercive, rewarding, and persuasive inducements are combined in various ways to constitute a general strategy of struggle, I discuss three sets of strategies that are varyingly regulated and have different combinations of inducements. The strategic approaches are nonviolent action, terrorism, and problem solving.

Nonviolent Action

In the concluding decades of the twentieth century, many nonviolent actions have been joined together in large-scale efforts to transform societies and to resist particular changes.[30] Sometimes participants in these efforts, and often the resisting authorities, have resorted to violence as well. Important examples include the civil rights struggle in the United States in the 1960s, the Solidarity movement in Poland in 1980–1981, the antiapartheid struggle in South Africa in the 1980s, the Palestinian Intifada resistance against Israeli occupation, 1987–1993, and the uprisings in Eastern Europe in 1989. These efforts have drawn on earlier experiences, including the women's suffrage movement resulting in 1920 in women attaining the right to vote in the United States, and the struggle for the independence of India from Great Britain, achieved in 1947.

These large-scale struggles included a great variety of nonviolent actions and together with other activities constituted a long-term strategy.[31] The various kinds of actions can be characterized in terms of their combination of the three primary inducements, as may be seen in figure 4.1. For example, a protest demonstration in which protesters march and carry banners expressing their views is largely an effort at persuasion, but it may also convey some threats, perhaps of electoral opposition. Many such actions would be located about the point "Na" in the figure. In most societies, such protests are regulated and government authorities may give or deny permission for demonstrations. And most, but certainly not all, demonstrations are carried out within authorized limits. Many demonstrations are rallies in support of one side in the struggle and may then be directed at intimidating their opponents.

More typically, nonviolent action refers to activities that have larger and more severe coercive components. This includes withholding goods or services, as in boycotts and strikes (located at point "Nb"). Such actions are often intended to communicate how important the goal is to those making the claim. They are often regulated and performed in compliance with the institutionalized rules.

Other nonviolent actions may be based on noncompliance to laws that the challengers regard as unjust, such as laws upholding segregation between ethnic communities. Such noncompliance can be carried out in ways that disrupt or prevent those who would practice segregation from doing so (point "Nc"

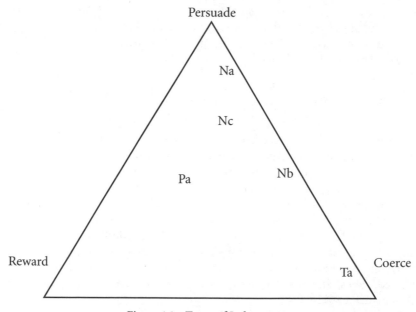

Figure 4.1   Types of Inducements

in the figure). This was the case with battles to desegregate public accommodations in the American South waged by civil rights organizations during the early 1960s. Their actions had highly coercive components but embodied persuasive elements as well, since they were conducted to avoid hurting the people whose actions they sought to change, even at the cost of enduring violence themselves. The actions were presented as demonstrating the importance to the nonviolent resisters of ending segregation, and indicating their view of it as immoral, but also demonstrating that this was done without hate and promising that once the segregated practices were ended, mutual benefits would follow.

Some nonviolent actions are presented by their adherents as offering rewards as well as being coercive, and the adherents seek to persuade opponents of the benefits to them in changing their objectionable conduct. The opponents are told, for example, that they will better satisfy their own value commitments to their country or to God.

Gandhi developed a comprehensive approach to principled nonviolence in the struggle he led for the independence of India from Great Britain.[32] His approach, termed *satyagraha*, or "truth force," has been influential throughout the world. Three concepts are fundamental in satyagraha: truth, nonviolence, and self-suffering. For Gandhi, truth is God; it is an end we seek, but since we cannot know absolute truth, its pursuit excludes the use of violence. Nonviolence does not imply the negative action of not harming, but positive love, of doing good to the evildoer. It does not mean acquiescence to the wrong, but resistance to the wrongdoer, even if that injures the wrongdoer. Self-suffering means inviting suffering upon oneself, not out of weakness but out of courage to refrain from violence even when it is possible to use violence. It is directed at moral persuasion.

Other advocates and practitioners of nonviolent action argue for its use on pragmatic grounds: it is effective and ultimately less costly in human life. They examine which strategies have contributed to reaching particular goals.[33] Conflict analysts recognize that in actual struggles, violent actions often occur in conjunction with nonviolent behavior.[34] Different organizations within each side may use alternative and often complementary nonviolent means, the mixture changing in the course of a conflict.

Whether principled or pragmatic, some features of nonviolent strategies tend to foster constructively waged rather than destructively waged struggles. Certainly, the adversary tends to be less dehumanized by the process; and indeed, nonviolent action often appeals to the empathy and reasonableness of the adversary. It can even garner respect from the adversary, often a goal of a people who have been viewed as inferior. As Martin Luther King, Jr., wrote in 1963 about the civil rights struggle, "The Negro's method of nonviolent direct action is not only suitable as a remedy for injustice; its very nature is such that it challenges the myth of inferiority. Even the most reluctant are forced to recognize that no inferior people could choose and successfully pursue a course involving such extensive sacrifice, bravery, and skill."[35]

Nonviolent action often gains effectiveness by attracting support and allies who are impressed by the demonstration of commitment and the lack of generalized threat such action seems to convey. This may be seen in trade union organizing and strike efforts. In the 1960s, Cesar Chavez mobilized consumer boycotts against grapes to support the strike efforts of the National Farm Workers Association (NFWA).[36]

Terrorism

People generally use the term *terrorism* to refer to methods they regard as immoral. Therefore it is more often attributed to the enemy than claimed by the perpetrators. Thus, what is terrorism to one side is a necessary military action or law enforcement to another. The term will be used broadly here, to include behavior that a variety of conflict groups have labeled as terrorism. But it will not encompass every such usage, since the term is often used metaphorically. An inclusive definition is proposed by Michael Stohl: "The purposeful act or the threat of the act of violence to create fear and/or compliant behavior in a victim and/or audience by the act or threat."[37] But the term is used more narrowly here for the use of violence against targets that are only peripherally associated with the adversary to be influenced. Moreover, the action is often covert; that is, the agents conducting the action do not always claim responsibility and sometimes even deny carrying it out. This makes it difficult to understand what goals are being pursued or how the means are viewed as advancing the cause.

Examples of terrorism include the bombing of a passenger airplane, such as Pan Am Flight 103 over Lockerbie, Scotland, on 21 December 1988; the bombing of the World Trade Center in New York City in 1993; and the bombing of the federal building in Oklahoma City on 19 April 1995. It also includes "state terrorism," as carried out in the assassinations and disappearances of citizens in Argentina, Chile, and Guatemala. In the latter two countries, the terrorism was conducted by military regimes that seized power after democratically elected governments were overthrown with the covert assistance of the U.S. Central Intelligence Agency.[38] Terrorism also includes the massive killings, labor-camp incarcerations and torture by "internal security" forces of Hitlerite Germany and of Stalinist Soviet Union. Terrorist tactics also may be elements of general strategies and incorporated into a conflict mode such as war, with aerial bombing of civilians and atrocities intended to drive people from their homes and lands.

Terrorism is highly coercive. It aims to intimidate others, whether to force them to yield power or to conform to the power of authorities. Terrorism has other coercive features. It may help generate conditions that destabilize the leadership of the opposition; it may provoke responses that antagonize others who then support challenges to that leadership.[39] It also may damage social and economic conditions by interfering with the tourist trade or other business sectors, and so undermine support for the governing authorities.

Often, terrorism is conducted as if the perpetrators seek to persuade the targeted opposition at least of the depth of their feelings and the strength of their convictions.[40] This may seem to enhance the intimidating character of the action, signaling such actions will persist. It may even be used to gain the attention of the inattentive. A cause is being announced, and indeed, an audience is gained as people try to understand why such actions are taken. Various terrorist actions, then, combine different degrees of coercive and persuasive inducements, but they tend to be at the predominantly coercive corner of figure 4.1, as indicated by the placement of "Ta."

Terrorism is generally regarded as the violation of fundamental rules of conflict behavior. Therefore, the victims are usually referred to as innocent. The perpetrators, however, either deny the targets' innocence or regard their deaths as an unfortunate but necessary part of a military struggle, as when military forces shell or bomb cities during wars.[41] Furthermore, the commission of terrorist actions at the behest of governments or their challengers are often covert.

Sometimes terrorism seems intended to punish the other side for its previous violent actions and to suppress such actions in the future. Insofar as the terrorist actions are punishing and revengeful, they may stiffen the enemy's resolve rather than achieve the desired change. Indeed, the terrorist acts may be largely expressive for some of the perpetrators. These qualities of terrorism tend to make struggles in which it is used destructive.

In any given usage, the many rationales for terrorism are varyingly combined, and different persons among the perpetrators may emphasize different purposes. For example, on 25 December 1994, a devout Palestinian Muslim blew himself up near a bus of Israeli soldiers close to the central bus station in Jerusalem.[42] In his farewell note to his family he wrote, "Holy war is our path. My death will be martyrdom. I will knock on the gates of Paradise with the skulls of the sons of Zion." The Qassam brigades, the armed wing of Hamas, issued a leaflet arguing that penetrating to that location was an intelligence and security achievement and explaining that the attack was a response to Israeli settlement activity in Arab areas of Jerusalem and to car-bombings of Muslim militants in Gaza and southern Lebanon.

Problem Solving

A third approach to conducting a struggle is to engage in exchanging information in order to solve what is regarded as a shared problem. This is an important mode of conflict resolution, but also a way to wage a conflict.[43]

The essential features of the problem-solving mode are that representatives of the contending parties discuss the nature of their shared problem, propose possible solutions, and consider ways to implement the solutions. The participants recognize the concerns of each other and seek ways in which they can be addressed in a mutually acceptable settlement.

Problem solving is typically tried at an early stage of a conflict and at various points when the parties in a conflict are seeking to de-escalate it. As with the nonviolent action and terrorism strategies, problem solving may be carried out by official agents of the contending parties or by other members of the adversary camps. Unlike the two other strategies, however, intermediaries often participate in problem solving, for example as facilitators or mediators. Furthermore, problem solving involves a joint decision-making process, rather than a unilateral imposition.

In the past few decades, one method of problem solving as a conflict resolution mode has greatly expanded; that is, workshops facilitated by intermediaries. This has been the case in ethnic and other communal conflicts within one country and in conflicts between countries. For example, such workshops have been conducted with Catholics and Protestants from Northern Ireland, members of various religious communities in Lebanon, Greek and Turkish Cypriots, Jewish Israelis and Arab Palestinians, and Argentinean and British representatives following the war over the Falkland/Malvina Islands.[44]

Even workshops among persons who lack authority to bind their respective parties may contribute to the de-escalation and resolution of the conflict over time. Nongovernmental agencies may help inform influential people in each side about the concerns of their adversaries. The understandings and options generated may become vitally relevant when the circumstances have changed and an opportunity for official de-escalating efforts arises. Sometimes the people with workshop experience themselves become part of the official problem-solving negotiations.[45]

In traditional competitive negotiations, in contrast, each party usually seeks to maximize its gain, often at the expense of the other side. Such negotiations usually involve an exchange of persuasive inducements, directed at changing the other side's position while rejecting influence by the other side's arguments. Although the negotiations sometimes include promises of benefits to the other side in exchange for benefits received, on the whole, each side takes a hard line, insisting on as much as it thinks it may get and threatening coercive consequences if it does not. Traditional negotiations may be accompanied by coercive actions, as when union-management negotiations are conducted while the union members are striking.

In problem-solving negotiations, efforts are made to understand the interests or needs of the other side and to discover possible solutions that maximize all the parties' goals. Mutual benefits result. Coercive inducements are minimized, but the negotiating parties may anticipate mutual losses if their search for mutual gain fails. Such problem-solving negotiations tend to be located at point "Pa" in figure 4.1.

Another way of conceptualizing problem solving as a conflict mode is presented in figure 4.2. An adversary's approach to a conflict varies along two dimensions, concern for one's self and concern for the relationship.[46] A low concern along both dimensions would be expressed by a conflict-avoidance approach. A high assertiveness and low cooperativeness orientation would be expressed by taking a competitive strategy. A low concern for one's self, but high concern for the relationship would be expressed as an accommodating strategy. Finally, a high concern in both dimensions would be characterized as a collaborating strategy, including problem-solving.

In official negotiations, no sharp dividing line between traditional competitive negotiations and problem-solving negotiations need exist. Although some negotiations are clearly traditional, many are mixed in character. For example, the disarmament negotiations in the 1950s between the U.S. and Soviet representatives had little problem-solving character: positions were stated and restated for home consumption and to posture for a larger audience, but there was little effort to find options that might contribute to both side's interests or needs.[47] The negotiations at Camp David in 1978 between the Israeli and Egyptian delegations, which was mediated by President Jimmy Carter and the U.S. delegation, had many attributes of a problem solving approach.[48]

A problem-solving mode is more likely to be used in domestic conflicts

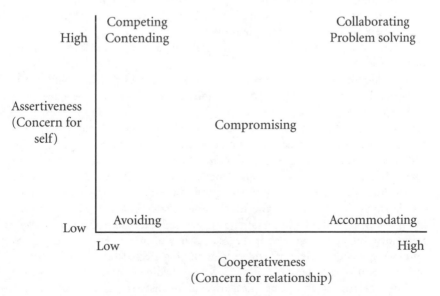

Figure 4.2   Conflict Modes

than in international conflicts. For example, it may be seen even in attempts to find accommodations among peoples with ethnic, linguistic, religious, and other communal differences within a single society. Often the efforts include negotiations among representatives of the different communities to find a constitutional formula to solve the problem they face. This may be seen in the negotiations leading to the transition of power in South Africa from a White-ruled country to one organized on the basis of equality in political rights of all peoples.[49] The problem-solving approach has also been advocated and utilized in labor-management relations.[50]

The three kinds of conflict strategies discussed illustrate various ways inducements are combined and conflict approaches are regulated. Obviously, there are many other kinds of conflict strategies, and they will be considered as we examine the various stages of conflicts.

Conclusions

Conflicts are pursued in a wide variety of ways. These strategies and modes are alternative ways for adversaries to reach a joint decision about matters in contention between them. Each side tries to use the method it prefers, and somehow in their struggle with each other they fashion the joint ways they wage their fight.

The conflict strategies and modes adopted are blends of coercive, rewarding, and persuasive inducements and are varyingly regulated. The choices are confirmed, modified, rejected, and remade as the struggle continues. Each party alters its strategies as its goals evolve, as it itself changes, as the other side responds, and as the environment alters, all partly as a result of the previous choices.

A conflict party generally uses many strategies in the struggle in which it is engaged. The strategies are used in various combinations at the same time and sequentially in the course of a struggle. This complexity is especially likely for conflict parties that are large and loosely coordinated. A party may be a broad coalition of organizations who are working toward similar goals, using different approaches and acting in competition as well as in concert with each other. For example, the 1960s' American civil rights movement included organizations using electoral political methods, judicial means, legal demonstrations, civil disobedience, and many other strategies and tactics. The pro-life movement in the United States, as it evolved after the 1973 *Roe v. Wade* Supreme Court decision, also includes a variety of organizations and groups employing a wide variety of strategies, including electoral political methods, judicial means, legal demonstrations, civil disobedience, and violence against persons performing abortions. Similarly, nationalist ethnic movements usually include a variety of organizations, each using a different set of strategies.

Notes

1. See William Brink and Louis Harris, *Black and White* (New York: Simon and Schuster, 1969), 264; Hazel Erskine, "The Polls: Speed of Racial Integration," *Public Opinion Quarterly* 32 (Fall 1968): 280–92; Joe R. Feagin and Paul B. Sheatsley, "Ghetto Resident Appraisals of a Riot," *Public Opinion Quarterly* 32 (Fall 1968): 352–62; and David O. Sears and T. M. Tomlinson, "Riot Ideology in the Los Angeles Riot: A Study in Negro Attitudes," *Social Science Quarterly* 49 (December 1968): 485–503.

2. Analysts of social conflicts have used many different terms to make these or similar distinctions. *Influence, threats,* and *promises* are the terms used by Morton Deutsch, *The Resolution of Conflict: Constructive and Destructive Processes* (New Haven, Conn.: Yale University Press, 1973). The terms *persuasion, inducements,* and *constraints* are used by William A. Gamson, *Power and Discontent* (Homewood, Ill.: Dorsey Press, 1968). Persuasion, coercion, and bargaining are distinguished by Ralph H. Turner, "Determinants of Social Movement Strategies," in *Human Nature and Collective Behavior: Papers in Honor of Herbert Blumer,* ed. Tamotsu Shibutani (Englewood Cliffs, N.J.: Prentice-Hall, 1970). Coercive, utilitarian, and normative bases of compliance are distinguished by Amitai Etzioni in *A Comparative Analysis of Complex Organizations* (New York: The Free Press, 1961). Threat, exchange, and love forms of power are distinguished by Kenneth E. Boulding, *Three Faces of Power* (Newbury Park, Calif.: Sage, 1989). Other writers stress the differences between threats and promises or between negative and positive sanctions. See, respectively, J. David Singer, "Inter-Nation Influence: A Formal Model," *American Political Science Review* 57 (June 1963): 420–30; and David A. Baldwin, "The Power of Positive Sanctions," *World Politics* 24 (October 1971): 19–38.

3. Johan Galtung, "Violence, Peace, and Peace Research," *Journal of Peace Research* 3 (1969): 168.

4. Galtung, "Violence, Peace and Peace Research," 171.

5. For an analysis of popular views about violence, see Monica D. Blumenthal, Robert L. Kahn, Frank M. Andrews, and Kendra B. Head, *Justifying Violence* (Ann Arbor: University of Michigan Press, 1972).

6. David Cortright and George A. Lopez, eds., *Economic Sanctions* (Boulder, Colo.: Westview, 1995).

7. This work is reviewed and developed in Marc Howard Ross, *The Culture of Conflict* (New Haven, Conn.: Yale University Press, 1993); also see Ashley Montagu, ed. *Learning Non-Aggression* (New York: Oxford University Press, 1978).

8. Leon V. Sigal, "Look Who's Talking: Nuclear Diplomacy with North Korea" (Social Science Research Council), *Items* 51 (June-September 1997): 31–36; also see his *Disarming Strangers: Nuclear Diplomacy with North Korea* (Princeton, N.J.: Princeton University Press, 1998).

9. President Lyndon B. Johnson during the war against North Vietnam offered aid for reconstruction, linked to ending the war; but this was not wholly credible and in any case reflected a grave cultural and political misunderstanding. See Doris Kearns, *Lyndon Johnson and the American Dream* (New York: New American Library, 1977), 278–82.

10. Baldwin, "The Power of Positive Sanctions."

11. There are many definitions of persuasion in the literature. One that incorporates many of the shared ideas is that persuasion is "symbolic activity whose purpose is to effect the internalization or voluntary acceptance of new cognitive states or patterns of overt behavior through the exchange of messages" (Mary John Smith, *Persuasion and Human Action* [Belmont, Calif.: Wadsworth, 1982], 7).

12. Sven Allard, *Russia and the Austrian State Treaty* (University Park: University of Pennsylvania State Press, 1970); and see Louis Kriesberg, *International Conflict Resolution* (New Haven, Conn.: Yale University Press, 1992).

13. Arthur M. Schlesinger, Jr., *A Thousand Days* (Boston: Houghton Mifflin, 1965).

14. James T. Tedeschi, "Threats and Promises," 155–91, in *The Structure of Conflict*, ed. Paul Swingle (New York: Academic Press, 1970).

15. Tedeschi, "Threats and Promises."

16. Margaret Mead, "Warfare Is Only an Invention—Not a Biological Necessity," *Asia* 40 (1940): 402–5.

17. P. H. Gulliver, *Disputes and Negotiations: A Cross-Cultural Perspective* (New York: Academic Press, 1979).

18. John Nef, *War and Human Progress* (Cambridge, Mass.: Harvard University Press, 1950).

19. In 1988, Amnesty International officials interviewed survivors of chemical weapon attacks on Kurdish citizens of Iraq. Cited in Judith Miller and Laurie Mylroie, *Saddam Hussein and the Crisis in the Gulf* (New York: Times Books, 1990), 52–53.

20. Gerard Prunier, *The Rwanda Crisis: History of a Genocide* (New York: Columbia University Press, 1996).

21. The official character of these policies was in varying degrees covert. For example, only in 1995 did Argentinean military officials begin to publicly acknowledge their participation in widespread killings of Argentineans (for example, by dropping sedated persons into the ocean from airplanes), during the period of rule by a military junta, 1976–1983. See *New York Times*, 27 April 1995.

22. John H. Leek, *Government and Labor in the United States* (New York: Rinehart, 1952); and Philip Taft, *Organized Labor in American History* (New York: Harper & Row, 1964).

23. Peter M. Blau, *Power and Exchange in Social Life* (New York: John Wiley, 1964).

24. Robert Axelrod, "An Evolutionary Approach to Norms," *American Political Science Review* 80 (December 1986): 1095–1111; and Michel Foucault, *Power-Knowledge* (New York: Pantheon, 1980).

25. See William Graham Sumner, *Folkways* (Lexington, Mass.: Ginn, 1906), 2–30.

26. Leonard R. Sayles and George Strauss, *The Local Union: Its Place in the Industrial Plant* (New York: Harper & Brothers, 1953).

27. The observation is based on personal, informal interviews with Catalans in Barcelona and other cities conducted in 1994. Juan Diez Medrano, *Divided Nations: Class Politics, and Nationalism in the Basque Country and Catalonia* (Ithaca, N.Y.: Cornell University Press, 1995).

28. See Thomas Hobbes, *Leviathan* (New York: Collier Books, 1962), originally published in 1651; and John Locke, *The Second Treatise of Government* (New York: Bobbs-Merrill, 1952), originally published in 1690.

29. Christopher Wright, "The Self-Governing of Commercial Communities," a report for the Arbitration Project, University of Chicago Law School, 1957.

30. Many case studies and synthesizing works are available, including Paul Wehr, Heidi Burgess, and Guy Burgess, eds., *Justice without Violence* (Boulder, Colo.: Lynne Rienner, 1994).

31. Gene Sharp provides a comprehensive analysis of the bases and varieties of nonviolent action in his *Politics of Nonviolent Action* (Boston: Porter Sargent, 1973).

32. Mohandas Karamchand Gandhi, *An Autobiography of My Experiments with Truth*, translated by Mahadev Desai, 2d ed. (Almedabad, India: Nvajivan, 1940), and Joan V. Bondurant, *Conquest of Violence: The Gandhian Philosophy of Violence*, rev. ed. (Berkeley: University of California Press, 1965).

33. Peter Ackerman and Christopher Kruegler, *Strategic Nonviolent Conflict* (Westport, Conn.: Praeger, 1994).

34. Charles Tilly and David Snyder, "Hardship and Collective Violence in France, 1830–1960," *American Sociological Review* 37 (October 1972): 520–32.

35. Martin Luther King, Jr., *Why We Can't Wait* (New York: The New American Library, 1963), 121.

36. See Donald C. Reitzes and Dietrich C. Reitzes, *The Alinsky Legacy: Alive and Kicking* (Greenwich, Conn.: JAI Press, 1987), 214–24.

37. Michael Stohl, "Demystifying the Mystery of International Terrorism," in *International Terrorism: Characteristics, Causes, Controls*, ed. Charles W. Kegley, Jr. (New York: St. Martin's Press, 1990), 83; also see other contributions in the volume.

38. Among the numerous accounts, see Victor Marchetti and John D. Marks, *The CIA and the Cult of Intelligence* (New York: Dell, 1974); Samuel Chavkin, *The Murder of Chile: Eyewitness Accounts of the Coup, the Terror, and the Resistance Today* (New York: Everest House, 1961); and Robert M. Carmack, ed., *Harvest of Violence: The Maya Indians and the Guatemalan Crisis* (Norman: University of Oklahoma Press, 1988).

39. This was emphasized by advocates of revolutionary violence in the 1960s, but generally proved unsuccessful in practice. See Frantz Fanon, *The Wretched of the Earth* (New York: Grove Press, 1966), and Regis Debray, *Revolution in the Revolution?* (New York: Grove Press, 1967).

40. Terrorist acts carried out by people who kill themselves in the process are an extreme example of such demonstrations of commitment. People who are willing to sacrifice themselves for their side are often honored by those in whose name they die.

41. For example, Abu Nidal, who is reputed to have directed terrorist attacks, explained his reasoning in an interview with the German weekly *Der Spiegel*, no. 42, 1985. He was asked, "If you are only an enemy of imperialism and Zionism, why is it that you seem to attack Jewish school children, synagogues and restaurants?" He responded, "The question isn't if we attack civilians or civilian Jews that we meet in our actions. The question is, when we attack, unfortunately these people are there in situations where the Zionist secret service, Mossad, is situated." Reprinted in Bernard Scheterman and Martin Slann, *Violence and Terrorism 90/91* (Guilford, Conn.: The Dushkin Publishing Group, 1990), 86.

42. *New York Times*, 26 December 1994.

43. For discussions of problem solving see, Howard Raiffa, *The Art and Science of Negotiation* (Cambridge, Mass.: Harvard University Press, 1982).

44. Accounts of some of these workshops may be found in Ronald Fisher, *Interac-*

tive Conflict Resolution (Syracuse, N.Y.: Syracuse University Press, 1997); and Jay Rothman, *From Confrontation to Cooperation: Resolving Ethnic and Regional Conflict* (Thousand Oaks, Calif.: Sage, 1992).

45. Herbert C. Kelman, "Contributions of an Unofficial Conflict Resolution Effort to the Israeli-Palestinian Breakthrough," *Negotiation Journal* 11 (January 1995): 19–27.

46. This formulation was introduced in R. R. Blake and J. S. Mouton, *The Managerial Grid* (Houston, Tex.: Gulf Publishing, 1964).

47. See Alva Myrdal, *The Game of Disarmament: How the United States and Russia Run the Arms Race* (New York: Pantheon, 1976).

48. See William B. Quandt, *Camp David* (Washington, D.C.: Brookings Institution, 1986); Saadia Touval, *The Peace Brokers* (Princeton, N.J.: Princeton University Press, 1982); and discussions later in this book.

49. John Kane-Berman, *South Africa's Silent Revolution* (Johannesburg: South African Institute of Race Relations, 1990); Allister Sparks, *Tomorrow Is Another Country* (New York: Hill and Wang, 1995); also see Hendrik W. van der Merwe, *Pursuing Justice and Peace in South Africa* (London and New York: Routledge, 1989).

50. R. R. Blake, H. A. Shephard, and H. S. Mouton, *Managing Intergroup Conflict in Industry* (Houston, Tex.: Gulf Publishing, 1964); and M. A. Rahim, *Managing Conflict in Organizations* (Westport, Conn: Praeger, 1986).

5

~~~~~

Adopting Conflict Strategies

A s soon as a contending party begins to move toward its goal, a way of attaining it has been chosen and new choices must be made as the conflict continues. The choices among possible alternatives may not be the result of much deliberation by anyone; or they may follow from deep and wide reflection and discussion. In either case, four sets of conditions jointly affect the strategies adopted in conducting a struggle: (1) the partisans' goals, (2) the characteristics of each adversary, (3) the relations between the adversaries, and (4) their environment.

Adversarial Goals

A major factor affecting how a conflict party pursues its goal is the goal itself. How people try to get what they want depends greatly upon what they want, since they often share understandings about what means are proper for particular goals. Generally, the strategies adopted are justified as serving to reach the desired end.

Many partisans want a close fit between means and ends, arguing that the means become the ends and therefore should be chosen so as to embody what is sought. Thus, they may reason that if a nonviolent, cooperative, and egalitarian relationship with another ethnic community is desired, a struggle using nonviolent methods would be more likely to succeed than violent ones. This was the reasoning of many activists in the 1960s' civil rights movement in the American South. Another illustration is provided by the adherents of the Solidarity movement in Poland. When it was suppressed by the communist-led government in 1981, many supporters simply "acted as if they were free." In many ways, they spoke, wrote, and met as they pleased, but discretely, while the government pretended not to notice.[1]

123

The means used by many of the American student activists and articulated by the Yippies during the late 1960s provides another illustration.[2] Simply acting spontaneously and outrageously was the way to disrupt and to change rigid social conventions; flaunting authorities was a way of reducing their legitimacy and control and thus liberating people. In the 1990s, some members of militia groups, drawing ideas and support from quite different sources, tried to reduce the U. S. government's power to set social policy for the country and regulate social conduct. They reasoned that they could advance their cause by refusing to follow those regulations and prepared themselves to resist with arms if necessary the government's implementation of those rules.[3]

These examples show that partisans in a conflict may justify a particular method as correct because it seems to actualize their goal. Methods, however, are often seen to contribute to reaching a goal indirectly and may sometimes even appear contradictory to the goal, as in the adage, "if you seek peace, prepare for war," or more generally, "the best defense is a strong offense." Members of a conflict unit tend to formulate connections between means and ends that they regard as common sense.

Conflict group members, however, frequently differ in values and beliefs about which strategy is best for the goal sought. The differences arise from variations in ideology, personality, past experience, interests, and many other circumstances, and are particularly likely to be important in large, heterogeneous conflict parties.

Despite the disagreements about what the appropriate means are, it is possible to discern tendencies for certain means to be chosen for particular goals. Thus, in conflicts that partisans regard as largely dissensual rather than consensual, conflict modes with significant components of persuasive inducements tend to be used. After all, in dissensual conflicts an alteration in the values or beliefs of the adversary is what is often sought. In that case, some degree of conversion of the opponent is needed. Since conflicts typically combine consensual and dissensual components, and since factions within a conflict party may stress different inducements depending on their own perspectives, the partisans on each side may disagree regarding the choice of conflict modes. For example, consider the alternative approaches that Black liberationists or women's liberationists have taken in the United States. Some have emphasized the consensual nature of their struggle against Whites or men, respectively, arguing that both sides want the same things and the other side is taking more of those things at the expense of the exploited, deprived side. They are likely to favor conflict modes with large coercive components. Other liberationists have emphasized the dissensual nature of the conflict, arguing that both sides are the losers under the prevailing ways of thinking, and liberation from stereotypes and prejudice would be liberating for everyone. On the basis of that view, conflict modes with large components of persuasion and reward would be favored.

The greater the perceived incompatibility of the goals in a consensual conflict, the greater the tendency for the adversaries to choose conflict modes with major coercive and even violent components. For example, data from a study of the strategies used by American challenging social movement organizations from 1800 to 1945 indicate that the goal of displacing or destroying the target was moderately correlated (.36) with accepting the ideology that violence was legitimate or necessary under some circumstances.[4] More specifically, in the civil rights struggle in the 1960s, many members of the Congress of Racial Equality (CORE) believed that their goals could be achieved with nonviolent action and its persuasive power because they believed that discrimination rested on isolated attitudes that were not deeply rooted and grounded in material interests.[5] Another example may be seen in a study of strikes and mutinies; those in which secession or seizure of power was sought were likely to use violence, imprisonment, or killing of superiors, while those in which improvement of interests was sought used work stoppage as their main weapon.[6]

Goals also vary in either desiring the adversary to initiate a new policy or action or in desiring the adversary to stop doing what it has undertaken. Strategies with positive sanctions rather than threats are likely to be regarded as appropriate for the former goals; while threats are likely to be seen as more suitable for the latter goals, since rewards might be seen as paying a possibly recurrent bribe.

A conflict group may have goals that primarily benefit nonmembers (e.g., to end slavery) or which benefit members either as a collectivity (e.g., to establish cultural autonomy for an ethnic community) or as an aggregation (e.g., to provide for equality of individual opportunity). Goals for members as an entity are more likely to seem to require coercion than are goals for individual constituent members.

Finally, one or both of the adversaries may be seeking either greater separation or greater integration between them. Thus, in communal struggles, one ethnic group may be striving for greater autonomy or even secession from the polity controlled by another ethnic group, for example, as have the Kurds in Iraq and in Turkey. One group may even seek to expel or destroy another group, by ethnic cleansing or genocide. Clearly, such goals would require extremely brutal means to be attained. On the other hand, an ethnic group may strive for closer integration with other groups. Specifically, they may seek equal opportunities in the economic and political systems in which they had been subordinated, as have Blacks in the United States during the civil rights struggle. If the adversaries seek a more integrated relationship, they are more likely to try to use persuasion and take a problem-solving approach.

In short, conflict partisans generally select modes that they believe will help them attain what they seek. In that sense, the ends help determine the means chosen and the means tend to change as goals are modified in the course of a struggle.

Partisan Characteristics

The means of conflict that partisans adopt often appear to observers as inappropriate for the goals ostensibly sought. The choice seems driven by other considerations. Indeed, while partisans generally explain their own choice of strategies by reference to the goals they seek and their circumstances, they often attribute the adversary's choice to characteristics of that adversary.[7] Indeed, there are likely to be justifications for that attribution. A strategy is chosen partly on the basis of a conflict group's internal predispositions, ideology, social structure, and resources.

Predispositions

Members of conflict parties have cultural traditions, ideological beliefs, religious convictions, socialization experiences, and other characteristics that predispose them to prefer some conflict methods rather than others. But what appears to be predispositions may be merely the group's response to the situation in which it is located. In any case, the predispositions interact with other circumstances in shaping the choices made in a struggle. These issues can be usefully studied by considering the preferences for various strategies favored by different categories of people in the same society regarding the same or similar conflicts. In this section, for example, persons of different socioeconomic statuses and of different genders are compared.

There is scattered evidence that persons of low income, education, ethnic status, and other indicators of socioeconomic rank are less likely than those of high rank to use or to support the use of institutionalized modes of conflict and more inclined to employ relatively militant and violent conflict modes. This is sometimes viewed as an indication of a subculture of violence among persons of low socioeconomic standing. In popular stereotyping, they are seen as "primitive" and uninformed.

The nature of the relationship between preferences about strategies and socioeconomic status needs to be empirically examined. Many public opinion surveys support the generalization that higher ranking persons tend to favor institutionalized and nonviolent modes, compared with low-ranking persons.[8] These findings are not consistent, however. They vary over time and with the conflict. These variations can help explain the nature of the relationship between different socioeconomic positions and support for alternative conflict modes.

For example, at the outset of the U.S. military engagement in Vietnam, respondents with many years of education were much more likely than those with few years of education to support "taking a stronger stand." As the war went on, the consensus among the elites broke down and support for the war fell. The educational differences lessened, as the college-educated respondents' support dropped.[9] Support for U.S. military spending may also be considered as an indicator of support for coercive strategies in international relations. Indeed, during the 1970s in the United States, the years of education a respondent had were positively associated with thinking the U.S. government was spending too much money on military defense.[10]

Analyses of the changing strength and direction of these relationships indicate that socioeconomic ranking affects opinions about the government's use of military means in international conflict due to the tendency of higher-ranking people to be attentive to the issue and to be influenced by the prevailing elite views. Lower-ranking persons tend to have less confidence in the leadership of established institutions and be more skeptical of the policies they would pursue [11]

In the Israeli-Palestinian conflict, lower status Israeli Jews have been relatively more militant in opposition to Palestinians than higher ranking Jews. For example, in a survey conducted in January 1995, during a difficult period in Israeli–PLO negotiations, respondents were asked, "Should talks be stopped or continued if terrorism continues?" The respondents with fewer years of education were slightly more likely than those with more education to answer, "stop the talks."[12] On the other hand, among Palestinians in the occupied territories and in Gaza-Jericho, in March 1995, during the period of slow and troubled negotiations between the PLO and the Israeli government, the more educated Palestinians were somewhat *more* likely to oppose continuing negotiations and *more* likely to support armed attacks against Israeli targets, compared with the less educated.[13]

For Jews and Palestinians in these surveys, political party identification was a much stronger correlate of strategic preferences than socioeconomic position. The respondents' ideology, the specific conflict and its phase, and the perception of the adversary were much more determining of strategy preferences than were general subcultural predispositions.

These findings indicate no consistent and strong tendency for persons of relatively lower class and status rank to support institutionalized rather than noninstitutionalized conflict modes and of nonviolent rather than violent modes. Insofar as such relationships are found, they are not likely to be substantially due to class or status subcultural differences in these regards. Rather, the differences are more likely explained by differences in trust and confidence in societal institutions and in the leaders of those institutions.

Gender socialization seems to be the source of significant differences in predispositions regarding conflict methods. Gender, based on the biological differences between males and females, is socially constructed in every society.

Although universal, cultures vary greatly in the content of the roles of men and women. Masculine and feminine may be regarded as overlapping tendencies along many dimensions or treated as a set of qualities with little overlap between those attributed to the roles of men and of women. Feminists and other analysts of gender have pointed out that in the United States and many other societies, masculinity has traditionally stressed competitiveness, dominance, assertiveness, and readiness to inflict and accept pain and even death for honor, while femininity tends to emphasize relationships with others, nurturance, caretaking, and warmth.[14]

In most of the theorizing and analyzing of the relationship between gender and preferences regarding conflict methods, women and men are compared as separate categories, not as persons varying in degree of femininity and masculinity. Nevertheless, a variety of evidence indicates consistent, but small differences between men and women in preferences about modes of conflict. For example, in public opinion surveys about international conflicts, women are usually less likely to support the use of military means than are men. The gender differences are usually statistically significant, but the magnitude of the differences are small.

Traditional gender roles tend to be more evident and given more salience among persons in lower socioeconomic strata than in higher strata.[15] This is reflected in the findings that within low socioeconomic strata, women are much more likely than men to oppose the use of violence or the threat of violence, while within high socioeconomic strata, the differences are small.[16]

The effects of gender on the preferences about how to struggle have also been examined in research in which the use of alternative conflict approaches are studied. Research has included observation, simulations, and self-reports regarding the alternative used in various kinds of conflicts. The research has included studies of the choice of the conflict-handling styles identified in figure 4.2: competing, collaborating, compromising, avoiding, and accommodating. Interestingly, very few differences between men and women have been consistently found.[17] For example, research using self-reports has found only small differences, women reporting competing less and compromising more than men.[18] The popular expectations of large gender differences in conflict-handling strategies may lead people to incorrectly perceive and attribute differences in conduct to gender and so confirm their expectations.

On the whole, members of large social groups have general predispositions providing support for a wide variety of approaches to conflict. Selection from that array depends on other, more specific characteristics of the partisans as well as the relations between the adversaries and their social context.

Group Ideology

Clearly, in many conflicts, a group's ideology drives and channels conflict behavior. Broadly conceived, ideology refers to general ways of thinking, often implicit, which offer interpretations of the social world in which the group functions and guides its actions. Narrowly conceived, ideology provides an explicit analysis of the group and its place in the larger social context. On the basis of that analysis, it prescribes conduct to advance the values and interests of the group and its members. The discussion here focuses on ideology, narrowly defined.

Popularly, we think of ideologies as what totalitarian political parties create and promulgate, as in the cases of Nazism and Bolshevism. Their adherents extolled an ethnicity or a class and provided reasons for its dominance; they set forth goals and the means to achieve the goals, and provided the rationale for a leader and a political party to have the absolute right to interpret the ideology. But ideologies are usually less comprehensive and authoritarian, with adherents debating the analysis and the prescriptions their ideology sets forth.

Ideologies, as understood here, refer to religiously based as well as secular interpretations of the world and how to live in it. Religions usually provide a vision of how individuals and communities should treat each other, including when they are in conflict. The universalistic religions that are prevalent in the contemporary world assume the equal and shared humanity of everyone. This provides the ethical basis for seeking solutions to conflicts that incorporate the partial truths known to the various disputants in a more comprehensive shared truth. It also provides the basis for rejecting violence and killing. These beliefs are central in some religious denominations whose members adhere to pacifism; for example, within Christianity the historic peace churches include the Society of Friends (Quakers), Mennonites, and the Church of the Brethren.[19] Pacifist traditions also exist or have existed among some adherents of Catholicism, Judaism, Hinduism, Buddhism, and other major religions.

Other interpreters of the same holy writings, however, find support for the use of violence in the service of God's will. Undoubtedly, many wars have been fought by followers of one religion against adherents of another religion, and by members of one religious sect against another. Nonreligious identities and interests usually significantly overlap with religious ones, and the religious beliefs may provide a justification for injuring and killing others.

The emergence of a terrorist underground group within Gush Emunim, an Israeli messianic movement, is illustrative.[20] The Israeli military victory in the Six-Day War of 1967 brought about the reunification of Jerusalem and the military occupation of the Golan Heights, the Sinai, and the West Bank (Judea and Samaria). Many messianic religious Jews succeeded in establishing some Jewish settlements in Judea and Samaria, even in localities with dense Arab populations, such as Hebron. They were the forerunners of the Gush Emunim, established in 1974. As Arab Palestinian attacks on Jewish settlers in the occupied territories increased, an underground group within Gush Emunim planned and carried out several terrorist operations beginning in 1980 with attacks on Palestinian mayors. In 1984, the Israeli secret service discovered and disrupted plans to blow up five Arab buses full of passengers, and the group was put on trial and imprisoned. The group's actions had vigilante qualities but also had support from rabbis associated with Gush Emunim.

Many ideologies analyze why a group of people continues to suffer injustice, using that analysis to formulate a strategy to overcome the injustice. Frantz Fanon's writing, influential in the 1960s and 1970s, offers a powerful example.[21] He examined how the colonizer dehumanizes the native, turning him into an animal. To overcome this violence, the colonized person also must use violence, and through violent struggle, the colonized frees himself and gains a new sense of power and self-respect. This was considered essential in winning a national liberation struggle against colonialism.

Social Organization

Among the many aspects of a conflict group's internal social structure that affect the choice of a conflict strategy, the primary one for analyzing and resolving social conflicts is the relationship among those who represent one of the antagonistic parties in a conflict and the constituent groups who support, challenge, or otherwise seek to influence them. This is what sets intergroup conflicts apart from interpersonal conflicts. In intergroup conflicts, some persons represent and commit their constituencies in the struggle, while in interpersonal conflicts the antagonists act relatively independently in relation to any constituency.

The relations among those who claim to speak for a conflict group in its adversarial interactions vary greatly. In some groups, for some goals, and in some periods, leaders are easily able to mobilize constituent support for the conflict strategies they choose. For other groups, goals, and times, various coalitions of elite constituent groups shape the external policy and determine the modes to be used. For still other groups, goals, and times, rank-and-file constituents set narrow limits regarding the conflict strategies employed. The nature of these internal relationships matters because the various component groups tend to have different preferences and interests regarding strategic approaches. Furthermore, as the relationships among them change, shifts in the strategies adopted are likely to occur. This is an important factor in the escalation and de-escalation of conflicts.

The experience, interests, and preferences of the many constituent groups within a conflict party vary with the character of the struggle. For example, in highly regulated conflicts, leaders are more prone than their followers to prefer to use the established conflict procedures, while followers or important segments of them tend to favor relatively antagonistic and coercive modes. On the other hand, when the conflicts are not highly regulated, particularly if the conflict party is becoming mobilized, the leaders tend to resort to relatively confrontational strategies. This is broadly stated; examples and research findings provide more of the necessary specification.

To illustrate, a study of trade union leaders in the United States in the late 1940s found that the highest trade union leaders tended to be less militant than lower-ranking union officials.[22] Lower-ranking officials were more suspicious of management intentions, presumably because the national leaders were more deeply involved in negotiations and other interactions with management, developing mutual dependence and understanding.

More generally, studies of elite groups' preferences regarding ways to conduct foreign policy reveal variations reflecting self-interests, general orientations, political ideology, network alliances, and other factors.[23] Their different positions and influence relative to the public and to elected national officials vary with the foreign policy issue and with the time frame being considered. Thus, analyses of American foreign policy indicate that the public is likely to be involved and have some autonomy in forming opinions over a long period of time about foreign policy issues in which national security and economic security are important.[24]

The massive shifts in American military spending in the 1970s illustrate many of these matters. At the beginning of the decade, support for increased defense expenditures was extraordinarily low, among the public in general and nearly all elite groups; and Department of Defense appropriations had sharply fallen. By the end of the decade, public opinion was strongly in favor of increased military spending and Department of Defense appropriations were rising and were about to rise sharply.[25]

Changes in public opinion and elite views, new officeholders, shifts in government policy, and major external events affected each other in a complex interaction over time.[26] For example, at the beginning of the decade, the public's opposition to increased defense expenditures was related to opposition to U.S. military involvement in the Vietnam War and distrust of U.S. military and other institutional leaders. By the mid-1970s, the salience of the Vietnam War had decreased and conventional sentiments of patriotism, national solidarity, and tough-mindedness were associated with growing support for increased arms spending. By the end of the 1970s, public opinion had shifted to favor increasing military expenditures. Although some elite groups still favored cutting back defense spending (notably, religious and educational leaders), others had shifted to support more spending (notably political and business leaders). These changes, and then the taking of U.S. diplomats as hostages in Iran and the Soviet invasion of Afghanistan in 1979, provided an opportunity for effective political mobilization in favor of increased U.S. military expenditures.

Finally, the leaders' need to sustain constituency support if they are to remain leaders has an important implication. Having an external enemy may appear to be an effective way of rallying support. More particularly, using conflict methods that commit the constituencies to the course set contributes to that aim. Using violence can have that effect. A leader of a terrorist group, of a state, or of an ethnic separatist organization by inducing his or her followers to commit violence on persons designated as enemies makes it difficult for them to withdraw. They need to justify their bloody actions; they risk retribution from the enemy if they fail; and their compatriots in violence are bonded by their actions to continue the struggle. This pattern may be especially likely for ethnic groups that are culturally similar to the groups from which they seek to distinguish themselves, for example the Kurds, Basques, and Croats.[27]

Resources Available for Struggle

Adversary groups vary greatly in the resources they possess to use particular conflict strategies. Hence, each group tends to select from among the strategies it believes it can employ. Thus, consider the implications of the numerical size of the conflict group as a resource. Members of a relatively small nongovernmental group believing they lack the capability of openly challenging their adversary with other means may resort to terrorism.[28] They recognize that to wage guerrilla warfare the group needs relatively large numbers of fighters and a supporting social environment. Similarly, nonviolent direct action requires a large number of participants to be effective, and a goodly number is also needed for mutual support and protection. The likely costs and benefits of nonviolent action depend to a significant degree upon the number of participants.[29]

Rioting, too, requires a large number of participants; this gives each one a sense of security and support. For example, research about racial disorders in the United States between 1961 and 1968 found that the absolute number of non-Whites in a city was by far the single most important factor in accounting for disorders.[30] Presumably, the grievances of Blacks were sufficiently widespread and rioting so generally an accepted form of protest that the more Blacks there were, the more incidents that might trigger a riot would occur, and the more people there were available for rioting. Riots, depending in part on milling and contagion, require congeries of people. Streets filled with people who are young enough to feel that they can take risks may begin engaging in protest activity that draws in other participants.[31]

In general, the particular resources available to group members channel their selection of a conflict means. Groups with resources that can be conditionally awarded to an adversary, such as continued service or electoral votes, may choose to offer or withhold that resource. For example, a dominant class may offer concessions to prevent a revolt, as did the Japanese rulers during the Meiji restoration of 1868–1873.[32] Groups skilled in manipulating symbols are likely to try strategies with high degrees of persuasion.

A conflict party has a limited repertoire of conflict techniques.[33] These tend to be the methods members previously used and found effective or at least promising. They generally emerge from the members' routine conduct; for example, as a coercive inducement, factory workers can stop working. Not having a particular capability effectively precludes using it. This does not mean that having a capability ensures its use, only that the capability makes its use possible. An implication of these observations is that expanding the repertoire of conflict methods that adversaries possess increases the likelihood that an appropriate means of struggle will be adopted. Thus, adversaries with the resource of problem-solving conflict resolution skills will be able to select a conflict mode incorporating them. This is a strong argument for training members of social movement organizations in nonviolent strategies, for training schoolteachers and students in mediation skills, and for training police in nonprovocative methods of crowd control.

In summary, among the many internal characteristics that affect the choice of means of struggle, it appears that general predispositions are less significant than characteristics pertaining directly to employing particular strategies, for example, having the capability to do so, and adhering to an ideology legitimating their use.

Relations between Adversaries

Conflict modes are not unilaterally chosen; rather, the adversaries influence each other's strategic selections. How this occurs in the course of a struggle's escalation and de-escalation are examined in subsequent chapters. At this time, I discuss the effects of three relatively stable aspects of the adversaries' relationship: (1) the kind of integration between the antagonists, (2) how they perceive and feel about each other, and (3) the degree of symmetry in the resources each controls.

Integration between Adversaries

Adversaries are mutually integrated insofar as their rates of interaction are high with each other relative to their interaction with other parties, and insofar as they have common and complementary interests relative to conflicting ones. The degree and nature of integration, affects not only the emergence of a conflict, but also the conflict mode used in waging the conflict.

Among highly integrated adversaries, violent conflict modes are less likely to be employed than among interacting adversaries who are not highly integrated. This flows from several implications of integration. The crosscutting ties usually associated with integration reduce support for choosing means that presume enmity toward the adversary. The interdependence that is inherent in integration raises the costs of resorting to conflict means that are destructive of the relationship. And the greater likelihood of shared understandings and institutionalized rules for managing conflict among integrated adversaries increases the probability that adversaries will use modes of conflict that are nonviolent and relatively low in coercion.

A wide variety of research results are consistent with these lines of reasoning. They indicate that crosscutting ties and other aspects of integration inhibit the use of highly coercive conflict or illegitimate means between adversaries and even provide the basis for the use of problem-solving conflict modes. For example, Kerr and Siegel's study of the rate of strikes in eleven industrial countries found that the propensity to strike was generally high in mining and the maritime industries; medium-high in lumber and textiles; medium in the chemical and printing industries; medium-low in clothing and services; and low in railroad, agriculture, and trade.[34] The authors concluded that one important determinant of the interindustry differences in the propensity to strike was the location of the workers in society. Workers who form "isolated masses" are particularly prone to strike. For example, miners, sailors, and longshoremen tend to have separate communities, relatively homogenous work roles, and low mobility out of the occupation.

An example of another kind of crosscutting mechanism is provided by a systematic analysis of conventional and rancorous conflicts in eighteen New England communities.[35] The fluoridation of water and two other issues were studied in each community. The use of illegitimate tactics, as volunteered by informants, identified rancorous conflicts. The study found that acquaintanceship between opponents was substantially lower in rancorous communities than in conventional communities. Furthermore, communities in which there was high crosscutting on the issues were more likely to have conventional conflicts than were communities with high cleavage.

Certain kinds of crosscutting ties inhibit or facilitate choosing particular conflict modes. For example, since men are most often the warriors in external conflicts, crosscutting bonds among the potential warriors is particularly relevant to the choice of war or other modes of violent conflict. This can be seen in cross-cultural research that finds that societies with matrilocal residence patterns tend to have a sense of solidarity and lack intervillage warfare, while patrilocal residence societies are plagued by more dissension, fights, and feuds.[36] This follows because among societies whose members marry outside their villages, in those with the patrilocal residence pattern, the bride moves to the husband's village; while in societies with a matrilocal residence pattern, the husband moves to the bride's village. Consequently, in patrilocal societies the men live in the same village with their brothers, while in a matrilocal society they live with their in-laws and face the possibility of fighting with their brothers in a conflict with another village.

In interstate conflicts too, integration provides the basis for applying negative sanctions short of violence and increases the likelihood that problem-solving approaches will be tried and will be effective. A variety of research findings support these expectations. For example, Karl W. Deutsch and his colleagues analyzed the emergence of "security communities," peoples within a territory who have a sense of community and have institutions that assure, for a long time, that social problems will be resolved without recourse to large-scale physical force.[37] Examples of such security communities include "amalgamated" cases, such as the United Sates since 1877, England-Scotland since 1707, Italy since 1859, and Switzerland since 1848, and "pluralistic" cases, such as Norway-Sweden since 1907, United States–Canada since the 1870s, and England-Scotland between the late 1560s and 1707. Three conditions seem essential for the success of both amalgamated and pluralistic security communities: the compatibility of major values relating to political decision making, the capacity of the participating units to respond to each other, and mutual predictability of behavior. Furthermore, in amalgamated security communities they found unbroken links of social communication both geographically between territories and socially between different strata, and there was a wide range of communication and transactions between the peoples.

Other research has examined relations between rival states or pairs of neighboring states. For example, Naroll, Bullough, and Naroll selected major civilizations from the second century B.C.E. through the eighteenth century C.E.[38] They examined the relationship of war frequency to many characteristics of twenty pairs of rivals during that period and found that general cultural exchanges were negatively related to war frequency ($-.44$) as was trade ($-.35$). Other studies have examined the onset of interstate war as related to trade. For example, Domke studied wars between 1870 and 1975 and found that countries that were more involved in foreign trade were less likely to be involved in wars.[39] Several other studies have examined the relationship between trade and conflict among pairs of states, finding that higher levels of trade lead to lower levels of conflict.[40]

Although high integration between parties generally reduces the likelihood that violence will be used between them, it does not preclude it. The shared culture may allow for certain kinds of violence. Furthermore, once a conflict erupts between integrated parties, the use of coercion may escalate into violence, even of a brutal kind, as the parties endure severe losses resulting from the vulnerability arising from their mutual dependency and as the parties feel betrayed by those previously close. Finally, as noted earlier, leaders sometimes resort to violence as a way of establishing differences and disrupting bonds that otherwise would be constraining.

Adversaries' Views and Feelings Regarding Each Other

A critical feature of adversary relations with each other is the readiness of each party to respond to the other's requests. If the opponents treat each other as legitimate and are responsive to each other, then problem-solving modes of conducting emerging conflicts between them are relatively likely. This is supported by one of the few well-documented empirical findings about the occurrence of war: democratic societies rarely if ever make war on each other.[41] Furthermore, democratic dyads are much less likely than nondemocratic dyads to engage in any kind of militarized dispute.[42] It is likely that the leaders and peoples of such societies recognize important common values, shared norms, and common interests. It is also likely that legitimacy is granted to the policies each government pursues, and they have shared understandings about how conflicts are to be managed.

The content of understandings and expectations adversaries share affects which strategy each party will use. For example, American employer hostility to trade unions helps account for the violent and often bloody history of trade union organization in the United States.[43] In the past, collective bargaining has been less institutionalized in the United States than in other industrialized, democratic societies. Consequently, American union members have been more likely to be involved in strikes and for longer periods than union members in other pluralistic industrial societies.[44] Another indication of the importance of institutionalization of the relationship is the finding that over the decades, the average length of strikes has been reduced.

Adversaries nearly always have a past history with each other or with others they regard as similar. They bring that past experience to bear in deciding how to act toward one another. Thus, it might be expected that countries that have been wartime allies subsequently would be less likely to make war on each other than those who previously had been at war with each other. However, quantitative analysis of pairs of countries who have fought wars against each other does not indicate strong tendencies for countries to sustain relations either as allies or as enemies.[45] On the whole, they often shift from being antagonists in one war to allies in another.

Historic enmities do exist, but for that to be sustained apparently requires that other conditions be satisfied. If in the past adversaries fought and one side feels it was humiliated, it may seek revenge.[46] Generations of young people may be taught about such humiliations, and learn to demonize their enemy, opening up the possibility of using dehumanizing conflict modes. Some ethnic conflicts have been plagued by such traditions, providing political leaders with sentiments to be mobilized, as between the Hutus and Tutsi in Rwanda and the Serbs, Croats, and Bosnians in the former Yugoslavia.

Sometimes, then, one conflict party holds views about an adversary that justifies its use of particularly harsh conflict modes. Those views may derive from political or religious ideologies or accounts of past atrocities. By those views, the adversary may even be considered to be subhuman or evil and therefore its interests and concerns can be disregarded. For example, during World War II, in accord with Nazi racist ideology, Germans treated even the anti-Soviet Russians, Ukrainians, and other peoples of the Soviet Union as inferiors. Rather than be won over as allies, they were driven to support the Soviet government.[47]

Resource Balance between Adversaries

The strength and variety of possible inducements one party has relative to its adversaries affects not only the emergence of a conflict, as discussed in chapter 3, but also the choice of conflict modes. Most theorizing and research on this matter has focused on the relationship between recourse to violence and the balance of coercive strength, particularly the capability of using physical violence. Therefore, this analysis of resource balance between adversaries concentrates on that relationship.

Two contrasting views of coercive power differences as an explanation for resort to violence have often been argued. According to one line of reasoning, a large power imbalance is expected to inhibit or deter the weaker party from coercively challenging the stronger one, since the weaker fears the anticipated failure of challenging the stronger party. By the same reasoning, the stronger party may be able to attain its goals, even aggrandizing ones, merely by its dominance and the threat of coercion. Consequently, relationships in which one party has a clear preponderance of power are not likely to be marked by violent conflict. On the other hand, some analysts argue that a symmetrical balance of power will inhibit either side from instigating a violent conflict. Unless one of the parties has considerable certainty that it will win a violent struggle, it will avoid initiating one.

The area in which these contrasting views have been most thoroughly examined pertains to the incidence of wars. Much of this work presumes a "realist" perspective, viewing each state as a unitary actor, rationally calculating the costs and benefits of waging war to maximize its power, and considering military force as the primary means to serve that end.[48] Each of the two lines of reasoning regarding power preponderance and power balance can be argued, using the "realist" approach. The research results, however, do not consistently support either argument.[49]

Reasons for failing to find a consistent association between state power relations and initiating wars abound. Many of them flow from criticisms of the "realist" approach. For example, states are not unitary actors; rather, governments respond to diverse domestic pressures and themselves include persons and groups with varied interests and perspectives. Also power cannot be measured only by the capability of doing violence and cannot be assessed without relationship to the goals toward which it is directed.

Even putting aside these problems of the "realist" approach, another reason for the failure in finding a consistent relationship between power differences and the onset of war is suggested by the work of Bruce Bueno de Mesquita.[50]

He tries to explain the onset of war, utilizing two influential theoretical approaches. First, he postulates that a leader seeks to maximize his expected utility; in other words, the policymaker is guided by a desire to maximize the net benefits he expects from his policy choices. Bueno de Mesquita further argues that the decision to go to war is generally made by an individual, a strong leader.

Second, he utilizes the theoretical approach regarding the importance of uncertainty in decision making and variations in preferences regarding risk taking. Uncertainty refers to the degree to which the probability of a course of action being successful is unknown. Each individual has his own preferences regarding risk and uncertainty. Persons who are risk averse require much more confidence in success than do those who are risk acceptant. Increased uncertainty enhances the differences between persons who tend to avoid risks and those who tend to accept risks. An implication of this reasoning is that individuals, even having the same expectations about the outcome of a war, may rationally make different choices about going to war. Even for rational actors, the immediate external conditions, therefore, do not determine the choices of conflict mode.

Despite the considerable research about wars, there is little agreement about explanations for the incidence of wars or for the outbreak of particular wars. One difficulty in achieving better grounded knowledge is that wars actually are not homogenous; they vary greatly and different explanations probably pertain to different kinds of wars.[51] They may be between rival states, or between complex alliances, or between a large expanding empire and a small neighboring people. They may be fought for more or less total goals, and by more or less total means.

Another difficulty is that although wars are generally studied in order to learn how to avoid them, relatively little research has been done about wars that have been averted. In the present analysis, we consider how conflicts emerge and what the alternative ways are in which they are conducted. Wars, in their manifold variety, are only one way among many to wage interstate struggles.

Of course, we should also examine evidence from conflict domains other than interstate relations about the relevance of resource differences in choosing a conflict mode. Labor-management relations is another relatively well-studied domain. On the basis of reasoning about power differences, we would expect that trade unions would resort to strikes to improve the conditions of their members when the strikers' chances of success are greatest. Indeed, strikes tend to be more frequent during upturns in the economy, and therefore, when labor is in shorter supply.[52] This indicates that it is not increased grievances that accounts for the choice of institutionalized coercive means to wage a conflict, but it is the opportunity to be successful in doing so.

These considerations cast additional light upon the findings that revolutions and uprisings often occur when previously improving conditions show a downturn. As discussed in chapter 3, this is usually interpreted as expressions of increased dissatisfaction resulting from an increased gap between attainments and expectations. But increased dissatisfaction alone does not lead to such actions. Some group must be held responsible and action to change them seem possible. It is when the ruling government is held responsible that noninstitutionalized coercive means tend to be undertaken. This is even more likely if the deterioration in conditions is attributable to the incompetence of the authorities. Such incompetence not only reduces their legitimacy, but makes them appear weak and vulnerable, inviting rebellion. The deteriorated conditions and the authorities' reduced legitimacy also mean that they have fewer resources available to be traded for continued obedience. Thus, Theda Skocpol's analysis of the French, Russian, and Chinese revolutions shows how they broke out when the governments had been weakened by their international overextension.[53]

An authoritarian government that allows for greater freedom of communication among its citizens in order to win support by reducing the citizen's sense of oppression often confronts rising opposition and sometimes protests, demonstrations, and uprisings. This occurs in part because the government may be seen as showing its weakness and revealing its internal divisions. Moreover, eased communication may make it possible for previously oppressed individuals to become aware of their shared discontent and take increasingly bold collective protest actions.[54] This was the case in the Soviet Union, East Germany, Poland, and Hungary after the death of Joseph Stalin in 1953.[55] It was the case even more dramatically with the changes introduced by Mikhail Gorbachev in the Soviet Union and Eastern Europe in the late 1980s.

On the whole, it is reasonable to conclude that power differences affect the choice of a conflict mode, but not strongly and consistently. The effects vary with the degree of differences along many dimensions of power. Furthermore, the degree of integration between the adversaries and the conceptions adversaries have of each other also affect their choices of conflict mode. In addition to the relationship between the adversaries, the choices depend not only on the previously discussed internal factors and the goals sought, but also on the larger social context within which the adversaries contend.

Social Context

The discussion of the social context significantly affecting the adversaries' strategic choices, is organized in four categories: (1) the institutions of the opponents' social system, (2) the norms and prevailing ways of thinking in their environment, (3) the roles of other parties, and (4) other systemic features of their environment.

Institutions

Adversary relations are embedded in larger social systems. This is most obvious in the case of interacting groups within countries with established governments; countries generally have judicial, legislative, and executive institutions for managing many of the conflicts arising among persons in a family, a factory, a community, or a country. The regulations for handling such disputes are institutionalized and relied upon. Even when informal means of dispute settlement are undertaken, they are conducted in the shadow of the law and the power of the state. Hence, the widespread and growing use of mediation in community dispute resolution centers and other forms of alternative dispute resolution (ADR) might be more accurately designated complementary dispute resolution (CDR).

Where a government is open to popular participation and regarded by its citizens as legitimate, even conflicts with the potential of breaking up the country may be managed in a problem-solving mode. Thus, ethnic, linguistic, religious, and other communal divisions in many countries have been a basis for brutal widespread violence in struggles for control of the state or for secession from the state. Yet, in many countries such struggles have been pursued with little or no violence, sometimes using the existing political system and often incorporating *ad hoc* negotiations among representatives of the contending parties. For example, this has been the case in Canada, regarding the relations between largely French-speaking Quebec and the rest of Canada, and in Belgium, regarding the relations between its French-speaking and Flemish-speaking citizens.

When the state itself represents one of the communal groups or a single ruling elite, problem-solving modes are much less likely to be used. If the government's domination is challenged, the challenge is likely to include resort to violence by the state and the challengers. This is illustrated by the very severe violence in Sri Lanka between the government dominated by the Sinhalese and the Liberation Tigers of Tamil Eaalam (LTTE), the secessionist organization of the Tamils.[56] The Sudan provides another instance of great violence, between the government dominated by Muslims in the north and the non-Muslim peoples in the south.

The world, obviously, lacks global institutions with the capability of a state to oppress segments of the world or with the authority to reach binding decisions, for example, regarding conflicts among states or between states and ethnic communities, or between nongovernmental groups. The parties generally resolve the conflicts among themselves by themselves, often with coercion and even through wars. But, as noted in many places in this work, transnational organizations can and do contribute to problem-solving dispute settlement modes. The contributions have been growing in recent years but still vary in availability for different regions of the world.

Norms and Prevailing Ways of Thinking

All or many of the members of a social system often share general understandings about what are the appropriate means to be used in pursuing and
settling conflicts. In the international domain, for example, ideas about national sovereignty and the right of governments to monopolize the legitimate
use of violence internally are widely shared. Consequently, war has long been
considered a legitimate way to pursue foreign policy. Consequently, too, governments have widely asserted the right to treat people in the territory they
rule as they wish, without other governments having any right to intervene.
In recent decades, ideas of sovereignty have been changing. International
norms that limit the rights of states to harm their citizens or to act aggressively
against other states have been evolving. Consensus about human rights, for
example, has been growing and with it a legitimate basis for intervention in
the internal affairs of countries.

Certainly, within a society norms and understandings about how various
groups should conduct themselves when in conflict are widely shared and
often quite detailed. They constrain the adversaries' choice of conflict modes,
making some choices unlikely while increasing the likelihood of others. The
context of such norms varies with the culture of the members of a social
system.

Other Parties

Protagonists in a fight are never alone. Each has possible allies and additional enemies who may join the conflict on one or another side. In addition,
groups who are part of the constituency of a protagonist may defect or may
increase its involvement in the struggle. Other groups may seek to intervene
to pursue a mediating role. All these groups also help, wittingly or unwittingly, to shape the changing choices of a conflict mode.

An adversary's beliefs about these other parties and their possible actions
profoundly shape the methods adopted in waging a conflict. Actions are often
avoided in fear of alienating constituents or of driving uninvolved parties to
the opponent's side. Often actions are chosen in hopes of getting the attention
and sympathy of potential allies.

Thus, for the leaders of the U.S. civil rights movement of the later 1950s
and early 1960s, large demonstrations and nonviolent direct action appeared
to be an effective means because they were persuasive to many citizens and
government leaders who might support legislation and other actions to end
discrimination and to foster integration and equal opportunity in the South.
Police attempts at repression in 1963 in Birmingham and elsewhere, as well
as vigilante terrorism, vividly revealed the prevailing oppression.[57] Those responses to the nonviolent actions enhanced support for the Blacks' demands

and greatly aided in the 1964 passage of civil rights legislation by the U.S. Congress.

Parties who are not directly engaged as partisans in the focal struggle often affect the choice of conflict modes by serving as models, advocates, teachers, and supporters of particular modes. Demonstrations, strikes, riots, even revolutions sometimes seem to spread as if by contagion. Jerome H. Skolnick, surveying the student protests of the 1960s, observes,

> Despite the differences among student movements in developed and underdeveloped countries, it is clear that a process of mutual influence is at work among them. For example, the white student movement in America received inspiration in its early stages from dramatic student uprisings in Japan, Turkey, and South Korea. American activists have been influenced by street tactics earned from Japanese students and by ideological expressions emanating from France and West Germany. The French students were certainly inspired by the West Germans, and the Italians by the French.[58]

Geographic contagion within the United States was observable in the urban riots in 1967, particularly for the disorders centering around Newark and Detroit.[59]

Advocates of particular strategies of conflict have written about the virtues and effectiveness of those strategies and have influenced others to try them out.[60] This has been true of nonviolent direct action, guerrilla action, and police suppression. Some advocates have visited locales where conflicts were emerging in order to consult and provide training in particular conflict strategies. Sometimes, governments provide training to soldiers, police, or terrorists from other countries, to enhance their use of coercive methods in their home countries. Often, without support from such outside groups, large-scale organized resistance or repression could not be undertaken or sustained.

Systemic Features

Whether the social context for a conflict is the world, a country, or an organization, it has features of a social system. We will discuss two structural features of those systems that significantly affect the choice of conflict mode and that have received particular scholarly and policy attention: the distribution of resources among the constituent members and the degree of integration among the members.

Resource Inequality

The earlier discussion of the preponderance or balance of power inhibiting the recourse to violence and war is applicable to the system level as well as to the dyadic relationship between two adversaries. The research about the incidence of wars in relationship to different power systems, whether unipolar, bipolar, or multipolar, however, has not yielded consistent results.[61] One reason for this may be that research focusing on polarity regards polarity as a discrete variable, often treated as dichotomous. That assumes a monotonic relationship between the incidence of war and either power preponderance or balance. But it may be that either extreme power concentration or extreme power diffusion reduces the likelihood of war, but a moderate degree of power dispersion increases the likelihood of war, the relationship being not monotonic but curvilinear.

Some research, using an index of power concentration among the major states in the international system, treated concentration as a continuous variable. Evidence of a curvilinear relationship between concentration and the incidence of wars among major states was found, wars being less likely with either high or low levels of concentration. The evidence is less clear for other kinds of wars.

Clearly, the relationship between any one measure of systemic power inequality and all kinds of violence cannot be large. There are too many dimensions of power and kinds of violence for that. Moreover, many other dimensions of inequality, as well as the other aspects of the system as a whole, affect the choice of a conflict mode.

Integration

The general level of integration in the system as a whole may affect adversaries' choices of conflict modes, even aside from the degree of integration between them. Higher overall levels of integration increases the interest and capability of other actors to affect the adversaries' choice of mode. In general, we would expect that high levels of integration would generate an effective interest in members of the system to constrain adversaries from choosing disruptive conflict modes such as wars.

Research relevant to these arguments has been conducted related to the incidence of international wars. One set of studies has examined the possible effects of the general level of integration, measured by the growth of international governmental and of international nongovernmental organizations. The results have not consistently supported the expectations about the level of integration so measured inhibiting wars.[62] It is likely the level of integration at the international level, indicated by the network of international organizations, is simply not great enough to markedly impact on the likelihood of wars in the system as a whole.

Many thinkers have argued that the growth of world trade would inhibit recourse to international wars. States would avoid wars when they are especially likely to be disruptive of trade benefits. Indeed, there is evidence that the level of international trade is inversely related to the incidence of wars among major states and among nonmajor states.[63] The relationship is quantitatively large and statistically significant.

Conclusions

We have mapped out the four sets of factors that shape the choice of a conflict strategy: the adversarial goal, the characteristics of the adversary, the relations between the adversaries, and their social environment. They combine in various ways, changing in the course of a struggle, to constrain the choice of strategies and resulting conflict modes.

General predispositions, relating to internal adversary characteristics, influence the selection of conflict means. But on the whole, they are less significant than characteristics pertaining directly to employing particular strategies, for example having the capability and adhering to an ideology legitimating a particular conflict method. Furthermore, the relatively proximate circumstances that the adversaries face are especially important. These significantly include the adversaries' conduct toward each other.

The Norwegian sports strike against the Nazi-backed Quisling government during the German occupation of Norway in World War II illustrates how goals, internal characteristics, relations between adversaries, and the social context combine to affect the selection of a conflict strategy.[64] The implementation by many Norwegians of a nonviolent resistance campaign during wartime occupation of their country was an impressive achievement. The many factors discussed in this chapter can jointly account for the choice. The power differences between the German military forces and the militarily defeated Norwegians would seem to limit the forms of resistance. Underground armed resistance groups were maintained but could not operate openly on a large scale. The Nazis wanted to indirectly govern people they ideologically believed to be "racially" like Germans, using a puppet regime. A sports strike could engage masses of people and yet not seem to threaten vital interests of the adversary. Yet, the issue could and did take on high symbolic significance, demonstrating defiance of the Quisling government and support for other forms of resistance. The failure of the government to overcome the strike further undermined its authority. This strengthened the resistance and its efforts to thwart other policies of the Nazis.

Knowledge of the many factors and processes that shape the selection of a conflict strategy provide us with the tools needed to account for conflict escalation and de-escalation, as examined in subsequent chapters. That knowledge also has policy relevance, indicating possible levers to move in order to bring about the adoption of one conflict mode rather than another.

Notes

1. Timothy Garton Ash, *The Magic Lantern: The Revolution of '89 Witnessed in Warsaw, Budapest, Berlin, and Prague* (New York: Random House, 1990). I was in Poland in October 1985, participating in a conference about social movements, focusing on Solidarity. The participating faculty, students, and activists spoke openly of their engagement in Solidarity and about their sentiments and activities during the suppression. On Solidarity, also see Louis Kriesberg and Bronislaw Misztal, with Janusz Mucha, eds., *Social Movements as a Factor of Change in the Contemporary World*, vol. 10 of *Research in Social Movements, Conflict and Change* (Greenwich, Conn.: JAI Press, 1988).

2. The "Yippies" were created in preparation for mobilizing people to demonstrate at the 1968 Democratic Party convention in Chicago. As Abbie Hoffman reports, Paul Krassner, Jerry Rubin, and he came up with the idea. "Y" was their symbol and Yippie followed after hippie, and Yippie would stand for Youth International Party. See, Abbie Hoffman, *Revolution for the Hell of It* (New York: Dial Press, 1968), 81.

3. James William Gibson, *Warrior Dreams: Violence and Manhood in Post-Vietnam America* (New York: Hill and Wang, 1994); and Gary Wills, "The New Revolutionaries," *New York Review of Books*, 10 August 1995, 50–55.

4. If there were no relationship, the correlation coefficent would be 0.0, and if the correlation were perfect, it would be 1.0. The data are from Homer R. Steedlly and John W. Foley, "The Success of Protest Groups: Multivariate Analyses," *Social Science Research*, 1979, reprinted in William A. Gamson, *The Strategy of Social Protest*, 2d ed. (Belmont, Calif.: Wadsworth, 1990), table 1, 188.

5. Inge Powell Bell, *CORE and the Strategy of Non-Violence* (New York: Random House, 1968), 59.

6. Cornelis J. Lammers, "Strikes and Mutinies: A Comparative Study of Organizational Conflicts between Rulers and Ruled," *Administrative Science Quarterly* 14 (December 1969): 558–72.

7. Fritz Heider, *The Psychology of Interpersonal Relations* (New York: Atheneum, 1975), 296–97; Harold H. Kelley, "The Process of Causal Attribution," *American Psychologist* 28 (1973): 107–28; and Mary John Smith, *Persuasion and Human Action* (Belmont, Calif.: Wadsworth, 1982), 142–63.

8. For example, see Monica D. Blumenthal, Robert L. Kahn, Frank M. Andrews, and Kendra B. Head, *Justifying Violence* (Ann Arbor: University of Michigan Press, 1972); also see W. McCord, J. Howard, B. Friedberg, and E. Howard, *Life Styles in the Black Ghetto* (New York: W. W. Norton, 1969).

9. See John E. Mueller, *War Presidents and Public Opinion* (New York: John Wiley & Sons, 1973), 122–36; also see Louis Kriesberg, Harry Murray, and Ross A. Klein, "Elites and Increased Support for U.S. Military Spending," *Journal of Political and Military Sociology* 10 (Fall 1982): 275–97.

10. Louis Kriesberg and Ross A. Klein, "Changes in Public Support for U.S. Military Spending," *Journal of Conflict Resolution* 24 (March 1980): 79–111.

11. Seymour Martin Lipset and William Schneider, *The Confidence Gap: Business, Labor, and Government in the Public Mind* (New York: The Free Press, 1983).

12. See Asher Arian, "The Peace Process and Terror: Conflicting Trends in Israeli

Public Opinion in 1995" Memorandum No. 45 (Tel Aviv: Tel Aviv University, Jaffee Center for Strategic Studies, February 1995).

13. Thus, among respondents with fewer than nine years of education, 17 percent opposed continuing negotiations, compared with 31 percent among those with university degrees. Similarly, among the respondents with fewer than nine years of education, 27 percent supported armed attacks against Israeli targets, compared with 47 percent of those with university degrees. Data are from Public Opinion Poll #16, conducted and reported by the Center for Palestine Research and Studies (CPRS), P.O. Box 132, Nablus, West Bank.

14. For example, see Terrell A. Northrup, "Personal Security, Political Security: The Relationship between Conceptions of Gender, War, and Peace," in *Research in Social Movements, Conflicts, and Change*, vol. 12, ed. Louis Kriesberg (Greenwich, Conn.: JAI, 1990) and Nancy C. M. Hartsock, "Masculinity, Heroism, and the Making of War," in *Rocking the Ship of State*, ed. Adrienne Harris and Ynestra King (Boulder, Colo.: Westview, 1989).

15. See Donald Gilbert McKinley, *Social Class and Family Life* (New York: The Free Press, 1964). The salience of socioeconomic rank for self-images is likely to be less among low-ranking persons than among high-ranking persons.

16. This was indicated, for example, in responses to a 1964 national survey question regarding "taking a stronger stand" in Vietnam; see Louis Kriesberg, *Social Conflicts* (Englewood Cliffs, N.J.: Prentice-Hall, 1982), 128.

17. Loraleigh Keashly, "Gender and Conflict: What Does Psychological Research Tells Us?" in *Conflict and Gender*, ed. Anita Taylor and Judi Beinstein Miller (Cresskill, N.J.: Hampton Press, 1994).

18. See Thomas L. Ruble and Joy A. Schneer, "Gender Differences in Conflict-Handling Styles: Less Than Meets the Eye?" in *Conflict and Gender*, ed. Taylor and Miller.

19. Peter Brock, *Pacifism in the United States: From the Colonial Era to the First World War* (Princeton, N.J.: Princeton University Press, 1968); and Robert L. Holmes, ed., *Nonviolence in Theory and Practice* (Belmont, Calif.: Wadsworth, 1990).

20. The Gush Emunim had its sources in messianic Jewish thought, which was further stimulated by the Israeli victory in the Six-Day War of 1967. The disciples of Rabbi Zvi Jehuda Kook, believing that the messianic age was at hand, urged the incorporation of Eretz Israel (the land of Israel, which included Judea and Samaria) into the State of Israel. Gush Emunim was founded in 1974 in reaction to the 1973 Yom Kippur War. It viewed the 1978 Camp David Accords between Egypt and Israel as a grave challenge. The Israeli government was seen to be committing an error that might stop a divine process. A few members thought to overcome this sin by blowing up the Muslim Dome of the Rock on the Temple Mount in Jerusalem. This was not approved by the rabbis who were consulted. See Ehud Sprinzak, "Fundamentalism, Terrorism, and Democracy: The Case of Gush Emunim," *New Outlook* 31 (September–October 1988):8–14. Interviews with two leaders of Gush Emunim (bloc of the faithful), Rabbi Moshe Levinger and Hanan Porat, also appear in the same issue.

21. For example, in the Basque region of Spain, during the 1960s, the ETA (Basque acronym for Basqueland and Freedom) evolved as an organization of Basque nationalism. It undertook a violent campaign, influenced by Frantz Fanon's analysis of decolo-

nization and the experience of Algeria. See Daniele Conversi, "Domino Effect or Internal Developments? The Influences of International Events and Political Ideologies on Catalan and Basque Nationalism," *West European Politics* 16 (July 1993): 245–70. Also see Frantz Fanon, *The Wretched of the Earth* (New York: Grove Press, 1966); Mostafa Rejai, *The Comparative Study of Revolutionary Strategy* (New York: David McKay, 1977); and Jorge Castenero, *Compañero: The Life and Death of Che Guevara* (New York: Knopf, 1997).

22. C. Wright Mills, *The New Men of Power* (New York: Harcourt, Brace, 1948).

23. See, for example, C. Wright Mills, *The Power Elite* (New York: Oxford University Press, 1956); Arnold M. Rose, *The Power Structure* (New York: Oxford University Press, 1967). The many studies of the military-industrial complex and of decision making about defense expenditures and weapons procurement provide evidence that domestic relations shape decisions about these matters.

24. See Barry B. Hughes, *The Domestic Context of American Foreign Policy* (San Francisco: W. H. Freeman, 1978).

25. President Nixon's request for Department of Defense (DoD) appropriations in January 1969 (for fiscal year 1970) was sharply down from President Johnson's January 1968 request. For an analysis, see Kriesberg, Murray, and Klein, "Elites and Increased Public Support for U.S. Military Spending."

26. Kriesberg, Murray, and Klein, "Elites and Increased Public Support for U.S. Military Spending."

27. See Daniele Conversi, "Violence as an Ethnic Border: The Consequences of a lack of Distinctive Elements in Croatian, Kurdish and Basque Nationalism," in *Nationalism in Europe: Past and Present*, ed. Xusto Beramendi, Ramon Maiz, and Xose M. Nunez (Santiago de Compostela: University of Santiago Press, 1994).

28. Obviously, in the case of state terrorism, government resources may be very great, and even if some terrorist acts may be conducted by factions of state police or security agencies, a policy of state terrorism requires the engagment of large numbers of people and authoritarian or totalitarian controls.

29. Anthony Oberschall, "The 1960 Sit-Ins: Protest Diffusion and Movement Take-Off," in *Research in Social Movements, Conflict, and Change*, vol. 11, ed. Louis Kriesberg (Greenwich, Conn.: JAI, 1989).

30. Seymour Spilerman, "The Causes of Racial Disturbances: A Comparison of Alternative Explanations," *American Sociological Review* 35 (August 1970): 627–49.

31. Youth are disproportionally involved in violent disruptions. See Lewis A. Coser, *Continuities in the Study of Social Conflict* (New York: Free Press, 1967), 65–71; National Advisory Commission on Civil Disorders (Kerner Commission), *Report of the National Commission on Civil Disorders* (New York: Bantam, 1968). Compared to the middle-aged and elderly, youth tend to feel invulnerable and have fewer assets that are hostage to those with superior power.

32. Theda Skocpol, *States and Social Revolutions: A Comparative Analysis of France, Russia, and China* (Cambridge: Cambridge University Press, 1979).

33. Charles Tilly, *From Mobilization to Revolution* (Reading, Mass.: Addison-Wesley, 1978), 156.

34. Clark Kerr and Abraham Siegel, "The Interindustry Propensity to Strike: An International Comparison," in *Industrial Conflict*, ed. A. Kornhauser, R. Dubin, and

A. M. Ross (New York: McGraw-Hill, 1954). Other studies of interindustry strike propensity in France and in Italy did not find the same pattern. See Edward Shorter and Charles Tilly, *Strikes in France, 1830–1968* (Cambridge: Cambridge University Press, 1974); and David Snyder and William R. Kelly, "Industrial Violence in Italy, 1878–1903," *American Journal of Sociology* 82 (July 1976): 131–62. Certainly, variations in economic conditions, legislation about collective bargaining, and structures of industries exist from country to country and also affect the rate of strikes.

35. William A. Gamson, "Rancorous Conflict in Community Politics," *American Sociological Review* 31 (February 1966): 71–81.

36. George Peter Murdock, *Social Structure* (New York: Macmillan, 1949), 204–6; and Robert A. LeVine, "Socialization, Social Structure, and Intersocietal Images," in *International Behavior*, ed. Herbert C. Kelman (New York: Holt, Rinehart & Winston, 1965).

37. Karl W. Deutsch, Sidney A. Burrell, Robert A. Kann, Maurice Lee, Jr., Martin Lichterman, Raymond Lindgren, Francis L. Loewenheim, and Richard W. Van Wagenen, *Political Community and the North Atlantic Area* (Princeton, N.J.: Princeton University Press, 1957).

38. Raoul Naroll, Vern L. Bullough, and Frada Naroll, *Military Deterrence in History* (Albany: State University of New York Press, 1974). For each civilization in each century, they chose the most conspicuous state and its major rival and then randomly selected one decade from each century, yielding twenty pairs of rivals.

39. William K. Domke. *War and the Changing Global System* (New Haven, Conn.: Yale University Press, 1988).

40. Mark Gasiorowski, "Economic Interdependence and International Conflict: Some Cross-National Evidence," *International Studies Quarterly* 30 (1986): 23–38; and Solomon W. Polachek, "Conflict and Trade," *Journal of Conflict Resolution* 24 (March 1980): 55–78 (this was a study of thirty countries between 1958 and 1967). Also see David Morse Hopkins, "Conflict and Contiguity: An Empirical Analysis of Institutionalization and Conflict in Contiguous Dyads," unpublished Ph.D. dissertation, Syracuse University, 1973.

41. For analyses and debates about the absence of war between democracies, see R. J. Rummel, "Libertarian Propositions on Violence within and between Nations," *Journal of Conflict Resolution* 29 (September 1985): 419–55; Bruce Russett, *Grasping the Democratic Peace: Principles for a Post–Cold War World* (Princeton, N.J.: Princeton University Press, 1993); and Scott Gates, Torbjorn L. Knutsen, and Jonathon W. Moses, "Democracy and Peace: A More Skeptical View," *Journal of Peace Research* 33, no.1 (1996): 1–10.

42. Bruce Russett, "The Democratic Peace: 'And Yet It Moves,' " *International Security* 19 (Spring 1995): 164–75.

43. Philip Taft and Phillip Ross, "American Labor Violence: Its Causes, Character, and Outcome," in *Violence in America*, ed. Hugh Davis Graham and Ted Robert Gurr (New York: Bantam, 1969); also see Jeffrey Haydu, "Managing 'The Labor Problem' in the United States ca. 1897–1911," in *Intractable Conflicts and Their Transformation*, ed. L. Kriesberg, T. A. Northrup, and S. J. Thorson (Syracuse: Syracuse University Press, 1989).

44. Arthur M. Ross and Donald Irwin, "Strike Experience in Five Countries, 1927–1947: An Interpretation," *Industrial and Labor Relations Review* 4 (April 1951): 323–42.

45. Richardson found that of the 186 pairs of opposed belligerents in wars from 1820 to 1929, 48 percent had fought against each other in the past and only 29 percent had been wartime allies. Singer and Small, using somewhat different indicators, found that of the 209 who had ever fought in opposition between 1816 and 1965, 19 percent had fought in opposition at least once before, but 21 percent had been partners in the past. See Lewis F. Richardson, *Deadly Quarrels* (Pittsburgh: Boxwood, 1960); also see J. David Singer and Melvin Small, *The Wages of War, 1816–1965: A Statistical Handbook* (New York: John Wiley, 1972), 345.

46. Thomas J. Scheff, *Bloody Revenge: Emotions, Nationalism, and War* (Boulder, Colo.: Westview, 1994); and Vamik D. Volkan, *The Need to Have Enemies and Allies* (Northvale, N.J.: Jason Aronson, 1988).

47. For example, George Fischer, *Soviet Opposition to Stalin: A Case Study in World War II.* (Cambridge, Mass.: Harvard University Press, 1952).

48. Most influentially developed in Hans J. Morgenthau *Politics among Nations* (New York: Alfred A. Knopf, 1950); among recent discussions, see John Vasquez, *The War Puzzle,* (Cambridge: Cambridge University Press, 1993).

49. Singer, Bremer, and Stuckey found that in the nineteenth century, wars among major states were less likely when power is dispersed, consistent with the balance of power argument, but in the twentieth century, wars were less likely when capability was concentrated, consistent with the preponderance argument. See J. David Singer, Stuart A. Bremer, and John Stuckey, "Capability Distribution, Uncertainty, and Major Power War, 1820–1965," in *The Correlates of War, I: Research Origins and Rationale,* ed. J. David Singer (New York: The Free Press, 1979).

50. Bruce Bueno de Mesquita, *The War Trap* (New Haven, Conn.: Yale University Press, 1981).

51. Vasquez, *The War Puzzle.*

52. It is true that business upturns also tend to be accompanied by price increases and a fall or slowing down of real income; but the relative power interpretation seems particularly compelling in that strikes to organize unorganized workers show the same pattern as do strikes to secure wage increases and other benefits. See, for example, K. G. J. C. Knowles, "'Strike Proneness' and Its Determinants," *American Journal of Sociology* 60 (November 1954): 213–29; Albert Rees, "Industrial Conflict and Business Fluctuations," in *Industrial Conflict,* ed. A. Kornhauser, R. Dubin, and A. M. Ross (New York: McGraw-Hill, 1954); and Lillian Christman, Walter R. Kelly, and Omer R. Galle, "Comparative Perspectives on Industrial Conflict," in *Research in Social Movements, Conflicts, and Change,* vol. 4, ed. Louis Kriesberg (Greenwich, Conn.: JAI, 1981).

53. Skocpol, *States and Social Revolutions.*

54. These points are developed in the resource mobilization approach to social movements. For example, Mayer N. Zald and John D. McCarthy, *The Dynamics of Social Movements* (Cambridge, Mass.: Winthrop, 1979).

55. Paul Kecskemeti, *The Unexpected Revolution: Social Forces in the Hungarian Uprising,* (Stanford, Calif.: Stanford University Press, 1961); Ted Robert Gurr, *Why Men Rebel* (Princeton, N.J.: Princeton University Press, 1970), 118–19; and Brian Crozier, *The Rebels: A Study of Post-War Insurrections* (London: Chatto & Windus, 1960).

56. The Sinhala, predominantly Budhist, make up about 75 percent of the popula-

tion of Sri Lanka, and the Tamil, mainly Hindu, constitute about 18 percent of the population. In addition, about 7 percent of the population are Muslims, who mostly speak Tamil. See David Little, *Sri Lanka: The Invention of Enmity* (Washington, D.C.: United States Institute of Peace Press, 1994).

57. The effects upon national opinions of demonstrations and the local reactions against them were not forgotten by Martin Luther King, Jr., and his associates in planning, conducting, and interpreting their nonviolent actions. See Martin Luther King, Jr., *Why We Can't Wait* (New York: Harper & Row, 1963).

58. Jerome H. Skolnick, *The Politics of Protest* (New York: Simon & Schuster, 1969), 86.

59. National Advisory Commission on Civil Disorders (Kerner Commission), *Report of the National Commission on Civil Disorders* (New York: Bantam, 1968), 114.

60. Daniele Conversi, "Domino Effect or Internal Developments? The Influences of International Events and Political Ideologies on Catalan and Basque Nationalism," *West European Politics* 16, no. 3 (July 1993): 245–70; and Ronald Pagnucco and John D. McCarthy, "Advocating Nonviolent Direct Action in Latin America: The Antecedents and Emergence of SERPAJ," in *Religion and Politics in Comparative Perspective*, ed. Bronislaw Misztal and Anson Shupe (Westport, Conn.: Praeger, 1992).

61. Michael Haas, "Social Change and National Agressiveness, 1900–1960," in *Quantitative International Politics*, ed. J. David Singer (New York: The Free Press, 1968); Dina A. Zinnes, "Empirical Evidence on the Outbreak of International Violence," in *Handbook of Political Conflict: Theory and Research*, ed. Ted Robert Gurr (New York: The Free Press, 1980); and Edward D. Mansfield, *Power, Trade, and War* (Princeton, N.J.: Princeton University Press, 1994)

62. See, for example, Paul Smoker, "Nation State Escalation and International Integration," *Journal of Peace Research* 1 (1967): 60–74; and J. David Singer and Michael Wallace, "Intergovernmental Organization and the Preservation of Peace, 1816–1964: Some Bivariate Relationships, *International Organization* 24 (Summer 1970): 520–47.

63. Mansfield, *Power, Trade, and War*, 233.

64. Richard B. Gregg, *The Power of Nonviolence*, rev. ed. (New York: Schoken Books, 1966); Gene Sharp, *The Politics of Nonviolent Action*, 3 vols. (Boston: Parter Sargent, 1973); and Paul Wehr, *Conflict Regulation* (Boulder, Colo.: Westview, 1979).

6

Escalating Conflicts

T oo often, struggles become terribly destructive. Many of them persist at great cost to all parties and become seemingly intractable. Partisans themselves often feel dismay that a conflict has so badly deteriorated, as illustrated in the anguished statements of many people from the former Yugoslavia who experienced the brutal fighting there in the 1990s. We want to investigate how such escalation occurs, and also how it is averted. The focus in this chapter is on the processes of escalation and the conditions that foster escalation.

Conflict escalation generally refers to increases in the *severity* of coercive inducements used and increases in the *scope* of participation within a conflict. Changes in these two dimensions often occur together; as more people are mobilized for a fight, they are able to undertake greater coercive action. Changes in each dimension, however, can also occur in different directions. Thus, as participation dwindles for one of the adversaries, the remaining members may, in desperation, resort to more extreme methods. On the other hand, expanding participation may incorporate other persons with less commitment to the struggle's cause.

Increased *severity* of coercion includes greater threats as well as harsher negative sanctions actually imposed. Most often, the level of coercion is indicated by measures of direct violence, typically the number of persons killed. Sometimes it is refined by calculating the proportion of combatants or the population on each side who are killed or the number of deaths per month or year of the conflict.

Most attention is given here to increases in coercive inducements, including coercive nonviolent as well as violent sanctions. The costs borne by the targets of nonviolent actions, such as boycotts, could be used as indicators of severity. Increases in the application of persuasive inducements or of positive sanctions are not readily calculable, but they also may escalate. The costs incurred by the party using noncoercive inducements might be used as indicators of such escalation, but little research has been done utilizing such indicators.

Increased *scope* generally refers to increases in the number of parties engaged in the struggle. Thus, a general war, involving several countries, is of wider scope than a war between two states. But scope, in this discussion, also refers to increases in the proportion of people in each party who are directly engaged in the fight. For example, total war means that a high proportion of the state's citizens are engaged in waging the war or in bearing the costs arising from it. In limited wars, the scope is smaller, since a relatively small proportion of the country's population is engaged in the fight. Total and limited wars also differ in the severity of the violence used.

Conflict escalation is not necessarily destructive. Although many escalating actions are usually destructive, some tend to be constructive. Furthermore, although escalating conduct may be a step along the road toward a mutually destructive result, it may also be a step toward a more just and mutually beneficial relationship.[1]

Destructively waged struggles entail relatively great losses to one or more of the contending parties, and they develop self-perpetuating mechanisms. The mechanisms themselves often have destructive qualities; these include the adversaries' dehumanization of each other, the growth of vested interests in continuing the struggle, and reinforcement of the wish for revenge. Mutually destructive conflicts are prone to persist for a very long time, in conflicts between large-scale collectivities, even from generation to generation. This was the case for French-German rivalry and enmity, marked by wars in 1870, 1914–18, and 1939–45.

Processes of Escalation

The escalation of conflicts has long been a major topic of scholarly analysis.[2] Escalation may occur inadvertently, in a series of incremental steps without the opponents having carefully considered the implications of their actions. However, escalation may also be a calculated policy to step up the pressure against an opponent, either gradually or abruptly. Escalation is driven by changes within each of the conflict parties, by evolving patterns of interaction between the adversaries, and by developments affecting previously uninvolved parties who join the struggle.

Internal Changes

Processes of escalation internal to one of the adversaries include those occurring within individual minds or within organizational structures. Those developments may result in well-calculated or ill-considered escalation. In this discussion, I give special attention to processes that contribute to the unwitting destructive escalation of conflicts.

Social-Psychological Processes

Many theories and research findings in social psychology provide insights, helping to explain conflict escalation. Cognitive dissonance theory, for example, suggests that individuals seek consistency between what they do and what they think they should do.[3] Consequently, once having committed an action, they seek to justify it in their own minds. After one has suffered an ordeal in order to join a fraternity or a military unit, the value of being a member of that group must be regarded as great so as to maintain self-respect in having chosen to put up with the ordeal. It follows that as persons expend resources to hurt or support injuring other humans, they tend to regard the cause for which those actions were taken as more and more important. As the cause becomes more valued, ever more harmful acts are justified.

Entrapment is another process contributing to conflict escalation. It refers to "a decision making process whereby individuals escalate their commitment to a previously chosen, though failing, course of action in order to justify or 'make good on' prior investments."[4] We all experience entrapment when we are put on hold when telephoning a company or when we are waiting for a bus; the longer we wait the more we want to walk away but the more difficult it seems to do so, having already invested so much time waiting. Having sunk resources into a fight, sinking more and more resources seems justified in order to attain the goal of the struggle and so justify what has already been expended in money, honor, or blood. This ever-increasing commitment and allocation of resources may go much beyond the original value of the goal, but the combatants are trapped into continuing and even escalating the struggle.

In addition, selective perception occurs in many ways that contribute to conflict escalation. People tend to notice phenomena that fit their expectations so that once a struggle has entered a stage of mutual recrimination and contentiousness, even conciliatory conduct by the adversary is likely not to be noticed or, if noticed, be discounted and considered deceptive.

Moreover, thinking is impaired when people feel they are threatened and must respond with urgency. Policymakers, in what they regard as a crisis, experience such pressures.[5] Under those circumstances, fewer alternatives are considered; and, previous conduct, even if ineffective, tends to be repeated.

Finally, we must consider emotions that play significant roles in the development of struggles that are protracted and destructive. Thus, fear and anger are likely to be aroused when people feel attacked, and the tendency to express those emotions by inflicting harm on the presumed attacker certainly contributes to conflict escalation. Shame and humiliation and the resulting desire for revenge are other emotions that fuel struggles.[6] They may be culturally elaborated and channeled, as in the institutions of duels, feuds, and wars. Unacknowledged, these feelings may hamper using constructive ways to wage a struggle.

Organizational Developments

As an intergroup conflict persists and particularly as coercive inducements are used, the adversaries may change in ways that tend to escalate the struggle further. Three interrelated developments of this kind are particularly noteworthy: leadership identification with external conflict, mobilization of partisans, and raised expectations.

Since leaders generally represent their constituents in conflicts with outsiders, they are predisposed to become identified with the group's already established oppositional goals and the means chosen to pursue them. They are prone to becoming so entrapped because the costs are particularly high for them to admit that the course of action being pursued is a failure. Typically, they have publicly claimed the course of action undertaken to be the correct one. For them to admit their conduct has been mistaken may be regarded as acknowledging the opponent's course as having been correct, and that may appear to be catering to the enemy. This would subject the leaders to charges of weakness and submission to the enemy. Finally, in external conflicts, failure is easier to obscure because the constituents have less ground for forming an independent judgment than in internal affairs.

This analysis presumes that the leaders believe they may be replaced by challengers. Indeed, competition and rivalry among alternative leaders tends to foster conflict escalation. For example, a study of civil rights leaders in fifteen American cities in 1964–65 found that militancy (measured by responses to four agree-disagree questions) was lower among leaders in cities with minimal competition and higher in cities with competition.[7] Demonstrations, although short-lived, were also more frequent where there was competition.

Growth in the relative influence of leaders who are "hard-line" and who specialize in coercive inducements also contributes to conflict escalation. As a fight persists and increasing reliance is placed on coercive means, the advocates and managers of those means tend to gain influence. For example, in an interstate conflict, once the armed forces become engaged, military leaders assume greater predominance.[8] Usually, as the fight goes on, those who are reluctant or who are critical of the means being used are silenced, are forced out of the leadership circle, or withdraw. The remaining leaders can then escalate the struggle, with less and less challenge. This happened within the U.S. government leadership circle as it escalated U.S. military engagement in Vietnam in the 1960s.[9]

Even among less highly organized adversaries, as a conflict intensifies, shifts in the leadership occur. These changes often enhance the influence of the more intransigent persons. The new members of the leadership circle are less likely than the established leaders to have had nonconflicting relations with the adversary, and they are less likely to have a stake in the *status quo*. For example, in community conflicts, the new leaders who take over the conduct of the conflict are rarely former community leaders. They lack the constraints of maintaining previous community positions, and are not as subject to the cross pressures felt by members of community organizations.[10]

Leadership changes, however, sometimes also contribute to de-escalation, as when the established leaders are challenged by relatively moderate alternative leaders. Considered in more detail later, this kind of pressure is most likely to occur in later stages of a struggle, in particularly heterogeneous conflict units, with adversaries who are consistently conciliatory, and in relatively regulated conflicts.

The other set of internal developments contributing to conflict escalation is related to changes among the constituencies within each adversary. At the early stages of a conflict, as members begin to share their experiences, their information about deprivations and their sense of grievance tend to increase. For example, an important component of the American women's liberation movement has been the "consciousness-raising" group. In these small groups, women meet to share their accounts of their lives as women. Hearing each other's stories, they learn that some difficulties that had seemed personal and singular are really general and societal, and therefore require societal solutions, not simply personal accommodations.

The membership composition of partisan groups may also tend to change in ways that foster escalation. As a fight goes on, and as participation widens, persons who are predisposed to use more intense means join the struggle. One reason this happens is particularly pertinent for members of oppressed groups. The most deprived members of such groups generally become involved in a struggle when possible gains have become credible. But their feeling of grievance, once aroused, is likely to be greater than among persons who had the resources to initiate the struggle. The newly aroused also tend to be less moderate because they are less constrained by understandings earlier arrived at with the adversary and are less likely to have experienced finding compromises with opponents.

Evidence for elements of this argument can be found in a national study of opinions regarding civil liberties for communists, atheists, and others expressing minority views, which was conducted in the United States during the period of intense anticommunist sentiment, often called "McCarthyism" in reference to U.S. Senator Joseph McCarthy.[11] On the whole, the national sample of community leaders interviewed was more tolerant of the rights of nonconformists than was a cross section of the public at large. A 1966 national survey of Blacks and of Black civil rights leaders also provides evidence for some of the arguments presented.[12] The leaders, compared with Blacks in general, were less satisfied about the progress being made by Blacks and were more militant about the goals to be pursued, but nevertheless were less likely to say they would engage in violent conduct.

The composition of a group also changes as some people withdraw from it. If conflict behavior is escalating, the members who prefer not to engage in higher magnitudes of conflict tend to withdraw, and those willing to engage in more severe behavior become increasingly dominant. But such intensification may actually reduce the scope of the conflict, measured by the number of persons or groups engaged in the fight.

The third organizational change that contributes to conflict escalation is the heightened commitment to the goal and the increased conviction that it is attainable. This is likely to occur at an early stage of a struggle as a conflict party rallies its forces but has not yet experienced the other side's punishing sanctions. Before difficult tests of strength occur, a group's conviction of victory is likely to grow as its forces mobilize. Within the insularity of the partisan group, mutual reassurances go unchecked, reinforcing a sense of power. If there are also some initial gains, the support for escalation is likely to grow rapidly. This is particularly true for people in a state of collective excitement and emotional contagion. Such swellings of feelings may be short-lived, but they can escalate swiftly in the form of riots and unregulated strikes. This is illustrated in the American student strikes of May 1970, reacting to the U.S. military invasion of Cambodia and the subsequent killing of student protestors at Kent State University and Jackson State University.[13] About 1.5 million students left classes and about a fifth of the U.S. colleges were closed down, many to the end of the school year.[14] Almost continuous rallies were held at colleges where announcements of "shut downs" at other institutions were proclaimed. The élan and the confidence that victory would soon be won sustained relatively extreme actions, as universities were barricaded and sit-ins conducted, at least for a few days. Some students expected that the strike would expand beyond those in France in 1968 when workers and students joined together in a great wave of strikes.[15]

Expectations also change in accord with the social-psychological mechanisms previously discussed. These mechanisms are often used by leaders, intellectuals, and activists to mobilize partisans for the perpetuation and escalation of a conflict. Leaders may "wave the bloody shirt," exclaiming how much has already been sacrificed in the struggle and urging that those losses should not be in vain, that the struggle must be continued until victory is won. The pain suffered is used to spur further struggle.

Leaders of a gang, a guerilla army, or a country sometimes commit followers to the struggle by requiring them to participate in acting violently against enemies. In accord with cognitive dissonance theory, those people will tend to justify their actions and come to believe in their positive value. At the very least, they are likely to feel compromised and unable to return to their former position.

Finally, conflict parties with specialized agencies for waging fights, such as armies or police, may escalate coercive behavior quickly, once those units begin operations. The agencies, following their standard operating procedures, often pursue policies that are inappropriate for the particular circumstances in which they are undertaken.[16] This can result in unforeseen escalation.

Once military forces engage in operations, whether ordered to do so by civilian authority or not, the level of coercion is often much greater than had been anticipated. This has been true in civil wars and in military replacement of civilian governments, as well as in waging interstate wars.[17] The outbreak of World War I is a frequently cited example of how plans for mobilization and military actions, once triggered, seemed to initiate uncontrolled escalation, hence, the image of unconstrained wildness when "the dogs of war are unleashed."[18]

Changes in Relations between Adversaries

Once a conflict erupts, the relations between the adversaries change in ways that tend to escalate the fight. Three such changes are fundamental: (1) the logic of contentious interaction, (2) the expansion of the issues in contention, and (3) the polarization of relations.

The Logic of Contentious Interaction

As adversaries exchange contentious behavior, each reasonably expects that the other will increase its pressure unless it is prevented or deterred by greater coercion. In this way, the expectations become self-fulfilling prophecies. Acting on the premise that the other side is guided only by a drive for power and influenced only by coercion tends to produce confirming behavior.[19]

Emotional responses contribute to the reverberation of coercive acts between opponents. If one party is harmed or even threatened by a rival, it is more likely to respond with hostility rather than acquiescence.[20] That hostility is then reciprocated, after which the parties may come to feel that revenge and damaging the other side have become goals in themselves. Runaway escalation then ensues.

Furthermore, as one side imposes negative sanctions upon the other, those sanctions themselves become issues. For example, when American women were struggling for suffrage, they picketed the White House. They were harassed by the police, and many were arrested. When maltreated in prison, they went on hunger strikes that resulted in forced feeding.[21] For members of the women's movement, such behavior by the opposition created new issues of contention; and many passive observers became supporters of the women's cause.

Such expansion of issues is often inadvertent. One party misperceives how the opponents will respond and commits acts that result in greater escalation than was intended by either party.[22] This may occur when one party tries to intimidate its opponent and instead provokes a harsh counteraction. This may also occur when a threat is made with the expectation that it will suffice, but is only a bluff. If the opponent is not intimidated and the bluff is called, the threatener has an additional reason to carry out the threat or lose credibility and face. Both sides have taken a step up the escalation ladder that was not intended, and the conflict has escalated to a higher level than either believed appropriate for the original subject of their quarrel.

If one of the parties commits extreme coercive acts, the other is likely to perceive the perpetrator as brutish and subhuman, perhaps as evil. Such views then allow or even justify harsh countermeasures. The brutish enemy presumably can only understand brutish acts. Soon, each side is treating the other inhumanly, but feels it is acting out of necessity.

It is even possible, sometimes, that humiliating and brutalizing the enemies makes them appear despicable and less than human, and thus their further degradation is made more justifiable. For example, this may occur in prison camps, or even in battle, when pleas for pity by the vulnerable soldier make him seem contemptible.[23]

Finally, once a struggle has begun to deteriorate destructively, even efforts to dampen the conflict may feed the flames of escalation. If one of the parties makes a conciliatory gesture or responds less aggressively than anticipated, the other may interpret that as a sign of weakness. The weakness then serves as an invitation to escalate demands and pressure. Then, to restore credibility and demonstrate resolve, the previously conciliatory party may stiffen its posture and raise its own demands. The conflict escalates as the stakes are raised.

Expansion of the Issues

Once a struggle has begun about one issue, additional and more general ones usually surface. Contentious issues that had been denied or hidden are frequently raised when parties have begun to fight each other. There is less need to deny them, and the overt struggle may seem a good time to "settle accounts."[24]

Such issue expansion is particularly likely when there are deep cleavages of fundamental values or interests among members of a community, organization, or other social system. For example, a community controversy over the inclusion of particular books in the school library may be generalized to a fight about educational philosophies.[25]

A relatively minor issue in dispute may take on great symbolic significance, once a struggle has gotten under way. What might be a minor matter between friends, has great significance between enemies. For example, control of a piece of land might seem easily divisible or a matter for which compensation could be made. But in a dispute with an enemy, the piece of land may be endowed with symbolic value and be prized even more because denying it to the enemy would be gratifying.

Polarization of Relations

As a conflict emerges and develops, the adversaries tend to become increasingly isolated from each other. For example, before war actually erupts between governments, they tend to withdraw from joint membership in international organizations.[26] As conflict parties reduce the number of non-conflicting relations, they are less and less constrained by cross pressures and crosscutting ties and are freer to indulge in more severe means.

Polarization is aggravated by the tendency of partisans to try to win bystanders to their side. Insofar as a party feels morally superior and confident that the people not yet engaged in the struggle will be their allies if they must choose sides, it will urge them to do so; or, if it believes it can, it may insist that other parties join with it. For example, the striking coal miners in Harlan County, Kentucky, sang in the 1930s, "You either are a union man or a thug for J. H. Blair. Which side are you on, man, which side are you on?" Or, as Eldridge Cleaver said during the civil rights struggle, "If you're not part of the solution, you're part of the problem." More forcefully, the German Nazis insisted, "If you are not for us, you are against us."

The polarization in relations between antagonists reduces the opportunities to communicate about noncontentious issues as well as contentious ones. Members of each camp, with little contradiction, tend to reinforce each other's negative stereotypes of the adversary, further dehumanizing the enemy.

Involvement of Other Parties

Once an overt struggle has begun, parties not initially engaged may see an opportunity to gain significant benefits by joining the fray.[27] The struggle may provide an opportunity to inflict harm and weaken an old foe, or it may be an opportunity to win a portion of the spoils that a victory might yield. Sometimes, a party will intervene out of obligation to support its friends or allies who are in the fight.

Intervention does not require direct engagement in the war, revolution, strike, or protest movement in order to escalate the conflict. The provision of weapons, funds, or other implements of struggle enables the combatants to raise the magnitude of the means being used and to sustain the struggle. Thus, a study of civil strife in 114 countries found that external support for dissidents correlated .37 with the length of the civil strife and .22 with its pervasiveness.[28]

Certainly, during the cold war, many local conflicts in Africa, Central America, Asia, and the Middle East were exacerbated and perpetuated by the superimposition of the conflict between the USSR and the United States. Each superpower would lend support to the enemy of the government supported by the other. Another example is provided by ethnic groups struggling for autonomy or independence who are sustained by members of the same ethnicity in other countries.

Other parties also tend to become engaged in a struggle because as the partisans pursue their goals, they sometimes infringe on the interests of non-engaged other parties. For example, in World War I, Germany used submarines to attack shipping to Great Britain, sinking U.S. vessels.[29] The German government announced unrestricted submarine warfare would begin 1 February 1917. Furthermore, the German government secretly telegrammed an offer to the Mexican government. It proposed an alliance, in the event the United States entered the war, promised Mexico would reconquer its lost territories, and suggested inviting Japan to join the alliance. The secret telegram was discovered and confirmed in March and, in conjunction with the submarine warfare, created a popular storm of outrage in the United States. On 2 April 1917, President Woodrow Wilson asked for a declaration of war against Germany.

In summary, as a fight escalates, the means of waging it tend to become increasingly removed from the underlying conflict. Consequently, the conflict may be considered to have more and more "unrealistic" qualities. Or, as the partisans are likely to argue, one might say that the objective conflict has shifted and that the adversaries have more at stake as the way of waging it has escalated.

Conditions and Policies Generating Destructive Struggles

Processes of escalation produce destructive struggles of long duration under some conditions but not others. We now examine the factors resulting in the adoption of destructive conflict modes. We also analyze how these modes are related to the duration of a conflict. Before doing so, we need to discuss two terms referring to particular kinds of prolonged struggles: *protracted* and *intractable conflicts.*

Protracted conflicts refer particularly to deep-rooted, identity-based conflicts. As Edward E. Azar has used the term, it is "the prolonged and often violent struggle by communal groups [religious, ethnic, racial, or cultural] for such basic needs as security, recognition and acceptance, fair access to political institutions, and economic participation."[30]

Intractable conflicts also refer to prolonged conflicts; in the case of large-scale conflicts, those that persist for more than a generation. They appear to resist efforts at resolution, and many members of the enduring adversary groups tend to consider their goals to be irreconcilable. These views are supported by the development of vested interests in waging the struggle. The conflicts tend to be waged in a self-perpetuating pattern of destructive interaction.[31] Protracted conflicts and intractable conflicts are best considered as processes, varying over time, and not as fixed qualities that are either present or absent.

Not all struggles become destructive and long lasting. Some quickly de-escalate, as one side to some degree unilaterally imposes a settlement or the adversaries more or less mutually construct an acceptable outcome. The conflict may also continue escalating, constructively or destructively, until it ultimately de-escalates.

In any prolonged conflict, even one characterized as protracted, the contentious conflict behavior fluctuates in severity. For example, the cold war between the United States and the Soviet Union was particularly intense in three periods: in 1948 and 1950 with the Soviet blockade of West Berlin and the North Korean invasion of South Korea, in 1962 with the Cuban missile crisis, and in the early 1980s with the Soviet intervention in Afghanistan and the militant U.S. policy.[32] The conflict also had many periods of thaw, including 1955 with the end of the occupation of Austria, 1963 with the Partial Nuclear Test Ban agreement, and 1972 with the signing of several arms control agreements.

What is of particular interest here is how some conflicts become prolonged and come to be regarded as intractable. We will examine how the conflict strategies chosen, the issues in contention, the changes within the adversaries, the interaction among the adversaries, and the social context all contribute to that development. We will examine how certain conditions and policies in each area contribute to a conflict being waged destructively. No single factor or policy wholly determines the course of a struggle. Therein lies many possibilities for averting a prolonged and destructive struggle.

Strategy Chosen

The conflict strategy undertaken by each adversary profoundly affects the likelihood of their struggle escalating destructively, since it influences the opponent's choice of conflict strategy, and also impacts the party that has undertaken the strategy as well as the kind of intervention made by other parties. Some strategies tend to limit escalation and others to foster it, either constructively or destructively. The selection too often is made with little attention to these kinds of long-term consequences.

Impact on Party Undertaking Conflict Strategy

Any strategy in pursuit of contentious goals has costs for the party applying that strategy, and those costs tend to impose limits on the escalation of a conflict. That might seem to be obvious. The more burdensome the costs, relative to the capabilities available, the less potential there is to sustain, let alone escalate, the conflict. Strategies that impose heavy costs affecting large proportions of the conflict unit, can be borne only for a short time. But assessing costs is difficult. Objective indicators may fail to capture the subjective experience of costs. For example, even war deaths or casualties are not always strong indicators of how long parties continue a war or escalate it.

Furthermore, the means of struggle used may provide gratifications, some of which are emotional. For example, consider not only the fears and pains of participating in sit-ins and protest demonstrations during the civil rights struggle, but also the pride. One participant in the civil rights movement in the early 1960s tells of thousands of students marching to a southern city jail in support of a group that had been arrested. The police attacked them, and he reports proudly,

> When I was able to see again (after the tear gas attack) I saw some of the girls getting themselves together. Some went back to the campus in an ambulance; they had been hit in the legs with nightsticks. And all of them—their clothes were torn and they were many of them bleeding—they were all standing in line again. In that few minutes they had pulled themselves back together and they were singing as loud as they could, "I'm gonna sit at the welcoming table." And the police stood there and didn't say a word.[33]

Feelings of collective solidarity, excitement, pride in your group's bravery, and pleasure in making history and proving one's self are all exhilarating, and those feelings enable participants to endure great discomfort and pain. Although such emotions cannot be sustained for long, they leave feelings of loyalty and commitment that help sustain a conflict group.

When a conflict party becomes differentiated enough to have persons whose careers are devoted to waging conflicts and using a particular method or of providing the infrastructure for it, the development of a vested interest in continuing the struggle and employing that means has begun. How important such vested interests become depends on the costs they impose and what the alternatives are for the people engaged in the struggle. In some countries, being engaged in armed struggle, whether as military officers or as guerrilla leaders, may provide relatively attractive careers.

Use of certain modes fosters antagonism toward the opponent. Harming the opponent needs to be justified, especially if partisans must be mobilized for a sustained campaign of inflicting injuries. Having undertaken such a strategy, the conflict party will tend to depict the opponent as not merely wrong on the issue in contention but also as evil and posing a great threat. Pressure may even be brought to bear on those who question such depictions, referring to them as traitors to their own side.

After the end of World War II, many U.S. leaders wanted to ensure American military, economic, and political engagement in Europe and the world generally. The Soviet/communist threat was dramatized in order to mobilize support for maintaining U.S. military forces in Europe and for the establishment of NATO. This break with traditional U.S. policies needed to be justified by a transcendent threat, and the Soviet threat was exaggerated, to provide the needed justification.[34]

Conflict strategies that do not engender vested interests in the struggle or the dehumanization of the opponent are less likely than those that do to result in prolonged, destructively waged conflicts. This is one of the arguments made for nonviolent strategies that oppose an adversary's policy or actions but insist that the perpetrators of the policies or actions are humans with a core of goodness.

Impact on the Adversary

The conflict strategy chosen by one party often significantly affects how its adversary reacts. The conflict strategy may be varyingly severe, adhering to or crossing boundaries of what is regarded as appropriate. Using strategies that the targets regard as outrageous often provokes severe countermeasures. Moreover, efforts at intimidation generally provoke responses of defiance.

For example, research on serious interstate disputes from 1863 to 1964 indicates that the use of threats tended to produce extreme responses, either of defiance or of compliance.[35] The inducements examined included threat (military violence and punishment, military violence, other threats), promise (with reward or other promises), and carrot and stick. The responses were comply, placate, mixed placate and defy, ignore, and defy. Inducements involving promises were somewhat less likely than those with threats to produce extreme responses; rather, the responses tended to be placate, mixed, or ignore. Placate or mixed responses, involving alternatives, may be the start of negotiations toward a mutually acceptable settlement. Among relatively evenly matched adversaries, threats were particularly likely to produce defiance, and defiance was associated with escalations leading to war. Threats or promises, when specified, tended to be reacted to by compliance or defiance; and if unspecified, those inducements were disproportionally ignored.

Some strategies tend to be unspecified and ambiguous even in regard to who is acting and with what purpose. For example, terrorism is often conducted by persons whose identity is secret. Specific goals are not always articulated, unless there is an overt agency that is understood to speak for the underground elements. In the case of riots or covert resistance, there may be no authoritative interpreters of the actions. The target persons and groups are then relatively free to define who is committing the acts and for what objectives and not engage in negotiations or other noncoercive means of settling the conflict. The alleged perpetrators and their supporters are often not considered legitimate negotiating parties, and may be regarded as inhuman by many members of the target groups.

Finally, some strategies are intended to provoke the adversary to escalate the conflict. The expectation is that when the other side escalates, allies and supporters will be gained, offended by the escalating leap. For example, the Cuban revolutionaries, led by Fidel Castro, were a small group until the revolution was about to succeed. The revolutionaries committed acts that provoked the government. The government forces, under the direction of Fulgencio Batista, the self-appointed president, undertook increasingly harsh and indiscriminate countermeasures, antagonizing many segments of the population. The government became isolated and fell in January 1959. As Che Guevara, one of the Cuban revolutionary leaders and theoreticians, said at the time,

> The dictatorship tries to operate without the showy use of force; forcing the dictatorship to appear undisguised—that is, in its true aspect of violent dictatorship of the reactionary classes, will contribute to its unmasking, which will intensify the struggle to such extremes that then there is no turning back.[36]

This strategy was considered an effective way to create a revolutionary situation and Che Guevara and many others attempted to follow it in several countries, but the strategy proved unsuccessful when tried in other countries.

Effects on Other Parties

Finally, the conflict strategies being used affect the likelihood of other parties joining the fight and so increasing its scope. The actions may seem so offensive to some of the people not yet engaged in the fight that they join the struggle to stop the perpetrators of the outrageous acts. The actions may also seem so admirable that supporters and allies rally to join those whose actions they admire. Such increases in the scope of the conflict tend to speed its end if those who join the fray add overwhelming resources to one side. For example, in the civil rights struggle against Jim Crow segregation laws in the U.S. South, many people throughout the nation were appalled by the violence of local authorities and admired the nonviolent actions of the protesters. Eventually, federal intervention and legislation contributed significantly to the abolishment of legally sustained segregation.

If, however, external parties bring the adversaries into balance, they may enable the contending parties to persist in the fight. Many struggles, particularly in Third World countries, were sustained during the cold war as the U.S. and Soviet governments, and governments associated with them, gave assistance to opposing sides. This was the case most directly in the Korean War and the war in Vietnam, and indirectly in the prolonged Arab-Israeli conflict. Associated governments also provided military assistance to adversaries in civil and interstate wars. For example, Cuba sent troops to help defend Angola's government against South Africa–backed guerrillas in 1975–90.[37]

Attention is often given by partisans to acting and portraying their actions so as to win over supporters and dissuade parties not yet engaged in the conflict from joining it on the side of their adversaries. Depending on the values and interests of those possible entrants to the conflict, such considerations may limit the conflict's escalation.

Of course, the conflict methods being used may also bring about efforts by those not engaged to enter as intermediaries to impose a cessation of the conflict behavior. Thus, within a society, many methods of conducting a fight are regarded as illegal, and the government and its agents are generally seen as legitimate imposers of the legal limits. The existence of institutions to manage fights also provides an alternative for the adversaries themselves to use, rather than settling the fight between themselves.

Contentious Issues

Matters in contention vary greatly in their disposition for escalation. Matters that are regarded as of vital interest by one or more of the adversaries have great potential for escalation. The party defending what it believes to be essential to its existence will use whatever means it has that it believes will be effective against a threat to its existence. Thus, labor strikes about union recognition or about attempts to weaken the union are more likely to escalate to violence than are strikes about wages and hours.[38]

What is regarded as vital generally differs among various factions or groups within each side of a large-scale conflict. What is consequential is whose interests receive the highest priority. This may be readily recognized in coalitions in which the vital interest of a minor member binds other members whose vital interests are not as directly engaged. For example, during the war in Vietnam, the survival of the South Vietnamese government was certainly in its vital interests and the U.S. government persisted in the war in part in deference to those interests. On the other hand, the Cuban missile crisis in 1962 did not escalate more than it did because the Soviet leadership negotiated a deal with the U.S. government, without including the Cuban government as a negotiating partner.[39]

In general, issues that involve many parties are prone to escalation. This is supported by systematic studies of interstate disputes. For example, a study of 960 militarized disputes between 1816 and 1976 found that 22 percent of the multiparty disputes escalated to war, while only 5 percent of the dyadic disputes did.[40]

Dissensual issues have a higher escalating potential than issues that are largely consensual. Disputes involving ideological and general value or moral issues can attract more parties than those involving concrete consensual matters. Furthermore, dissensual matters in contention appear to the partisans as difficult to divide and not amenable to compromise. Dissensual issues also foster conflict escalation because the opponent is often viewed as wrong in principle and not merely on the wrong side of an issue. Therefore, constraints on conduct may be reduced, particularly if the other side is considered immoral. Once one is engaged in a struggle, the advancement of one's side against an evil "other" can be supported by the fervor of a religious crusade.

Matters regarded by adversaries as being integral to their personal or collective identities are particularly prone to escalation and resistant to resolution.[41] This is a source of the intensity with which ethnic conflicts are sometimes waged. Thus, in a country with two or more ethnic communities whose people speak different languages, the state may be dominated by one ethnic group and require that education and cultural activities all be conducted in its language. Some members of the other group may well view this as an effort to destroy them as a people.

The formulation of the adversaries' goals also has varying escalating dispositions. Thus, insofar as the goals are collective rather than aggregate, escalation is more likely. Collective goals generally require group reallocations of resources or of evaluations, and that seems more threatening to the targeted adversary than the individual accommodations required in aggregate goals. Furthermore, collective goals require a relatively open acceptance of the claims of those working to achieve the goals. Finally, institutionalized and minimally coercive means are more likely to be seen as appropriate and effective by those seeking aggregate rather than collective goals. For example, an ethnic group's struggle for equal opportunity and even the possibility of assimilation is often more amenable to problem-solving conflict modes than an ethnic group's struggle for autonomy or independence.

In addition, the greater the number of issues in contention and the greater the grievances, the more fuel there is to feed the fire of escalation. Thus, although community variations in the social conditions of Blacks have not been found to be related to the outbreak of urban riots in the 1960s, the riots' severity has been. For example, in one study, the percentage of non-Whites living in ten-year-or-older housing was highly correlated (.86) with the severity of the riots.[42]

Finally, each side in a struggle forms contentious goals to resolve the conflict. The nature and the magnitude of the incompatibility of those goals profoundly affect the course of their struggle. Of course, the adversaries may misperceive the degree of incompatibility; if they exaggerate it and act on the basis of their perceptions, they may unduly perpetuate and escalate the conflict.

For example, there is evidence that during much of the cold war, the governments of the United States and the Soviet Union each said they feared the expansionism of the other side and claimed not to be expansionist, even believing that the other side must know that it was not really expansionist.[43] In those circumstances, continuing hostility, mutual threats, and recurrent crises remained likely. However, since both governments' goals were limited and generally defensive, the escalation was usually constrained. In the end, the Soviet-American rivalry did not escalate into the feared nuclear war but was nonviolently transformed. This transformation largely resulted from the profound internal changes in the Soviet Union. However, those were a product not only of the inherent problems of the communist system and the burdens of waging a cold war but also of the accommodationist elements of the West's policies.[44] The openness of the West, the engagement between the Soviet people and the peoples of Europe and the United States, and the assurance that vital interests were not threatened encouraged the initial moves toward basic change in the Soviet Union, leading in a few years to the dissolution of the USSR. All this suggests that misperceptions contributed to perpetuating the cold war, and the actuality of limited goals contributed to containing the potential escalation.

Internal Developments

Earlier, we discussed many social-psychological and organizational processes internal to a conflict party that could be conducive to conflict escalation. Now we consider the internal circumstances and policies that affect those processes so that they actually contribute to escalation.

Homogeneity

Adversaries with relatively little internal diversity tend to sustain increases in the severity of a conflict. The social-psychological processes and organizational developments fostering escalation tend to reinforce each other. Given the similarities of the members of the conflict party, members are likely to respond similarly to events and to drown out dissident murmurs. Conversely, internal diversity provides a basis for limiting escalation and fostering de-escalation since various segments of a heterogenous adversary tend to have different priorities relating to the struggle. Furthermore, the costs of waging the struggle are likely to be unevenly experienced. Such differences can provide the grounds for opposing escalation and prolongation of the struggle.

Leaders are likely to foster homogeneity, instituting policies to build support for the goals of the struggle, and portraying the enemy as a grave threat to vital interests and identities. Insofar as they are effective in these policies and alternative voices are absent, their constituency is less open to overtures or divisive efforts by the adversaries.

In general, homogeneity and policies fostering it reduce the likelihood that members of an adversary group will consider alternatives to the belligerent course under way. Furthermore, they are less likely to be responsive to their opponents and insensitive to the witting and unwitting conciliatory signals from the other side; thus, opportunities for de-escalation are missed and the struggle escalates.[45]

Nevertheless, in any large conflict party, some variations in orientation toward the adversary are generally present. In international relations, the differences between hard-liners and accommodationists have been frequently noted.[46] The differences are derived not only from personality characteristics, but also from varying beliefs about the efficacy and legitimacy of threats and violence, and about the possibility of compromising their goals. Where hard-liners direct foreign policy, destructive escalation is likely.

Differentiation

Opponents with specialized agencies to wage struggles are more capable of increasing the severity of a conflict, without widespread constituency support. This has been seen as an advantage of professional rather than conscript armies for waging wars that lack popular appeal. More generally, training, discipline, threat of punishment, a sense of honor, and loyalty to comrades in arms combine to keep combatants risking their lives, even when the odds of avoiding death or injury are poor.

In some circumstances, however, it is the very lack of coordination and control that can result in escalating events. In many struggles, the persons in direct confrontation are not under effective control of their superiors, which often results in conflict escalation. For example, the Chicago police who acted against the demonstrators at the 1968 Democratic Party convention used more violence than was probably intended, constituting and provoking further escalation.[47] The shooting of students at Kent State in May 1970 was an unplanned act of escalation that led to further escalation; it exemplifies the loss of control that sometimes occurs when violence is threatened.[48]

Interaction between Adversaries

How adversaries respond to each other's contentious conduct usually makes the most significant immediate contribution to the escalation of a conflict. Almost any reaction, including nonresponse, can be part of an escalating dynamic, as the following discussion of nonresponse and of over- and under-reaction indicates.

Nonresponse

Ignoring an adversary's contentious behavior often escalates a conflict, as the adversary resorts to more extreme conduct in order to arouse attention from the mass media and get a response from the opposing party that is acting inattentively. Nonresponse is often experienced as a denial of significance and is therefore humiliating.

Often, in ongoing struggles, the adversaries mutually acknowledge each other as they fight each other, but deny the other side's legitimacy. That threatens the very existence of the party whose legitimacy is rejected. This is often a fundamental feature and cause of intractable conflicts.

For example, until Anwar al-Sadat, president of Egypt, dramatically visited Jerusalem in November 1977, none of the Arab states had recognized the state of Israel or would publicly meet with its representatives. This conveyed the message to Israelis that they faced implacable enemies who would destroy their state. Conversely, until the Israeli government and the Palestine Liberation Organization (PLO) mutually recognized each other in September 1993, the Israeli government would not recognize the PLO as representing Palestinians, and most Palestinians saw that as a denial of their collective existence as a people.

Overreaction

Once adversaries are engaged in a conflict, their contentious interaction tends to escalate in severity, as one side or both seeks to impose a settlement by increasing the coercive pressure. Escalation is particularly likely if the step up in severity exceeds the normative expectations of the other side. The reaction may be of such outrage that the acts are counterproductive—they fail to intimidate and provoke intensified and broader struggle. For example, in 1968, after students at Columbia University occupied several university buildings as part of a protest, university administrators decided to call in the city police to remove the students. In the eyes of many students and faculty, the police "bust" delegitimated senior university administrators. Furthermore, faculty and students who actually witnessed the police clubbing students and dragging them from the seized buildings were much more likely to regard the police action as brutal than were those who only heard or read about it.[49]

At least within the context of American civil society and the limits of legitimate coercion, the more severely authorities react to social protest, the more likely the protest is to escalate. For example, a study of colleges that had demonstrations against certain kinds of campus recruitment in 1967 found that the more severe the control measures were against civil disobedience, the more likely the protest was to expand.[50]

The story of the American civil rights struggle in the 1950s and 1960s can be read as the counterproductive effects of violent acts of intimidation (see table 6.1). Such efforts at repression by state and local government officials and by private citizens were particularly counterproductive against the well-articulated and disciplined nonviolent civil rights campaigns.

At the societal level, the theoretical explanations of resource mobilization, political process, or rational choice suggest that domestic political violence would tend to be greatest in societies with intermediate levels of repressiveness. In countries with relatively high levels of consistent repression, dissent and opposition would be suppressed. In societies with relatively little repres-

TABLE 6.1
Major Events in the Civil Rights Struggle, 1954–1967

1954	In *Brown v. Board of Education,* developed and argued by the National Association of Colored People (NAACP), the U.S. Supreme Court bans segregation in public schools.
1955	To end bus segregation, the Montgomery Improvement Association, with Dr. Martin Luther King, Jr., as president, launches bus boycott in Montgomery, Alabama.
1956	December 21, after more than a year of people boycotting the buses and legal actions, the Montgomery buses are desegregated.
1957	At previously all-White Central High in Little Rock, Arkansas, 1,000 paratroopers are called by president to restore order and escort nine Black students.
1960	February, the sit-in protest movement begins at a Woolworth's lunch counter in Greensboro, N.C., and spreads across the nation.
1961	Freedom rides begin from Washington, D.C. Groups of Black and White people ride buses through the South, challenging segregation.
1962	Two killed, many injured in riots as James Meredith is enrolled as the first Black student at the University of Mississippi.
1963	Police arrest King and other ministers demonstrating in Birmingham, Alabama, and turn fire hoses and police dogs on the marchers. 250,000 attend the March in Washington, D.C., urging support for pending civil rights legislation. September 15, four girls killed in bombing of the Sixteenth Street Baptist Church in Birmingham, Alabama.
1964	Three civil rights workers are murdered in Mississippi. July 2, President Johnson signs Civil Rights Act of 1964.
1965	Selma, Alabama, voting rights campaign waged. August 6, President Johnson signs Voting Rights Act of 1965, authorizing federal examiners to register qualified voters and suspend devices aimed at preventing African Americans from voting.
1968	April 4, King assassinated in Memphis, Tennessee, unleashing violence in more than 100 cities.

sion, opposition could be expressed nonviolently. There is consistent evidence of such a curvilinear relationship between the repressiveness of governments and domestic political violence. For example, several cross-national, quantitative studies have been conducted relating political violence to regime repressiveness and other factors. Typically, regression analysis has been used, sometimes for the same years and sometimes lagging violence five years after the measure of repressiveness. The expected curvilinear relationship has been consistently found.[51]

The quiet order of a society with a repressive regime is considered here to be a relatively destructive condition. Struggles resulting in overturning a repressive regime would contribute to a relatively constructive outcome. How constructively waged struggles may produce such outcomes is considered in later chapters.

Regarding interstate conflicts, a great deal of theorizing and research has been done about the effectiveness of military strength as a way of preventing wars. On the one hand, the argument of traditional "realists" is that wars are prevented by having the military strength to deter attack. On the other hand, critics of that approach argue that as each side arms to deter the other, the resulting arms races generate mutual fear and hostility and escalate disputes into wars.

The evidence indicates that arms races increase the likelihood that serious interstate disputes will escalate to war.[52] This is the case when the dispute is between states who are rivals and contiguous. The evidence does not indicate that an arms race by itself will result in a war, but that it contributes to a resort to war in the context of an ongoing crisis or militarized dispute. Furthermore, bullying strategies in militarized situations tend to escalate disputes into war.[53]

One form of overreaction is an overgeneralization in identifying the enemy. In those circumstances, employment of violence may be indiscriminate or threats to use violence tend to be broad, injuring or threatening to injure persons who are not directly engaged in the struggle. Those impacted by the broadness of the attack are made parties to the fight, thus increasing the scope and probably the severity of the struggle.

Even punitive reactions by authorities, if they are narrowly focused and limited, are likely to avoid escalation, particularly if legitimate channels for protest are available. For example, consider the evolution of the Puerto Rican national independence movement. Shortly after World War II, steps toward the establishment of commonwealth status for Puerto Rico were taken by the U.S. Congress, President Harry Truman, and the Puerto Rican Legislative Assembly.[54] Some Puerto Ricans, however, favored independence, and in 1950 a group of Puerto Rican nationalists unsatisfied with the electoral strategy of the political party favoring independence, the *Partido Independentista Puertorriqueno* (PIP), occupied two towns in Puerto Rico and attacked the governor's mansion. The towns were retaken and the attack repulsed; thirty-three persons were killed, and arrests were made throughout Puerto Rico. Two Puerto Rican nationalists also attacked Blair House where President Truman was living while the White House was undergoing repairs. One of the attackers and a police officer were killed. Later, in 1954, after the commonwealth status had been overwhelmingly approved in Puerto Rican elections, four nationalists entered the visitors' gallery of the U.S. House of Representatives, shooting wildly.

During the 1950s, the PIP sought to dissociate itself from those nationalist tactics. The nationalist activities remained relatively isolated, and the PIP garnered few votes in subsequent elections. Instead, support for statehood as an alternative to commonwealth status has increased but has not won majority support. Social and economic developments, suppression of violent attacks and avoidance of general repression, and the openness of the electoral political process have limited the appeals of independence and channeled the struggle within the political system.

Underreaction

Mild or conciliatory reactions to threats or challenging acts sometimes perversely result in conflict escalation. The 1938 meeting in Munich where the British and French governments yielded to Nazi Germany's demands regarding its incorporation of the Sudetenland region of Czechoslovakia is the most notorious example of the escalating consequences of a policy of appeasement.

Even resistance that is overwhelmed may also result in the opponent raising its demands, since goals generally expand as the opportunity allows. For example, after the communist North Korean military forces crossed the 38th parallel in June 1950, they quickly moved south occupying more and more South Korean territory. U.S. military forces, aiding the South Korean forces under United Nations authority, fell back but then advanced. They did not stop when they reached the old border, the 38th parallel, but continued northward. Even suggestions of establishing buffer zones below the Yalu River bordering the People's Republic of China were ignored. As Richard Neustadt observed, "Appetites rose as the troops went forward."[55]

The risk of an underreaction is that it appears to signal weakness and whets the appetite of the adversary. It may, however, offer enough to the challenging party that the conflict shifts to a less-confrontational mode and de-escalating negotiations may be initiated. The Mexican government's response to the uprising in the state of Chiapas, in southeastern Mexico, is illustrative. On 1 January 1994, hundreds of armed Indian peasants, members of the Zapatista Army of National Liberation, stormed four towns in Chiapas. Some police officers were killed, and the Mexican army moved in to suppress the action that bordered on open rebellion; a very bloody, destructive struggle appeared likely. But very quickly, the government chose a more conciliatory strategy and negotiations between the federal government and the Zapatistas regarding fundamental reforms were undertaken.[56]

We have noted that either a too hard or a too soft reaction can escalate a struggle, each under differing circumstances. The discussion indicates that narrowly focused and proportionate responses characterize a likely effective middle course. Furthermore, acknowledgment of the opponent's legitimate needs and the availability of nonviolent channels contribute to avoiding destructive escalation. In chapter 7, which deals with de-escalation, we will examine strategies of response that are neither too hard nor too soft, and that contribute to constructive escalation and de-escalation.

Social Context

As discussed in chapter 5, the social context of a struggle influences the adoption of conflict strategies in many ways, for example by providing models of effective policies and as the source of interventions. Those and other contextual processes and factors therefore also affect the shift from less to more severe sanctions and from smaller to larger struggles.

Linkages

The extent to which each partisan in a fight is linked with other persons, groups, and organizations is critical in the expansion of a struggle's scope. Thus, friends and relatives tend to be drawn into interpersonal fights. Thus, too, as suggested by resource mobilization theory, organizations allied by ideology, previous alliances, or other network connections tend to be mobilized for assistance once a struggle has begun. This is also demonstrated by the evidence that interstate alliances tend to spread a dyadic militarized dispute or war to a multiple-party war or world war.[57]

Other Conflicts

Another important aspect of the context of a particular struggle is the partisans' engagement in other struggles. Thus, when an additional conflict becomes superimposed on a given struggle, both tend to escalate and be prolonged. For example, in 1936, when the rebellious military forces led by General Francisco Franco sought to overthrow the elected Spanish government, the Fascist states of Germany and Italy gave extensive military assistance to the rebels.[58] The Soviet government and nongovernmental anti-Fascist organizations from many countries in the world came to the aid of the Spanish government and the forces loyal to it. The Spanish Civil War was long and bloody, in part because the internal adversaries thought they could persist and triumph with external support. This was true for the Fascists, who overwhelmed the Spanish government forces in 1939.

Sometimes, too, a conflict within one of the major adversaries in a particular struggle, rather than being subordinated in the struggle against a common enemy, escalates. One or both sides in the subordinate conflict may regard the larger struggle as an opportunity to escalate its own fight. In the shadow of the larger struggle, brutal suppression or genocidal policies may be undertaken. Thus, the genocidal suppression of Armenians by the Ottoman authorities occurred when the Ottoman Empire was engaged in World War I.[59]

Intervention

Other parties in the social environment generally play significant roles affecting the course of a struggle. They may act to escalate or prolong a conflict by joining the struggle on one side, helping to sustain it, and so gain advantages for themselves. They may also pursue policies to contain the conflict, barring support to all sides in the struggle. Finally, they may provide intermediary services to facilitate a de-escalation of the struggle. Actors outside a given struggle affect the struggle's escalation and likely outcome by their inaction as well as action. Partisans, particularly those who feel weak, seek assistance from those not yet involved in the struggle. The failure to intervene, then, appears at least as acquiescence in the way the conflict is going.

Conclusions

Clearly there are many factors, processes, conditions, and policies that may contribute to the escalation of struggles and their prolongation, often in a destructive manner. The policies pursued by partisans and outsiders can have such effects intentionally, but frequently they are unintentional. Better understanding of how various policies affect the likelihood of destructive escalation can help reduce its unwanted occurrence.

The number of processes that combine to account for the deterioration of struggles is illustrated by the terrible fighting in the former Yugoslavia.[60] As we discussed, several processes internal to each adversary party foster conflict escalation and prolongation, often of a destructive character. These include social-psychological processes relating to cognitive dissonance, entrapment, and emotional reactions to the stress of struggle. One implication of cognitive dissonance is that if people can be induced to act in a brutal manner, they need to justify their conduct, blaming the other side for their brutality is a likely justification. Entrapment is another process that makes interrupting an escalating conflict difficult, as the costs make yielding seem more and more like a betrayal of those already sacrificed. For many, the emotional burden of facing and having endured great pain and fear evokes feelings of humiliation and rage. These insights help make explicable the surprisingly brutal escalation of fighting among persons identified as Serbs, Croats, and Bosnians.

The internal organizational developments discussed also contribute to explaining the destructive escalation of conflicts between certain ethnic groups in the former Yugoslavia. Political leaders in each community mobilized support for themselves, as the communist ideology and party structure dissolved, by making appeals to ethnic solidarity and in hostility to other ethnic communities. Once the struggle escalated into extreme violence, many people fled and accommodationist voices were stilled. The interaction among the communities deteriorated in a series of reciprocated acts, as policies within each piece of territory ruled by the dominant community offered little assurance of security to the minority communities.[61] The vital interests of other communities were accorded little legitimacy by the leadership of each community. Despite considerable integration between members of the various communal groups in many parts of the former Yugoslavia, once the ethnic cleansing, mass executions, and systematic raping was taking place, polarization between the communities was extremely difficult to bridge.

Other parties were attentive to this increasing destructive escalation, but their policies were generally ineffective in stemming the deterioration. Private relief organizations, United Nations specialized agencies, and many governments helped to alleviate the worst misery of the refugees and other victims of the struggle. But, the policy inconsistencies among the major states attempting to control the conflicts prevented the implementation of a coherent strategy of intervention. For example, Croatia and Bosnia-Herzegovina were encouraged by Germany and other European states to declare independence, without first providing assurances for the ethnic Serbs living in the territory of what were to become new countries. Mediation efforts were conducted, but were often undermined by changes in the fighting situation or by suggestions that a better deal might be forthcoming, for example, for the Bosnian government, which had lost much territory. Only later did more forceful intervention and mediation stop the killing. How struggles that have escalated into a destructive intractable conflict finally have been transformed and become tractable is discussed in the next chapter.

Notes

1. See Morton Deutsch, *The Resolution of Conflict: Constructive and Destructive Processes* (New Haven, Conn.: Yale University Press, 1973); and Adam Curle, *Making Peace* (London: Tavistock, 1971).

2. For example, see James Coleman, *Community Conflict* (New York: The Free Press, 1957); and Terrell A. Northrup, "The Dynamic of Identity in Personal and

Social Conflict," in *Intractable Conflicts and Their Transformation*, ed. Louis Kriesberg, Terrell A. Northrup, and Stuart J. Thorson (Syracuse, N.Y.: Syracuse University Press, 1989).

3. Leon Festinger, *A Theory of Cognitive Dissonance* (Evanston, Ill.: Row, Peterson, 1957).

4. Joel Brockner and Jeffrey Z. Rubin, *Entrapment in Escalating Conflicts: A Social Psychological Analysis* (New York: Springer-Verlag, 1985), 5.

5. Considerable research has been done on these matters, based on social-psychological experiments, case studies of international crises, and other kinds of data. See for example, James A. Robinson, Charles F. Hermann, and Margaret C. Hermann, "Search under Crisis in Political Gaming and Simulation," in *Theory and Research on the Causes of War*, ed. Dean G. Pruitt and Richard C. Snyder (Englewood Cliffs, N.J.: Prentice-Hall, 1969); Raymond Cohen, *Threat Perception in International Crisis* (Madison: Wisconsin University Press, 1979); and Patrick J. McGowan and Charles W. Kegley, Jr., eds. *Threats, Weapons, and Foreign Policy* (Beverly Hills, Calif.: Sage, 1980).

6. Thomas J. Scheff, *Bloody Revenge: Emotions, Nationalism, and War* (Boulder, Colo.: Westview, 1994).

7. Gerald A. McWorter and Robert L. Crain, "Subcommunity Gladiatorial Competition: Civil Rights Leadership as a Competitive Process," *Social Forces* 46 (September 1967): 8–21.

8. Fred Charles Ikle, *Every War Must End* (New York: Columbia University Press, 1971).

9. See the account of U.S. policy making regarding Vietnam in David Halberstam, *The Best and the Brightest* (New York: Fawcet, 1973).

10. Coleman, *Community Conflict*, 12.

11. Samuel A. Stouffer, *Communism, Conformity, and Civil Liberties* (New York: Doubleday, 1955).

12. William Brink and Louis Harris, *Black and White* (New York: Simon & Schuster, 1969), appendix D.

13. The Ohio National Guard fired into a milling crowd of students at Kent State University, killing four persons and wounding nine others. See Kenneth J. Heinman, " 'Look Out Kid, You're Gonna Get Hit!' Kent State and the Vietnam Antiwar Movement," in *Give Peace a Chance: Exploring the Vietnam Antiwar Movement*, ed. Melvin Small and William D. Hoover (Syracuse, N.Y.: Syracuse University Press, 1992).

14. Charles DeBenedeti and Charles Chatfield, *An American Ordeal: The Antiwar Movement of the Vietnam Era* (Syracuse, N.Y.: Syracuse University Press, 1990), 278–80.

15. Based on personal interviews with students at Syracuse University at the time it was shut down by protesting students.

16. For example, when the Soviet rocket units built the bases in Cuba for the nuclear-tipped missiles, they did so following their standard procedures, laying out on the ground their insignia. That certainly eased the task of discovering the bases by U.S. intelligence flights. See Graham Allison, *The Essence of Decision* (Boston: Little, Brown, 1971).

17. For example, Chile had a long tradition of political civility, but this was brutally interrupted in 1973. The democratically elected government led by Salvador Allende,

had been subjected to destabilizing efforts, many undertaken by the U.S. government, including covert actions by the Central Intelligence Agency. A military junta led by General Augusto Pinochet seized power on 11 September 1973 and unleashed a bloody repression. See Samuel Chavkin, *The Murder of Chile* (New York: Everest House, 1982).

18. Thus, the German kaiser seemed to feel that once mobilization had been ordered, he was unable to halt or even modify the next steps, and the war came. See Barbara W. Tuchman, *The Guns of August* (New York: Macmillan, 1962).

19. John A. Vasquez, *The War Puzzle* (Cambridge: Cambridge University Press, 1993).

20. Ted Robert Gurr, *Why Men Rebel* (Princeton, N.J.: Princeton University Press, 1970), 35; Leonard Berkowitz, ed., *Roots of Aggression* (New York: Lieber-Atherton, 1969); and Vasquez, *The War Puzzle*.

21. Eleanor Flexner, *Century of Struggle* (Cambridge, Mass.: Harvard University Press, 1959), 251.

22. That international conflicts are often initiated by drift is developed by Charles Lockhart, *Bargaining in International Conflicts* (New York: Columbia University Press, 1979), 140–41; also see Glenn H. Snyder and Paul Diesing, *Conflict among Nations: Bargaining, Decision Making, and System Structure in International Crises* (Princeton, N.J.: Princeton University Press, 1977), 96–97.

23. Henry Near, ed., *The Seventh Day: Soldiers Talk About the Six-Day War* (London: Penguin 1971).

24. Ikle, *Every War Must End.*

25. See Robert Shaplen, "Scarsdale's Battle of the Books," *Commentary* 10 (December 1950): 530–40.

26. Kjell Skjelsbaek and J. David Singer, "Shared IGO Memberships and Dyadic War, 1865–1964," paper presented to the Conference on the United Nations, Center for International Studies, 1971.

27. Harry Eckstein, ed., *Internal War: Problems and Approaches* (New York: The Free Press, 1966).

28. Gurr, *Why Men Rebel*, 270–71.

29. Barbara W. Tuchman, *The Zimmermann Telegram* (New York: The Viking Press, 1958).

30. Edward E. Azar, "The Analysis and Management of Protracted Conflicts," in *The Psychodynamics of International Relationships, vol. 2,* ed. Vamik D. Volkan, Joseph V. Montville, and Demetrios A. Julius (Lexington, Mass.: Lexington, 1991), 93.

31. See Louis Kriesberg, "Moving Middle East Conflicts into and out of Intractibility," presented at a conference, Intractable Conflicts and the Potential for Peacemaking: The Middle East in the 1990s, held at the University of Dayton, 3 March 1992. For discussions of various aspects of intractable conflicts, see Louis Kriesberg, Terrell A. Northrup, and Stuart J. Thorson, eds., *Intractable Conflicts and Their Transformation* (Syracuse, N.Y.: Syracuse University Press, 1989). Also see Louis Kriesberg, "Intractable Conflicts," in *Handbook of Interethnic Coexistence,* ed. Eugene Weiner (New York: Continuum Press, 1998).

32. Kriesberg, *International Conflict Resolution.*

33. Inge Powell Bell, *CORE and the Strategy of Non-Violence* (New York: Random House, 1968), 115.

34. Theodore J. Lowi, "Making Democracy Safe for the World: National Politics and Foreign Policy," in *Domestic Sources of U.S. Foreign Policy*, ed. James Rosenau (New York: The Free Press, 1967); J. David Singer, ed., *The Correlates of War*, vol. 1. *Research Origins and Rationale* (New York: The Free Press, 1979).

35. See Russell J. Leng, "Influence Strategies and Interstate Conflict," in *The Correlates of War*, vol. 2, ed. J. D. Singer (New York: The Free Press, 1980).

36. Ernesto Guevara, *"Che" Guevara on Revolution*, ed, Jay Mallin (New York: Delta, 1969), 30. Guevara participated in another such attempt in Bolivia and was captured and killed there in 1967.

37. See Louis Kriesberg, "Regional Conflicts in the Post–Cold War Era: Causes, Dynamics, and Modes of Resolution," in *World Security: Challenges for a New Century*, ed. Michael T. Klare and Daniel C. Thomas (New York: St. Martin's Press, 1994). Also see Jorge I. Dominguez, "Pipsqueak Power: The Centrality and Anomaly of Cuba," in *The Suffering Grass: Superpowers and Regional Conflict in Southern Africa and the Caribbean*, ed. Thomas G. Weiss and James G. Blight (Boulder, Colo.: Lynne Rienner, 1992).

38. Anthony Oberschall, "Group Violence: Some Hypotheses and Empirical Uniformities," paper presented at the meetings of the American Sociological Association, 1969.

39. The Cuban government objected to the agreement. See Ole R. Holsti, Richard A. Brody, and Robert C. North, "Measuring Affect and Action in International Reaction Models: Empirical Materials from the 1962 Cuban Crisis," *Journal of Peace Research*, nos. 3–4 (1964): 170–89.

40. Charles S. Gochman and Zeev Moaz, "Militarized Interstate Disputes, 1816–1976: Procedures, Patterns, and Insights," *Journal of Conflict Resolution* 28 (December 1984): 585–616; also see review of literature by Vasquez, *The War Puzzle*, 191 ff.

41. Northrup, "The Dynamic of Identity."

42. Jules J. Wanderer, "An Index of Riot Severity and Some Correlates," *American Journal of Sociology* 74 (March 1969): 500–505.

43. William A. Gamson and Andre Modigliani, *Untangling the Cold War* (Boston: Little, Brown, 1971).

44. Kriesberg, *International Conflict Resolution*.

45. George H. Quester, "Wars Prolonged by Misunderstood Signals," *The Annals of the American Academy of Political and Social Science* 392 (November 1970): 30–39.

46. Vasquez, *The War Puzzle*, 200–216. Also see Snyder and Diesing, *Conflict Among Nations*; and Eugene R. Wittkopf and Michael A. Maggiotto, "Elites and Masses: A Comparative Analysis of Attitudes toward America's Role," *Journal of Politics* 45 (May 1983): 303–34.

47. Daniel Walker and others, *Rights in Conflict: A Report to the National Commission on the Causes and Prevention of Violence* (New York: Bantam, 1968); and John P. Robinson, "Public Reaction to Political Protest: Chicago 1968," *Public Opinion Quarterly* 34 (Spring 1970): 1–9.

48. The President's Commission on Campus Unrest, *Campus Unrest* (Washington, D.C.: U.S. Government Printing Office, 1970).

49. Among those who did not see the police action, 28 percent of the faculty and 41 percent of the students thought the police action was brutal, compared with 66

percent and 74 percent of the faculty and students, respectively, who did see it. See Allen H. Barton, "The Columbia Crisis: Campus, Vietnam, and the Ghetto," *Public Opinion Quarterly* 32 (Fall 1968): 331–51.

50. For example, in only 2 percent of the cases in which there was no confrontation did the protest expand; in 50 percent of the schools in which police were used, protest expanded; and in 73 percent of the cases in which some demonstrators were arrested by the police, there was expansion of the protest. See William R. Morgan, "Faculty Mediation of Student War Protests," in *Protest! Student Activism in America*, ed. Julian Foster and Durward Long (New York: Morrow, 1970). For an analysis of the effects of various Israeli government responses to Palestinian resistance, see Marwan Khawaja, "Repression and Popular Collective Action in the West Bank: A Test of Rival Explanations," *Sociological Forum* 8 (March 1993): 47–71.

51. Studies have included from twenty-five to forty-eight countries, for periods in the 1950s, 1960s, and 1970s. See Erich Weede, "Some New Evidence on Correlates of Political Violence: Income Inequality, Regime Repressiveness, and Economic Development," *European Sociological Review* 3 (September 1987): 97–108; Edward N. Muller, "Income Inequality, Regime Repressiveness, and Political Violence," *American Sociological Review* 50 (February 1985): 47–61; Erich Weede, "Income Inequality and Political Violence Reconsidered," *American Sociological Review* 51 (June 1986): 438–41; also see Jennifer G. Walton, "Correlates of Coerciveness and Permissiveness of National Political Systems: A Cross-National Study," M.A. thesis, San Diego State College, 1965, cited in Gurr, *Why Men Rebel*, 250.

52. Vasquez, *The War Puzzle*, 177–84; Michael D. Wallace, "Armaments and Escalation: Two Competing Hypotheses," *International Studies Quarterly* 26 (March 1982): 37–51; and Henk W. Houweling and Jan G. Siccama, "The Arms Race—War Relationship: Why Serious Disputes Matter," *Arms Control* 2 (September 1981): 157–97.

53. Russell J. Leng and Hugh Wheeler, "Influence Strategies, Success, and War," *Journal of Conflict Resolution* 23 (December 1979): 655–84.

54. Arturo Morales Carrion, *Puerto Rico: A Political and Cultural History* (New York: W.W. Norton, 1983), 276 ff.

55. Richard Neustadt, *Presidential Power* (New York: John Wiley, 1960), 127. Also see Glenn Paige, *The Korean Decision* (New York: The Free Press, 1968).

56. John Ross, *Rebellion from the Roots: Indian Uprising in Chiapas* (Monroe, Maine: Common Courage Press, 1995); Phillip L. Russell, *The Chiapas Rebellion* (Austin, Tex.: Mexico Resource Center, 1995); and Raul Trejo Delarbre, *Chiapas: La Guerra de las Ideas* (Mexico, D.F.: Editorial Diana, 1994).

57. Vasquez, *The War Puzzle*, 233.

58. Hugh Thomas, *The Spanish Civil War*, 3d ed. (New York: Harper & Row, 1977); and Sheelagh M. Ellwood, *The Spanish Civil War* (Oxford: Blackwell, 1991).

59. See Rouben P. Adalian, "The Armenian Genocide: Revisionism and Denial," in *Genocide in Our Time: An Annotated Bibliography with Analytical Introductions*, ed. Michael N. Dobkowski and Isidor Walliman (Ann Arbor, Mich.: The Pierian Press, 1992); Vahakn N. Dadrian, "The Documentation of the World War I Armenian Massacres in the Proceedings of the Turkish Military Tribunal," *International Journal of Middle East Studies* 23 (1991): 549–76.

60. Misha Glenny, *The Fall of Yugoslavia* (New York: Penguin, 1992).

61. During the Second World War, Nazi Germany established the Independent State of Croatia; the Croatian fascists, the Ustashas, killed hundreds of thousands of Serbs, Jews, Gypsies, and members of the Croat opposition. The Serbs in Croatia feared the emergence of a Croat-dominated state. The new president of Croatia, Franjo Tuchman, made no gesture of reconciliation, which might have alleviated some of the fear felt by the Serbs. See Glenny, *The Fall of Yugoslavia*, 10–82.

7

De-escalating Conflicts

very struggle de-escalates eventually. However intractable and destructive a struggle may be, at some time it decreases in the severity of the
means used and/or in the number of parties engaged in the struggle.
Those decreases are not always a prelude to a conflict's ending, but when a
conflict does end, de-escalation has generally preceded it. In the 1990s, a series
of remarkable de-escalating transformations occurred in many regions of the
world. The cold war between the United States and the Union of Soviet Socialist Republics, which had dominated the world system and threatened a
nuclear catastrophe, was transformed and then ended. In South Africa, after
decades of often violent struggle about the maintenance of the oppressive
system of apartheid, constructive escalation contributed to the shift to a fundamental de-escalation, leading toward a constructive outcome. Remarkable
shifts toward de-escalation also occurred in the relations between the Palestine Liberation Organization (PLO) and the Israeli government and among
the British and Irish governments and the Republican Catholics and Unionist
Protestants of Northern Ireland.

Although such dramatic transformations command our attention, the
transitions from escalation to de-escalation and the implementation of de-
escalation policies have not been systematically researched and analyzed. Contributions to that analysis are made in this chapter, examining how escalation
ceases and resistance to actual de-escalation is overcome. Some of the processes producing de-escalation are the same ones discussed earlier as contributing to escalation; but in different circumstances, they have different effects.
The changing conditions that make de-escalation probable are also examined,
focusing on seemingly intractable struggles. Finally, we analyze the policies
that partisans and intermediaries may pursue that help de-escalate conflicts.

Processes of De-escalation

The processes of de-escalation, like those of escalation, occur within each adversary, in the relations between the adversaries, and also among other parties in the social environment. In the case of large-scale, long-lasting struggles, generally the effects of these various processes must converge and reenforce each other for de-escalation of protracted conflicts to proceed.

Internal Processes

Within each adversary, both social-psychological and organizational developments contribute to conflict de-escalation. They contribute to members of an adversary group considering their own responsibility for the conflict's course rather than simply blaming the other side. They also help in reframing the conflict so that a mutually beneficial outcome seems possible. We examine those processes as they occur under varying conditions, particularly conditions that are modifiable by policy choices.

Social-Psychological Processes

In chapter 6, we discussed how cognitive dissonance, entrapment, and certain other cognitive and affective processes contribute to conflict escalation. Here we consider how the effects of these and related social-psychological processes contribute to de-escalating movement.

Cognitive dissonance theory suggests that if people can be brought to make conciliatory moves toward an adversary, they will tend to justify their actions and value what they have done. Evidence for this can be found in survey data about approval of the country's president. This assumes that people regard actions taken in the name of an entity with which they identify, such as their country, as their own. For example, there is much evidence that Americans will "rally-round-the flag." That is, they will support a military action or other forceful foreign policy initiative of their government or president, and even increase their approval of the president during that period.[1] Leaders anticipating this, may more readily undertake escalating moves. There is also survey evidence, however, that approval of the president will rise if he undertakes a conciliatory action.[2] That is less widely assumed and therefore less likely to affect conduct.

In any case, once having undertaken conciliatory actions, as with confrontational actions, legitimate leaders can count on at least initial support and approval. If the actions prove beneficial and there is reciprocation, de-escalating movement is likely. This is illustrated by the approval won by President Richard M. Nixon for his conciliatory initiatives in the early 1970s toward the Soviet government and the Chinese government that contributed so much to the rapid movement toward détente between the United States and the USSR and between the United States and the People's Republic of China.

Once actions toward de-escalation have been taken, the goal previously sought may become devalued. That is a way to bring consistency between the values desired and the actual conduct. Aesop's fox gave up trying to get the grapes it could not reach, explaining they were sour anyway. This "sour grapes" mechanism helps explain how at least some people handle thinking they had been wrong. Thus, many Whites in the South, once the struggle to maintain legal segregation was defeated, recognized many moral and economic benefits from the newly emerging relations and began to regard the old segregation system as wrong.

Entrapment, another process usually fostering escalation, can be controlled to help avoid escalation. A variety of experimental evidence indicates, for example, that if, at the start, individuals set limits on how far they will go, prior to embarking on a possibly entrapping course, they will tend to avoid entrapment.[3] Public commitment probably strengthens that effect. This supports the actions that the U.S. president and/or Congress have taken in the 1990s, limiting the time commitment for U.S. participation in peacekeeping missions. However, in a conflict situation, if adversary "A" knows that conflict party "B" has set a limit, "A" may try to push "B" to that limit and a little beyond, winning the fight.

Entrapment tends to be avoided if people reflect on the risks of entrapment, for example, by having been told about the concept of entrapment or having experienced it dramatically. The gradual increase in American engagement in the war in Vietnam is widely considered a powerful example of entrapment; the engagement crept up and up and disengaging then became extremely difficult. The danger of entrapment has influenced U.S. foreign policy and military doctrine since then, but it has not always resulted in an avoidance of any escalation.[4] One response has been to intervene with overwhelming force, and for specific goals, when the decision to escalate has been made. This was the strategy in the U.S.-led war in 1991 to end Iraqi annexation of Kuwait.[5] Another response has been to "cut losses" and end the struggle when it escalates markedly. Thus, U.S. military forces were withdrawn from Lebanon immediately after 241 U.S. Marines were killed in the 23 October 1983 truck-bombing of their barracks in Beirut, Lebanon.[6]

Finally, the response may be to avoid entering a struggle in which creeping escalation and entrapment seems likely. Thus, a concern to avoid repeating the Vietnam experience has inhibited U.S. military intervention on the ground in the fighting within the former Yugoslavia. Anthony Lake, then President Bill Clinton's national security adviser, reflecting about the situation in Bosnia observed in early 1995, "There are a lot of practical lessons that come out of Vietnam. Think ahead. Don't make commitments that you can't meet. And don't just wander into something."[7]

Yet certain aspects of entrapment sometimes contribute directly to de-escalation. Once adversaries have taken initiating actions to de-escalate their conflict with each other, the process of entrapment may contribute to keeping them on that course. Taking de-escalating action in a conflict usually has some costs, and each adversary therefore has made some investment in this course. The dynamics of entrapment is that one or both sides may find itself making greater and greater concessions in order to proceed consistently. Even though one or more parties, therefore, may feel trapped, it may yield more than it had anticipated in order not to lose the investments already made. After all, the party abandoning the movement toward settlement would appear inconsistent and be admitting that its previous actions had been mistaken.

Other conflict-escalating effects of the emotional and cognitive processes discussed in chapter 6 also can be controlled and even contribute to de-escalation. Thus, the effects of earlier personal experiences interfering with accurate perceptions of current situations and relationships can be reduced by awareness of such risks. Such insight can be learned from training in workshops, personal therapy, and by reflection. Furthermore, persons who represent conflict groups in adversarial relations may be selected in ways that reduce the likelihood that they tend to be greatly affected by emotional processes that dispose them to engage in destructive conflict. Thus, persons selected through open, nonviolent means are probably less prone to engage in destructive conflict escalation than those who have won leadership by their own manipulative and violent conduct.

Additional cognitive and affective processes significantly contribute to conflict de-escalation. Sympathizing and empathizing with others are such processes, and certain policies and experiences can trigger and sustain these processes, even between enemies. A person sympathizing with another person feels along with that other human, and is emotionally moved by the other's feelings.[8] Being sympathetic to another person or members of another group tends to inhibit acting to inflict harm on them; indeed, it would evoke actions to help them.

The construct of empathy, compared with sympathy, stresses taking the role of the other, without losing one's identity.[9] Among the several components often noted as constituting empathy, four are particularly relevant for ameliorating conflict escalation. First, empathy includes accurately perceiving the other person's feelings and thoughts relating to the conflict. Second, the empathetic person experiences those feelings and thoughts "as-if" they were his or her own. Third, the person distinguishes his own thoughts and feelings from those of the person with whom he empathizes. Finally, empathy includes communicating the experience of empathy. This may be most fully realized in a therapeutic or intimate interpersonal relationship, but some degree of these various components also occurs in more mundane relations and in social conflicts.

Varying proportions of the members of a conflict party may empathize, in different degrees, with their adversary. Signs of empathy may be seen in the novels, plays, and statements by Whites in South Africa regarding the circumstances of Blacks there.[10] Empathy occurs among members of each side toward members of the other, for example between some Israeli Jews and Arab Palestinians.[11] Such empathy helps construct plausible and credible de-escalating steps.

Organizational Processes

Several processes within one or more conflict parties contribute to de-escalation. Under certain conditions, leadership competition may foster de-escalation rather than escalation. The development of a constituency for accommodation is an important condition for the emergence of a viable alternative leadership; the emergence of alternative leadership, in turn, tends to give legitimacy to further dissent from the hard-line policies sustaining conflict escalation.

Constituencies for de-escalation arise from many sources. The costs of continuing a struggle grow as the struggle goes on, raising doubts about the benefit of the goals sought. Moreover, the burdens of a long, escalating struggle often become increasingly unequal. The unfairness of that inequality arouses dissent and withdrawal of support; in a war, this may take the form of draft riots, desertion, and flight. This is illustrated by the Russian Imperial army's 1917 resistance to the war against Germany and its allies, resulting in Russia's withdrawal from the war.

Leaders sometimes seek to stifle dissent among their constituencies in order to sustain a struggle. But trying to suppress dissent often drives people into further opposition. Branding people as disloyal can provoke acts of disloyalty. This even occurs in democratic societies, such as the United States.[12]

Dissent and opposition to official hard-line policies can be mobilized readily insofar as groups of people favoring accommodation with the adversary are already present and are linked by networks of communication. Thus, in the United States during the 1960s, opponents to the U.S. intervention in Vietnam were able to mobilize demonstrations and other acts of resistance by their ties to previous peace movement organizations, to traditional peace churches, to student organizations, and to civil rights organizations.[13]

As a struggle escalates, increased severity of the means used by an individual or faction within a conflict party sometimes crosses the boundary of majority opinion regarding acceptable conduct, and the movement as a whole suffers. When a small group of persons affiliated with a cause commits what most affiliated persons regard as outrageous acts, the cause may lose constituent support and legitimacy. We noted this in the struggle for Puerto Rican independence. To some degree, this also happened in 1970 in the struggle for the independence of Quebec from Canada.[14] In the 1960s, the Quebec separatist movement grew rapidly, and the Front de Liberation du Quebec (FLQ), a tiny Maoist organization, carried out bombings and conducted robberies for funds. These actions culminated in October 1970 with the kidnapping of two officials, one of whom was killed. Prime Minister Trudeau invoked the War Measures Act, and the FLQ was made illegal. Violence as a means of winning independence was generally repudiated, and since then the separatist movement has used electoral and negotiation methods.

In the 1990s, many acts of violence in the United States were directed at physicians who performed abortions and at clinics where abortions were provided. This prompted reactions that tended to marginalize the more extreme groups within the right to life movement and encouraged moderation in means; even efforts to search for common ground with supporters of the freedom of choice movement were advanced.

The processes that limit consideration of alternatives in times of crises tend to engender further escalation. Some circumstances and policies, however, can reduce those destructive effects. Decision making by a broad and diverse group of persons and procedures that foster free discussion ensure consideration of alternatives. President John F. Kennedy's handling of the Cuban missile crisis, in this regard, is often regarded as exemplary.[15] When President Kennedy was presented evidence of Soviet missiles in Cuba, on 16 October 1962, he called together a small but diverse group to consider possible responses. The group met secretly for six days, considered several possible responses, gathered information about the alternatives, and discussed each. In order to encourage open discussion and to avoid early closure on a decision, the president did not participate in all discussions.

Finally, once de-escalation has gotten under way, several organizational processes can come into play that make turning back difficult. The road to peace sometimes becomes a slippery slope. Leaders who have undertaken the first de-escalating steps are reluctant to appear to have made a mistake by changing the course they have begun. Furthermore, their actions sometimes have actually altered the relations within their party and with other organizations, so that new vested interests in continuing to de-escalate have emerged. Particularly if large, public steps have been taken, the new course may seem irreversible. For example, after the 13 September 1993 mutual recognition between the PLO and the Israeli government and the agreement to establish Palestinian control in Gaza and Jericho, the signatories were committed to continuing the peace process path they had entered.[16] Nevertheless, if significant elements of either side can rally opposition to the process, a new leadership may gain control and interrupt the accommodation.

Interaction Processes

As discussed in chapter 6, three general processes pertaining to the interaction between adversaries foster conflict escalation: the logic of contentious interaction, the expansion of the issues at stake, and polarization. But other processes, also relating to adversary interaction, often contribute to de-escalation. These include reciprocity in interaction, issue containment, and linking between adversaries.

Reciprocity in Interaction

This analysis of reciprocity builds on the earlier discussion of the possible escalating consequences of over- and underreaction. In certain circumstances, an overreaction may suppress the adversary. Thus, a very strong escalation by one side may force the other to yield; the severe sanctions effectively force the other side to lower its resistance or to discontinue the struggle. Such impositions are unusual, however, unless the goals in contention are not highly significant to the imposed-upon party. Underreaction, within certain circumstances, may also bring about a de-escalation or even the termination of a struggle. Thus, one side may present such great concessions to its adversary that the adversary's goals are well satisfied, escalation does not occur, and the struggle de-escalates and may even cease.

The focus of this analysis is on struggles that are mutually de-escalated. Those de-escalations are more likely to be constructive than are unilaterally imposed de-escalations. Three related processes of adversary interaction help avoid destructive escalation and unilateral imposition: reacting equivalently, learning about the struggle and the adversary, and developing shared norms. In the first process, each side reacts in a measured and equivalent level to the other. In this scenario, one or both sides avoid acting in ways they think may be provocative or may invite an aggrandizing move by the other side. The response selected by President Kennedy and his advisors to the Soviet emplacement of missiles in Cuba in 1962 was a "quarantine." It was not a dismissal of the matter as of little consequence or simply a protest at the United Nations, nor was it a provocative air strike or an invasion of Cuba. President Kennedy had recently read Barbara Tuchman's book *The Guns of August*, about the outbreak of World War I, and was determined to allow time and space for discovering acceptable ways out of the crisis, avoiding a runaway escalation of words and actions.[17] Having drawn that lesson from history, he took what he regarded as a measured response, which would not provoke an escalating interaction. He also communicated directly with Soviet chairman Nikita S. Khrushchev, inviting interaction, and he closely monitored the operations of the U.S. quarantine.[18] The actions by each side during the crisis were roughly equivalent.[19]

The second interaction process that is often de-escalating is learning from experience with the adversary. Learning about conflicts in general or about a particular struggle encompasses a wide variety of phenomena.[20] Here, it refers to adversaries understanding more about each other and their conflict as they contentiously interact in recurrent disputes. As each side learns more about the other, each makes better estimates of how the other side will react to its actions. That reduces the likelihood of unintentional and ineffective escalation.

Learning occurs at the collective level as well as at the individual level, and over a period of months or years. For example, the governments of the United States and the USSR, over years, became more familiar with each other's thinking about arms control and nuclear nonproliferation and developed ways to cooperate in these areas. Studies also indicate that officials representing their government in international conflicts learn much about their adversary.[21]

Finally, adversaries sometimes develop shared norms guiding some arenas in which they are in contention. The rules themselves may be matters of dispute for a time, but once agreed upon, they provide guidance for waging a conflict that constrains the antagonists from escalating very far. Thus, collective bargaining between management and union representatives is carried out about certain matters, but not all matters about which workers and managers may disagree. In international affairs, normative regimes sometimes develop to stabilize and manage particular areas of recurrent disputes.[22]

Issue Containment

Although issues in a struggle often expand and spill over, incorporating other divisive matters, such expansion is not inevitable. An adversary may purposefully remain focused on a specific goal in order to isolate the opponent and concentrate its own energies. In 1963, Martin Luther King, Jr., and the Southern Christian Leadership Conference (SCLC) led the Blacks of Birmingham, Alabama, in an economic boycott, in demonstrations, in sit-ins, and into jail.[23] The success of the campaign is frequently attributed to the violence of the agents of social control as they sought to intimidate the demonstrators, thereby generating federal and other intervention, which supported the strikers. Although the local civil rights leaders did expand their goals to include national concerns, the local strategy remained paramount. King's group kept focused on Birmingham's economic elite and their goals were precise: they included desegregation of public facilities in downtown department stores, fair hiring procedures in retail stores and city departments, and appointing a biracial commission to set a timetable for the desegregation of the public schools. A variety of tactics were used, but the focus on specific goals was sustained.

As a struggle persists, issues can begin to contract. One of the adversaries, failing to attain its grand goals, may find settling for what it can get to be its best option. A conflict party that believes it is unable to impose its preferences will come to recognize that it must deal with its adversary. The great matters in contention between them tend to be broken down into more manageable subissues. When adversaries fractionate the conflict into specific issues, some may appear easily settled and trade-offs among several issues may seem possible.[24]

Finally, inflammatory issues may be contained by the development of superordinate goals; these are shared goals that are given primacy over the contentious ones. One kind of superordinate goal that sometimes emerges when a conflict persists is a mutual avoidance of destruction. Adversaries who think that continued escalation risks giving both sides their worst outcome may decide to coordinate their conduct to avoid such a result.[25]

Developing Ties between Adversaries

As a struggle persists and even escalates, some members of each side sometimes communicate with members of the other in order to facilitate a de-escalation of the conflict. They serve as quasi mediators, conveying information and suggestions between the antagonistic parties.[26] They also may develop bonds with each other and thus form an interest group within their own camps to de-escalate the conflict.

If the conflict persists with recurrent confrontations, the representatives of the opposing sides themselves often develop shared expectations about how the next confrontation will be handled. If previous confrontations were contained and settled in a mutually acceptable fashion, the next one is likely to be guided by the previous experience. This is particularly likely in a setting with an ongoing relationship between the adversaries, for example within a business organization.

Processes of Involvement with Other Parties

Adversaries contend with each other within a social context of many other parties, and some of the ways those other parties relate to the adversaries can foster de-escalation. First, they sometimes provide models of the way de-escalation may occur, or at least provide the vision that de-escalation is feasible. Thus, to bring about the transformation of Rhodesia to Zimbabwe and end internal warfare, a system of transition was negotiated in 1979, mediated by Lord Carrington. This helped provide a model for arrangements in Namibia and other countries as well, to establish a system of transition for implementing cease-fires and providing procedures to legitimate new governments, for example, through monitored elections.[27]

Second, other parties often set limits to the escalation of a conflict, and intervene to enforce those limits. Thus, the state generally enforces certain constraints on the struggles between groups within a society. Such outside intervention may impose a cessation of the use of particularly destructive means to ensure that one of the adversaries is not too badly damaged. Increasingly, international governmental organizations and other governments have intervened within countries when its government has exercised extreme violence on its own people.

Finally, other parties frequently serve as intermediaries to assist the contending parties in finding a way to de-escalate their conflict, as examined in chapter 8. They may facilitate the antagonists' accepting a move toward de-escalating their struggle, for example, by providing a face-saving way out of the fight. This includes offering a proposal that an adversary would reject if made by its enemy, but accepts when suggested by a mediator. The intermediaries may also forcefully intervene and help impose a settlement of the conflict, but such intervention often only freezes the conflict at its current status.

Changing Conditions

De-escalation, in large measure, occurs as a result of changes in the conditions that underlay the emergence of a conflict in the first place and sustained its escalation. Those changed conditions provide a new context so that processes contributing to conflict de-escalation are likely to have significant effects. Finally, those changed conditions increase the likelihood that de-escalating policies pursued by partisans and by intermediaries will be undertaken, and with effectiveness.

We examine changing conditions within one of the adversaries in a struggle, in the relationship between them, and among other parties not directly engaged in the struggle. This discussion will draw illustrative material particularly from three conflicts that have undergone profound transformation after many decades of struggle: the conflicts (1) between the United States and the Soviet Union, (2) between Israeli Jews and Arab Palestinians, and (3) between Blacks and Whites in South Africa. To aid in the discussion, a chronology of major de-escalating events in each struggle are presented in tables 7.1, 7.2, and 7.3.

These chronologies indicate that de-escalating transformations are long, cumulative processes. They are not brief, clearly delineated events. Neither is the transition from escalation to de-escalation a single event; rather it is a shift produced by pressures building over time. Even if there are astounding moments of change, they usually follow from many less-visible trends.

TABLE 7.1

U.S.-USSR De-escalation Chronology

1949, May	End of Soviet blockade of West Berlin.
1955, May	Austrian State Treaty signed by United States, USSR, France, and United Kingdom, ending occupation of Austria.
1962, October	End of Cuban Missile Crisis.
1963, June	Hot line established, U.S.–USSR.
1963, August	Partial Nuclear Test Ban signed by United States, USSR, and United Kingdom.
1972, May	SALT I, ABM, Basic Principles of Mutual Relations signed by United States and USSR.
1975, August	CSCE, Helsinki Final Act signed.
1985, March	Gorbachev chosen as general secretary of Communist Party.
1987, December	INF signed by United States and USSR.
1989, November	Berlin Wall falls.
1991, August	Coup against Soviet government fails, Communist Party disbanded.
1991, December	Soviet Union breaks up.

TABLE 7.2

Israeli-Palestinian De-escalation Chronology

1974, November	Arab states at Rabat declare that the PLO is the sole representative of the Palestinian people.
1976, April	Palestinian nationalists win municipal elections on West Bank.
1978, September	A Framework for Peace in the Middle East agreed at Camp David.
1985, February	Jordanian-PLO accord on negotiations with Israel.
1987, December	Palestinian uprising (Intifada) begins.
1988, July	King Hussein announces Jordan's disengagement from the West Bank.
1988, December	United States and PLO enter into direct communications.
1991, October	Middle East Peace Conference in Madrid.
1993, January	Start of secret, unofficial meetings in Oslo, Norway, between PLO officials and private Israeli representatives.
1993, September	PLO and Israeli government sign the Declaration of Principles, and Arafat and Rabin shake hands.
1994, May	Cairo Agreement for "self-rule" in Gaza and Jericho.
1994, August	PLO and Israeli government sign "Preparatory Transfer of Powers and Responsibilities in the West Bank."
1994, October	Israeli-Jordanian peace treaty signed.
1995, September	Israel and PLO sign interim agreement to transfer authority in most of occupied territories.

TABLE 7.3
South African De-escalation Chronology

1969, September	National Party expels right-wing dissidents.
1985, April	Repeal of prohibition of marriages between Whites and others announced.
1985, September	White South African business leaders and newspaper editors hold talks with ANC in Lusaka, Zambia.
1986, April	Law requiring Blacks to carry pass books repealed.
1986, October	The general synod of the Dutch Reformed Church resolves that the forced separation of peoples cannot be considered a biblical imperative.
1989, August	Frederik Willem de Klerk elected President of SA.
1990, February	Nelson Mandela unconditionally released from prison.
1991, June	Group Areas Act and Population Registration Act repealed.
1991, September	National Peace Accord signed.
1992, March	De Klerk wins Whites-only referendum to negotiate end of White minority rule.
1993, November	New constitution approved.
1994, April	Mandela elected president of South Africa.

Internal changes

Many kinds of changes within one or more of the adversary parties play critical roles in a struggle's de-escalation. These often result from other internal developments, but to some degree also come from the interaction between the parties engaged in the struggle and other outside factors. In this section, I give particular attention to internally driven changes, relatively unrelated to the struggle itself.

In many conflicts, the adversaries are sustained by confidence in the justness and morality of their cause. A waning of that conviction can greatly contribute to a de-escalation of the struggle. Such a weakening can be seen in the gradually declining faith among Soviet citizens in communist ideology and the Soviet system.[28] It can also be seen in the undermining of apartheid's legitimacy, among Whites in South Africa. This was attested to, for example, by the withdrawal of approval from the Dutch Reformed Church in the mid-1980s. In the Israeli-Jewish and Arab-Palestinian struggle, however, Jews have not slackened in their faith in Zionism and the Palestinians have not lost their sense that they have suffered a great injustice by the establishment of a Jewish state in Palestine. Nevertheless, many people in each camp had come to acknowledge the authenticity of the other's claims, and that has meant modifying their own claims.

The evident failure of past militant strategies is a powerful stimulus for partisans to consider turning to a more accommodationist approach. Adversaries generally seek to advance their own interests and to win as much as possible, and tend to rely on coercive, often violent, means. The transition to transformation often arises from a realization that those means were not achieving what was intended. Indeed, past policies may come to be seen as undermining the attainment of the ends sought.

How dissatisfaction with old militant policies contributes to the transition to de-escalation and sometimes to the transformation of the struggle is readily illustrated. For example, in the South African case, White-supported apartheid was official policy, intended to ensure White domination by an elaborate form of segregation, discrimination, and control. But in actuality, integration and mutual dependence among the so-called racial communities was increasing despite apartheid. Indeed, some actions of the South African government were slowly reducing Black-White inequality. For example, John Kane-Berman reports, "In 1983/84 white education was budgeted to consume 53% of state education money, but five years later the white proportion had declined to 40%."[29]

In the conflict over the maintenance of White domination, both sides' efforts at unilateral imposition by the mid-1980s were clearly failing. The armed struggle by the African National Congress (ANC) had not forced an end to apartheid. Yet neither had the South African government's police repression and military attacks suppressed the ANC.

Certain changes in the relative influence among the constituent parts of an adversary group are important precursors of a de-escalating transition. The emergence into prominence of groups interested in an accommodation with the adversary may lead to a shift in goals and means. The Palestinian uprising, the Intifada, which began in December 1987, provides a paradoxical example. It escalated the intensity of the struggle against the Israeli occupation, but also contributed to a moderating shift in the position of the PLO. The PLO leadership, seeking to represent all Palestinians, outside as well as inside the territories occupied by Israel, had long stressed the needs and desires of those Palestinians outside to return. This was viewed as especially threatening by the Israeli government, and harsh means of struggle were attempted by the PLO to compel Israeli change. An important component of the PLO, therefore, was the fighters in the armed struggle. The Intifada, however, increased the relative importance of the Palestinians in the occupied territories and their emerging local leadership. For those Palestinians, shaking off Israeli control of their lives was the primary objective.

For the PLO leadership to sustain its position, it needed a new political role. To represent the Palestinians in the occupied territories in their struggle, the PLO leadership, among other efforts, sought to open a dialogue with the U.S. government and be recognized as the representative of the Palestinians. Extensive negotiations through several channels were conducted regarding a PLO statement satisfying certain U.S. government conditions. Finally, on 14

December 1988, Chairman Arafat said he accepted, "the right of all parties concerned in the Middle East conflict to exist in peace and security . . . including the state of Palestine, Israel and other neighbors according to resolution 242 and 338. . . . We renounce all forms of terrorism, including individual, group and state terrorism."[30] Thus, a year after the Intifada had begun, the U.S. government agreed for the first time to open a dialogue with the PLO.

Finally, some internal changes demand attentiveness by an adversary's leaders and divert them from external affairs, particularly antagonistic foreign relations. Beginning in the mid-1970s, the Soviet economy was clearly stagnating and living conditions were deteriorating. Life expectancy actually began to decline, unlike in any other industrially developed country.[31] Improving relations with the West offered the prospect of limiting the immense military defense expenditures and gaining access to Western technological developments and more and better consumer products. In 1985, Mikhail Gorbachev was chosen by the Communist Party to lead it and the Soviet Union into a period of domestic reforms, and an accommodation with the West was regarded as a requisite for that.

A change in the population of Israel also contributed to a change in the Israeli government and its readiness to be more forthcoming in negotiations with the Palestinians. This change in part resulted from one of the Soviet actions, which was at least partly aimed at winning approval in the West: the Soviet government increased the freedom of movement of the Soviet people. Consequently, the number of Soviet Jews who entered Israel rapidly grew. The costs of absorbing them in Israel competed with the costs of subsidizing Jewish settlers in the occupied territories. The Labor Party, promising greater attention to the needs within Israel itself, won the election in 1992, aided by the votes of the Jews from the former Soviet Union. The Labor Party government undertook more earnest negotiations with the Palestinians than had been the case earlier and in September 1993 reached an accord with the PLO. In addition, the increased number of Jews from the former Soviet areas enhanced Jews' confidence about their future in the Middle East, easing the risk of conceding more authority to the Palestinians.

Changes in the Relationship

Changes in the relations between the adversaries that undermine the prospects of any of them unilaterally imposing a solution greatly contribute to a shift toward de-escalation. This frequently means that the adversaries are in a stalemate, and no party anticipates that the balance of forces will change to enable it to triumph. Furthermore, if the stalemate is highly unsatisfactory, so that the parties wish to escape from it, they are in what Touval and Zartman have called a "hurting stalemate."[32] Such circumstances are often a prelude to a negotiated settlement of a conflict.

One other component is frequently critical for a transition away from escalation: the prospect of a better alternative than remaining in the stalemate. The alternative is a formula providing a mutually acceptable solution that appears to be attainable. A necessary element in any such formula is that the opponents do not threaten each other's most significant interests. Somehow, each side must convince the other that it accepts the other's legitimacy.

For seemingly intractable conflicts, to pass through a transition to a mutually acceptable de-escalation, each side minimally should not appear to be threatening the other's right to its collective existence. The nature of that collectivity and the form of existence, however, may take many shapes. The bargaining about the shapes of each can go on for a long time, even as part of a constructive struggle within the context of a legitimate political system. It should also be recognized, however, that the contention about the nature of the collectivities and their relations is often not symmetrical. The adversaries differ in resources, and one side usually gains more of what it wants than the other side does.

Many of these points can be illustrated in the de-escalating transition of the Israeli-Palestinian conflict. The acceptance by each side of the other's collective legitimacy, as the other side defined it, took many years of struggle. Many in the PLO leadership over the years came to accept as unalterable what they had wished had never happened: the creation of a Jewish state in part of what they regarded as their land—Palestine. They had come to reconcile themselves to a Palestinian state alongside Israel, a two-state solution. Some Palestinians continued to reject that solution, and many others claimed more for their state than the Israelis were offering.

Prior to the 1967 war, when the Israeli army took possession of the Gaza strip, the Sinai, the West Bank, the Golan Heights, and East Jerusalem, the Israelis might well have accepted a two-state solution or would have agreed to the control of those territories by various Arab states. But after the war, the options shifted. Jerusalem was unified and incorporated into Israel. Jewish settlements in the occupied territories were established, particularly after the Likud Party victory in 1977.

Gradually, Israeli consensus about a possible settlement of the conflict with the Palestinians broke down. Many Israelis wanted to retain control over the West Bank, providing the Palestinians with limited autonomy there; a solution unacceptable to the PLO when it was offered in the course of many exploratory negotiations in the 1980s. Other Israelis increasingly came to believe that a more fundamental separation was desirable, accommodating more of what the Palestinians were becoming willing to accept. They came to believe that Israel could not remain a democratic Jewish country and also rule or incorporate the Palestinians in the occupied territories. They preferred to be democratic and Jewish than to hold the land and the Palestinian inhabitants.

By the early 1990s, the latter view was strengthened by the experience with the Palestinian Intifada. It helped impose a recognition by Israeli Jews of the national character of the Palestinians. In the occupied territories, an infrastructure separating Jews and Palestinians was being constructed. The changing position of the PLO was increasingly acknowledged, and Hamas had arisen as a more intransigent adversary of Israel, making the PLO seem an even more acceptable negotiating partner for the Israelis.

In South Africa, the social and economic relations between Blacks and Whites had been undergoing a fundamental change in the 1980s. Despite the official policies of apartheid, the communities were becoming increasingly interdependent. Black people had voted with their feet; they had migrated to the urban centers and integrated industry and residential areas, violating the official pass requirements.[33] It is important to recognize that although the ANC demanded the transfer of power to a government chosen by a majority of the people, as Benyamin Newberger observes, it "recognized the equal right of whites to South Africa as their native land."[34] That reassurance was available to be recognized by Whites.

The American-Soviet relationship also underwent many profound social, political, and economic shifts in the course of the cold war. The United States had overwhelming global dominance at the outset, but that gradually declined as more centers of economic power developed. The Soviet Union, although lacking the global economic and military reach of the United States, by the end of the 1960s had achieved the capability of waging a nuclear war that could destroy much of the United States; and so a balance of terror existed. But at the same time, neither side had immediate goals that threatened vital interests of the other. Beginning with détente in the early 1970s, arms control agreements and many other measures appeared to demonstrate a mutual acceptance of each other as superpowers. After years of negotiation in the Conference of Security and Cooperation in Europe (CSCE), the Helsinki Final Act was signed in 1975. This provided assurance to the Soviet Union of the inviolability of the borders established in Europe after the end of the Second World War, including the western shift of Soviet borders and the division of Germany. With that assurance, the Soviet Union and the East European countries it dominated reduced their barriers to Western influence.

Changes in Context

The presence of associated conflicts often plays a major role in the social context of the focal struggle being considered. Shifts in the salience of those other conflicts impact upon the possible de-escalation of the struggle regarded as primary. For example, the shift to détente in the early 1970s was fostered by changes in the salience of several other conflicts.[35] Thus, the Soviet-Chinese antagonism had increased, indicated by the bloody border skirmishes in 1969.

That provided an incentive for each of them to be less intransigent toward the United States. On the other side, the U.S. engagement in the war in Vietnam was an overwhelming concern in 1969, when Richard M. Nixon was elected president. He and his advisors reasoned that an acceptable way out of Vietnam might be found by being more accommodating to the Soviet Union and the People's Republic of China, playing one against the other and isolating North Vietnam. Furthermore, the newly elected Social Democratic government of West Germany undertook a policy of accommodation with the Soviet Union, East Germany, and other countries of eastern Europe, which eased and indeed fostered American-Soviet accommodation.

End of the Cold War

The cold war's demise, marked by the fall of the Berlin Wall in 1989, Soviet agreement to Germany's reunification and entry into NATO, and finally, the dissolution of the Soviet Union in 1991, impacted many conflicts throughout the world, including the struggles in South Africa and the Middle East. Policies pursued by many of the parties involved in each of those conflicts were based on the existence of the cold war, and these policies tended to perpetuate each conflict. The end of the cold war required changes in those policies.

For South Africa, the collapse of communism in Europe undermined the National Party's argument that it was fighting communism by its anti-ANC policy and its armed intervention in neighboring countries. Relatedly, the South African government could only expect more opposition to its policies from the U.S. government. Moreover, the ANC's reassurances about the economic policies it would pursue if it gained political power seemed more credible under the new conditions. A new government strategy was needed.

The end of the cold war weakened support for both the Israelis and Palestinians. It lessened the value of Israel to the United States as an ally in the struggle against communism, and therefore threatened reduced support. On the other side, and more significantly, Soviet support for the PLO was lessened and Chairman Arafat was encouraged to find an accommodation with Israel. After the dissolution of the Soviet Union, Russia was even less likely to be antagonistic to U.S. policies in the region.

Other Regional Conflicts

The outbreak or the ending of intense armed combat in an adjacent region is likely to profoundly affect the course of the focal struggle being considered. For example, either may help forge new alliances or weaken support for one or more of the adversaries in the primary conflict.

In the Middle East, two regional wars involving Iraq greatly affected the Israeli-Palestinian conflict. First, the 1980–88 war following Iraq's invasion of

Iran drained Arab attention away from the Palestinian cause and added to the Palestinians' sense that they were on their own. This contributed to the outbreak of the Intifada and widespread Palestinian support for it.

The Iraqi attempt to incorporate Kuwait unleashed an intense war as U.S. and allied forces drove the Iraqi army out of Kuwait. The war divided the Arabs, particularly weakening the positions of the Palestinians, the PLO, and Jordan, who had not joined the anti-Iraqi government coalition. Furthermore, the threat Saddam Hussein was able to raise by appealing to popular anti-Israeli sentiments, was a powerful incentive for the U.S. government to try to settle the Israeli-Arab conflict and help sustain the Arab governments with which it was allied in the war against Iraq. The war also appeared to leave the United States as the dominant regional as well as the dominant global power. The U.S. government's incentive and ability to play a major intermediary role after the war were evident and led to the Middle East Peace Conference in Madrid, according to a formula brokered by U.S. secretary of state James Baker.[36]

Economic Changes

The increasingly integrated global economy also has impacted on each conflict being discussed. For example, growing global integration meant that the international economic sanctions against South Africa were becoming more and more burdensome. The increasingly integrated global economy also contributed to the pressure felt by Soviet leaders to change their stagnating economy in order to function effectively within the global economy.

Beginning in the early 1980s, economic conditions in many Arab countries deteriorated for most people. The great flow of income that the success of OPEC had generated for some Arab countries in the 1970s now slowed down. This contributed to the felt need to settle the Arab-Israeli conflict.

Economic expansion, which is a goal shared by all the adversaries, encourages cooperation and facilitates finding win-win outcomes. For example, the growth of the economy in the United States in the 1960s facilitated the integration of women, Blacks, and other minorities into the economy and, hence, into the general society.

Summary

A combination of several changes is generally needed to bring about a transition into a de-escalating movement, particularly for protracted conflicts. The changes occur within one or more adversary, in their relations, and in the social context. Quite different combinations of changed conditions can bring about the shift toward de-escalation. Thus, if a stalemate is very painful, then the formula to escape from it need not be as attractive as when the stalemate is more bearable.

The nature of the de-escalation and the resulting outcome is also likely to differ, depending upon the particular combination of conditions. There is little reason in theory or in experience to believe that the result of conflict de-escalation or termination will be equitable for all the adversaries. Some adversaries are likely to fare better than others, but none is likely to gain all that it might have wanted in the heat of a struggle.

The changing conditions create opportunities, but no guarantees, for successful de-escalating efforts. In each of the major de-escalations described here, many counterforces and events were evident; they created a quite different set of expectations for many of the participants and observers at the time. The adverse circumstances as well as those conducive to constructive de-escalation must be recognized. No single kind of de-escalating effort will work for every conflict in every situation. A particular set of policies and a particular set of conditions must match for de-escalation movement to occur, as discussed in the next section.[37]

De-escalation Policies

In selecting a policy to de-escalate a conflict, a sound analysis of the prevailing conditions and trends relating to the struggle should be made. It ought to be obvious that one tool does not fit all problems; having a hammer in hand should not make a person think that everything to be fixed requires hammering.[38] Consideration should be given to the stage of escalation the conflict has already reached, how the conflict is like and unlike others, and the nature of de-escalation desired. In addition, a wide range of alternative policies and possible undertakers of the policies should be reviewed. All these tasks are rarely fully completed by persons engaged in a struggle or in trying to ameliorate it, but engaging in them tends to improve performance. It is the goal of this analysis to assist in those tasks by examining possible de-escalation policies in order to better specify which policies, executed by different persons, are likely to attain particular goals under specific circumstances.

Analytic Parameters

Alternative de-escalation policies are examined in terms of the level of escalation a struggle has reached and the level of de-escalation the policies are targeted to achieve.[39] This discussion differentiates among four starting levels: little escalation, sharp escalation (or crisis), protracted stalemate, and asymmetrical imposition, even though these levels tend to be mixed in actual struggles. Thus, a crisis may erupt in the context of a low level of struggle or in the context of a protracted stalemate. Furthermore, various segments of a large-scale conflict may be in different stages simultaneously. For example, while at the societal level a struggle may be relatively stalemated, in one community one side may be sharply escalating the fight.

Starting Levels

Before conflicts become protracted and destructive, they exhibit a relatively low level of overt struggle, whose seriousness is too often unrecognized. One or more of the adversaries makes demands, probes for responses, threatens, or otherwise begins trying to gain its goals. Such actions, often precursors of much more severe conflicts in the near future, should serve as early warnings that a disastrous struggle may develop. Appropriate policies following such actions, by the partisans or by intermediaries, can often avert destructive escalation. Clearly, averting destructive escalation at an early stage is generally less costly, less risky, and more likely to be enduringly effective than it would be once the conflict has become protracted. Nevertheless, adversaries often think that others will prevent the conflict from escalating badly and meanwhile they must strive to reach their contested goal. Possible intermediaries generally do not act since they see high risks of failure and little potential gains, even if they succeed.

Efforts at de-escalation, particularly by intermediaries, often occur when a conflict has markedly escalated. Among the many forms of sharp escalation, one form is much examined in international relations—the crisis. Definitions of international crises abound, but they generally include at least the following elements.[40] A crisis denotes an increase in the severity of antagonistic interactions between two or more states, elevating the probability of military hostilities, and destabilizing their relationship. It is important to recognize that the catalyst to a crisis is not inherent in particular actions but depends on how those events are perceived by the recipient of the actions. A sense of crisis arises when the actions are viewed as a threat to basic values, as requiring a response in a limited time, and as increasing the likelihood that military means will need to be used in the response.

Crises occur not only in relations between states. They also occur between a state and a challenging agent within a country, for example a separatist movement. They occur among nonstate actors such as organizations and individuals. In these cases, military hostilities may not be likely, but a radical escalation in the intensity of the antagonistic exchanges and a rupture of the relationship are threatened and sometimes occur. For example, confrontations have sometimes escalated tragically as the members of a religious community and government authorities reject the claims made by the other. This was the case in 1993 when the compound of the Branch Davidians near Waco,

Texas, was besieged for fifty-one days and then stormed, resulting in a fire that consumed the people in the compound.[41]

In addition to crises, escalation surges occur when one of the parties greatly intensifies its means of struggle. In community and societal conflicts, this may take the form of disorderly outbursts such as riots and widespread demonstrations. Within organizations, it may occur when subordinates refuse to follow orders, as in a military mutiny or when buildings are seized by protesting persons and groups, as happens when prisoners take control of parts of a prison or students occupy and hold college buildings.

The third starting level is that of protracted, seemingly intractable struggle, a stage receiving increasing attention by scholars and policymakers.[42] In these long-standing struggles, neither side is able to impose a settlement on the other, nor is either willing to accept the terms insisted upon by the other in preference to continuing the struggle.

Finally, some conflicts are at a stage where one side is increasingly dominating the other, and able to impose its preferred settlement. Partisans often stress asymmetrical imposition. For two reasons, I give little attention to how one side defeats or destroys the other. First, that course is unduly emphasized by analysts and activists alike, to the neglect of other courses of development. Second, it is a relatively rare course for a struggle to take. In large-scale conflicts, even if one side defeats the other, the adversary can and often does renew the fight at a later time. The relationship, in any case, generally persists in some form, and one or another kind of mutual accommodation is inevitable. Admittedly, in the short run for many conflicts and particularly for interpersonal and small-scale conflicts, the total defeat of one side or the rupture of the relationship may occur. Sometimes one party may even be destroyed or dissolved.

De-escalation policies are also analyzed in terms of four kinds of goals: (1) preventing destructive escalation, (2) stopping the ongoing violence, (3) de-escalating the mutual antagonism, and (4) using problem-solving means. The first two goals are relatively short term, while the second two are relatively long term. These policies, whether pursued by elements in one of the adversary parties or by other parties, are intentionally directed at de-escalation. They are mapped out in table 7.4 and analyzed below. Policies that contribute to constructive de-escalations receive the most attention.

From Low Level of Escalation

Everyone acknowledges that it is easier to stop a conflict from escalating destructively, if the struggle has not persisted for a long time and not escalated greatly. This underlies the high interest among conflict resolution professionals in the potential of preventive diplomacy and in early warning. Much of

TABLE 7.4
Policies for Constructive De-escalation

Starting situation	Short-term goals		Long-term goals	
	By partisans	By intermediaries	By partisans	By intermediaries
Low-level escalation	De-link issues; nonviolent action; measured reciprocity.	Provide mediation; isolate conflict.	Reduce inequalities; foster shared identities.	Develop supportive norms, institutions; introduce more stakeholders.
Sharp escalation	Allow time; face-saving.	Mediation; face-saving; suggest formula.	Reframe conflict; avoid provocation; CBM.	Mediation; develop crosscutting ties.
Protracted struggles	Conciliatory signals; tract 2; accept responsibility; reassure adversary.	Mediation; isolate conflict.	GRIT; TFT; Training in conflict resolution; CBM; introduce more stakeholders.	Develop superordinate goals; foster communication.

this interest is directed at possible intervention by those not engaged as partisans in the struggle.

Despite the interest in early warning, the problem is not so much not knowing that a conflict is likely to escalate badly, but that the political will is low when the profile of a conflict is low.[43] First, this is because intervention even at an early stage generally calls for the use of resources, and there usually are many more pressing claims on resources. Second, potential intervenors tend to believe that there is a good chance that intervention will not be necessary. Third, what actions actually will be effective are uncertain, a good reason for caution. Fourth, ineffectively interfering will be regarded as a failure. Finally, little credit is likely to be won by preventing a conflict from deteriorating, since most people will hardly have noticed or believed that a disaster was averted. Many of these considerations also affect leaders of an adversary group so they are not likely to pursue de-escalatory policies. The presentation of effective early de-escalation policies, then, should not only contribute knowledge about what to do to prevent destructive escalation, but also address the lack of popular understanding and support for such efforts.

Short Term

Conflict partisans and intermediaries can pursue a variety of policies that tend to prevent conflicts from escalating destructively and turn them toward constructive de-escalation.

Partisans' policies. As earlier discussions have shown, how a challenging group pursues its goals and how the other side responds, greatly affect the likelihood that a struggle will de-escalate constructively rather than escalate destructively. For example, conflicts in which challenging groups use relatively nonprovocative methods, such as conventional protest or nonviolent resistance, are less likely to escalate destructively than those in which challenging groups resort to violence. Similarly, conflicts in which the challenged parties respond in an equivalent way rather than by overreacting tend not to escalate destructively.

De-escalation is likely to be fostered insofar as the partisans keep the issues in contention narrowly focused and isolated from other issues about which they might also fight. Destructive escalation tends to be limited if participation does not spread. One way that can be prevented in societal disorders is to reduce or counter inflammatory rumors of outrages. For example, in periods of rioting, urban organizations have provided centers where citizens could seek verification about stories they had heard.

Intermediaries' policies. In the case of international conflicts or communal conflicts with transnational links, outside parties may strive to prevent the conflict from spreading into neighboring countries or try to stop or limit the sale of weapons in the country where the struggle is under way. Policies to stop a conflict's spreading is illustrated by the conduct of the United Nations and other international organizations and governments in limiting the scope of the wars in the former Yugoslavia. Thus, at the request of the president of the Yugoslav Republic of Macedonia, in December 1992, the UN Security Council authorized the deployment of troops under command of the United Nations Protection Force (UNPROFOR) along the Macedonian border with Albania and the successor Yugoslavia (Serbia and Montenegro). The troops not only acted as a deterrent to the spread of war, but also mediated border encounters and succeeded in achieving a withdrawal of soldiers on both sides.[44]

Within many social systems, agencies frequently exist that provide mediation, information gathering, facilitation, and consultative services to defuse nascent conflicts. For example, the U.S. Justice Department, during the civil rights struggle in the 1960s, helped by mediation to prevent White resistance and intimidation that would generate destructive escalation. In labor relations, federal and state agencies offering mediating services for collective bargaining provide a mechanism to help defuse disputes that might otherwise be waged with great intensity for a long time.

Nonofficial mediators or officials acting informally may also intervene to help settle community disputes, as is sometimes done by political and religious leaders. They often have bonds crossing religious and ethnic lines and use such connections to bring together leaders from disputing communal groups.

Long Term

Long-term de-escalation policies include the promotion of crosscutting ties; institutionalized procedures for resolving conflicts; improvement of the social, economic, and cultural way of life of the disadvantaged in the social system; and the creation of shared identities and vested interests in advancing that shared identity.

Within a society, policies fostering those conditions include establishing an electoral system that is conducive to broad political parties that are not based on a single ethnic, religious, or other exclusive identity. They also include educational systems and curricular material that emphasize shared identities, without denigrating relatively narrower ones. They further include the development of legitimate procedures for protecting fundamental rights of the disadvantaged members of the society.

From Sharp Escalation

Great interest is exhibited by policymakers, analysts, and the public at large in the outbreak of crises and other sharp escalations, and research about policies that enable adversaries to avoid destructive escalation has been done, at least in some conflict arenas.

Short Term

One of the essential qualities of a crisis is the sense of urgency engendered among the partisans. That urgency often hampers taking actions that would avoid a disastrous escalation. One way to increase the likelihood of crisis de-escalation is for one or more adversaries to allow time for the other side to reflect on its course of action and not be pushed into a corner and face humiliation. This is exemplified in some degree by the U.S. government's responses in the Berlin crisis of 1948–49 and the Cuban missile crisis of 1962.

Although the 1948 Berlin blockade contributed greatly to the emergence of the cold war, it did not erupt into military hostilities, with even more destructive consequences.[45] In June 1948, the Western powers (U.S., U.K., and France) announced their decision to economically integrate their occupation zones in West Germany and in West Berlin and to institute a new currency. To stop this action in Berlin, the Soviets imposed a blockade of all Western land transportation across East Germany, into or out of West Berlin. A U.S. airlift was undertaken, and in July, the U.S. National Security Council recommended expanding the airlift and seeking negotiations, rejecting the use of force. This reduced pressure for both sides and allowed time to find a way out of the crisis. Negotiations to end the crisis began in August 1948, and an agreement was finally reached in May 1949, with the Soviet withdrawal of all restrictions and the Americans, French, and British accepting a meeting of the foreign ministers to consider the future of Germany and Berlin.

In the October 1962 Cuban missile crisis, too, the alternative chosen by President Kennedy and his advisors to bring about the Soviet withdrawal of its missiles deployed in Cuba was not a military attack, but a naval quarantine. This provided time for the Soviets to consider alternative responses and for negotiation between the concerned parties to find a formula for a way out of the crisis. The formula included the withdrawal of the missiles, the promise that the U.S. government would not try to overthrow the Cuban government, and the covert understanding that the United States would close its missile base in Turkey.

In domestic crises, hostages are often a crucial component, since they provide leverage for a small, relatively powerless group to counter the overwhelming power of state forces. The common understanding among police officers and other officials in responding to hostage situations is to be patient and to negotiate with those holding hostages but not to accede to their demands. For persons not part of a larger group who have seized a hostage in desperation, this strategy generally works. With persons who are acting as part of larger organizations and identities, the negotiations are more difficult. Government officials are concerned about precedents and sometimes use the negotiations as ruses in preparation for storming the location where the hostages are held. Such stormings have often resulted in tragic losses and enduring difficulties, as the cases of MOVE in Philadelphia and Attica prison in New York illustrate.[46]

Long Term

Among the many ways to foster de-escalation from sharp escalations is to develop institutions and procedures that reduce the likelihood of such events. This may take the form of improving the communication between the adversaries, making it swifter and better understood. For example, after the Cuban missile crisis, the U.S. and Soviet governments established the "hotline," a direct telephone line between the offices of the heads of the U.S. and the Soviet governments.

Another long-term strategy is to develop groups, networks, or organizations including persons from opposing sides. These persons may sometimes be the primary representatives or advisors to them. Getting to know each other and their views reduces the likelihood of misunderstandings that may exacerbate conflicts. The crosscutting networks also provide channels for quickly considering alternative paths out of a sharp escalation when that occurs. For example, many communities have labor-management councils and interreligious and interethnic dialogue groups for these very purposes. Such organizations also exist in international relations and have played a role in the transformation of the American-Soviet conflict. The Pugwash movement and the Dartmouth meetings are particularly noteworthy in this regard.[47]

In addition, confidence building measures (CBMs) were developed in East-West relations in Europe to reduce the chances of sharp escalations. These measures included, for example, each side notifying the other in advance of large-scale military maneuvers and each side allowing representatives of the other to observe the maneuvers. Such measures provided reassurance, avoided misunderstandings, and thus contributed to the end of the cold war. This idea has been discussed and to some extent implemented between other sets of international and domestic adversaries.[48]

Finally, a basic policy to prevent conflicts from escalating destructively is to prevent provocative acts from happening. General agreements, even among unfriendly parties, can implement methods to reduce or even stop particular provocative actions. For example, politically motivated airplane hijackings were widespread in the 1960s, but they have been greatly reduced by improved security measures at airports and by international agreements to deny havens to hijackers.

From Protracted Struggle

Many large-scale conflicts persist for generation after generation, appearing to be intractable. They persist in self-perpetuating ways with varying degrees of destructiveness. I will discuss some of the many policies that enable adversaries to move out of such conflicts and into more constructive ways of conducting or of resolving them.

Short Term

Even profound and long-term conflict transformations have small beginnings. Tactical policies are crucial in initiating and sustaining long-term change.

Partisans' policies. A fundamental issue in protracted struggles is that one or more sides feels that its basic interests are threatened and it must fight on to sustain them. A crucial step in turning away from such a vision is for all sides to undertake actions that counter those feelings. When such actions are made on a reciprocal basis, appear credible, and seem irreversible, protracted and intractable conflicts are in transition. In each of the three cases of intractable conflicts being discussed here, variations of such actions can be seen. The transformation in American-Soviet relations that brought about the end of the cold war occurred over a long time. There were periods of thaw in the cold war and with them normalization of some aspects of American-Soviet relations; the actions of each side and the treaties signed by all parties indicated an acceptance of each other's continuing survival and even superpower status. The Reagan administration's renewal of the cold war rhetoric and conduct turned out to be relatively brief, confined largely to Reagan's first term.

The threat to each other's collective existence was felt most intensely by the Israeli Jews and the Palestinians. For decades, each did not recognize the other's legitimacy and would not even meet each other officially and publicly. The PLO, under the leadership of Chairman Yasser Arafat, gradually moderated its goals so that it came to accept the continuing existence of a Jewish state in Palestine. The Israeli government, even while led by the nationalist Likud Party, came to acknowledge the existence of a Palestinian people, though it continued to resist negotiating with the PLO as the representative of the Palestinians. The Israeli political leaders had for decades characterized the PLO as a terrorist organization. The mutual recognition each other's legitimacy, manifested in the signing of the Declaration of Principles (DOP) and the handshake of Chairman Yasser Arafat and Prime Minister Yitzhak Rabin on 13 September 1993, therefore, was a transforming event.

In South Africa, too, Whites and Blacks lived together, but Blacks generally felt that their basic rights were denied to them collectively and individually, while Whites generally felt that to recognize those rights would undermine their own existence in the country. Yet, here too, earlier steps had been taken that made possible finally the direct, problem-solving negotiations. Notable among those steps was the 1990 unconditional release of Nelson Mandela, the leader of the previously banned African National Congress (ANC) after twenty-seven years in prison. The release was celebrated in great public ceremonies that made the commitment to peaceful negotiations appear irreversible. Public spectacles and media events are useful in making such commitments.[49] Furthermore, Frederik W. de Klerk expressed regrets and apologized for the harm done to Blacks by Whites in South Africa by apartheid, which was certainly a major conciliatory gesture enhancing his credibility among the Blacks.

Policies to build support for de-escalation among members of one of the adversaries also are necessary for large-scale protracted conflicts, particularly communal ones, since these conflicts are especially dependent on the sentiments of the rank-and-file members of the opposing sides. Many such policies may be undertaken by persons in leadership offices and in alternative groups. The mobilization effort may be part of a long-term policy, or a short-term effort to rally support for a particular action. Mobilization may be attempted, for example, by social movement organizations arranging a demonstration or a campaign of protest against officials reluctant to change. Mobilization may also be sought by officials who hold major ceremonies that serve to make a public commitment to the transformation process. The officials may also hold a referendum to gain constituent support and campaign to get it. This was done, for example, in South Africa, and the government won a referendum in March 1992, in which only Whites voted, to negotiate the end of White minority rule.

Of course, significant internal opposition to ending a protracted conflict, on terms not unilaterally imposed, is very likely. Once the transition toward a joint solution has begun, opposition often intensifies. How leaders handle that opposition to continuing with de-escalating moves is crucial. They may attempt to suppress it, placate it, or co-opt it, with varying degrees of success.[50] Yet, having entered this path, the leaders of the opposing sides have a mutual interest in helping their negotiating partners stay in power and maintain support from their constituents. This poses a fundamental dilemma. The leaders must both reassure their own followers that the course taken will yield what they want and also reassure their former opponents they will not lose what they have sought.

In South Africa, de Klerk and Mandela, each facing challenges from within their camps, used a wide array of tactics to maintain credibility with the opposing side, to mobilize support from their own side, and to block disruptive actions by opponents from their sides. Opposition to the movement toward resolving the struggle in South Africa included many threats and acts of violence. In April 1993, Chris Hani, a major and popular figure in the ANC was assassinated by an immigrant from Poland who was a member of the right-wing Afrikaner Weerstandsbeweging. The assassin was captured after an Afrikaner woman telephoned the police, providing his license plate number. Nelson Mandela spoke that evening on national television in a successful effort to prevent the negotiations under way from being derailed, saying,

> Tonight I am reaching out to every single South African, black and white, from the very depths of my being. A white man, full of prejudice and hate, came to our country and committed a deed so foul that our whole nation now teeters on the brink of disaster. A white woman, of Afrikaner origin, risked her life so that we may know, and bring to justice this assassin. . . . Now is the time for all South Africans to stand together against those who, from whatever quarter, wish to destroy what Chris Hani gave his life for—the freedom of all of us.[51]

Mandela and de Klerk discussed how to sustain the negotiations despite this crisis. The ANC organized protest demonstrations to allow for nonviolent expressions of anger and resentment; the government, for its part, arrested a member of the Conservative Party in connection with the murder.

During the Israeli-Palestinian de-escalation of 1993–94, intense challenges were faced by the leadership of both sides. For example, upon the announcement of the DOP in September 1993, Chairman Arafat was bitterly attacked by many Palestinians for negotiating the agreement privately and even more fundamentally for surrendering so much to the Israelis. Opposition was mounted by an organization rivaling the PLO, the Islamic-based organization

Hamas. On the other side, Prime Minister Rabin was criticized for risking too much; he was opposed vigorously by the Likud Party and by some of the Jewish settlers in the occupied territories. For a variety of reasons, leaders on neither side acted as clearly to overcome dissent from within their camp as did the leaders in South Africa.[52] And that eroded each side's ability to sustain support for the long-term de-escalating strategy they had formally embraced.

The attacks on Prime Minister Yitzhak Rabin, prior to his assassination in 1995, had risen to great intensity, condemning him as a traitor to the Jewish people. But, his assassination shocked nearly all Israelis. Those who had been particularly vehement in the denunciations of Rabin and the peace process initially were somewhat marginalized and the new prime minister, Peres, led the government in a speedy implementation of the interim agreement that had been signed shortly before Rabin was killed.[53]

In the transition phase of the cold war's transformation, opposition on both sides had to be overcome. When Mikhail Gorbachev was chosen to be the new head of the Communist Party and of the Soviet government early in 1985, his initial actions were not radical: focusing on reducing the sale of alcohol and allowing for more ownership of small plots of land.[54] When Gorbachev began more radical changes domestically and internationally, there was some popular resistance in the Soviet Union. In the United States, the initial response was great skepticism and resistance to reciprocation by traditional cold warriors in the Reagan administration and outside it. But the earlier opposition to the Reagan administration's renewed cold war policies offered alternative responses, and President Reagan himself recognized the changed Soviet stance, even crediting his own previous policy as a cause.[55]

Intermediaries' policies. Particularly in enduring struggles, when the adversaries are frozen in mistrust, mediators and other intermediaries often play critical roles in facilitating direct or indirect de-escalating negotiations. In the Israeli-Arab/Palestinian conflict, the U.S. government has often played critical mediating roles. This has included helping to construct a formula that would enable adversaries to begin negotiations, a particularly challenging task when the opposing parties do not recognize each other and do not officially meet. Thus, the U.S. government, following the war against Iraq, sought to initiate comprehensive peace negotiations between the Israeli government and the neighboring Arab governments, and the Palestinians. After much shuttle diplomacy, a complex formula was constructed by Secretary of State Baker and his associates. It consisted of three arenas for negotiation: a general conference (preferred by Arab governments), bilateral meetings between Israel and each neighboring Arab government (long sought by the Israelis), and regional meetings on issues of common concern such as water, security, and refugees (to provide a wider mix of countries and matters of possible mutual benefit). Palestinians would be represented within the Jordanian delegation, and their relationship to the PLO somewhat veiled. The general conference was held briefly in Madrid in October 1991, bilateral negotiations followed, as did the regional meetings later. A breakthrough had been achieved, but progress then languished until the Israeli government changed in the election of June 1992, when the ruling Likud Party was defeated by the Labor Party.

After making little progress in bilateral negotiations between the Israelis and the Palestinians (but only indirectly with the PLO), a back channel for negotiations was secretly opened. The negotiations were initiated by unofficial, and still illicit, conversations between an Israeli Jewish academic, Yair Hirschfeld and a prominent PLO official, Abu Alaa, Arafat's director of finances. [56] Their first secret meeting was in London, in December 1992, arranged by the Norwegian sociologist Terje Rod Larsen. Hirschfeld's previous contacts with Palestinians and with Israeli government officials made the meeting possible and hopeful. Soon the Norwegian government was supporting small regular meetings between Hirschfeld and a former student of his, the historian Ron Pundik, with Abu Alaa and two aides, Hassan Asfour and Maher al Kurd. Terje Larsen's research institute served as host and provided cover. The Israelis sent reports of their meetings to Yossi Beilin, the new deputy foreign minister, who read them but offered no advice. The small group, in intensive discussions, developed the idea of a joint declaration of principles envisaging free elections in the occupied territories and the gradual establishment of Palestinian authority. Beilin informed Foreign Minister Peres and Prime Minister Rabin; Peres was enthusiastic and Rabin skeptical but open to new suggestions. Later, Israeli officials joined the talks and the intense negotiations continued until the Declaration of Principles was initialed on 20 August 1993. By giving their tacit, but secret go-ahead, both the Palestinian and Israeli leadership could explore and construct the formula for a major peacemaking move without arousing internal resistance until a deal had been struck.

Long Term

Moving out of intractable struggles takes a long time. Many small steps usually must be taken before more significant ones can be made. The effectiveness of each action is likely to be enhanced if actions are considered as a series of steps along a considered path. In addition, in large-scale struggles many de-escalating actions often must be taken by many partisans and intermediaries at the same time, and those efforts are likely to be more effective if they are well coordinated.

Partisans' policies. Two major strategic approaches to change from a confrontational relationship to a more cooperative one have been presented in the literature. One is graduated reciprocation in tension-reduction (GRIT), as set forth by Charles E. Osgood, and the other is a tit-for-tat (TFT) strategy, as discussed in the work of Anatol Rapoport and Robert Axelrod.[57] According to the GRIT strategy, one of the parties in conflict unilaterally initiates a series of cooperative moves; these are announced and reciprocity is invited, but the conciliatory moves continue for an extended period, whether or not there is immediate reciprocity. GRIT was first prescribed in the early 1960s as a strategy for the United States to induce reciprocation from the Soviet Union.

While GRIT strategy was inferred from social-psychological theory and research, the TFT strategy was derived from game theory, particularly work on the prisoners' dilemma (PD) game. The strategy reasons that in a series of PD games, the payoffs are cumulative and the player's strategy can be based on the other player's prior behavior. Experimental research and computer simulations of iterated games of PD indicate that cooperative relations often emerge and the most successful strategy for developing cooperative relations and yielding the highest overall payoff is for one player to initiate the series of games by acting cooperatively and afterward simply reciprocating the other player's actions, whether a cooperative or a noncooperative action.

Analysts have assessed these strategies by examining actual de-escalating interactions, particularly in the protracted U.S.-Soviet conflict. For example, Amitai Etzioni has interpreted the de-escalation in American-Soviet antagonism in 1963 as an illustration of the GRIT strategy.[58] He views it as beginning with President Kennedy's 10 June speech at American University announcing a unilateral halt to the atmospheric testing of nuclear weapons; the Soviets reciprocated and other cooperative moves were soon made, including the signing of the Limited Nuclear Test Ban in August 1963. The initial moves, however, were to some extent orchestrated by indirect communication between President Kennedy and Premier Khrushchev.[59]

A quantitative and case analysis of reciprocity in relations between the United States and the Soviet Union, between the United States and the People's Republic of China (PRC), and between the Soviet Union and the PRC was conducted by Joshua S. Goldstein and John R. Freeman, for the period 1948–89.

It is ironic that GRIT was offered as a strategy to be undertaken by the U.S. government to break out of the cold war, but its most spectacular enactment was undertaken by a Soviet leader. Gorbachev announced a change in policy toward the United States and Western Europe and made many conciliatory moves. Goldstein and Freeman characterize it as super-GRIT. It led, they say, to normalized relations with China. It also transformed relations with the United States, although initially, as the Soviets offered concessions, U.S. demands were raised. But Gorbachev's policy of saying "yes, yes" until the U.S. government could no longer say "no, no," successfully resulted in cooperative moves by the U.S. government.

Another long-term de-escalation policy is to strengthen shared identities. In the South African case, the sense of identity that Whites, Blacks, and coloreds shared in being South African and living in their beautiful country was strong and mutually recognized. In the Israeli-Palestinian case, however, the peoples have only a few, and relatively nonsalient, unifying identities—such as being Middle Eastern. Zionism as it became state doctrine was and is exclusive, insisting that the Land of Israel is for Jews. Arab and Palestinian nationalism has tended to be exclusive as well, even if less-sharply articulated than Zionism; but more recently, some Islamic activism has became quite exclusive.

Policies pursued by nongovernmental persons and organizations are also important in long-term de-escalating strategies. In South Africa, the gradual shift from confrontation to negotiation was fostered by changes in the White establishment's economic thinking. The increasing emphasis on the free market and efficiency undermined the wish to maintain White purity. Blacks who shared the business ideology values were increasingly incorporated into the establishment, and this was regarded as a way of preserving the existing socioeconomic system. Hendrik W. van der Merwe reports that in 1985 and 1986 "more than two dozen delegations of white and black South African businessmen, academics, church leaders and others met with the ANC in Lusaka," outside of South Africa. [60]

South African Blacks used a variety of strategies to end apartheid and gain political rights in a unified South Africa. Generally, the strategies pursued were chosen with some consideration of their effects on the long-term relationship between Whites and Blacks in South Africa. The ANC at the outset pursued a nonviolent strategy, but in the early 1960s, the decision was made by the ANC, with Nelson Mandela's urging, to sanction the formation of MK (Umkhonto we Sizwe—the Spear of the Nation) to use violence and conduct an armed struggle. This led to the imprisonment of Mandela and the banning of the ANC. Mandela explains the kind of violence he advocated: "For a small and fledgling army, open revolution was inconceivable. Terrorism inevitably reflected poorly on those who used it. . . . Guerrilla warfare was a possibility, but since the ANC had been reluctant to embrace violence at all, it made sense to start with the form of violence that inflicted the least harm against individuals: sabotage. Because it did not involve loss of life it offered the best hope for reconciliation among the races afterward."[61] Even violence can be modulated and constrained by long-term considerations.

Actually, the struggle waged by Black South Africans was largely nonviolent, but did become more extensive and intensive in the 1980s. The Blacks had a high rate of trade union membership, and strike activity was frequent; rent strikes, in which rent payments were withheld to force improvements in housing conditions, were also conducted.

The Palestinian Intifada was generally viewed by the Palestinians as nonviolent.[62] It included extensive boycotts of Israeli products and the development of alternative economic and social structures. The stone throwing by the youth was considered symbolic, and at the beginning, knives and guns were not used. But in the opinion of Israeli Jews, the Intifada was a challenge to the occupation and rock throwing was extremely violent, threatening their lives when driving in the occupied territories. The Israeli military response suppressing the stone throwing resulted in the image around the world of soldiers catching Palestinian youth, beating them, and breaking their bones. This was effective in gaining attention and sympathy for the Palestinians, but it further embittered their relations with the Jews.

Policies pursued by segments of an adversary group to influence the leadership's relationship with the group's common opponent are also important. For example, after President Sadat's visit to Jerusalem in November 1977, the Peace Now social movement arose within Israel to pressure the Likud-led Israeli government to be more forthcoming in its negotiations with the Egyptian government.[63] Pressure on the Israeli government also was exerted by other groups opposed to any concessions or accommodation with the Palestinians; notable among such groups were those of religiously motivated settlers, such as the Gush Emunim, discussed in chapter 6.

Sometimes even the dominant faction in an adversary party can be the source of long-term policies to bring about fundamental changes in relations with its opponent. This was the case in the Soviet Union starting in 1985 with the ascension to power of Mikhail Gorbachev. He and his associates believed that reform of the Soviet system was necessary to sustain itself as a super-power. The changes they instigated were not widely popular and indeed were not radical, but they did create the opportunity for those who desired change to generate pressure for more. Clearly, the forces for change soon gained enough strength to transform the Soviet Union, and they could not be stopped.

Finally, it should be noted that the failure to control and coordinate action sometimes undermines de-escalation too, once it has been undertaken. Insofar as the struggle has generated hostility and mistrust between the antagonists, de-escalating efforts must be clear and consistent to be effective. Subordinates carrying on routine activities or exhibiting extra zealousness may disrupt de-escalation progress. For example, in 1960, the heads of government of the United States, Great Britain, France, and the Soviet Union were to meet in Paris as part of a nascent movement to reduce East-West tension.[64] A high-flying U.S. reconnaissance plane, a U-2, was shot down over Soviet territory. As a result, the meeting was canceled and the de-escalation movement was interrupted. Some segments of the side undertaking to de-escalate the struggle sometimes so oppose the policy that they attempt to sabotage it. They may commit acts of violence against the adversary and so provoke responses that will escalate the conflict again. This has been the case many times in the Israeli-Palestinian peacemaking efforts.

Intermediaries' policies. Outside actors may also foster de-escalation over the long run. They may do this as interested parties, seeking to stop what they regard as abhorrent conditions and to bring about what would be a just outcome.

The UN, the United States, and many IGOs and NGOs pressured the South African government with sanctions relating to trade and investment and participation in cultural and sports events. These sanctions impacted not only the government but all the people in South Africa. The impacts were unequally borne and had a variety of effects, but they contributed to a widespread feeling of isolation and beleagurment among Whites. Blacks were encouraged by the external support, even though they also suffered economic strains. In the short run, increases in sanctions were associated with increased strike activity by Black workers but were associated with decreased numbers of Black workers on strike a year after the increased sanctions. [65]

The Israeli government was subjected to similar pressure in the UN General Assembly; but generally, the line taken by the United States and others foiled sanctions, arguing that the Israeli government needed reassurance of its security so that it would feel safe to make concessions.

Intermediaries also often pursue long-term de-escalating strategies. These include actions to develop better mutual understandings and to foster recognition of possible mutual interests; the actions may be organizing dialogue groups and problem-solving workshops. They may also entail large-scale assistance programs to help develop institutions for managing social conflicts or to help reduce economic problems.

Intermediaries have played important roles in the transformation of American-Soviet relations, but that is not widely acknowledged in the United States. For example, the Conference on Security and Cooperation in Europe (CSCE), which formulated the Helsinki accords signed in 1975 by thirty-five countries including the United States, contributed immensely to the transformation of the cold war. The neutral and nonaligned countries represented at the CSCE meetings played important roles in negotiating the agreement.[66]

Conclusions

This chapter has focused on conflict de-escalation, and particularly on how the adversaries jointly create the transition away from intractability. Admittedly, not much attention was given to unilateral impositions of settlements; clearly that is de-escalation of another sort. We have noted that asymmetries in resources, particularly coercive capabilities, profoundly shape the course of de-escalation, but a more extended discussion of that is left for chapter 9 on the termination of struggles.

It suffices at this time to observe that at every stage of conflict development, the shape of its future course and its likely outcome are affected by the structure of the adversaries' relationship, and their relative coercive strength. This is particularly the case when the parties are not highly integrated with each other and when they tend to rely on coercion in making joint decisions with each other. For example, in Snyder and Diesing's influential study of international crises between 1898 and 1973, they concluded that fourteen out of their sixteen cases ended without war. However, in two of them the outcome was a more or less equal compromise, two others ended in partial compromises, and the remaining twelve cases ended in one-sided capitulation. They conclude that the outcome of an international crisis "pretty closely reflects the 'inherent bargaining power' of the parties that derives essentially from the relative valuation of their interests and their relative disutility for war or risk of war."[67] But they also noted that resolve and the importance of the issues at stake for the opposing sides were important factors. Furthermore, a crisis is usually an episode in a larger struggle, not the whole conflict.

In this chapter, we examined the processes, conditions, and policies that help explain how struggles can move toward settlement without one party simply imposing its will on another. In concluding, I emphasize the implication of the previous analysis for the pursuit of constructive de-escalating policies. The choice of policies and their effectiveness depends on the existing circumstances and the goals sought. It is easier and certainly less costly to the antagonists to avoid destructive escalation in the first place than to attempt de-escalation after the conflict has been raging for a long time. But there are risks and costs to taking actions before a conflict has visibly deteriorated. For potential intermediaries, de-escalating interventions may seem unnecessary, or at least difficult to mobilize support for. Furthermore, the preventive action may fail and those undertaking it are likely to bear the blame for further deterioration. For representatives of one of the adversaries, the risks and costs of premature de-escalation are even greater. They are likely to appear weak and be accused of losing what they might have won if the struggle had been continued and even intensified. A better understanding of ways to escalate and de-escalate a fight constructively can contribute to reducing those risks and costs.

De-escalation strategies, even constructive ones, are not implemented smoothly, since no party is wholly in charge and none gets all that it wants. Every side has many components, and the policies pursued by an adversary are manifold and often inconsistent. At the same time, the fundamental external conditions keep changing. Consequently, de-escalating transformations are usually long processes, and do not move in a unidirectional fashion. Indeed, just when a transformation has actually occurred is more frequently recognizable retrospectively than prospectively.

The conditions underlying a communal or other large-scale conflict and the changes in these conditions do not wholly determine whether or not a conflict can be transformed or whether that conflict is being waged constructively. Nor can any person or group, no matter how powerful a role that person or group plays, wholly determine that a conflict will be waged constructively rather than destructively. There is always a complex interaction between the prevailing conditions and the long- and short-term policies pursued by the protagonists and by the intermediaries.

These interactions have two sets of implications. First, the underlying conditions set parameters within which the policies can be pursued. The conditions are more constraining for short-term policies than for long-term ones, which may be directed at modifying the conditions themselves. Second, those persons and groups seeking to limit the destructiveness of a conflict or transform it into a constructively waged one need to use an appropriate set of short-term and long-term policies. The policies are more likely to be effective and enduring insofar as they are consistent with the direction in which conditions are changing.

More can be said about which policies can help prevent, limit, or transform destructive conflicts. One useful policy is to minimize reliance on violence, particularly violence that threatens the opponent's existence or that is humiliating and provocative. The previous analysis also suggests the power of nonviolent inducements. Those can be coercive, as when coalitions are built and allies are mobilized to support the goals being pursued in the struggle. This is illustrated by the transformation of the cold war as well as the successes of the civil rights movement in the United States in the 1960s and of the ANC in South Africa. Mobilization of support requires framing the contentious issues in ways that are appealing to broad constituencies. Those persuasive efforts were also directed at the constituents of the opposing side, and that too helps account for the way the struggles discussed in this chapter actually developed. The adversaries influenced each other by their words and deeds; the power of persuasive ideas was most forcefully demonstrated by the changes within the Soviet Union, particularly among the elites.

Finally, consideration by each side of the concerns and fears of the other opens avenues for conducting a constructive struggle and a constructive de-escalation. That consideration must be conveyed convincingly, which is difficult in the midst of an intense and protracted struggle. But the efforts were made and contributed greatly to the transformation of the struggles analyzed in this chapter.

These matters have been discussed here with particular emphasis on the transition away from seemingly intractable conflicts. There is no single path from an intractable to a tractable conflict, from a destructive to a constructive struggle. The paths out can lead in quite different directions, to greater integration in South Africa, to greater separation between Israelis and Palestinians, and to acceptance of the opponent's ideology, as happened in significant ways within the Soviet Union. Changing conditions converge to form new conjunctures of circumstances and new opportunities for movement. Furthermore, various groups in those circumstances can introduce policies to change the course of the ongoing conflicts.

A critical component of successful new policies is reformulation, a new vision of the nature of the relationship between the adversaries. This may be the result of new ways of thinking, perhaps arising from changes within one or more adversaries, changes in the concrete broader situation, and changes in the relationship between the adversaries. After all, social conflicts are socially constructed, and they often can be restructured and reframed so they become a shared problem that requires a joint solution.

Such visions are expressed in new ways of thinking about the relationship between the erstwhile enemies. They also are expressed in alterations in the set of parties primarily engaged in the conflict and its resolution, excluding intransigent parties or including accommodative new parties. The addition of accommodative new parties is particularly manifest in the interventions of intermediaries, discussed in chapter 8.

The de-escalation process must proceed in a broad step-by-step fashion, preparing for and sustaining any agreements reached. What is also especially important is that the changes be done consistently and unequivocally, be in depth, and not be attempts to squeeze as much as possible from the adversary. For leaders in each party, however, it is important to sustain a balance between relations with adversaries and with their constituents. Maintaining support from constituents is critical, but that is best thought of in terms of their long-term best interests.

A basic finding of this analysis is that transforming transitions come about when a new way of thinking about their conflict becomes dominant in each of the primary adversaries. They each come to believe that the strategy they had been pursuing cannot triumph or they cannot gain more by continuing it, and an accommodative strategy promises to offer a better alternative. This is a more general statement than the suggestion that a negotiated settlement is reached when the adversaries are in a hurting stalemate and a formula for a settlement seems possible and acceptable. [68]

While force and coercion are sometimes critical, the argument advanced here is that the de-escalation of intractable conflicts is not necessarily the result of immutable, large-scale forces or of the actions of a few brave and wise persons. Many circumstances need to converge, and these must be interpreted in new ways in order for a seemingly intractable conflict to pass beyond a transition favoring de-escalation and become fundamentally transformed. Resistance and reversals are likely, and they too must be considered.

Notes

1. John E. Mueller, *War, Presidents, and Public Opinion* (New York: John Wiley, 1973), 58–59, 220–25.

2. Susan Borker, Louis Kriesberg, and Abdu Abdul-Quader, "Conciliation, Confrontation, and Approval of the President," *Peace and Change* 11 (Spring 1985): 31–48.

3. See Joel Brockner and Jeffrey Z. Rubin, *Entrapment in Escalating Conflicts: A Social Psychological Analysis* (New York: Springer Verlag, 1985), 193–222.

4. Brockner and Rubin in their *Entrapment in Escalating Conflicts*, 246–48, examine how, despite the Vietnam experience, the U.S. intervention in El Salvador during President Ronald Reagan's administration exemplifies entrapment.

5. Bob Woodward, *The Commanders* (New York: Simon & Schuster, 1991), 306–7.

6. William B. Quandt, *Peace Process: American Diplomacy and the Arab-Israeli Conflict Since 1967* (Washington, D.C: The Brookings Institution; Berkeley: University of California Press, 1993), 348–49.

7. Quoted in Jason DeParle, "Inside Mr. Inside," *New York Times Magazine*, 20 August 1995, 39.

8. Arnold P. Goldstein and Gerald Y. Michaels, *Empathy: Development, Training, and Consequences*, (Hillsdale, N.J.: Lawrence Erlbaum Associates, 1985), 7–9. To take the role of other persons is a basic human capability and essential for the development of a sense of self. See George H. Mead, *Mind, Self and Society* (Chicago, Ill.: The University of Chicago Press, 1934).

9. Goldstein and Michaels, *Empathy*, 4–7.

10. Alan Paton, *Cry, the Beloved Country* (New York: C. Scribner's Sons, 1948); and Nadime Gordiner, *July's People* (New York: Viking, 1981).

11. For example, see Rafik Halabi, *The West Bank Story: An Israeli Arab's View of Both Side's of a Tangled Conflict* (San Diego: Harcourt Brace Jovanovich, 1985), original publication 1981, translated from the Hebrew by Ina Friedman; David Grossman, *The Yellow Wind* (New York: Farrar, Straus and Giroux, 1988), translated from the Hebrew by Haim Watzman.

12. Morton Grodzins, *The Loyal and the Disloyal* (Chicago: The University of Chicago Press, 1956).

13. See discussions, for example, in John Lofland, *Polite Protestors: The American Peace Movement of the 1980s* (Syracuse, N.Y.: Syracuse University Press, 1993); Sam Marullo and John Lofland, eds. *Peace Action in the Eighties* (New Brunswick: Rutgers University Press, 1990); and David S. Meyer, *A Winter of Discontent* (New York: Praeger, 1990).

14. Kenneth McRoberts, *Quebec: Social Change and Political Crisis*, 3d ed. (Toronto: McClelland and Stewart, 1988).

15. Arthur M. Schlesinger, Jr., *A Thousand Days* (Boston: Houghton Mifflin, 1965), 830–31.

16. In December 1993, I traveled with a group of the U.S. Interreligious Committee for Peace in the Middle East, to Israel, Syria, Egypt, and Jordan. We spoke with government officials, academics, and other personages, with varying opinions about the Declaration of Principles agreed to by the Israeli government and the PLO. Nearly everyone spoke of the irreversibility of what had happened.

17. Robert F. Kennedy reports the president's conversation after the quarantine was announced, and his concern to avoid the miscalculations of the Germans, the Russians, the Austrians, the French, and the British who "somehow stumbled into war, he said, through stupidity, individual idiosyncrasies, misunderstandings, and personal

complexities of inferiority and grandeur" (Robert F. Kennedy, *Thirteen Days: A Memoir of the Cuban Missile Crisis* [New York: W. W. Norton, 1971], 40).

18. Richard Ned Lebow and Janice Gross Stein, *We All Lost the Cold War* (Princeton: Princeton University Press, 1994), 110–45.

19. Ole R. Holsti, Richard A. Brody, and Robert C. North, "Measuring Affect and Action in International Reaction Models: Empirical Materials from the 1962 Cuban Crisis," *Journal of Peace Research*, nos. 3–4 (1964): 170–89.

20. George W. Breslauer and Philip E. Tetlock, eds. *Learning in U.S. and Soviet Foreign Policy* (Boulder, Colo.: Westview, 1991).

21. For example, Henry Kissinger, as national security advisor and then secretary of state in President Nixon's administration, on the basis of his experience negotiating with Soviet officials, modified his thinking about the way various issues might be linked, taking a step-by-step approach and not trying to require particular linkages. See Deborah Welch Larson, "Learning in U.S.-Soviet Relations: The Nixon-Kissinger Structures of Peace," in *Learning in U.S. and Soviet Foreign Policy*, ed. Breslauer and Tetlock.

22. Stephen Kramer, ed., *International Regimes* (Ithaca, N.Y.: Cornell University Press, 1983).

23. Aldon D. Morris, "Birmingham Confrontation Reconsidered: An Analysis of the Dynamics and Tactics of Mobilization," *American Sociological Review* 58 (October 1993): 621–36.

24. Roger Fisher, "Fractionating Conflict," in *International Conflict and Behavioral Science*, ed. Roger Fisher (New York: Basic Books, 1964).

25. Louis Kriesberg, "Coordinating Intermediary Peace Efforts," *Negotiation Journal* 12 (October 1996): 341–52.

26. Louis Kriesberg, "Varieties of Mediating Activities and of Mediators," in *Resolving International Conflicts*, ed. Jacob Bercovitch (Boulder, Colo.: Lynne Rienner, 1995).

27. Allan T. Griffith, "International Diplomacy and Democratic Legitimation in Zimbabwe and Namibia" (M. Litt. diss., Oxford University, 1992). For the Rhodesian transformation, see Henry Wiseman and Alistair M. Taylor, *From Rhodesia to Zimbabwe: The Politics of Transition* (New York: Pergamon, 1981).

28. For example, Vladimer Shlapentokh, "Attitudes and Behavior of Soviet Youth in the 1970s and 1980s," *Research in Political Sociology*, vol. 2 (Greenwich, Conn.: JAI, 1986), 199–224.

29. John Kane-Berman, *South Africa's Silent Revolution* (Johannesburg: South African Institute of Race Relations, 1990), 8.

30. Quandt, *Peace Process*, 373.

31. Christopher Davis and Murray Feshback, *Rising Infant Mortality in the USSR in the 1970's*, U.S. Department of Commerce, Bureau of the Census (Washington, D.C.: U.S. Printing Office, 1980); and John Dutton, Jr., "Changes in Soviet Mortality Patterns, 1959–77," *Population and Development Review*, no. 5 (June 1979): 267–91.

32. See Saadia Touval and I. William Zartman, eds., *International Mediation in Theory and Practice* (Boulder, Colo.: Westview, 1985). For further discussions of this concept, see Louis Kriesberg and Stuart J. Thorson, eds., *Timing the De-Escalation of International Conflicts* (Syracuse, N.Y.: Syracuse University Press, 1991).

33. Kane-Berman, *South Africa's Silent Revolution*.

34. Benyamin Neuberger, "Nationalisms Compared: ANC, IRA, and PLO," in *The Elusive Search for Peace: South Africa and Northern Ireland*, ed. Hermann Giliome and Jannie Gagiano (Cape Town: Oxford University Press, 1990), 65.

35. Louis Kriesberg, *International Conflict Resolution: The U.S.–U.S.S.R. and Middle East Cases* (New Haven, Conn.: Yale University Press, 1992).

36. Quandt, *Peace Process*, 383–412.

37. For discussions of timing and ripeness, see Louis Kriesberg and Stuart J. Thorson, eds., *Timing the De-Esclation of International Conflicts* (Syracuse, N.Y.: Syracuse University Press, 1991); and I. William Zartman, *Ripe for Resolution: Conflict and Intervention in Africa* (New York: Oxford University Press, 1989), originally published in 1985.

38. Loraleigh Keashly and Ronald J. Fisher, "Complementarity and Coordination of Conflict Interventions: Taking a Contingency Perspective," in *Resolving International Conflicts*, ed. Jacob Bercovitch (Boulder, Colo.: Lynne Rienner, 1995).

39. I have discussed this in presentations at professional meetings, and an elaboration of it appears in Louis Kriesberg, "The Phases of Destructive Conflicts and Proactive Solutions," in *The International Politics of Ethnic Conflict: Prevention and Peacekeeping*, ed. David Carment and Patrick James (Columbia: University of South Carolina Press, 1998).

40. This discussion draws from Michael Brecher, *Crises in World Politics* (Oxford: Pergamon, 1993), 2–25; also see Glenn H. Snyder and Paul Diesing, *Conflict among Nations* (Princeton: Princeton University Press, 1977).

41. Dick J. Reavis, *The Ashes of Waco: An Investigation* (New York: Simon & Schuster, 1995); and James Tabor and Eugene V. Gallagher, *Why Waco?* (Berkeley: University of California Press, 1995).

42. Edward A. Azar, Paul Jureidini, and Ronald McLaurin, "Protracted Social Conflict: Theory and Practice in the Middle East," *Journal of Palestine Studies* 29 (Fall 1978): 41–60; Louis Kriesberg, Terrell A. Northrup, and Stuart J. Thorson, eds. *Intractable Conflicts and Their Transformation* (Syracuse, N.Y.: Syracuse University Press, 1989).

43. Louis Kriesberg, "The Phases of Destructive Communal Conflicts and Proactive Solutions."

44. United Nations, *United Nations Peacekeeping, Update: December 1994* (United Nations dp/1306/Rev.4, 1995), 71–2; United Nations, *The United Nations and the Situation in the Former Yugoslavia*, United Nations Reproduction Service, DPI/1312/Rev.4, 1995, 31; and John Marks and Eran Fraenkel, "Working to Prevent Conflict in the New Nation of Macedonia," *Negotiation Journal* 13 (July 1997): 243–52.

45. Michael Brecher, *Crises in World Politics* (Oxford: Pergamon, 1993), 84–85, 250–53.

46. In 1985, the Philadelphia police, when blocked from serving a search warrant, dropped a bomb on the house where the MOVE community lived. Their house and sixty other row houses on the block were burned, with eleven people killed, including five children. See Hizkias Assefa and Paul Wahrhaftig, *Extremist Groups and Conflict Resolution: The MOVE Crisis in Philadelphia* (New York: Praeger, 1988). In 1971, prisoners at the prison in Attica, New York, seized forty-three hostages and controlled part

of the prison for four days; after unsuccessful negotiations, the prison was stormed and ten hostages and twenty-nine prisoners were killed in the retaking of the prison. See *Attica: The Official Report of the New York State Special Commission on Attica* (New York: Praeger, 1972); and John Irwin, *Prisons in Turmoil* (Boston: Little, Brown, 1980).

47. Michael J. Pentz and Gillian Slovo, "The Political Significance of Pugwash," *Knowledge and Power in a Global Society*, ed. William M. Evan. (Beverly Hills, Calif.: Sage, 1981); Louis Kriesberg, "International Nongovernmental Organizations and Transnational Integration," *International Associations* 24, no. 11 (1972): 520–25; Gennady I. Chufrin and Harold H. Saunders, "A Public Peace Process," *Negotiation Journal* 9 (April 1993): 155–77; and Joseph Rotblat, *Scientists in the Quest for Peace; A History of the Pugwash Conferences* (Cambridge, Mass.: MIT Press, 1972).

48. Shai Feldman, ed., *Confidence Building and Verification: Prospects in the Middle East*, JCSS Study no. 25 (Jerusalem: The Jerusalem Post; and Boulder, Colo.: Westview, 1994).

49. See Daniel Dayan and Elihu Katz, *Media Events: The Live Broadcasting of History* (Cambridge, Mass.: Harvard University Press, 1992).

50. Gavan Duffy and Nathalie Frensley, "Community Conflict Processes: Mobilization in Northern Ireland," in *International Crisis and Domestic Politics*, ed. James W. Lamare (New York: Praeger, 1991).

51. Nelson Mandela, *Long Walk to Freedom* (Boston: Little, Brown, 1994), 530.

52. Unlike the South African case, neither side had a widely shared vision of a common future together. Furthermore, the rejectionists on each side still had important external support.

53. The withdrawal of Israeli occupation forces from Hebron, however, was delayed and remained as a matter of contention when the Likud came to power in 1996, under the leadership of Benjamin Netanyahu.

54. I visited Moscow in that spring, and in conversations with several academicians, with and without ties to the Communist Party and the government, I was often told that more radical action would be forthcoming. Gorbachev was securing his base before undertaking the needed wide-ranging reforms.

55. In 1989, while some hard-line observers doubted that real changes were happening in the Soviet Union, some others proclaimed the West with the Reagan Doctrine had defeated the Soviet Union. See "Bulletin: We Won!" *Review and Outlook, Wall Street Journal*, 24 May 1989, A14. For a discussion of this and an alternative explanation for the ending of the cold war, see Louis Kriesberg, "Explaining the End of the Cold War," Occasional Paper Series, no. 2, June 1990. The Program on the Analysis and Resolution of Conflicts, Syracuse University.

56. At the time of the first meeting, Israeli law banned contact with the PLO; this law was abrogated by the Israeli Knesset on 19 January 1993. For a detailed account, see Amos Elon, "The Peacemakers," *The New Yorker*, 69 (20 December 1993): 77–85; and David Makovsky, *Making Peace with the PLO: The Rabin Government's Road to the Oslo Accord* (Boulder, Colo.: Westview, 1996).

57. See Charles E. Osgood, *An Alternative to War or Surrender* (Urbana: University of Illinois Press, 1962); Anatol Rapoport, "Escape from Paradox," *Scientific American* 217 (1967): 50–59; and Robert Axelrod, *The Evolution of Cooperation* (New York: Basic Books, 1984).

58. Amitai Etzioni, "The Kennedy Experiment," *The Western Political Quarterly* 20 (June 1967): 361–80.

59. Based on personal interviews with Norman Cousins and Ted Sorenson. Also see Norman Cousins, *The Impossible Triumverate* (New York: Norton, 1972); Louis Kriesberg, "Noncoercive Inducements in U.S.-Soviet Conflicts: Ending the Occupation of Austria and Nuclear Weapons Tests," *Journal of Political and Military Sociology* 9 (Spring 1981): 1–16; and Louis Kriesberg, *International Conflict Resolution*, 83, 112.

60. Hendrik W. van der Merwe, *Pursuing Justice and Peace in South Africa* (London: Routledge, 1989), 102.

61. Mandela, *Long Walk to Freedom*, 246.

62. Don Peretz, *Intifada* (Boulder, Colo.: Westview, 1990).

63. Kriesberg, *International Conflict Resolution*, 68; also see Simona Sharoni, *Gender and the Israeli-Palestinian Conflict* (Syracuse, N.Y.: Syracuse University Press, 1995).

64. David Wise and Thomas B. Ross, *The U-2 Affair* (New York: Random House, 1962).

65. William Kemfer, Anton D. Lowenberg, H. Naci Mocan, and Lynne Bennett, "Foreign Threats and Domestic Actions: Sanctions against South Africa," in *Justice without Violence*, ed. Paul Wehr, Heidi Burgess, and Guy Burgess (Boulder, Colo.: Lynne Rienner, 1994).

66. For example, see the discussion by Janie Leatherman, *Principles and Paradoxes of Peaceful Change* (Syracuse, N.Y.: Syracuse University Press, forthcoming). For a discussion of the role of neutral countries in reaching the agreement on control of arms on the seabed, see Bennett Ramberg, *The Seabed Arms Control Negotiations*, Monograph Series in World Affairs, vol. 15 (Denver: University of Denver, Graduate School of International Studies, 1978).

67. Glenn H. Snyder and Paul Diesing, *Conflict among Nations* (Princeton, N.J.: Princeton University Press, 1977), 498.

68. Saadia Touval and I. William Zartman, eds., *International Mediation in Theory and Practice* (Boulder, Colo.: Westview, 1985).

8

Intermediary Contributions

Persons or organizations providing intermediary services often contribute significantly in de-escalating conflicts, and in reaching and sustaining agreements. The services include actions by persons filling social roles such as mediators, arbitrators, and fact finders; and they include similar actions provided by persons who do not fill such socially recognized roles.

Mediation is central in the field of conflict resolution, and the number of people and organizations serving as mediators has expanded greatly in the 1980s and 1990s.[1] They are increasingly active in the fields of international relations, industrial relations, environmental disputes, interethnic relations, divorce proceedings, commercial relations, and fights among students. A variety of intermediary activities, provided by different kinds of persons, are analyzed in this chapter; but most attention is given to mediating activities provided by persons playing the role of mediator.

Intermediaries frequently contribute to speeding an escape from a destructive struggle, and often contribute to reaching an agreement that reflects a broader range of interests than would be the case without their participation. They also often increase the likelihood that an agreement between the adversaries is fair and enduring. However, intermediaries frequently fail in one or more of these goals or can even hamper success. To understand intermediary contributions, it is important to distinguish between the activities performed and the persons conducting particular sets of activities in playing distinct social roles.

Intermediary Activities

The activities that may contribute to de-escalating and resolving a struggle are many and varied, but we will focus on the subset of mediating services.

De-escalating intermediary activities include forcefully intervening to stop certain kinds of overt conflict behavior, as police forces sometimes do. They include giving support and assistance to the side that might otherwise be forced to yield, and so help to create a stalemate. De-escalating efforts also include helping set limits on the way the conflict is waged, by withholding support or threatening sanctions against the parties that prolong or escalate the struggle. The activities also include providing models of alternative ways for adversaries to find mutually acceptable accommodations and monitoring agreements reached. With the consent of the antagonistic parties, intermediaries also may settle a dispute by *arbitration*, providing binding decisions about the terms of settlement.

The activities that can contribute to constructive conflict de-escalation and settlement are usefully first discussed separately from who performs them. Afterward, we can examine the various kinds of people who play diverse roles in providing the services. This will allow us to analyze what different kinds of actors can do with varying effectiveness. No single intermediary can perform all possible de-escalating or even mediating activities, since many are incompatible with each other. Some can be done well by one kind of an intermediary, and some by another kind. We begin by listing possible mediating services, indicating their great variety.

Provide a Space for Communication

An important, and minimally intrusive, intermediary service is to provide a place for adversaries or their representatives to meet. Sometimes adversaries want to meet to explore possible de-escalating moves but do not want this known until they work out an agreement about the nature of the move. This was the case for the 1993 meetings between the PLO and Israelis in Oslo. Sometimes each adversary prefers not to meet in the other's space, fearing that it would appear to be the supplicant. A neutral location avoids that symbolic loss of face.

Provide Information

As a struggle escalates, the antagonists are increasingly likely to misinterpret the actions and words of each other, exaggerating their hostility and intransigence. It is difficult to cross those barriers. Transmitting information from one side to another with relatively little distortion contributes significantly to constructive de-escalation. Thus, information about how the struggle is viewed by the other side is an essential component of constructive de-escalation. The information also may be about the other side's readiness to de-escalate, the terms of a possible settlement, and the risks of continuing or escalating the struggle.

Providing such information so that an opponent can hear it from and about an enemy requires that the transmitter have the confidence of the recipient, and it may require considerable skill on the part of the intermediary. The transmission may be made more acceptable by omitting particularly provocative elements of the message or by explaining the context from the other side's point of view.

Help Adversaries to Begin Negotiations

A variety of intermediary activities can help adversaries undertake negotiations by making success seem more likely and by reducing the costs of failure. Intermediaries can explore with the antagonists in a struggle what set of negotiating partners, agenda, and context would make negotiation seem worth trying. The formula for negotiations, presented by the intermediary, is likely to have more appeal and legitimacy than if proposed by any one of the partisans alone. This is illustrated by the actions of Secretary of State James Baker in arranging the 1991 Middle East peace conference held in Madrid.

Intermediaries can reduce the risks for adversaries of entering into negotiations with each other in several ways. The adversaries generally indicate to the intermediary that they are serious in their effort to find a mutually acceptable settlement, and that becomes a kind of commitment to the intermediary, aside from any commitment they may make to each other.

In addition, intermediaries help in finding a formula for who the negotiating partners will be. The choice of parties to be engaged in the de-escalating effort involves three competing principles. One is to exclude the intransigents so a deal can be made. The second is to include all those who have the capability to disrupt an agreement if one is reached. The third is to maximize participation by all those with a stake in the outcome. Difficult choices often must be made about the relative weight given to each principle. The choice may change after the initial negotiations are undertaken.

Help Penetrate Emotional Barriers

The hostile feelings that hamper members of one side accurately perceiving the other or believing that it is trustworthy may be reduced in many ways by intermediaries. A mediator sometimes meets with each side privately, sympathetically listening to expressions of anger, hate, or fear of the enemy. Members of an adversary party, having vented such emotions out of the enemy's hearing are then more able to carry on without showing such feelings and provoking the other side.

An intermediary may also make suggestions that help build mutual appreciation between the adversary representatives. Thus, the intermediary may suggest to one side that it make a unilateral gesture or symbolic gift that would be difficult for the other side to misinterpret. A gesture as simple as an acknowledgment of the bravery of the adversary and its past sacrifices may be moving and effective. Such gestures, if effective, can win the adversary's attention and a fresh look at the other side.

Intermediaries may propose other techniques to penetrate emotional barriers. They may suggest that representatives from each side take turns listening to each other and summarizing what the other side's representative said. The exercise improves hearing what the other side says and also enhances the other side's feeling that it has been heard. Another, less-formal technique, is to work together on some collective task (preparing a meal or arranging an excursion) and having teams with members from different sides undertake various aspects of the task.[2]

Help Stall Deterioration

As a conflict persists in escalation, it generally deteriorates into increasing destructiveness. An outside party's engagement in trying to de-escalate the conflict can enable both sides to at least halt the slide toward further destructiveness. The adversaries may freeze the conflict then, until a more opportune time develops to move toward a substantive de-escalation. The intermediaries can do this by engaging adversaries in prolonged negotiations, raising the costs of escalating violence. They sometimes also intercede to stop further violence, often in agreement with the adversaries. The UN peacekeeping missions exemplify this kind of service.

Save Face

Once in a fight, each side finds it difficult to appear to accept the ideas of the enemy. If an idea is voiced by an intermediary, it can be accepted without seeming to yield to the adversary. Furthermore, the idea may be accepted out of respect for the intermediaries or in deference to the relationship with them. An adversary, recognizing these considerations, rather than offer an idea on its own sometimes suggests that the intermediary make it. This was done, for example, in the Israeli-Egyptian negotiations in 1978 at Camp David, mediated by President Jimmy Carter and his associates.[3]

Similarly, a commitment can be made to an intermediary, without appearing to bow meekly to an opponent's demands.[4] To illustrate, in the 1973 negotiations between the Israeli and Egyptian governments mediated by Henry Kissinger, the Israelis wanted a commitment from Egypt to reopen the Suez Canal and allow Israeli shipping to use the canal. President Sadat, not willing to appear to be limiting Egyptian sovereignty, refused. The commitments were made to the U.S. government, which conveyed them to the Israeli government.[5]

Another way for adversaries to save face is to have the mediator take the blame for a mistake. If something goes wrong in the negotiation arrangements, the relationship between the adversaries is less likely to be damaged if the mediator accepts responsibility than if one of the adversaries is accused of a blunder or a deception.

Change Procedures

Negotiators sometimes become frozen in unproductive procedures, and suggesting new procedures may break the impasse. The procedure is often changed by bringing in high-ranking representatives of the opposing sides, who have more authority to take new positions. Or, difficult issues frequently are delegated to specialists on the issues in contention to discuss options in small working groups. Establishing small negotiation groups to work on a subset of issues is a way to fractionate a conflict, resolving pieces of the total conflict one at a time.

The negotiation setting can be physically changed by altering seating arrangements, making them more informal. The style of discussion can be changed by altering the format, perhaps by having a facilitator, in addition to a chair.[6] The facilitator moderates the discussion of proposals, at first allowing only clarifying questions. The facilitator then summarizes what has and has not been agreed to, setting the stage for new proposals to deal with the matters not yet in agreement.

Help Invent New Options

Once a conflict has persisted or has become severe, the adversaries tend to become locked into the positions they have previously staked out. Each side sees the other's preferred outcome as unacceptable and thus, sees continuing or escalating the struggle as better than accepting those terms. Mediators often can help reframe the struggle and suggest ways to construct new options for consideration.

Mediators can sometimes be more inventive than the opposing sides because they recognize the underlying interests that the negotiators for each side are trying to advance. Furthermore, they are not likely to be committed to the previous terms of settlement offered by the adversaries themselves, and therefore are freer to think of new alternatives.

Intermediaries often help adversaries think of new options. One way this is done is to bring together a few members of the opposing sides to informally discuss their relationship and identify a variety of possible solutions to the problem they face. This may occur in the context of problem-solving workshops, discussed later in this chapter. It may also be promoted by setting aside time for "brainstorming." Members of the negotiating sides are encouraged to suggest possible solutions, putting aside likely difficulties in implementing them. The rule is to be imaginative and uncritical of one's own or of each other's suggestions. Only after many options have been mentioned can the necessary critical discussion begin.

Finally, intermediaries—particularly mediators—may encourage a different style of discussion.[7] For example, when a person says, "no, no, no" to a proposal from another party, the mediator may say, "what if the other person had said such and such, would that be better?" Then, if the person says, "That's better, but it's not enough," the mediator may ask, "What would you add to improve it?" The idea is to show participants how to get beyond rejecting a proposal to thinking about how to make it acceptable.

Represent Persons Not Represented in the Negotiations

Conflicts generally affect many more parties than those represented in any set of negotiations, and those parties have a stake in the outcome. Intermediaries may be able to represent the more diffuse interests of others by upholding general norms of fairness. Intermediaries may also be expected to represent the interests of absent others, for example, the general public, consumers, taxpayers, or future generations. In the 1978 Camp David negotiations between the Israeli and Egyptian governments, President Jimmy Carter lent support to developing a comprehensive peace, taking into account the interests of important parties not participating in the negotiations, particularly the other Arab governments, and the Palestinians.[8]

Construct Deals

Often mediators actively shuttle between opposing sides, learning what each side wants, what each will give up, and what each will not abandon. On that basis, an intermediary may develop a possible settlement and propose it to the opposing sides. This may become the basis for further negotiations as the intermediary modifies the proposed plan, taking into account the criticisms of each side. The mediator repeatedly modifies the plan and presents all negotiating parties this single negotiating text, which each side is asked to accept as a whole.[9] The mediator may be more or less active in formulating the proposals, varying from combining elements of the positions of both sides to creatively constructing a deal that he or she tries to sell.

Add Resources

Since expanding the size of the pie makes it easier to divide, intermediaries sometimes help the adversaries to find additional resources that they can share. To illustrate, community groups contending about access to limited

sport facilities may be encouraged to go together to city hall requesting increased facilities that they would share. Sometimes, intermediaries directly
assist in those efforts.

Some intermediaries themselves contribute resources that sweeten the settlement deal, resources that none of the adversaries will or can credibly contribute to the settlement. Consider how in August 1970, the U.S. government
mediated a cease-fire in the war of attrition between Egypt and Israel. The
Israelis feared that the Egyptians would use the cease fire to move their anti-
aircraft missiles forward to be better able to repel Israeli air attacks when
fighting broke out again. The cease-fire would forbid this, and the U.S. government offered assurances that it would monitor any violations. If they occurred, the United States would sell the Israelis advanced weapons to destroy
the missiles. This greatly contributed to helping the parties reach an agreement. The agreement, nevertheless, was violated when the Egyptians did deploy their missiles forward; the U.S. government then did sell the promised
weapons. In this case, the Israeli distrust of the Egyptian government was
reinforced. Years later, the U.S. contributions were more enduringly successful. In 1979, when an Israeli-Egyptian peace treaty was finally negotiated with
the successor Egyptian government, the assistance to each side and the monitoring services promised and provided by the U.S. government were crucial
in reaching and sustaining the agreement.

Generate Pressures for an Agreement

Intermediaries, even relatively nonintrusive mediators, often pressure one
or more of the adversaries to reach an agreement. One mild source of pressure
is the obligation felt by the adversaries toward the intermediary with whom
the parties have a nonantagonistic relationship. Having invested time and
taken the risk of seeking to help bring about a settlement, the adversaries
frequently are hesitant to walk away from the negotiations or appear to fail,
as this may seem disrespectful of the intermediary's efforts.

Sometimes the pressure applied by an intermediary is much more direct.
Time pressures may be imposed, as when the intermediary says that he or she
will stop current efforts as of a certain date in the near future. President
Jimmy Carter, for example, set a deadline for his mediation of the negotiations between President Sadat and Prime Minister Begin, at Camp David.

The intermediary pressure may be applied to one side more than another.
One way this is done is to threaten public accusations that the failure to reach
agreement is due to the intransigence of one party. In addition, a powerful
intermediary may more or less directly threaten to impose negative sanctions
on the recalcitrant party. To illustrate, President Carter, at the Camp David
negotiations, reports what he privately said to President Sadat at a difficult
point in the negotiations:

I explained to him the extremely serious consequences of his unilaterally break-ing off the negotiations: that his action would harm the relationship between Egypt and the United States, he would be violating his personal promise to me, and the onus of failure would be on him. I described the possible future progress of Egypt's friendships and alliances—from us to the moderate and then radical Arabs, thence to the Soviet Union. I told him it would damage one of my most precious possessions—his friendship and our mutual trust.[10]

Rally Support for an Agreement

Intermediaries often provide support for an agreement, which helps give it legitimacy for the negotiators' constituencies. An intermediary may even tes-tify to how well the negotiators for each side strove to protect the interests of their respective constituencies.

An intermediary, insofar as it represents a broader community, frequently is seen as validating the fairness of the agreement. Furthermore, the interme-diary's engagement in the negotiations can be regarded by both sides as help-ing to guarantee that the agreement reached will be honored, since the mediator has an interest in ensuring that its efforts appear successful.

Summary

In short, many activities that intermediaries can and do perform enhance the de-escalating process. These activities may speed initiating and concluding settlements; they may contribute to the fairness of a resulting agreement and help ensure its implementation. Some of these activities, however, are incon-sistent in the sense that the same person or group cannot perform them si-multaneously. Sets of them tend to be gathered together and carried out by incumbents of particular social roles.

Intermediary Roles

Intermediary activities are generally conducted by persons filling a recognized, intermediary social role, for example, as fact finder, facilitator, mediator, en-forcer, or arbitrator.[11] A social role is a position about which a set of expecta-tions are generally shared. Thus, an arbitrator is expected by the incumbent of that role and by the parties submitting a dispute to make a binding decision to settle the matter in contention.

One reason to discuss activities apart from the actor is to more easily exam-ine variations in social expectations about the functions to be performed by incumbents of various roles. This is especially important in understanding the work of mediators. Some mediators and parties to mediation expect that the mediator will carry out largely facilitative activities and avoid appearing to pressure any sides or intrusively suggest solutions. But other mediators and parties to mediation often have other expectations, for example to bring extra resources to the table and to actively help construct a deal.

Differences in expectations between the opposing sides or between the parties in the dispute and the mediator are obviously a source of difficulty in the effective conduct of mediation. Formal mediation is generally improved if the expectations are made explicit and agreement about them reached among all the parties engaged in the mediated negotiation. In each mediation, the adversaries and the mediators develop, by a process of implicit or explicit negotiation among themselves, at least a partially shared understanding of the role the mediator will play.

Mediator Roles

The wide variety of mediator roles and their dimensions deserve our attention, including those roles that are not regarded by some analysts and practitioners as embodying true or good mediation. After discussing the variety of social roles and the kinds of persons who fill them, I will examine the factors that help shape the roles.

Quasi Mediator

At one margin of what might be regarded as a mediator role are members of one of the adversary parties who carry out some go-between activities. They usually are not recognized as mediators and are referred to here as quasi mediators.[12] Nevertheless, they frequently convey information from the adversary back to their own side. In international relations, ambassadors are expected to inform their home government about the thinking of the government to which they are assigned. In the light of their insights, they may even suggest new options to their home government.

In the course of negotiations, one or more members of the negotiating team may help breach the barriers of mistrust by his side, by testifying to the sincerity and trustworthiness of members of the opposing side. They may even explore the possibility of the other side accepting a particular option and then seek their own side's acceptance of the idea. For example, during the 1978 Camp David negotiations between the Israeli and Egyptian governments, some members of the Israeli delegation, notably Ezer Weizman and Moshe Dayan, acted as quasi mediators between President Anwar al-Sadat and Prime Minister Begin.

Another noteworthy illustration of quasi mediation is provided in the context of the early 1980s U.S.-Soviet negotiations about the deployment of intermediate-range nuclear weapons in Europe.[13] The U.S. government wanted the

Soviets to remove all their intermediate-range missiles targeted on Western Europe (the SS20s). Only on that condition would the United States not deploy Pershing II and cruise missiles in Europe to target the Soviet Union. The Soviets rejected that possibility. To break the impasse, the chief of the U.S. delegation to the negotiations in Geneva, Paul Nitzi, and the head of the Soviet delegation, Yuli Kvitinski, privately and without informing their superiors worked out a compromise in their walks in the woods of Geneva. Once they had reached an agreement between themselves they tried to win acceptance from their respective governments, but failed.

Ad Hoc Informal Go-Between

In many different kinds of conflicts, persons acting as individuals or as representatives of religious or political organizations often carry messages back and forth between adversaries who are in such intense conflict that direct communication is difficult. They often set severe limits on the range of activities that they will perform as go-betweens. This has been the case for the work of a few Quakers in the protracted and severe struggle between the Sinhalese-dominated government of Sri Lanka and the separatist organization of the minority Tamils.[14] Conditions of their mediation include that the parties respect the anonymity of intervention and that each party has veto power regarding the continuation of the mediation. This makes it clear that the mediators have no agenda of their own beyond helping the adversaries negotiate with each other.

Consultant and/or Trainer

Increasingly, persons and organizations provide training and consultation services in conflict resolution methods. They are based in academic, governmental, business, religious, and philanthropic settings. The training includes developing skills in negotiation, active listening, mediation, strategic planning, and many other aspects of conducting a constructive struggle. The consultation often includes such training and also helps in developing conflict-management systems. Such intermediary activity is often carried out with one of the sides engaged in a struggle, but sometimes is provided to all sides. It frequently is undertaken before intense struggles erupt, and sometimes after the struggles have become protracted.

Training in conflict resolution and alternatives to violence are increasingly offered in schools at all levels, in prisons, in governmental and business organizations, and in churches and other voluntary associations. The training may be part of managing adaptations to changes in the composition of the membership, for example, as women and minorities become more significant participants in the organizations.

Consultations generally are short-term activities, often conducted with only one party to the conflict. Nevertheless, they can provide information about a struggle, and facilitate developing alternative ways of conducting it, or reducing its destructiveness.

Facilitator in Problem-Solving Workshops

A relatively new form of conflict resolution utilizes a workshop structure. A convenor, often academically based, brings together a few members of the opposing sides and guides and facilitates their discussions about the conflict in which they are engaged. The participants are often persons with ties to the leadership of their respective parties, or have the potentiality to become members of the leadership in the future. The workshops usually go on for several days, moving through a few stages of discussion.

The workshops have evolved through the experience of John Burton, Leonard Doob, Herbert Kelman, Edward Azar, Ronald Fisher, and others.[15] Workshops often have been held in connection with protracted international and intranational struggles, such as those in Northern Ireland, in Cyprus, and between Jewish Israelis and Arab Palestinians.

Workshop members generally do not attempt to negotiate agreements. Former members of workshops, however, sometimes act as quasi mediators upon returning to the adversary group to which they belong. Furthermore, they later sometimes become participants in official negotiations, as has been the case with former members of some of Herbert Kelman's workshops who subsequently participated in the early negotiations between the PLO and the Israeli government.[16]

Problem-solving, interactive workshops are one kind of what is often referred to as "track-two diplomacy" in international relations.[17] Track one is the official mediation, negotiation, and other exchanges conducted by governmental representatives. Track-two channels include much more than problem-solving workshops, and are best viewed as multitrack.[18] Among the many nonofficial channels are transnational organizations within which members of adversarial parties meet and discuss matters pertaining to the work of their organizations.[19] Another kind of nonofficial track includes ongoing dialogue groups with members from the adversary parties discussing the issues in contention between their respective countries or communities or organizations.

Facilitators and Members of Dialogue Groups

A few members of adversary groups sometimes develop an ongoing series of meetings at which they discuss particular aspects of the struggle in which their groups are engaged.[20] Such nonofficial, regular meetings between well-connected persons from adversary parties often play significant roles in providing a channel of communication and discussion of possible solutions to contentious issues. Members are acting as unofficial mediators; but their actions are done consciously and are known to the leaders and others in the groups to which they belong. In addition, persons with experience in such dialogue meetings apply this method to other conflicts, and so are acting with little ambiguity as an intermediary. Finally, some organizers of workshops have extended their problem-solving workshops into a series of meetings, becoming a kind of dialogue group between representatives of opposing sides. Examples of each of these kinds of dialogue groups can be found in many domestic conflict arenas, including industrial relations and community inter-religious and interethnic relations, and the international arena.[21]

In 1957, nuclear physicists and others involved in the development of nuclear weapons and strategies about their possible use, working in the United States, Great Britain, and the Soviet Union, began to meet and exchange ideas about ways to reduce the chances of nuclear warfare. The first meetings were held in Pugwash, in Nova Scotia, Canada, at the summer home of Cyrus Eaton, who provided the initial funding. This evolved into what has come to be called the Pugwash Conferences on Science and World Affairs.[22] In the 1950s, 1960s, and 1970s, discussion at the meetings contributed to the signing of the Partial Test-Ban Treaty, the Nonproliferation Treaty, the Biological Weapons Convention, and the Antiballistic Missile Treaty. Later meetings helped build consensus for the Strategic Arms Reduction Treaties I and II, the Intermediate Nuclear Force Treaty, and the Chemical Weapons Convention. In 1995, the Pugwash Conferences and Joseph Rotblat, its executive director, won the Nobel Peace Prize for their work.

Another important international example of track-two diplomacy is the Dartmouth Conference.[23] At the urging of President Dwight D. Eisenhower, Norman Cousins, then editor of the *Saturday Review*, brought together a group of prominent U.S. and Soviet citizens as a means of keeping communication open when official relations were especially strained. The first meeting was at Dartmouth College in 1960, and many meetings followed, providing a venue for the exchange of information and ideas such that participants could serve as quasi mediators.

With the end of the cold war, a more direct mediating role has evolved through one of the task forces that the Dartmouth Conference established in 1982. Following the collapse of détente at the end of the 1970s, members of the conference established a task force on arms control and one on regional conflicts to examine what had gone wrong. Reflection on the process and the phases of development of the Dartmouth Conference provided the basis for two members of that task force, Gennady Chufrin and Harold Saunders, to cochair another set of conferences, called the Tajikistan Dialogue.[24] Meetings among a wide range of Tajikistanis were begun in 1993, following a vicious civil war that erupted after the Soviet Union dissolved and Tajikistan became independent. Meeting frequently, the sustained dialogue group moved through five stages: (1) People decided to engage in dialogue to resolve intolerable problems they had. (2) They came together to map the elements of the problems and the relationships responsible for them. (3) They uncovered the underlying dynamics of the relationships and began to see ways to change them. (4) Together they planned steps to change the relationships. (5) They devised ways to implement their plan. In practice, participants sometimes remained at one stage for several meetings, and even returned to an earlier stage when circumstances changed.

Finally, short-term problem-solving workshops sometimes have grown into an organized series of workshops, with the same participants, constituting a continuing workshop. This is the case for the Israeli-Palestinian continuing workshop organized by Herbert Kelman and Nadim Rouhana.[25] It met four times between November 1990 and July 1992. Each workshop, lasting three or four days, followed ground rules designed to facilitate analytic discussion leading to joint thinking about the conflict. The third-party facilitators steered the participants through two major phases: first, concerns and needs were presented, and second, joint thinking about solutions and barriers to reaching them were undertaken.

Facilitators and Nonaligned Parties in Conferences

Large, multilateral meetings are often a setting in which conflicts involving many parties are negotiated. Some participants in such conferences play important intermediary roles, and some parties provide intermediary services without filling clearly defined roles. The social roles include convenors, facilitators, and mediators. Participants in multilateral conferences sometimes include parties who are clearly opposed and others who are not aligned with either side, and tend to perform mediating or facilitating functions.

In large multilateral conferences, some of the participants serve as mediators between opposing coalitions. In international affairs, this proved to be the case for the General Assembly of the United Nations and the negotiations about arms control during the cold war. Neutral and nonaligned powers have also been quite significant in the case of negotiations related to the Conference on Security and Cooperation in Europe, which concluded with the 1975 Helsinki Accords, and has since evolved to become the Organization on Security and Cooperation in Europe.

Local conflicts relating to environmental issues such as water usage, disposal of radioactive waste, or the location of a garbage-burning facility often involve numerous parties. A variety of conference formats may be used to bring many of the stakeholders together to find an acceptable solution to their conflicts.[26] For example, between 1981 and 1990, the management of the South Platte River in Nebraska and Colorado was the subject of controversy among persons engaged in sport fishing, raising cattle, and farming, as well as residents desiring fresh water for household uses, and environmentalists desiring the preservation of the natural habitat for sandhill cranes and endangered whooping cranes.[27] In the late 1970s, the State of Colorado initiated plans to build a large reservoir at the Two Forks site, where the north fork joined the main stem of the South Platte River. The conflict escalated in 1985 when the U.S. Army Corps of Engineers joined the Denver Water Board in supporting the dam project.

The controversy was resolved in a mutually satisfactory way. As the protests mounted, then Colorado Governor Richard Lamm convened a meeting of business, environment, and government leaders to discuss the issue. A series of conferences were also held at various Colorado universities involving scientific, recreational, agricultural, business, and environmental interests. At these meetings, the implications of the project for various parties were analyzed and alternatives discussed, including water conservation and small-scale development projects. In part because of this, when the Environmental Protection Agency's director William Reilly ordered a full review of the project in 1989 and then terminated plans for the dam in 1990, the conflict did not escalate.

The conflict over the habitat of the spotted owl in the forests of Oregon, however, did escalate into a much more intense and protracted struggle between the timber industry and environmentalists. Extensive meetings and conferences were not held at the beginning of the conflict; rather, the conflict began with confrontations and escalated. In 1990, the Fish and Wildlife Service declared the spotted owl to be an endangered species, and several months later, a forest service biologist released a report noting that the Sierra National Forest habitat was critical to the spotted owl's survival. In response to law suits brought by national environmental organizations, a federal court ordered that five million acres of the eight million acres of federal forest be set aside to protect the spotted owl. Later, when President George Bush's administration acted to ease those federal restrictions and open another two million acres to logging, the fight escalated further. The struggle was at a high level of tension when Bill Clinton took office as president. He convened a conference at which the many interested parties could meet and try to identify possible compromises. Shortly thereafter, the president announced a compromise, but it failed to satisfy either side and the general issue remained before the country. The struggle had persisted in being viewed as a zero-sum conflict and as ideologically significant. Furthermore, organizations from outside the immediate region had entered the fight, according it great symbolic importance.

Institutionalized Mediator

The typical mediator role is one that functions within a widely shared consensus. In many large-scale social systems, this means that mediators operate within the context of a legal system, and are likely to provide many of the services noted earlier. But even among the institutionalized mediators, various activities are combined in particular roles and by particular role players, while other activities are combined in other roles and by other incumbents.

In many countries, institutionalized mediation is most developed in the realm of labor-management relations. Even in such contexts, there are important variations in the social roles and how they are played. For example, Deborah M. Kolb compared official labor mediators in two different institutional settings: the Federal Mediation and Conciliation Service (FMCS) and a state board of conciliation.[28] She found that the mediators of the FMCS thought of themselves and acted as orchestrators, assisting the union and management to reach an agreement. The mediators in the state board regarded themselves and acted as dealmakers, actively constructing a package acceptable to both sides and using persuasion and even manipulation to win acceptance.

In recent years, alternative dispute resolution (ADR) has greatly expanded in many conflict arenas. Thus, throughout the United States, ADR is conducted in neighborhood conflict-resolution centers. In some judicial districts, mediation is mandated as part of the judicial process, as in child custody disputes between divorcing parents.

When the mediator functions within a highly institutionalized setting, the failure to reach a negotiated agreement tends to be followed by conflict-settlement procedures that are even less under the control of the parties to the dispute. Recourse to judicial proceedings is likely to follow or an executive branch agency imposes a settlement. Sometimes, however, the conflict escalates to a struggle in which each adversary resorts to coercion attempting to unilaterally impose its desired outcome.

Ad Hoc Facilitator

In many conflict arenas, major institutions provide mediators when conflicts erupt or their escalation is anticipated. The nature of the social role of these mediators and the services they provide is quite variable. In many urban conflicts, a mayor or governor may request that someone serve as a mediator to help manage or resolve the conflict. Usually, there is little preexisting consensus about the kind of mediator role the designated person will assume. Sometimes, in a difficult conflict, a series of mediators may be asked to try to help settle the dispute. This happened, for example, in the long (December 1962–March 1963) New York City newspaper strike.[29]

Some religious organizations are highly engaged in humanitarian work in various parts of the world, and some of their members provide informal, facilitative mediation. For example, various members of the Society of Friends have served in this way in several conflicts around the world. This was true in the 1967–71 Nigerian civil war, when the eastern region struggled unsuccessfully for independence as the Republic of Biafra.[30]

Ad Hoc Dealmaker

In many settings, an influential personage is called upon to help settle a dispute. This may be a political or religious leader in the community or society. He or she may have the authority to act as an arbitrator but more often acts as a dealmaking mediator. The dealmaker may have few resources to offer benefits or threaten losses and will mostly employ persuasion and manipulation.

An illustration of an ad hoc dealmaker can be seen in the handling of the 1972 dispute regarding a proposed low-income housing project in Forest Hills, a middle-class neighborhood in the borough of Queens, New York.[31] The mayor of New York, John Lindsey, requested a Queens lawyer, Mario Cuomo, to act as a fact finder to help resolve the dispute. Cuomo's role evolved, and he formulated a compromise for which he sought to mobilize general support, and which became the basis for the solution adopted by the political decision makers.

In international relations, often the dealmaker-mediator has many resources that can be used to help reach an agreement. These are mediators with muscle, or, using an old Chicago political term, *clout*. President Jimmy Carter was such a mediator at the 1978 Camp David negotiations between the Israeli and Egyptian governments, which resulted in the peace treaty between Israel and Egypt. The president could provide political cover for the concessions that each side felt would otherwise be fearful to make, could provide Israel with alternative sources of oil and military security if needed, and could provide Egypt with the prospects of badly needed economic assistance.

Summary

Mediator roles vary significantly in their degree of intrusion and activism.[32] At one extreme, some mediation roles involve only facilitative activities, and at the other extreme, they include deal making or even near-imposition of settlements. Activities at different ends of this continuum generally do not mix well within a single mediator role. This is one reason that different kinds of mediation are often carried out by different mediators in sequence or in parallel.

Many advocates of mediation in the context of the recent growth of conflict resolution practice stress that mediators only facilitate the disputants reaching an agreement themselves. The power to make an agreement lies in the disputants' own hands. This is counterpoised to a legal system in which judges and jurors determine the outcome of the dispute. But this discussion demonstrates that many other kinds of mediation also occur.

Although the parties to a dispute are the ones who ultimately select the mediator role and sometimes the person(s) who occupy the role, they frequently face some degree of pressure to accept mediation. In large part, this depends on the institutional setting. In certain areas of labor-management relations, laws require a governmental effort at mediation. Once parties enter into a mediation process, the variation in pressure and influence they experience is great.

Shapers of Mediator Roles

Mediator roles are socially constructed by all members of the social system in which they are enacted, even though the inputs of different members have varying strength. Furthermore, they are negotiated anew among the parties undertaking an actual mediating effort. Four major kinds of determinants of mediator roles warrant examination here: the cultural setting, the institutional context, the characteristics of the conflict, and the characteristics of the mediator.

Cultural Setting

Every social system, whether a society or an organization, has a culture with rules about how conflicts should be managed. These generally include rules about mediation. In traditional societies, mediators tend to be political or religious leaders of their communities; and they use the resources of their positions to help resolve the conflict.[33] In many small traditional societies, the goal is to heal the rupture that the conflict may have caused and to ensure that cooperative relationships within the community are sustained. For example, in traditional Hawaiian culture, interpersonal conflicts are regarded as entanglements, which are unfortunate as when fishing lines or nets become entangled.[34] Conflict resolution, therefore, is called *ho'oponopono*, or disentanglement. In this process, still in practice, the disputants are gathered together by a high-status community member who knows them. Prayers are offered, a statement of the problems is made, and for each problem, the leaders asks questions and a discussion follows, channeled through the leader. After a period of silence, confessions are made to the gods (or God) and to each disputant, and then restitution is arranged. Each problem is dealt with in this fashion, and then the disputants forgive each other, releasing each other from guilt. After a closing prayer, the participants share something to eat.

In highly differentiated societies, especially in Western societies, the judicial system tends to focus on the disputants and strives to determine who is right and who is wrong. Yet even in such societies, mediation is often used to

discover or construct a mutually acceptable agreement between the disputants. The mediation process, nevertheless, tends to be different in large, relatively bureaucratized societies than in small, traditional societies. Disputes
tend to be treated in relative isolation, the mediator roles tend to be profes-
sionalized, and the value of mediator neutrality is emphasized. The previous
discussion of the various mediator roles should demonstrate, however, the
great variability among kinds of mediation, in every society.

Institutional Context

The nature of the mediator role clearly varies with its institutional setting.
Some mediator roles are part of the same hierarchical structure as the disputing parties. The mediators in those roles operate with considerable authority
deriving from their position. A conflict unresolved by mediation is likely to
be decided by other third-party processes, such as litigation or administrative
authority.

Many mediator roles, even in highly differentiated societies, are quite informal and without institutional support, and the resources such mediators have
at their disposal are generally small. Sometimes they consist of little more than
personal ties with each side, the knowledge brought from previous mediating
experience, and the information attained in the very process of the mediation.
Thus, in interpersonal conflicts, even in large, bureaucratized societies, a local
priest or a bartender may mediate informally and represent the concerns of
the local set of social relations.

In many settings, the institutions are relatively sparse or weak for managing
particular conflicts among particular adversaries. Thus, in some societies, institutionalized procedures are not well developed for family disputes, since
they are considered private. Often communal conflicts are relatively inchoate
and therefore lack institutionalized means of being managed.

Characteristics of the Conflict

The scale and stage of a conflict, and the nature of the adversaries and their
relationship all affect the kind of mediation that tends to be used. In large-
scale conflicts, many kinds of intermediaries are likely to be engaged in the
mediation, sometimes at the same time. In small-scale conflicts, more often a
single person serves as the mediator, whether in a facilitative or deal-making
role.

Increasing attention is being given by analysts to specifying the kind of
intermediary intervention that is appropriate for various stages of a conflict.[35]
For example, unofficial roles and mediation that is largely facilitative are most
common and effective at early stages of a conflict.

Finally, the adversaries and the relationship between them strongly affect the kind of mediation practiced and the impact of the mediation. One important dimension of the relationship between adversaries in a conflict is the symmetry in resources between them. If adversaries differ greatly in resources, including legitimacy, the party with more tends to refuse mediation that seems to place the adversaries on an equal level. Official mediation tends to make visible that recognition. Consequently, an informal and relatively facilitative kind of mediation is more likely under those circumstances.

Adversaries with an ongoing relationship and with high levels of integration tend to utilize mediation or even arbitration in seeking to settle their disputes. Mediation or arbitration are expected to help reach a settlement quickly and prevent the escalation of antagonism, and so preserve the relationship.

Characteristics of the Mediator

Each kind of mediator can play only a particular range of mediator roles. For example, mediators with considerable material resources are likely to find it difficult to restrict themselves to a facilitator role; the adversaries tend to anticipate that such a mediator will use those resources to help fashion a deal.

In addition to organizational base and sponsorship, individuals obviously differ in style, as a result of past mediating training, experience, and personality. Such individual differences make some kinds of mediation especially congenial to particular persons, and provide a strong reason that no single way of filling a role will prove to be effective for every incumbent. Effective training for mediation takes that variability into account.

Summary

Mediator roles, like all social roles, are socially constructed by the adversaries and the mediators. They negotiate the nature of the mediation process and reach enough agreement to proceed, or the mediator does not gain access and does not mediate. Since many kinds of persons or groups can play mediator roles, and mediating functions can be provided by persons outside the formal mediator role, some mediating activities are often evident in social conflicts, inevitably so in large-scale conflicts.

Mediator Contributions

Having noted all the functions that mediators and other intermediaries may serve to foster constructive conflict de-escalation, we will consider what the actual contributions are. Although intermediaries can help adversaries in many ways, the adversaries must agree to accept the services of a mediator if someone is to play that role at all. If one or more of the adversaries refuses to do so or does so only begrudgingly, a mediator cannot act effectively. Consequently, one might argue that when the adversaries want to de-escalate their conflict, they will do so and the contributions of mediators are therefore only marginal. We must examine the evidence regarding the nature and magnitude of the contributions mediation efforts make to conflict de-escalation and settlement.

Meanings of Success

For many analysts, the ambiguities of the terms *effectiveness* and *success* have led them to categorize simply reaching a settlement with the participation of a mediator to be a successful mediation. If the overt struggle continues, the mediation is regarded as failed. Other analysts use several criteria of effectiveness, including durability of agreement, fairness of the agreement, and speed of reaching an agreement. Of course, even the assessment of each of these dimensions varies in difficulty. Measuring durability seems relatively straightforward, but even that can be uncertain when we consider the disputes about adherence to an agreement and to its implementation. Determining justness and efficiency are even more problematic, yet very important.

Which definition is chosen depends on the purposes of the definer and the definer's conception of the nature of mediation. For purposes of quantitative research, reliable categories that can fit many cases are needed. For this book, the contributions to a constructive outcome are of special interest, difficult as that may be to ascertain.

Another difficulty in assessing the contribution of mediation efforts is that the agreement, when it does come, depends on many factors in addition to whatever an intermediary has done. It is extraordinarily difficult to separate out the value added by an intermediary's actions. For some purposes, the testimony of the adversaries is an important indicator. Research findings indicate high rates of user satisfaction with mediation, typically 75 percent or higher.[36] But, to make an independent assessment of the contributions mediation makes, an analyst must use various kinds of comparative evidence of other mediating efforts in the same conflict at other times, of mediating conflicts in other similar conflicts, and of the consequences of similar conflicts lacking mediation.

A related issue is inherent in trying to answer the question, does mediation work? The issue can be put in terms of another question: compared to what? In the realm of many interpersonal, family, or public disputes, mediation is generally compared to adjudication. Within hierarchical organizations, the comparison may be to arbitration by higher authority, and in international relations the comparison may be to coercive diplomacy or to efforts at coercive imposition.

To assess the contributions of mediators in resolving conflicts, we will consider five issues. First, gaining mediator entry; second, contributing to reaching an agreement; third, contributing to the quality of the agreement; fourth, contributing to the implementation and durability of the agreement; and finally, coordinating mediation efforts. In this discussion, we will focus on persons enacting formal mediator roles, since the research has been so concentrated. Relatively little analysis has been done on informal mediation and on mediating services provided by persons not filling the role of mediator.

Gaining Entry

The intervention of mediators is anticipated and generally realized in many spheres of social life. For example, in countries with institutionalized collective bargaining, mediation is generally available and frequently used. Even in international conflicts, mediation by international organizations or by governments not engaged in the conflict frequently occurs. For example, Butterworth analyzed 310 international disputes between 1945 and 1974 and found that a mediator was involved in 82 percent of the cases.[37]

In the rapidly growing arena of disputes mediated through community dispute resolution centers, between one-third and two-thirds of the disputants to whom mediation is offered, refuse it.[38] In some matters, where mediation is required, interestingly, the likelihood of agreement and of user satisfaction is about the same for mandated and elective mediation.

Contributing to the Attainment of Agreements

Settlement rates for mediated disputes vary considerably across domains, ranging between 20 and 80 percent.[39] Analyses of international conflicts indicate that the involvement of intermediaries is associated with reduced likelihood that the conflict escalates and results in violence. Thus, an analysis of seventy-two major international conflicts between 1920 and 1965 found that 28 percent of those that were handled through procedures involving intermediaries had outcomes determined by violence, compared with 76 percent for those conflicts in which the adversaries did not use such procedures.[40]

Research evidence also indicates that mediators tend to speed reaching an agreement. For example, in social experiments, when a mediator intervened to make suggestions, the subjects made larger and more frequent concessions.[41] Apparently, the intervention enabled the negotiators to make concessions without considering themselves weak for doing so.

Observations and analyses of industrial disputes indicate that mediators are able to make suggestions and generate pressures that tend to result in concessions that hasten reaching an agreement.[42] A study of negotiations involving municipal governments and police and firefighter unions found that mediators using a relatively aggressive strategy of making suggestions was associated with narrowing the differences between the bargainers, particularly about nonsalary issues.[43]

Contributing to the Quality of Agreements

Reaching a settlement is not enough. The settlement should be regarded as a good one by the disputants, and also by other stakeholders it affects. A variety of evidence indicates that mediators often help produce agreements that are regarded as fair by analysts as well as those with a stake in the conflict. Experimental evidence, for example, indicates that third-party observers or mediators making even small interventions increase the pressures toward adhering to norms of fairness and equity.[44] Furthermore, experimental research indicates that mediators who are perceived to have high ability are especially likely to help produce settlements that yield high gains for the negotiators, perhaps because their suggestions can be readily accepted without losing face.[45]

There is evidence that mediated disputes result in agreements involving more equal sharing of resources and more compromise than *adjudicated* agreements. For example, divorce mediation resulted in more joint (rather than sole) custody agreements, and small claims disputes resulted in "awards going entirely to the plaintiff in almost 50 percent of the adjudicated cases, but in only 17 percent of the mediated ones.[46]

Observations and interviews with negotiators indicate several ways that mediators may help to produce relatively fair agreements and outcomes. One reason for this is that the presence of a trusted mediator who is considered skillful in mediation facilitates a fuller discussion of contentious issues.[47]

Contributing to the Implementation and Durability of Agreements

Compliance to mediated agreements appears to be relatively high. Thus, agreements reached in neighborhood justice centers have compliance rates of 67 to 87 percent; in the small claims area, full compliance was reported for the mediated cases, compared with 48 percent through adjudication.[48]

Several reasons for the relatively high compliance and durability of mediated agreements can be suggested. First, insofar as the disputing sides have participated in reaching an agreement, they are likely to feel that the agreement is fair and represents their interests, hence worthy of implementation and maintenance. The disputants' relations to the mediator are also important bases for honoring an agreement; disputants may have obligations to the mediator or wish to sustain their reputation with the mediator and therefore believe they should honor the agreement made with the assistance of that mediator. Particularly for mediators who have actively supported an agreement and have great resources, such considerations are important. For example, this has played an important role in the honoring of the 1979 Israeli-Egyptian peace treaty mediated by President Jimmy Carter.

Coordinating Intermediary Peacemaking Efforts

Whether consciously intended or not by any of the intermediaries, some of the activities they pursue seem to support each other, making them more effective jointly, than each would have been alone.[49] On the other hand, different activities performed by different intermediaries can interfere with each other, undermining all of them. The mutually supportive actions will be referred to as well-coordinated activities, and those that adversely affect each other will be termed poorly coordinated.

Two major types of coordination can be distinguished: sequential and simultaneous, and the many varieties of each. Intermediary activity may be coordinated over time in several ways. Thus, there are many examples of one intermediary preparing the ground or even initiating de-escalating negotiations and then having the negotiations taken up by a different set of mediators. Many instances of effective sequential complementarity can be cited, usually involving nonofficial or track-two methods preceding more traditional diplomacy.[50] Track two may prepare the groundwork for official negotiations.[51] At other times, negotiations are actually initiated in a nonofficial track and then handed off to an official negotiating channel. Sometimes, the traditional diplomatic channel has reached an impasse, and a new track is opened informally. When progress is made, the negotiations are returned to the official channel. This is illustrated in the 1993 negotiations between Israelis and the PLO, conducted in Oslo, Norway.[52] Finally, organizers of short-term problem-solving workshops sometimes have organized a series of workshops, with the same participants, which constitute a continuing workshop. This is the case for the Israeli-Palestinian continuing workshop organized by Rouhana and Kelman. These and earlier workshops involving Israeli Jews and Palestinian Arabs contributed in several ways to the later direct official negotiations between the Israeli government and the PLO.[53] For example, the understandings about each other's points of views and concerns, and possible ways to reconcile them, provided the basis for officials on each side to believe a mutually acceptable formula could be found.

Unofficial meetings and official back-channel conversations sometimes complement relatively traditional diplomatic activities when carried out simultaneously as well as sequentially. One way this occurs is when unofficial tracks parallel official negotiating tracks. For example, this was the case for the Pugwash and Dartmouth meetings during the years of U.S.-Soviet negotiations regarding many arms control measures.

In large-scale conflicts, various intermediaries and approaches generally need to be blended together to be effective. If they are well coordinated, their effectiveness enhances the efforts of any one approach. The coordination includes actions pursued simultaneously and sequentially, as illustrated in the 1989–92 peace process ending Mozambique's war.[54] Some organizations make efforts to coordinate a variety of intermediaries in conducting a set of activities. This is the case, notably, for the Carter Center's Programs on Conflict Resolution.[55]

The destructive and protracted character of many communal conflicts, despite multiple efforts to intervene and resolve them, indicates that the interventions are often ineffective. We must consider why they fail. To what extent is failure due to the nature of the conflict and the existing conditions and to what extent is it due to inappropriate intermediary actions? Was the time not ripe for the kind of interventions that were tried?[56] Does the very multiplicity of intermediary efforts often hamper effective de-escalation and reaching enduring mutually acceptable agreements? Does this occur because poorly coordinated efforts undermine each other as they convey inconsistent messages to the adversaries about what needs to be done? Were the wrong kinds of intermediaries used for the kinds of adversaries in the conflict? Under what circumstances do adversaries play one intermediary against another? Do intermediaries compete for attention and strain the capability of the adversaries' representatives to make appropriate responses?

Previous experience, theorizing, and research suggest answers to some of these questions.[57] Thus, possible intermediaries vary in the likelihood of effectively intervening in different kinds of conflicts. For example, conflicts within a country, between the government and challengers to the government, tend to be resistant to peacemaking interventions by other states, and even by international governmental organizations. Therefore, unofficial, facilitating intervenors are probably more likely to gain access.[58] The difficulty that governments and governmental organizations have in intervening in domestic conflicts has created a void that nongovernmental organizations increasingly fill, for example, the center established by former U.S. President Jimmy Carter.[59] Once negotiations have been initiated, however, intermediaries with resources are relatively more effective than are facilitating, nonofficial intermediaries to bring about an agreement and to help implement it.[60]

Various intermediary activities also differ in their likely effectiveness for different kinds of conflicts and at different phases of a conflict. Thus, consulting and conveying information between the adversaries is likely to be more effective than strong, deal-making activities at the prenegotiation stage of a conflict.[61]

For simultaneous intermediary activity to be effectively complementary, coordination is important. This is often aided by consultation among the intermediaries and agreement about the various roles each will play—for example, which one takes the leading role. Some complementarity may be unwitting, as when one intermediary threatens to put increasing pressure on one party, and another intermediary suggests a solution and a way out of the confrontation. Finally, sometimes having a secret channel allows for exploration of alternatives, undistracted by attention directed at relatively public channels.

Conclusions

Mediators and other kinds of intermediaries frequently try to ameliorate conflicts, seeking to speed an end to violence or other destructive conduct and to help achieve a durable and fair settlement. Undoubtedly, those efforts are effective in many kinds of conflicts in a variety of settings. Undoubtedly, too, such efforts frequently are not made and even when made are ineffective. In these conclusions, we discuss mediator intentions and practices as they affect the course of conflict de-escalation and settlement. We also review variations in their effectiveness under different conflict conditions.

The issue of mediator neutrality often has been a matter of contention. Many mediators and analysts of mediation stress that mediators should be neutral while playing the mediator role. Others argue that neutrality is not possible, and in any case is not necessary. Being trustworthy and honest with the disputants is sufficient to play the role effectively. To clarify this debate, we should recognize that neutrality in this context has a variety of meanings.

Neutrality of the mediator may refer to feelings and intentions, or to conduct as perceived by the disputants or observers, or to effects upon the disputants and the course of the conflict. Some mediators may be genuinely disinterested in the conflict or the disputants; this is more likely among mediators who play their role largely as facilitators. But even they may have strong interests in the use of particular processes and/or in reaching an agreement. Such concerns are likely to mean that whatever their neutrality about the dispute, their actions will have implications for the kind of settlement reached, thus affecting the conflict's outcome.

More often, the mediators are likely to have feelings and interests that are the bases for sympathy toward one party compared with another. How they act on such convictions, however, is another matter. Some may strive to act evenhandedly, or to be an advocate for both sides; others act to assist one side more than another, or to advance their own interests; finally, some try to serve the interests of stakeholders not represented in the negotiations. Such actions may be more or less energetically pursued.

In addition, how the disputants perceive the mediators' intentions, actions, and impacts influences the mediators' effectiveness. Some mediators, with past histories of relations with one or more of the parties in a conflict, may be regarded as too biased or untrustworthy to serve as a mediator. In many circumstances, particularly for potential mediators with great resources, disinterested neutrality is not expected by the disputants. Often, neutrality is not desired. One or more side may prefer a mediator who can enlarge the pie to be divided, who can leverage the other side, or who can ensure the compliance with any agreement reached. This is one of the attractions of U.S. official mediation for antagonists in the Middle East and in other regions.

Whatever the intentions or perceived conduct of mediators, the consequences of their efforts are not likely to be neutral. By their very act of mediation, they give some legitimacy to the parties among whom they are mediating. Of course, this is a reason for a party that does not recognize the legitimacy of an opposing side to refuse mediation in the conflict with that opposition. This is particularly the case for official mediation. By according legitimacy, the mediators tend to provide a measure of equality, at least in rights, to the adversaries.

Mediation is more or less effective, depending on the nature and stage of the conflict, the disputants, and their relations with each other. On the whole, the less antagonistic and the more integrated the relations between the adversaries, the better are the prospects for mediation.[62] The more intensely and destructively the conflict has been waged, the greater is the difficulty in undertaking mediation and doing so effectively. But if the antagonists believe they are unable to impose a victory and begin to search for a way out, mediation begins to appear attractive. Conflicts in which one side is more powerful than the other are more difficult to mediate than are conflicts in which the adversaries are relatively equal.

Some kinds of contentious issues are more amenable to mediation (and to resolution) than are others. For example, conflicts deriving from dissensus, value differences, or matters of principle are often more difficult to mediate than are conflicts deriving from consensus, or more compromisable substantive matters. Evidence supporting this generalization can be found in studies of international conflict, labor relations, and community mediation regarding environmental issues.[63] Furthermore, mediation is more difficult under conditions of resource scarcity, as noted in studies of labor mediation and in divorce mediation. Finally, mediation is more difficult the greater the disparity in goals and the greater the sense by any side that its vital interests are threatened.

Many other conditions relating to the mediation process, the mediators, and the adversaries' relations with possible mediators influence the effectiveness of mediating efforts. In certain cultural and institutional settings, mediation is likely to be seen as widely appropriate to help resolve conflicts. Furthermore, mediation is more likely to occur and more likely to be effective, if mediators are available whom the adversaries regard as legitimate and with whom they have ongoing relations.

Certainly, mediation is not a panacea for all conflicts. It can make important contributions, however, to preventing or controlling destructive conflicts. It contributes to the transition from escalation or stalemate to de-escalation; and contributes to constructing a mutually acceptable outcome. It also contributes to improving the equity and stability of the outcome. The size of such contributions depends on many conditions of a conflict, the kind of mediation efforts undertaken, and most significantly, the match between them.

Intermediary actions other than mediation also contribute to the amelioration and resolution of conflicts. These include interventions to separate contending groups. Sometimes this is done with the agreement of the adversaries, as is generally the case with United Nations peacekeeping forces; and sometimes this occurs without such agreement, as when police break up family or community fights. Other intermediary efforts are intended to reduce the presumed grounds for the conflict or to mitigate the damages caused by the fighting, as is attempted by the interventions of organizations advocating human rights or providing humanitarian assistance. These and other kinds of intermediary actions will be discussed in the following chapters, in the context of examining how conflicts end and what the consequences of the outcomes are.

Notes

1. Deborah M. Kolb and Associates, *When Talk Works: Profiles of Mediators* (San Francisco: Jossey-Bass, 1994).

2. Bryant Wedge, "A Psychiatric Model for Intercession in Intergroup Conflict," *Journal of Applied Behavioral Science*, 7, no. 6, (1971): 733, 761.

3. Jimmy Carter, *Keeping Faith* (New York: Bantam Books, 1982), 378 ff.

4. Jeffrey Z. Rubin and Bert R. Brown, *The Social Psychology of Bargaining and Negotiation* (New York: Academic Press, 1975).

5. Matti Golan, *The Secret Conversations of Henry Kissinger: Step-by-Step Diplomacy in the Middle East*, trans. R. G. Stern and S. Stern (New York: Bantam, 1976), 168–69.

6. Michael Doyle and David Straus, *How to Make Meetings Work* (New York: Playboy Press, 1976).

7. Ways that one mediator does this are reported in John Forester, "Lawrence Susskind: Activist Mediation," in Kolb and Associates, *When Talk Works*.

8. Carter, *Keeping Faith*.

9. This was done, for example, in the Israeli-Egyptian negotiations mediated by President Carter and his associates at Camp David. The idea has been advocated by Roger Fisher. See the discussion in Roger Fisher, "Playing the Wrong Game?" in Jeffrey Z. Rubin, ed. *Dynamics of Third Party Intervention: Kissinger in the Middle East* (New York: Praeger, 1981); and Roger Fisher, Elizabeth Kopelman, and Andea Kupfer Schneider, *Beyond Machiavelli* (New York: Penguin, 1996), 126–32.

10. Carter, *Keeping Faith*, 392. Also see Eileen F. Babbitt, "Jimmy Carter: The Power

of Moral Suasion in International Mediation," in Kolb and Associates, *When Talk Works.*

11. James Laue, "Intervenor Roles: A Review," *Crisis and Change* 3 (Fall 1973): 4–5.

12. Louis Kriesberg, "Varieties of Mediating Activities and of Mediators," in Jacob Bercovitch, ed. *Resolving International Conflicts* (Boulder, Colo.: Lynne Rienner, 1996).

13. Strobe Talbott, *Deadly Gambits* (New York: Knopf, 1984).

14. Thomas Princen, "Joseph Elder: Quiet Peacemaking," in Kolb and Associates, *When Talk Works.*

15. Ronald J. Fisher, *Interactive Conflict Resolution* (Syracuse, N.Y.: Syracuse University Press, 1997).

16. Herbert C. Kelman, "Contributions of an Unofficial Conflict Resolution Effort to the Israeli-Palestinian Breakthrough," *Negotiation Journal* 11 (January 1995): 19–27.

17. Joseph V. Montville, "Transnationalism and the Role of Track-Two Diplomacy," in W. Scott Thompson and Kenneth M. Jensen, eds. *Approaches to Peace: An Intellectual Map* (Washington, D.C.: United States Institute of Peace Press, 1991).

18. See John W. McDonald, "Further Explorations in Track Two Diplomacy," in Louis Kriesberg and Stuart J. Thorson, eds. *Timing the De-Escalation of International Conflicts* (Syracuse, N.Y.: Syracuse University Press, 1991).

19. William M. Evan, ed., *Knowledge and Power in a Global Society* (Beverly Hills, Calif.: Sage, 1981) and Louis Kriesberg, "International Nongovernmental Organizations and Transnational Integration," *International Associations* 24, no. 11 (1972): 520–25.

20. Many such dialogue groups have been organized between Jews and Palestinians in Israel and elsewhere in the world, working with Jews and Palestinians in the diaspora. For discussions about the theory and practice of such groups, see Fisher, *Interactive Conflict Resolution,* 121–41; and Haim Gordon and Jan Demarst, " From Dialogue to Responsibility: Bridging Conflict Resolution and Peace Education," in Louis Kriesberg, ed., *Research in Social Movements, Conflict and Change,* vol. 7 (Greenwich, Conn.: JAI Press, 1984).

21. Some communities have labor councils, at which management and union representatives meet regularly, and associations such as the Industrial Relations Association nationally and locally provide a forum for ongoing discussions. In the United States, local and national interreligious organizations provide a way for leaders of different religious communities to get to know each other and help each other when crises threaten.

22. Michael J. Pentz and Gillian Slovo, "The Political Significance of Pugwash," in Evan, ed. *Knowledge and Power in a Global Society;* and Joseph Rotblat, *Scientists in the Quest for Peace: A History of the Pugwash Conferences* (Cambridge, Mass.: MIT Press, 1972).

23. Gennady I. Chufrin and Harold H. Saunders, "A Public Peace Process," *Negotiation Journal* 9 (April 1993): 155–77.

24. Harold H. Saunders, "Sustained Dialogue on Tajikistan," *Mind and Human Interaction* 6 (August 1995):123–35.

25. Nadim N. Rouhana and Herbert C. Kelman, "Non-official Interaction Processes in the Resolution of International Conflicts: Promoting Joint Israeli-Palestinian

Thinking through a Continuing Workshop," *Journal of Social Issues* 50, no. 1 (1994): 157–78; and Nadim N. Rouhana, "The Dynamics of Joint Thinking Between Adversaries in International Conflict: Phases of the Continuing Problem-Solving Workshop," *Political Psychology* 16, no. 2 (1995): 321–45. In addition to Kelman and Rouhana, two other persons constituted the third party for the workshop: Harold Saunders and Christopher Mitchell.

26. Lawrence Susskind, *Breaking the Impasse: Consensual Approaches to Resolving Public Disputes* (New York: Basic, 1987), and Lawrence Susskind, *Dealing with an Angry Public: The Mutual Gains Approach to Resolving Disputes* (New York: Free Press, 1996).

27. For an analysis comparing the Two Forks dam and spotted owl conflicts, see Bruce W. Dayton, "Sources of Escalation in Natural Resource Conflicts: The Spotted Owl and the Two Forks Dam," unpublished paper, Syracuse University, March 1994. Also see Gail Bingham, *Resolving Environmental Disputes* (Washington, D.C.: The Conservation Foundation, 1990).

28. Kolb, *The Mediators.*

29. A. H. Raskin, "The Newspaper Strike: A Step-by-Step Account," in I. William Zartman, ed. *The 50% Solution* (New Haven, Conn.: Yale University Press, 1983).

30. See: C. H. Mike Yarrow, *Quaker Experiences in International Conciliation* (New Haven, Conn.: Yale University Press, 1978); Maureen R. Berman and Joseph E. Johnson, eds., *Unofficial Diplomats* (New York: Columbia University Press, 1977); Thomas Princen, *Intermediaries in International Conflict* (Princeton, N.J.: Princeton University Press, 1992); and Douglas Johnston and Cynthia Sampson, eds., *Religion, the Missing Dimension of Statecraft* (New York: Oxford University Press, 1994).

31. Mario Matthew Cuomo, *Forest Hills Diary: The Crisis of Low-Income Housing* (New York: Vintage Books, 1974).

32. Many analysts have made similar distinctions; for example, Princen, in *Intermediaries in International Conflict*, distinguishes between neutral mediators and principal mediators.

33. See, for example, P. H. Gulliver, *Disputes and Negotiations: A Cross-Cultural Persepective* (New York: Academic Press, 1979); and John Paul Lederach, *Preparing for Peace: Conflict Transformation across Cultures* (Syracuse, N.Y.: Syracuse University Press, 1995).

34. James A. Wall, Jr., and Ronda Roberts Callister, "*Ho'oponopono:* Some Lessons from Hawaiian Mediation," *Negotiation Journal* 11 (January 1995): 45–54; and E. Victoria Shook and Leonard Ke'ala Kwan, "*Ho'oponopono:* Straightening Family Relationships in Hawaii," in K. Avruch, P. Black, and J Scimecca, eds., *Conflict Resolution: Cross-Cultural Perspectives* (New York: Greenwood Press, 1991).

35. See Loraleigh Keashly and Ronald J. Fisher, "Complementarity and Coordination of Conflict Interventions: Taking a Contingency Perspective," in Jacob Bercovitch, ed., *Resolving International Conflicts* (Boulder, Colo.: Lynne Rienner, 1996); Cristopher Mitchell, "The Process and Stages of Mediation," in David R. Smock, ed., *Making War and Waging Peace: Foreign Intervention in Africa* (Washington, D.C.: United States Institute of Peace Press, 1993); Louis Kriesberg, *International Conflict Resolution: The U.S.-USSR and Middle East Cases* (New Haven, Conn.: Yale University Press, 1992); and Louis Kriesberg, "The Phases of Destructive Communal Conflicts and Proactive

Solutions" in David Carment and Patrick James, eds., *International Politics of Ethnic Conflict: Prevention and Peakeeping* (Columbia: University of South Carolina Press, 1998).

36. Kenneth Kressel and Dean G. Pruitt, "Conclusion: A Research Perspective on the Mediation of Social Conflict," in Kenneth Kressel, Dean G. Pruitt, and Associates, eds., *Mediation Research* (San Francisco: Jossey-Bass, 1989).

37. R. Butterworth, *Managing Interstate Conflict, 1945–1974* (Pittsburgh, Pa.: University of Pittsburgh Press, 1976).

38. Kenneth Kressel, Dean G. Pruitt, and Associates, eds., *Mediation Research* (San Francisco: Jossey-Bass, 1989).

39. Kressel, Pruitt, and Associates, eds., *Mediation Research*, p. 397.

40. Peter Wolf, "International Social Structure and the Resolution of International Conflicts, 1920 to 1965," in *Research in Social Movements, Conflicts, and Change*, vol. 1, ed. Louis Kriesberg (Greenwich, Conn.: JAI Press, 1978).

41. Jeffrey Z. Rubin and Bert R. Brown, *The Social Pyschology of Bargaining and Negotiation* (New York: Academic Press, 1975).

42. See Ann Douglas, *Industrial Peacemaking* (New York: Columbia University Press, 1962).

43. Thomas A. Kochan and Todd Jick, "The Public Sector Mediation Process," *Journal of Conflict Resolution* 22 (June 1978): 210–40.

44. Rubin and Brown, *The Social Pyschology of Bargaining and Negotiation*, 58–59.

45. David A. Brookmire and Frank Sistrunk, "The Effects of Perceived Ability and Impartiality of Mediators and Time Pressure on Negotiation," *Journal of Conflict Resolution* 24 (June 1980): 311–27.

46. Kressel, Pruitt, and Associates, eds., *Mediation Research*, p. 397. Such outcomes are not necessarily more just or fair.

47. Richard E. Walton, "Interpersonal Confrontation and Third Party Functions: A Case Study," *Journal of Applied Behavioral Sciences* 4, no. 3 (1968): 327–50.

48. Kenneth Kressel and Dean G. Pruitt, "Conclusion: A Research Perspective on the Mediation of Social Conflict," in Kressel, Pruitt, and Associates, eds., *Mediation Research*, 396.

49. Louis Kriesberg, "Coordinating Intermediary Peace Efforts," *Negotiation Journal* 12 (October 1996): 341–52; also see Christopher Mitchell, "The Process and Stages of Mediation," in David R. Smock, ed. *Making War and Waging Peace.*

50. See Joseph V. Montville, "Transnationalism and the Role of Track-Two Diplomacy," in W. Scott Thompson and Kenneth M. Jensen, eds., *Approaches to Peace: An Intellectual Map* (Washington, D.C.: United States Institute of Peace Press, 1991); and John W. McDonald. "Further Explorations in Track Two Diplomacy," in Louis Kriesberg and Stuart J. Thorson, eds., *Timing the De-Escalation of International Conflicts* (Syracuse, N.Y.: Syracuse University Press, 1991).

51. Chufrin and Saunders, "A Public Peace Process"; see also Saunders, "Sustained Dialogue on Tajikistan."

52. Amos Elon, "The Peacemakers," *The New Yorker* 69 (20 December 1993): 77–85.

53. Herbert C. Kelman, "Contributions of an Unofficial Conflict Resolution Effort to the Israeli-Palestinian Breakthrough," *Negotiation Journal* 11 (January 1995): 19–27.

54. Cameron Hume, *Ending Mozambique's War* (Washington, D.C.: United States Institute of Peace Press, 1994).

55. Dayle E. Spencer and Honggang Yang, "Lessons from the Field of Intra-National Conflict Resolution," *Notre Dame Law Review* 67, vol. 5 (1992): 1495–517; Janice Gross Stein. ed., *Getting to the Table: The Process of International Prenegotiation* (Baltimore, Md.: The Johns Hopkins University Press, 1989); I. William Zartman, *Ripe for Resolution: Conflict and Intervention in Africa*, 2d ed. (New York: Oxford University Press, 1989); and I. William Zartman, "Conflict Reduction: Prevention, Management, and Resolution," in Francis M. Deng and I. William Zartman, eds., *Conflict Resolution in Africa* (Washington, D.C.: Brookings Institution, 1991).

56. Zartman, *Ripe for Resolution*; and Kriesberg and Thorson, eds., *Timing the De-Escalation of International Conflicts*.

57. Michael S. Lund, *Preventing Violent Conflicts* (Washington, D.C.: United States Institute of Peace Press, 1996); Saadia Touval and I. William Zartman, eds. *International Mediation in Theory and Practice* (Boulder, Colo.: Westview, 1985); Elise Boulding, ed., *Building Peace in the Middle East* (Boulder, Colo.: Lynne Rienner, 1994); Carnegie Commission on Preventing Deadly Conflict, *Preventing Deadly Conflict* (New York: Carnegie Corporation of New York, 1997); Kriesberg, "Coordinating Intermediary Peace Efforts" and "The Phases of Destructive Communal Conflicts and Proactive Solutions."

58. Hume, *Ending Mozambique's War*.

59. Douglas Brinkley, "Jimmy Carter's Modest Quest for Global Peace," *Foreign Affairs* 74 (November-December, 1995): 90–100.

60. I. William Zartman, "Conflict Reduction: Prevention, Management, and Resolution," in Francis M. Deng and I. William Zartman, eds., *Conflict Resolution in Africa* (Washington, D.C.: Brookings Institution, 1991).

61. Zartman, "Conflict Reduction: Prevention, Management, and Resolution"; Loraleigh Keashly and Ronald J. Fisher, "Complementarity and Coordination of Conflict Interventions: Taking a Contingency Perspective," in *Resolving International Conflicts*, ed. Bercovitch; and Stein, *Getting to the Table*.

62. Kressel, Pruitt, and Associates, eds., *Mediation Research*.

63. For example, see Kressel, Pruitt, and Associates, eds., *Mediation Research*, and Bercovitch, *Resolving International Conflicts*.

9

Negotiations, Settlements,
and Outcomes

Conflicts do not simply disappear. After violent outbursts, after campaigns that are episodes within an extended struggle, and after a struggle that is waged for decades, conflicts cease and there is an outcome. The outcome may be the basis for new fights but also the foundation for integrative relationships. The ending of the struggle may be written down in an agreement the adversaries negotiate, or it may be the unstated acceptance of a new status quo. The outcome of a conflict, not just its cessation, is a matter of highest concern to the partisans in the struggle, and should be to analysts of social conflicts as well.

In the past, research and theory concentrated on the outbreak and escalation of conflicts. In recent years, however, popular as well as scholarly attention to the outcomes of struggles has begun to increase. The growth of the conflict-resolution field has directed attention particularly to the role of negotiations in settling, resolving, or otherwise ending a conflict. The major dimensions of possible outcomes are discussed in this chapter before we examine the various paths taken to reach a recognizable outcome, particularly the path of negotiations. Finally, we consider how the path taken to end the fight affects the struggle's results.

Outcomes

To talk about conflict outcomes presumes we know when a conflict has ended, but that is not always clear. The conflicts between social classes or between ethnic communities in the same country may be regarded as never-ending by many members of each side. Even within those enduring conflicts, nevertheless, particular struggles often are regarded by the opponents and others to have ended. Since a conflict exists when two or more parties manifest their belief that they have incompatible goals, when they no longer contest a particular goal, that conflict ceases. Typically, a symbolically important event, an explicit agreement, or an authoritative decision marks a profound change in the adversaries' beliefs. For example, the 1920 adoption of the amendment to the U.S. Constitution providing for women's suffrage ended the struggle over the right of American women to vote in the United States, and the 1979 Egyptian-Israeli peace treaty marked the end of a fundamental conflict between those countries regarding territory and recognition.

Admittedly, at some future time other contentious issues will arise, but probably in circumstances that make it reasonable to regard the conflict as a new one. In any case, for most analytic purposes, conflicts ending with explicit agreements and ratified by a process the adversaries deem legitimate mark the conclusion of a struggle. There may be factions within one or more parties to the conflict who are not reconciled to the terms of the agreement, but they are unable to effectively represent any of the major parties who had waged the struggle.

A struggle often incorporates many individual fights and campaigns, limited in time or locality, yet conducted in the context of a long-enduring struggle. To illustrate, consider the 1960s' struggle for civil rights for African Americans. It included many specific fights, some of which ended in negotiated agreements. For example, the massive nonviolent campaign in 1963 in Birmingham, Alabama, was directed to end segregation at lunch counters and public facilities in downtown stores, to establish fair hiring procedures, and to establish a biracial commission to set a timetable for the desegregation of the public schools. The sit-ins, boycotts, widespread arrests, other aspects of the campaign, and the responses to it resulted in negotiations with the local business elite, and on 10 May 1963 an agreement was reached granting many of the demands made by Dr. Martin Luther King, Jr., and the Southern Christian Leadership Conference (SCLC).[1] That campaign was over, but the civil rights struggle went on for other goals in Birmingham and the country as a whole.

Identifying a termination is problematic when no explicit agreement or widely recognized symbolic event occurs. Some conflicts gradually melt away, and it is unclear when the conflict was acknowledged to be over. Outside observers or analysts often use their own criteria to decide that the struggle has concluded. Given the frequent use of acts of violence or other coercive actions as an indicator of the existence of a conflict, the cessation of that conduct is often used as the indicator that a conflict has ended.

In large-scale conflicts, even major actions signaling the end of a struggle are frequently problematic since rejectionist factions may continue the struggle that the presumed authorized leadership has agreed to end. This has often been the case in the conflicts in Lebanon, Northern Ireland, the Basque region, and many other places.

However designated, when the conflict is deemed to have ended, the question then arises: on what terms has it been settled? The deal the adversaries strike in ending a conflict is obviously central to assessing the effectiveness of various strategies for waging the struggle and for settling it. Partisans in a fight usually think about a conflict as ending in victory or defeat. Indeed, that is what parties themselves often proclaim after a fight has ended, and those designations have important consequences. Such characterizations affect who will seek future redress and which conflict modes will be tried in the future. They do not suffice, however, to portray the social reality, since they do not allow for the multidimensional quality of actual outcomes. We first consider distributive outcomes: the degree of relative gains and losses among the adversaries, not assuming one side wins all and the other losses all. We then discuss joint outcomes: the extent to which the adversaries share benefits as well as costs. Outcomes with a high degree of shared benefits are often termed *integrative.*[2] The set of distributive and joint outcomes are shown in figure 9.1. Finally, we consider an additional outcome dimension: the degree of engagement or separation between the former adversaries.

Distribution of Gains and Losses

Adversaries often view the outcome of a fight in terms of the relative gains each side won, at the expense of the other. This zero-sum view of conflict is

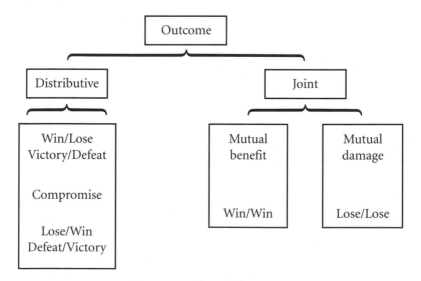

Figure 9.1   Types of Outcomes

widely taken, particularly regarding consensual conflicts, for example, about the allocation of money or land. Furthermore, the gains and losses are generally considered in terms of what was sought by each side as the conflict arose. Therefore, to make a demand and then fail to have it met is generally regarded as a loss, and will be so considered here. Of course, one side rarely wins everything it sought; some degree of compromise is almost inevitable. Even the Allies' demand for Japan's unconditional surrender in World War II was slightly tempered at the very end by the Allies' acceptance of the emperor remaining on his throne. On the other hand, the losing side may not lose as much as it feared it might, and therefore can claim some success. The gains and losses are rarely total, but one side usually gets more of what it sought than does the other side.

Assessing relative gains and losses is difficult because for many matters in dispute, the goals of the opposing sides are not clear, and various persons and groups within each side have somewhat different goals. Furthermore, the goals are likely to shift in the course of a struggle. An adversary tends to expand its goals when it is doing well in the struggle but contract them when it believes it is doing poorly.

Another possible anchoring point to assess gains and losses is the circumstance of each adversary when the conflict erupted. One or more of the parties in a struggle may end up worse off after the struggle has ended than they were before it began. Or, one or the other may think it is better off, even if it did not achieve what it set out to achieve in the struggle. Admittedly, the circumstances at the time the conflict erupted is ambiguous in retrospect and may also be disputed. Furthermore, the parties generally start off in unequal circumstances, and the fight may modify the balance without fundamentally changing the relative positions of the opponents. The party advantaged by the modification, however, may assert that it has gained.

From still another perspective, each side may regard its gains and losses relative to those of its opponent, so a party that inflicted pain on its opponent or prevented the opponent from attaining all that it sought may claim a victory. Although bruised and bloodied, the fighter can say, "You should see the other guy!" and claim triumph.

Finally, sometimes, merely resisting fiercely, under great odds, is proclaimed to be a defining event and a great achievement. It becomes the basis for mobilization in renewed later battles. For example, many Serbs celebrate the Battle of Kosovo, fought in 1389, in which they unsuccessfully resisted the invading Turkish army.

Generally, in this analysis, losses and gains are assessed by comparing them with the adversaries' ostensible goals at the outset of their struggle. This conception is closest to the partisans' sense that they won or lost the struggle. Nevertheless, the other considerations noted are often useful in interpreting the significance of various outcomes for the adversaries in the struggle. Furthermore, they allow leaders to interpret an outcome in a favorable light, even if the losses have been heavy. Finally, even a defeat in a campaign embedded within a protracted struggle can contribute to victory in subsequent campaigns: lessons are learned, allies are rallied, and constituents are mobilized.

An important implication of these observations is that both adversaries may regard the outcome as having given them some benefits. Indeed, most conflicts do end in a kind of compromise with each side gaining something of what it sought and failing to gain everything. The compromise may be the result of an exchange of concessions, sometimes reflecting a trade-off in gains in high-priority areas for concessions in low-priority areas. In ideologically driven conflicts and in some cultures about some matters, compromise has connotations of betraying sacred commitments. Although adversaries, in such circumstances, may deny they have agreed to a compromise, outside observers may view the outcome as embodying an exchange of concessions.

The ambiguities of outcomes and the rarity of one side totally overwhelming the other, make the attainment of a mutually acceptable outcome more feasible than it might otherwise appear. The changing character of goals and their varying importance for different elements in each side help adversaries find outcomes with some joint gains and minimal joint loses.

Joint Damages and Benefits

In addition to relative losses and gains for each side, conflict outcomes vary in the degree to which the parties have joint gains and losses. That is, one can look at the outcome in terms of the benefits and damages accruing to the opposing parties together. Furthermore, the outcome may be more or less mutually damaging or mutually beneficial, not simply in an additive sense, but as a shared result. Such joint possibilities are present in every outcome, but often are not part of either adversary's goals when entering a fight. They become more significant when the adversaries begin to consider ending a fight and are generally more salient when a problem-solving approach is taken in conducting the struggle.

For example, Walton and McKersie describe a union-management dispute regarding the issue of promotion that was transformed into a problem and then solved. Few senior employees were being promoted because management said they lacked the requisite skills. The union wanted to improve the promotional chances of employees with most years of service. Initially, the employees said they wanted more weight to be given to seniority. "After considerable discussion, it was agreed that the company would inaugurate a 'self-help' program for employees. It would pay for outside education and do everything possible to help the employees improve their skills in advance of promotion opportunities."[3]

Joint Damages

A struggle is usually costly to all or many of the adversaries. Each is hurt by the coercion inflicted by the other side, and both lose the resources expended in coercing each other. Furthermore, the losses are mutual in the sense that all sides forgo the benefits that might have accrued to them if they were acting cooperatively to achieve whatever shared objectives they had. Thus, revolutions often cause great damage to a society's economy, which takes decades to overcome.[4]

A struggle may end with the adversaries so weakened that parties not primarily engaged in the struggle are able to gain at the expense of the contending parties. Thus, the outcome of civil strife may be the domination of the contenders in one country by the government of another country. For example, the outcome of the very long civil war waged among many Lebanese groups between 1975 and 1991 was largely imposed and enforced by the Syrian government. In some cases, the opposing parties contribute to each other's destruction, as was the case in World War I, the outcome of which included the end of both the German and Russian ruling dynasties.

Mutual losses also take the form of embittered relations, mutual fear, mistrust, and hatred so that it is difficult afterward to engage in the cooperation that may be essential for either side to regain some of what had been lost in a bitter fight. This is often the legacy of communal fights, where members of each side experienced atrocious acts perpetrated by members of the other side.

Joint Benefits

Some conflict outcomes, on the other hand, are integrative, yielding the opponents much of what they most sought when they entered the conflict. They discover trade-offs that allow members of each side to gain what has the highest priority for them in exchange for concessions about matters to which they attach low priority. Given the opponents' different sets of preferences, a formula often can be found that maximizes the benefits that they can achieve together.[5] A labor-management agreement, for example, may provide enhanced job security, improved opportunities for training and advancement, and experimentation to increase productivity, and also yield higher profits.

Another important source of mutual benefits is the avoidance of mutual losses. Stopping a fight reduces the costs each side would bear in continuing the struggle. Even an outcome that favors one side more than the other may yield important mutual benefits. Thus, an agreement for power sharing among various ethnic communities, even if dominated by one, may be seen as mutually beneficial because the resulting stability allows for economic prosperity, which disorder would undermine. Thus, the accommodation in

Malaysia between the dominant Malays and the ethnic Chinese allows them all to "make money."[6]

Finally, mutual benefits may be attained at the expense of outsiders to the conflict. Adversaries may negotiate an agreement that gives them much of what they regard as important and passes on the costs to others. For example, labor-management negotiations in a company operating in a market that it tends to monopolize may reach an agreement whose costs of increased wages, salaries, and/or profits are largely paid for by the consumers of the company's products. In a sense, collusion between the representatives of the opposing sides may be integrative for them but yield a one-sided gain for the constituency of one side. For example, negotiators for one side may accept an unfavorable contract in exchange for personal gains awarded by the opposing side. While outcomes with high levels of joint benefits are regarded as constructive, this is not the case when the benefits are gotten at the expense of other parties.

Degree of Engagement or Separation

A quite different dimension is the degree to which the outcome betokens movement toward greater engagement or toward greater separation. To illustrate, ethnic or other communal groups within a society may move toward increased integration and away from segregation in the use of public facilities, in residential locations, and in occupational positions. Integration may extend to a gradual assimilation or to the preservation of group diversity. At the other extreme, separation may extend to expulsion or to population transfers between states; and it may include the division of territory into separate states. In between are various forms of coexistence with varying degrees of segregation, power-sharing, or federal systems with local autonomy. Similarly, within families, spouses may be highly involved with each other, sharing many aspects of their lives, or be relatively separated, sharing little and living quite independently. Relations between countries also vary in their degree of integration, with varying rates of trade, movements of people, or shared consumption of popular culture.

Clearly, there are many dimensions of integration, and persons and groups may be highly engaged along some dimensions and separated along others. Clearly, too, the degree of interaction or separation may be largely imposed by one side, or it may be a matter of mutual preference. Finally, we should note that the parties to large-scale conflicts are never unitary actors. Consequently, some elements of each side may feel that they gained much of what they wanted, while other factions feel they received little.

Constructive and Destructive Outcomes

Conflicts ending with great joint damages are widely recognized as destructive. Conflicts ending with great mutual benefit are widely regarded as constructive, unless the benefits are accrued at the expense of parties not engaged in agreeing to end the struggle. The degree to which conflicts ending with one side gaining more than the other should be regarded as constructive or destructive is not so simple. Victors are quick to proclaim that the outcome has enhanced many widely shared values and is constructive, and their interpretation often prevails.

In this work, we temper such judgments by taking into account the aspirations of all the parties involved in the struggle and the claims of equity and justice for all persons and peoples.[7] At a minimum, an outcome in which one side effectively denies the humanity of the members of the antagonistic side would not be considered constructive. Generally, struggles in which a person or group was defeated in its effort to gain basic human rights and a more just relationship with its opponents would not be regarded as a constructive outcome.

An improved relationship between the former adversaries is another marker of constructive outcomes. Usually, but not necessarily, this means that outcomes with increased engagement between the adversaries will be regarded as constructive. Separation when it is mutually sought and does not impose severe unequal costs on one side can be regarded as constructive, but more frequently one side imposes it on the other.

Since conflicts are not neatly bounded, the constructiveness of their out comes should not be assessed only in regard to those most directly engaged in ending a struggle. All the stakeholders are rarely involved in settling a fight; yet in determining how constructive the conflict outcome is, the more distant stakeholders should also be considered. Finally, characterizations should give weight to long-term considerations as well as short-term ones.

The discussion demonstrates that what is a constructive and what is a destructive outcome is not always clear. The designation is often disputed. But at the extremes, there is likely to be wide consensus, and in the vast middle range, variations in constructiveness in one or another regard may be specified. Hence, it is generally possible to characterize outcomes as being relatively constructive or destructive along specific dimensions.

Paths to Conflict Outcomes

Struggles are frequently ended by a negotiated agreement. But there are also several nonnegotiated ways to reach an outcome. These should be considered as well as the negotiation path, because they are the way many conflicts end, and because those alternatives must be kept in mind in order to understand the peculiarities of negotiation and its possible contribution to the resolution of a conflict. Although negotiation and nonnegotiation paths will be discussed sequentially, in actuality, they are often simultaneously blended together. For example, peace negotiations may be conducted concurrently with violent struggle.

Nonnegotiated Paths to Conflict Termination

Nonnegotiated terminations of conflicts are widespread, and are the predominant way many kinds of struggles are settled. Thus, many small-scale disputes, between neighbors, within extended families, and among members of work organizations are resolved without negotiations and written agreements. Even large-scale struggles sometimes quietly subside to low level contention after threatening to erupt into violent confrontation or after intense struggle. Unilateral actions may be taken, modifying the status quo, and they are acquiesced to by the other side.

Six types of nonnegotiated endings are distinguished here.[8] First, a settlement may be externally imposed, with varying degrees of concurrence between the adversaries. This includes, for example, arbitration, judicial proceedings, police intervention, or forceful intervention by an international organization.

Second, one side in the conflict may unilaterally force a capitulation by the other side. This includes dissolution of organized resistance by the defeated party. Mutinies, uprisings, and other disruptive challenges to authority are often simply suppressed. Capitulation may also arise from a restructuring of one of the parties, so that its representatives no longer contest the goals of the other side. This may result from a change in the leadership of one of the adversaries, especially a leadership whose policies did not represent what major elements of its constituency wanted.

Third, a fundamental conversion of one or both sides may arise from the experience with the conflict. Important members of one side may become convinced that the views of the adversary have great merit, undermining faith in their previous ideology or religious beliefs. Thus, many southern American Whites who believed in the propriety of segregation, became convinced in the course of the civil rights struggle in the South, that segregation was wrong and inconsistent with American values. Thus, too, in the 1980s, many persons in the Soviet Union increasingly found fault with the workings of the Soviet system and viewed the Western democratic and free market system as attractive.[9]

Fourth, a conflict may be settled by implicit bargaining, as each adversary takes actions, partly in response to what the other side has done, until a new mutual accommodation has been reached. The actions are left to speak for themselves, and each side makes its own interpretations of what has happened. This may reflect a kind of stalemate that neither side can overcome, but that is preferred by the adversaries to acknowledging the reality and giving it legitimacy. Thus, in some civil wars, the government may for years control the capital and many regions of the country while insurgents control a segment of the country.[10]

Fifth, one party to a conflict may raise and pursue a contentious issue, but meeting strong resistance, it may abandon the pursuit and the conflict becomes dormant. The challenge withdrawn, the overt struggle dwindles away. Or, a diffuse conflict may erupt in a demonstration or other protest and demands are voiced, but no settlement of the ostensible issues is reached and yet the protests cease. The grievance may remain, but the other factors essential to sustain the struggle are lacking.

Finally, one side may be exterminated or expelled from the social system that the victor controls. This may entail genocide or ethnic cleansing or other forms of driving people out of the organization, territory, or society ruled by the victors.

Note that in many instances of these terminations, the adversaries themselves may not openly acknowledge that the conflict has ended. This means that the belligerents in a struggle may disagree about when (or whether) a conflict has ended and what the terms of its settlement were. In addition, outside analysts or observers sometimes use their own criteria and judgment for regarding a conflict as terminated.

The relative frequency with which negotiation or one of these other paths are taken obviously varies greatly among different kinds of conflicts. Studies of these variations aid our understanding of the way conflicts end. A detailed analysis was made by Paul R. Pillar of the termination of the 142 interstate, extrasystemic, and civil wars fought between 1800 and 1980.[11] Interstate wars were waged among members of the state system; extrasystemic wars were imperial or colonial wars involving a member of the state system on only one side; and civil wars were waged within a member of the state system. The largest percentage of the 142 cases, 40 percent, ended in a negotiated settlement; in 26 percent of the cases, one side capitulated; in 18 percent, one side was exterminated as an organized force or was expelled; in 6 percent an international organization intervened and ended the conflict; in 5 percent one side withdrew from the conflict; and in 6 percent of the cases, one side was absorbed by the other.

The endings, however, varied greatly among the three kinds of wars. Among the 69 interstate wars, 55 percent were settled by negotiation, 16 percent by one side capitulating, and only 10 percent by extermination or expulsion. But negotiated endings were much less likely in extrasystemic wars or civil wars. Among extrasystemic wars, only 25 percent ended by negotiation, 38 percent ended in capitulation, and 23 percent ended by extermination or expulsions. Among civil wars, 29 percent ended by negotiation, 29 percent ended by capitulation, and fully 33 percent ended by extermination or expulsions. The stakes in civil wars and for those seeking freedom from imperial rule are high, and negotiating a termination is very difficult. So the struggle often goes on until one side is defeated. Even if a stalemate is reached, negotiating any recognition of that is much more difficult than in the case of interstate wars.[12]

Roy Licklider has analyzed all civil wars from 1945 to 1993, inclusive, using a definition that includes revolutions and wars of secession.[13] He constructed a data set of ninety-one cases, but discarded seven because violence had ended in those cases less than five years before 1994, too early for him to regard as ended. Of the remaining eighty-four cases, 32 percent (twenty-seven) were classified as still ongoing in 1994. Of the fifty-seven civil wars that had ended, consistent with other studies, he found that only 25 percent (fourteen) were ended by negotiation, while the others ended by military victory by one side.

In struggles in which the stakes are not so high as in civil wars or where institutionalized ways of managing the conflict are regarded as legitimate by the adversaries, negotiated conflict endings are highly likely. Most interpersonal and intergroup community and societal conflicts have those characteristics. More particularly, negotiated agreements are generally used to settle economic and political conflicts in most domestic settings.

Negotiated Paths to Conflict Termination

Negotiated agreements are emphasized in this book because it is often expected that they are more likely than nonnegotiated outcomes to reflect mutual accommodation. Negotiations are often expected to increase the chances that the conflict outcome will be constructive. They also are expected to increase the likelihood that the negotiators' constituents will support the agreement, and hence that the settlement will be enduring. The validity of these expectations are assessed in this and the next chapter. The growing literature on how negotiations can be done skillfully to maximize efficiency, mutual gain, social justice, and durability may contribute to understanding why those expectations are fulfilled in some cases and not in others.

Negotiation occurs in every aspect of social life, between companies buying and selling materials needed in production, among family members deciding where to spend a vacation, between a supervisor and a worker settling how long it will take to finish a task, or between governments setting the conditions to end a crisis. The negotiating parties, in all these cases, are trying to find the terms they will mutually accept to act jointly: either to transfer ownership of a house or to cease firing weapons at each other. But negotiating to end a fight tends to be unlike negotiating a sale of a commodity in several ways. First, in negotiating a sale, the seller usually has alternative buyers and the buyer typically can find alternative sellers. An agreement to end a fight, however, must be made between existing adversaries; peace is negotiated with enemies. Second, negotiations to end a fight usually occur after interactions with the adversary that have aroused anger and mistrust. But this is typically not the case in negotiating a purchase of a car or a house. Third, in a conflict, the alternative to not reaching an agreement is often to continue the fight and suffer ongoing costs. In a business transaction, the alternative usually is to end the interaction and to find alternative negotiating partners.

Negotiations to de-escalate or to end struggles, nevertheless, share some qualities with other kinds of negotiations. For example, the logic of the search for a mutually acceptable agreement is generally shared in all negotiations. Furthermore, negotiations, generally move through various stages: including each party preparing its positions, the parties arranging who will participate and what the agenda will be, each side setting forth its positions, exploring possible options, exchanging concessions, reaching an agreement, and implementing the agreement.[14] In addition, the nature of negotiations varies considerably, unrelated to whether they are part of an effort to settle a conflict or to sell a commodity. For example, the negotiating partners may anticipate an ongoing relationship with recurrent negotiations, or they may anticipate that after the agreement is reached, their interactions will cease or be unimportant. The negotiations may also vary in their scope, being about a narrow matter, part of a larger set of negotiations, or being about a wide range of matters at the same time. In examining negotiations to settle a struggle, therefore, some lessons can be drawn from other kinds of negotiations, but that should be done thoughtfully, taking into account the peculiarities of negotiations in the context of a conflict, and the degree to which the particular conflict or exchange context differs.

Theories and Strategies of Negotiation

People have reflected about negotiations for a very long time, since they are a universal aspect of social life. The reflections have produced general theories, suggested rules of conduct, and provided many observations about how negotiations are and should be conducted.[15] Much theorizing has been based on the analysis of actual behavior, seeking to predict or at least explain negotiating conduct. Some theorizing also has been deductive, based on certain assumptions about human nature or the logic of mathematical games. In either case, the reflections often take the form of admonitions, prescribing good negotiating behavior. One variation in these prescriptions underlies much discussion about negotiations and is particularly relevant here. At one extreme, negotiation is treated as a way of waging a contest, and the prescriptions are about how to win for yourself and your side. At the other extreme, negotiation is considered a way to reach mutually acceptable and even beneficial agreements, and the prescriptions aim to efficiently and effectively attain such outcomes for all parties in the negotiations.

Approaches to Negotiation

Although theoretical perspectives about negotiation vary along many dimensions, the previously mentioned one is fundamental and serves to organize this discussion. First, I contrast, at one extreme, the effort to maximize one side's advantage, and at the other extreme the effort to construct a mutually advantageous agreement. Then, the ways the two polar approaches complement each other and are combined will be examined. Negotiations in the context of conflict are of central interest throughout.

Maximizing One Side's Advantage

Traditionally, people view negotiations as a way to conduct a struggle. Consequently, each side tries to gain as much as it can, expecting that the gains will be at the expense of the other side. Some theorists tend to reason that this is inherent in negotiations and therefore each side must pursue this effort or risk being badly exploited. Others argue that negotiators generally believe that this is so and therefore act on that belief, making it effectively true, but that they might be led to believe otherwise.

In this discussion we start by examining the theoretical and applied approach based on the premise that the negotiating parties in a conflict relationship generally seek to maximize their gains relative to the other side. Adherents of this approach tend to take a hard line in negotiations, arguing that by firmly staking out a desired position and holding to it, negotiators will maximize their benefits. Conversely, making concessions will be viewed as indicating weakness and will invite increased demands or rigidity by the other side. From this perspective, conflicts are essentially zero-sum in character, and negotiations typically take the form of a series of concessions moving toward convergence somewhere between the initially stated positions.

In this approach, much attention is accorded to tough bargaining strategies. The advantages of staking out a relatively high opening position is emphasized. This follows from the negotiating parties' belief that a series of concessions by opposing sides will be made and an agreement most likely will be reached somewhere between the opposing opening positions, around the midpoint between them. The midpoint assumes salience as a focal point, barring other bases for making a particular division seem natural and legitimate, as discussed by Thomas Schelling.[16]

Persons using this approach give attention to the strategy of convincing the other side that significant concessions cannot be made. Tactics that seem to commit the negotiator to the position staked out and leave little room for maneuver are frequently made. For example, leaders, may make their positions public, even announce them prior to negotiations so that they would suffer a loss of face if they later backed down. They may also say that they cannot change their positions because of constraints imposed by their constituency, who would not support any concession. Negotiators also may assert that they are under strict instructions and are not authorized to make any concessions. Consider how Soviet intransigence in negotiations with the United States during the cold war was often attributed to the inability of Soviet negotiators to deviate from strict instructions.[17]

This traditional approach also tends to emphasize that one side may use or threaten to use coercion in order to convince its adversary that the alternatives will be more costly than the terms being offered. Indeed, in many cases, negotiations are conducted while a mutually coercive struggle is being waged, as happens when collective bargaining is conducted while a strike is on or peace negotiations are conducted while a war continues, as was the case for the U.S. negotiations with North Vietnam in the early 1970s. One side may even intensify the struggle to increase its bargaining power, whether by harming the adversary or strengthening support among coalition partners.

Duplicity is not so widely discussed in the scholarly literature, but its significance is noted by practitioners and feared by many members of each adversary party. One or more sides often provide deceptive or misleading information about their capabilities, alternatives, and preferences. The degree to which this is done, and is expected, varies by personality, social role, culture, and subculture.[18]

Problem Solving

The problem-solving approach has developed in part from critiques of the relatively traditional one-sided maximizing approach. Although derived from many analyses and practices, it has become increasingly recognized beginning in the early 1980s.[19] Game-theory models and social-psychological experimentation have revealed the many self-defeating dangers of seeking immediate unilateral gains. Prescriptions for an alternative approach that would serve the best interests of all or most of the negotiating parties began to emerge. These were skillfully set forth in a vastly influential book by Roger Fisher and William Ury, *Getting to YES*, published in 1981.

Fisher and Ury named their approach to negotiation, "principled," located between the hard-line and soft-line negotiation approaches. They argue that with positional bargaining, negotiators play either a soft or a hard game; but they should change the game and negotiate on the merits. For example, the goal for those following a soft line is agreement, and the goal for the hard-liners is victory, but the goal for those negotiating on the merits is a wise outcome reached efficiently and amicably. This means, for example, separating the people from the problem, focusing on interests and not positions, inventing options for mutual gain, and insisting on objective criteria in choosing options.

Advocates of this approach contend that in traditional negotiation bargaining positions are often set forth without adequate reflection about the underlying interests the positions are supposed to satisfy, so that gaining the positions becomes the goal, rather than satisfying the underlying interests. Indeed, more than one way to satisfy underlying interests frequently exist. If both sides examine their interests and explore various options to meeting them, it is often possible to discover options that substantially meet the underlying interests of all the negotiating partners. A variety of tactics can facilitate such a problem-solving strategy. For example, negotiators may ask questions, searching to understand what the other side's interests are, and try to acknowledge their understanding of how the other side sees them. Making such efforts contributes to converting a hostile negotiation session into a problem-solving discussion.

Another important technique is to generate many possible options to solve the problem. Special "brainstorming" periods may be set aside for this purpose. In such periods, all participants are encouraged to suggest solutions, and these ideas are not to be critiqued or discussed until very many options have been suggested. Only then, ideas that seem to be the basis for actual solutions are selected, examined carefully, and modified in discussion.

A related basic idea in this approach is that a conflict can be reconfigured, under certain conditions, so that a mutually beneficial or at least mutually acceptable agreement can be reached. Some of the methods that are used to bring this about are presented in I. William Zartman and Maureen Berman's *The Practical Negotiator*, published in 1982.[20] They emphasize the significance of constructing a formula in order to enter negotiations and reach an agreement.

To undertake negotiations, each adversary must come to believe that a joint settlement of some contested issues is possible. Moreover, joint action is needed, a unilaterally imposed settlement is not considered feasible, and each side acknowledges that the interests of the other side must be given some recognition. The diagnoses need not be totally shared, but they must be compatible for serious negotiations to be undertaken. As Zartman and Berman state: "negotiation is appropriate when the parties see that a problem can only be resolved jointly and when they have the will to end an existing situation they consider unacceptable, while admitting the other party's or parties' claim to participate in that solution."[21]

Such diagnoses come about by reframing the conflict so that it is no longer viewed as purely zero-sum, but that some common interests will be served by a joint solution. Such redefining occurs in several ways, as discussed in earlier chapters. Along with the redefinition, possible formulas for settling the conflict emerge. The formulas may begin to be constructed in the prenegotiation stage of a conflict or in the early negotiation sessions. The formula may be the result of mutual concessions, as occurs in negotiations following a traditional bargaining model. But they also may be constructed by reference to a general conception or principle. A combination of a general framework with concessions and trade-offs is likely for complex, multidimensional problems.[22]

This new formula may be related to a redefinition of the primary parties involved in the conflict. Conflicts that appear nonnegotiable for one set of parties may become negotiable for a subset of those parties or by including additional parties with a stake in the outcome.[23] To illustrate, the several interlocked conflicts in the Middle East offer many examples of shifting diagnoses and formulas for settlement. One recurrent difference in the diagnosis and of the possible formulas for resolution is whether the conflict is to be considered as a single, multifaceted conflict requiring a comprehensive settlement or a set of related conflicts best dealt with in a step-by-step fashion. Various parties have stressed one or the other formulation regarding the Arab-Israeli conflict at different times. Generally, prior to the Egyptian-Israeli peace treaty of 1979, the Arab governments had sought comprehensive negotiations, including Palestinian representation, while the Israeli government tended to seek bilateral negotiations with one Arab government at a time.

In 1977, President Jimmy Carter sought a comprehensive settlement and worked to organize a peace conference including Israel and all the neighboring Arab countries and Palestinian representatives within the Jordanian delegation. Anwar Al-Sadat, president of Egypt, came to believe that such a comprehensive meeting was doomed to fail, if it ever met: too many intransigent parties would participate. He decided to break open the barrier to peace by going to Jerusalem and opening a dialogue with Israel, and to the amazement of the world he did this in November 1977. Afterward, with the help of President Carter and the U.S. team of mediators, a treaty was negotiated and signed in March 1979. Sadat also tried to represent the Palestinians and to link Egypt's peace treaty with a resolution of the Palestinian issue, but he failed to do so.

Sadat was hailed as a great leader and peacemaker in Israel and most of the world, receiving the Nobel Peace Prize along with Israeli Prime Minister Menachem Begin. But Sadat was widely condemned by Arabs as a traitor and Egypt was ostracized by the Arab world. Clearly, different combinations of disputants will produce different formulas resulting in different solutions. Making agreements among those finding a formula to do so, may also outrage many others with a stake in the conflict.

Formulas, in a similar way, may be based by selecting one or two issues from the many in contention or by aggregating many issues to seek a comprehensive settlement. Each strategy, can be effective under particular circumstances. By disaggregating or fractionating a conflict, particular issues may be selected that appear relatively easy to solve.[24] They may appear to be less contentious and less risky. If successfully negotiated and implemented, they often become stepping-stones to agreements regarding more fundamental issues.

Aggregating several issues also can be the basis for a formula because linking issues facilitates trade-offs among them. Although negotiating parties may have opposing interests on many issues, the priority they assign to each issue is likely to be different. By linking the issues, Party A may give up to Party B what is much more valuable to B than to A and in exchange, Party B will give up what is more important to the other side than to itself.[25] For example, after the Israeli army seized and occupied all of the Sinai in 1956, the territory became a matter of contention between Egypt and Israel. The Israelis wanted security from military threats from Egypt, which it experienced before the 1956 war. Egypt wanted to regain sovereignty over its territory. Among other matters, the Egyptian-Israeli peace treaty of 1979 encompassed a trade-off: Egypt regained sovereignty over all of the Sinai, and Israel's security concerns were assuaged by the treaty provision severely limiting the presence of Egyptian military capability in the Sinai.

In general, in large-scale, protracted conflicts, comprehensive settlements are not likely to be successful in reaching an agreement or in transforming a conflict. An overall peace is more likely to be achieved on a step-by-step basis. This seems to have been the case for the transformation of the U.S.-USSR relationship over many years, which contributed to the fundamental change within the Soviet Union. In a quite different way, the transformation of the Arab-Israeli conflict occurred in a series of partial agreements between Egypt and Israel and then later by other agreements, building on each other.[26]

Finally, a formula may be based on a shared image of the future or an agreed-upon conception of the conflict as a problem. Particularly, in ethnic conflicts, having a shared vision of the future relationship between the contending communities is critical. The negotiators may anticipate an outcome in which their communities will become separate countries, or establish a system of autonomous regions, or construct a political structure providing power sharing among the different communities. In the case of an international environmental dispute, a problem-solving process is aided if the negotiators agree that they are confronting a shared ecological problem. This likelihood is enhanced when the negotiators from different countries share common professional outlooks and have developed personal relationships, and when nongovernmental representatives also participate.[27]

What is critical in the problem-solving approach is working together to find solutions. Some negotiators enjoy this prospect but consequently become mistrusted by their constituents. Innovative thinking can often make conflicts that seem nonnegotiable open to joint solutions, but such thinking must be convincingly communicated to significant segments of each side's members if the agreement is to be binding.

Combining One-Sided Maximizing and Problem-Solving Approaches

In the minds of some advocates of the traditional one-sided maximizing approach and of some advocates of the problem-solving approach, the two perspectives are incompatible. Some traditionalists, taking a hard line, argue that ultimately one side wins and the other loses and negotiation reflects and ratifies that reality. They dismiss the adherents of the other approach as being naive and unrealistic. Moreover, some critics of the problem-solving approach argue that it often fails to deal with the existing asymmetries of power and enduring injustices.[28]

On the other hand, some advocates of the integrative problem-solving approach contend that every conflict can be converted into a problem and then solved in a way that is mutually beneficial to those with a stake in the solution. They dismiss the adherents of the traditional approach as rigid and enamored of toughness. Each side seeking to advance its interests unilaterally fosters reliance on force and sustains or increases injustice.

In actuality, the two approaches are often complementary, one being more appropriate and effective under some circumstances than others. Most analysts and practitioners appear to believe that each of the two approaches can be carried too far, and think that in practice negotiators tend to synthesize the approaches and their prescriptions derive from both. Elements of such syntheses and complementarity need to be examined carefully.

An analysis of the conflict that is to be subjected to negotiation, it is widely recognized, is an important first step to effective negotiation. Such analyses require attention to the alternatives each side has if a negotiated agreement is not reached. For rational calculation, the best nonnegotiated alternative sets the minimum terms a party is willing to accept in negotiations. One or more side, however, may not fully estimate what its best alternative would be; its members may get caught up in the process of negotiation and consider not reaching an agreement to be necessarily a failure. A prescriptive admonition of many trainers and consultants of negotiation, therefore, is that a negotiating team carefully consider what is its best alternative to a negotiated agreement (BATNA).[29]

Advocates of the one-sided maximizing and of the problem-solving approaches tend to differ in how to affect the other side's BATNA. Persons utilizing the traditional approach tend to believe that it is necessary to change the external reality, often by increasing the costs to the other side of failing to accept the terms of the offer being made. Problem solvers, however, tend to argue that changing the other side's BATNA may be affected by changing the frame within which the conflict is viewed. Such changes may be brought about by persuasive efforts and by insights gained from exploring the perspectives of the opposing sides.

Another matter of significance to students and practitioners of negotiations is the appropriate time for undertaking de-escalating efforts. There may be widespread consensus that the effectiveness of de-escalating efforts, whether by partisans or by intervenors, depends on the timing of such efforts. But there is much less consensus about what is the ripe moment for what kind of strategy. Those taking a traditional approach tend to argue that until the adversaries have exhausted the coercive alternatives, de-escalating efforts are not likely to be effective. Ill-timed efforts to de-escalate a conflict will not be successful and can have undesired consequences.[30] On the other hand, problem-solving advocates tend to emphasize the value of de-escalating attempts in a wide variety of circumstances, arguing for finding the suitable long-term or short-term strategy for the particular circumstances.[31] An emphasis on constructing an acceptable formula in combination with a hurting stalemate having been reached between the adversaries is a kind of synthesis of the two approaches.[32]

Ethical issues confound the choice of either negotiating approach, as indicated by the moral critiques that can be made of each approach. Critics of the one-sided maximizing approach, for example, may argue that the failure to attend to possible mutually acceptable solutions tends to perpetuate struggles destructively and often results in imposed oppressive outcomes. On the other hand, critics of the problem-solving approach may argue that in the rush to find an accommodation between adversaries, evildoers are rewarded and injustices perpetuated or de-escalating efforts fail and reduce the chances for an agreement when the times are more suitable. As discussed in chapter 11, ethical issues need to be considered in specific empirical conditions, partly because the weighting given to various ethical considerations is influenced by the perceived probabilities of various conflict outcomes.[33]

According to the perspective taken here, the problem-solving approach should be broadly understood to include strategies of constructive struggle. Those strategies may foster conditions that encourage conducting problem-solving negotiations and reaching outcomes that minimize injustice. Such strategies also may include escalating a conflict by mobilizing broad support and adhering to policies that do not deny the humanity of the opponents. The inducements used in such strategies include large components of persuasion, the offering of rewards, and coercion that is minimally violent.

Finally, we should acknowledge that not all negotiations are serious attempts to resolve a conflict. Sometimes, negotiations are entered into by leaders of one party to demonstrate to their constituents or to a wider audience or even to elements in the opposing side that they are devoted to peace. They seek only to reveal the intransigence and unreasonableness of their counterparts. They may formulate positions they expect to be rejected, but that appear plausible to their own side. This was the case in the early years of the Reagan administration arms control negotiations with the Soviet Union.[34] In the disarmament negotiations in the early years of the cold war, both sides engaged in such tactics.[35]

Some negotiations, even those pursued for years, then, may be fraudulent. But even these may be transformed and become serious. Changes within one of the parties or changes in the ongoing struggle may produce a shift that facilitates earnest negotiations. The preceding negotiation sessions may turn out to have been useful, for example, by constraining the tendency toward escalation. Moreover, the negotiators may have established interpersonal relations with each other and each side may have learned enough about the other side's concerns that when the time is more suitable, they can move speedily toward a mutual agreement. This happened in the later years of the Reagan administration, when Gorbachev led the Soviet Union into the pursuit of a new foreign policy.

This suggests that one side may be able to transform the course of negotiations, even when the other side entered into them for self-serving reasons. Treating a stated position, even one suspected of insincerity, as a serious offer and subject to modification may commit the side making the offer to become engaged in serious negotiations. Mediators sometimes are helpful in this regard, as examined in chapter 8. They take a proposal submitted by Party A, objected to by Party B, and ask what changes would make it acceptable. They then take the modified proposal back to Party A to discover what additional modifications it requires to make it acceptable.[36]

Cultural Considerations

One-sided maximization and problem-solving approaches share similar cultural limitations. They tend to focus on independent actors engaged in episodes of social interaction, and that may reflect a particular cultural orientation. But other cultural views can be found. Thus, in some cultures, such as the traditional Chinese culture, conflict is viewed as a disruption of community relationships. Negotiation and accommodation is then seen as the right way to restore relations within the community in which the antagonistic parties live.

More generally, the distinction is often made, in this context, between individualistic and collectivist world outlooks.[37] European and North American societies are regarded as generally having individualistic cultures, emphasizing personal freedom and achievement. Non-Western societies, in contrast, tend to be collectivist, according high respect to authority and giving group welfare precedence over individual welfare. Conflicts within individualistic societies tend to be adjudicated within a legal framework based on individual rights, and that framework tends to characterize one side as right and the other as wrong. Conflicts in societies with collectivist cultures tend to be handled through conciliation in order to sustain group affiliation.

Regard should be given to such cultural orientations, but they should not be made into stereotypes, assuming that all members of a given society share the identical culture and there is no overlap among cultures. Within every society, individual differences exist as well as do subcultural variations by class, area of residence, gender, and many other factors. Moreover, cultures include a broad range of conduct, and persons in each culture are familiar with a wide variety of ways of conducting themselves while differing in their tendencies to act in a particular way in specific circumstances. For example, U.S. negotiators are often reported to go directly to the issues to be negotiated and try to reach an agreement quickly, while negotiators from many non-Western cultures think it is important to build a relationship within which the negotiations can be conducted and therefore take time to build that potential relationship.[38] But obviously there are circumstances when Americans, too, recognize that building a relationship is important and takes time, for example in courting a spouse or a customer.

As we consider negotiation and other paths to conflict termination, cultural variations should be kept in mind. We will treat one-sided maximization and problem-solving approaches broadly in order to minimize the cultural bias that otherwise would limit their applicability.

Forms and Stages of Negotiations

Negotiations sometimes are completed in a single session; but generally to settle large-scale conflicts, a series of sessions are conducted over a period of months or even years. The negotiations are conducted in a wide variety of forms and generally proceed through several stages. Before discussing the consequences of different negotiation approaches, those contexts need to be mapped out, because the likelihood and consequences of pursuing one or another strategy differ in those various settings.

Forms of Negotiation

Negotiations vary in their institutionalization, size, scope, isolation, privacy, and conflict setting. The variations reflect differences among struggles and their context, and they have significant implications for the results of the negotiations. The various characteristics of negotiations are not wholly independent of each other, but they will be discussed separately here.

Institutionalization of Negotiation Procedures

Every society has procedures for settling disputes; these are generally embodied in political institutions and judicial proceedings. Often, informal negotiations are integral to the working of these formal procedures. This obviously is the case in the negotiations among legislators drafting a piece of legislation. It occurs in adversarial legal proceedings when the lawyers, frequently with the encouragement of the judges, negotiate a settlement to the case before the dispute goes to trial.[39] But the agreement is made binding by the court.

Those formal legal and political procedures available to resolve disputes are an almost universal context for the relatively unofficial and informal methods, generally referred to as conflict resolution or as alternative dispute resolution (ADR). The disputants often recognize that if the informal procedures they are using do not result in an agreement, they have recourse to legal proceedings or to political action. ADR, then, serves as a complement to the formal and official procedures.

In the United States, as in many other large-scale societies, provisions are made for disputants to negotiate directly or with the support of conciliators and mediators. The arenas in which such direct negotiations are conducted often function with legally enacted rules about procedures. In the case of collective bargaining, legislation and previous contracts define what is good-faith bargaining and specify what is negotiable. In recent decades, understandings about informal conflict resolution procedures have developed in public policy disputes concerning environmental issues and concerning alleged discrimination by gender, age, or minority status.

The form of institutionalization, reflecting culture and institutional structures, influences which negotiation approach tends to be used. For example, in the Untied States, the adversarial style is deeply embedded in the political and legal culture. The founding document of the U.S. government, the Constitution, is based on a system of checks and balances, presuming that a struggle between different government units will preserve and protect liberty. A society in which individuals and groups seek their own advantage is thought best managed by having other individuals and groups contest them in an adversarial manner. This is evident in the way the American electoral and judicial systems function.

Elements of collective solidarity, mutual support, and shared responsibilities, of course, are also to be found in the American society. In recent years, conscious efforts have been made to promote less-adversarial methods to manage possibly conflictful relations and specific disputes. This has been true within work organizations, among groups differing in religion or ethnicity, and between groups differing in policy positions, for example about environmental matters. The conflict resolution movement and the promotion of the problem-solving approach to negotiation in many ways have been part of those efforts.[40]

Scale of Negotiations

Negotiations vary in scale by the number of parties engaged and by the number of persons representing each party. Although most theorizing about negotiations assumes two parties are engaged, actual negotiations increasingly include more than two parties. In international affairs, multilateral negotiations are becoming increasingly frequent, and are even conducted in large conferences. For example, the Law of the Sea was negotiated with more than 150 governments represented.[41]

The participation of many parties often enables some of them to provide intermediary services and so to foster a problem-solving approach. Some participating parties may not have as vital interests at stake as do the primary adversaries in the conference, and hence they are subjected to appeals for support from the major antagonists. This also encourages persuasive efforts, couched in terms of shared principles and objective criteria, appeals consistent with a problem-solving approach. This was evident in the extended Conference on Security and Cooperation in Europe (CSCE) negotiations, culminating in the Helsinki Accords.[42]

In negotiations involving large entities, each delegation is often numerous, with representation of diverse constituencies. Thus, in interstate negotiations, technical specialists, even military specialists, in each delegation may discover some commonalities in perspectives and experience not as well shared with other members of their own delegation. This can become the basis for alliances or at least increased channels of communication across delegation lines.

Scope of Negotiations

Everything about the relations between adversaries cannot be settled at the same time. A subset of issues is jointly chosen for negotiation, although the parties may not wholly agree about which matters should be subject to bargaining at a given time. Negotiations vary greatly in the significance and number of issues that are considered. They may include matters of vital concern to one or more parties or matters regarded as of insubstantial consequence; and they may include only a few items or encompass a great number and variety of issues.

Negotiations about many significant matters obviously are complex and are likely to require extended discussions. They pose difficulties, particularly for traditional negotiations, but opportunities for newer integrative negotiations, since the multiplicity of issues enhances the chances of finding advantageous trade-offs. Constructing a formula for a solution becomes increasingly important and hence more likely, since it will be more energetically sought.

Isolation of Negotiation Sessions

Negotiations vary in their degree of isolation in several senses. Some negotiations are brief, one-time sessions, while others are conducted in a series of sessions over many years. Some negotiations result in agreements in a relatively short time, and are regarded as unique agreements, but others are viewed by the negotiating partners as part of a series of possible agreements, and some are considered to be one in a series of recurrent negotiations to renew expiring past agreements. When agreements are viewed as the product of recurring negotiations, expectations about trade-offs over time may develop.

Some negotiations are conducted through one set of representatives in a single negotiating channel. For example, there may be only one official, highly visible channel and the negotiators take instructions and report back to the central authority of each negotiating party. But others are conducted through more than one channel. Thus, an official, but private "back channel" may be used in addition to the official and relatively public negotiation channel. Such a dual format was made famous (or infamous) when Secretary of State Henry Kissinger, while the official SALT I negotiations were being conducted, met privately with the Soviet ambassador to the United States and discussed the terms of a SALT I agreement. He explained later that he did so in conjunction with several other matters in Soviet-American relations, and explicit as well as implicit trade-offs were developed during those talks.[43]

In international relations, and other conflict arenas, various negotiation channels are used sequentially and concurrently with the official channel, often referred to as track-two or multitrack diplomacy.[44] Among the many nonofficial channels are transnational organizations within which members of adversarial parties meet and discuss matters pertaining to the work of their common organizations. Another kind of track includes occasional meetings or ongoing dialogue groups with members from the adversary parties discussing the issues in contention between their respective countries (or communities or organizations). Such meetings were held between Whites and Blacks in Rhodesia beginning before official negotiating efforts were attempted for the transition to majority rule and the establishment of Zimbabwe.[45]

Privacy

Negotiations are conducted with varying degrees of confidentiality. Some are conducted in public; for example, community members may be important witnesses to a political or religious leader's mediation of a dispute between neighbors. Even negotiations between large-scale entities may be public, with news media providing coverage and the negotiators discussing their positions with the general public. On the other hand, many negotiations are conducted in private and the processes considered confidential until they are concluded. Some negotiations are so confidential that only the participants and a few others are aware of them, and even the negotiators' constituents are not informed of them; the proceedings and sometimes even the agreements are considered secret.[46]

Several advantages accrue with confidential negotiations. The negotiators are able to be more flexible in considering each other's ideas and suggesting possible options, thus encouraging a relatively problem-solving approach. They are also able to be more flexible in making concessions, thus facilitating traditional negotiation. These arguments are supported by social-psychological experiments indicating that if negotiators are subject to attention and evaluation by their constituencies, they are more intransigent in their bargaining.[47]

There can be drawbacks to secret negotiations. The negotiators may reach agreements acceptable to them that do not reflect the interest of all their respective constituents or that may be neglectful of implications damaging to all sides. An open discussion of the agreement reached and a legitimate ratification process are ways to minimize those risks. Furthermore, confidentiality may be particularly effective and helpful at some stages in the negotiation process, but not at others. In general, it is particularly useful in the preliminary, prenegotiation stage. Explorations of possible agreements and steps to reach them can determine whether or not the time is ripe to undertake serious negotiations. For example, King Hussein of Jordan met secretly with Israeli leaders many times over decades, but no extended negotiations or public meetings were held until the circumstances fostered negotiations for the peace treaty concluded in 1994. The secret meetings helped manage the conflict between Jordan and Israel; and when the time was conducive to sign a peace treaty, the negotiations were able to proceed quickly.[48]

Conflict Setting

Many of the ways struggles vary affect the negotiation approach that is used and its likely effects. Three conflict variations that affect how a struggle comes to an end warrant particular attention here: the issues in contention, the relative importance of shared and of contested interests and values, and the timing of the negotiations in the context of the ongoing conflict.

The issues in contention obviously affect how a struggle ends. Many partisans in a conflict as well as analysts of conflict contend that some kinds of issues are particularly difficult to settle by negotiation. The heightened attention to ethnic, religious, and other communal-associated conflicts, and the destructiveness of some of them has indicated to many observers that such conflicts are particularly difficult to resolve.[49] They seem to involve values and cultural patterns that form part of a people's self-identity and are presumed to entail deeper commitments than political-economic issues and therefore to be harder to change than conduct. Others have argued that issues related to identity often involve symbolic issues that can be resolved relatively inexpensively.[50]

Licklider, in his previously described analysis of civil wars from 1945 to 1993, found "that identity and political civil wars are about equally likely to end in negotiated settlements."[51] This suggests that the apparent content of the issue in contention is not inherently more or less negotiable and amenable to compromise or to integrative solutions. The way the goals relating to the issues are framed is more significant. For example, the goals of a challenging identity group may be framed either in terms of collectively shared attainments or in terms of aggregated individual attainments. In the former case, benefits for the entity as a whole are sought, such as cultural autonomy or shared power arrangements. But in the latter case, benefits for individual members of a category are sought, such as equal access to educational and political institutions.

In general, goals formulated in terms of collective benefits are more likely to be seen as threatening to the dominant societal group than those to attain aggregated individual benefits. Even this tendency is affected by the dominant group's own goals for the society. Thus, in the United States, the widely shared ideology of individual rights gave legitimacy to claims of discriminated-against minorities for equal opportunities during the civil rights struggle of the 1950s and 1960s. Persuasive inducements and nonviolent coercion promised success to the challengers, and negotiated outcomes proved to be feasible.

The degree to which the adversaries share common values and interests profoundly affects the likelihood that their struggle will be brought to an end by negotiations. Thus, even in the period of apartheid, many of the people of South Africa, Whites and Blacks, thought of themselves as South Africans who shared the land. They increasingly came to believe that they could prosper only by working together or would destroy that hope and each other by seeking to impose one group's will upon the others.

Since every struggle has a course of development, different approaches to ending the struggle are likely to be effective at different times. If a conflict is in a period of relative de-escalation, negotiating agreements on specific issues in contention will appear relatively favorable and they are likely to be successfully undertaken. Thus, in the early 1970s, during the period of détente between the governments of the United States and the Soviet Union, several agreements and treaties were concluding on arms control and other issues. During periods of intense and protracted struggle, finding the right opportunity to undertake an appropriate peacemaking strategy is not self-evident. Attention is increasingly being given to discerning what constitutes the ripe moment to undertake particular de-escalating or peacemaking efforts.[52] Protracted struggles are strewn with the wreckage of failed initiatives.

In summary, the forms of negotiation are immensely diverse, and that diversity is shaped by the variability of conflicts and their social settings. A form suitable for certain conditions inevitably is wrong for other conditions. Knowing a large variety of negotiation forms therefore increases the possibility that those seeking to reach an agreement will be able to find an appropriate form for a specific conflict.

Negotiation Stages

That negotiations move through several stages is generally recognized, even if there is no consensus about identifying the stages. For analytic purposes here, seven stages are distinguished and discussed: prenegotiation, planning, initial presentations and analysis, search for options and formulas, drafting agreements, ratifying, and implementing. Different negotiation approaches and strategies are varyingly effective at each stage of negotiation.

Prenegotiation

In recent years, considerable attention has been devoted to the processes and conditions that bring adversaries to the negotiating table. In the chapter on de-escalation, we considered the circumstances and policies that foster efforts to negotiate a settlement to a conflict. At this time, we note the relatively proximate actions that occur prior to direct negotiations, particularly after protracted struggle.

An early phase of this prenegotiation stage is the signaling by one of the adversaries to the other that it is interested in reaching a negotiated settlement.[53] This is not a simple or easy matter. Adversaries often are mutually suspicious, and each side has been mobilized to sustain the positions staked out as its goals. Therefore, a leadership group thinking about making a conciliatory gesture as an overture to begin negotiations faces several risks. The other side may construe the overture as a sign of weakness and raise its demands; consequently, the leaders will appear foolish or weak to their followers. Another possibility is that the other side rejects the overture as a trick, aimed at appearing good to various audiences, but not serious; consequently, the overture may seem inept and be counterproductive.

Several policies can be followed to minimize the risks associated with signaling a readiness to start negotiations. One is to use unofficial intermediaries to discover whether the basis for negotiations exists for the parties engaged in the struggle. Another tactic is to conduct secret meetings between high-ranking representatives of each side to probe for possible formulas for negotiations. Such communications help ensure that the overture will be appropriately reciprocated. For example, prior to President Sadat's dramatic visit to Jerusalem in November 1977, the Israeli foreign minister Moshe Dayan and the Egyptian Deputy Premier Dr. Hassan Tuhami discussed formulas for peace at a secret meeting hosted and facilitated by the king of Morocco, in September 1977.[54]

Other policies involve taking a risk, and in doing so making the overture particularly attractive and credible. The fundamental transformation of the cold war between the blocs led by the United States and the Soviet Union were initiated in a series of statements and acts carried out the government led by Mikhail Gorbachev. In many ways, the actions and their effects on President Reagan, his administration, the American public, and the West generally were in accord with the idea of GRIT, previously discussed (see chapter 7). The Soviet actions, however, did entail substantial risks to the Soviet Union, much greater than those recommended by Osgood who directed his articulation of GRIT at the United States. Gorbachev had reason to believe that the risks of the West taking unilateral advantage of the Soviets' military downsizing and restructuring were manageable, given the American and Western opposition to the heightened militancy of the Reagan administration.[55] The internal risks to the Soviet system, however, were underestimated.

The covert exploration and the grand public commitment can also be effectively combined. The adversary leaders can give each other some assurances, and then the apparently bold public gesture can win over mistrusting elements of the antagonistic side and rally constituents to the new course the gesture seems to initiate. The spectacle of the president of the largest Arab nation flying to Jerusalem in 1977 and addressing the Israeli Knesset was highly dramatic and constituted an irrevocable act. The secret direct and indirect communications previously made ensured a warm response when President Sadat publicly expressed his readiness to go to Israel.

Another prenegotiation stage is the formulation of the structure for negotiations: this includes agreeing on the parameters of the negotiations, on the participants, and on the possible outcomes. Adversaries will avoid entering negotiations if they are convinced that the likely negotiated agreement will be worse than the status quo and deny them what they regard as minimally acceptable. Consequently, exploratory talks, through various intermediaries or directly between the adversaries' representatives at several levels, are often necessary before negotiations can begin.

Planning

Each party to negotiation, prior to entering the talks, generally reflects on what it seeks and how it proposes to reach its goals from the negotiations. In large-scale parties, difficult and complex negotiations are generally conducted among the various factions within each side who have a stake in the outcome. The goals of any large entity are always manifold, with varying priorities accorded different goals. The positions articulated for negotiation by each side reflect the relative influence of groups within that side.

It seems wise for each party entering negotiations to work out what it wants, what it will ask for, and what it will settle for prior to meeting with its negotiating counterparts. The negotiators will then enter discussions with detailed instructions about what they should try to get. But this fosters the traditional one-sided maximizing negotiation approach, and makes problem-solving negotiation more difficult. The problems in combining the internal and external negotiations are severe. Roger Fisher has suggested a strategy to reconcile them so as not to hamper a relatively problem-solving approach.[56] According to this strategy, the initial instructions should not include commitments, but directives, for example, to learn the other parties' views of their interests and concerns, to explain their own side's interests and concerns, and to generate a range of options that might satisfy both sides.

Initial Meetings and Analysis

What happens in the initial meetings varies with the negotiation approach being followed. In the relatively traditional approach, representatives of each side argue their positions. When those sessions are public, the staking out of commitments may subsequently hamper reaching a mutually acceptable agreement. In confidentially held negotiations and when the negotiations are anticipated to be lengthy, the initial sessions may involve a good measure of housekeeping matters: getting acquainted and agreeing upon ground rules. The procedural understandings may pertain to confidentiality, ensuring space for informal socializing, and scheduling some shared activities.

In these initial meetings, attention may be given to discussing the issues in contention and the concerns underlying the positions being taken, in order to ensure that each side understands how the other views the matters being negotiated. A shared analysis of the conflict may then emerge that sets the stage for viewing the conflict as a common problem the negotiators will seek to solve, rather than a contest each will try to win. Obviously, this is particularly important for the problem-solving approach. Regardless of the approach used, initial sessions of negotiations that are anticipated to be conducted over many meetings are often devoted to establishing an agenda and common priorities.

Inventing Options and Constructing Formula

At various stages in extended negotiations, sessions may be devoted to thinking of new options and constructing possible formulas for an agreement. Such sessions may be held at junctures in the extended negotiation process when an impasse seems to have been reached. The effectiveness of such sessions may be enhanced by changing the venue or composition of the negotiating teams, for example, by having subgroups of technical experts meet or by adding outsiders to discuss the issues or to help facilitate the sessions. In addition, discussions of possible trade-offs and formulas may occur in informal conversations over drinks at the bar or in side-channel meetings.

Drafting an Agreement

The product of a negotiated agreement is nearly always a written document and the processes of negotiation are directed at finding the words the negotiating parties can all accept. The more detailed and precise the terms of the agreement are, the more difficult the task of writing is, as provisions for likely but unwanted contingencies are considered and ways to counter them fashioned. An agreement that uses vague and ambiguous terms to paper over differences can be written much more easily. Of course, precisely written documents reduce the likelihood of later misunderstandings and alleged violations. Negotiators try to balance the urgencies of reaching an agreement with their concerns to forge an enduring agreement; as noted later, mechanisms can be instituted to minimize future disagreements arising from ambiguities in the document.

To reach complex agreements involving many items, another set of choices among approaches must generally be made. According to one strategy, a disposition is first reached on particular items and these are treated as settled. They may be the relatively easy items but agreeing on them helps create a sense of confidence and trust. Another approach sets aside the items settled early on but allows them to be reintroduced later when they may be renegotiated in the context of a larger trade-off among several items. A quite different approach is to agree upon general principles and then work out solutions to specific issues based on those principles. Finally, the agreement may be negotiated as a whole with changes made incrementally to a single negotiating text. The latter strategies fit better than the former with the problem-solving negotiation approach, but the best strategy may well vary from struggle to struggle and its cultural, historical, and social context.

Finally, the style of discourse used in negotiations can affect the speed with which an agreement is reached and its equity. Undoubtedly, there are cultural variations in how positions are put forward, discussed, accepted, and rejected. The style in the United States is generally viewed as direct, matter of fact, even hasty.[57] But even in the United States, effective negotiators are not confrontational. There is evidence that effective negotiators tend to ask more questions of their counterparts than do less effective negotiators, and they do not preface their remarks with "I disagree."[58] They tend not to attribute feelings and motives to the other side but clearly identify their own thoughts and feelings.

Signing and Ratifying

The negotiation process is not over, even when the negotiators have final-ized an agreement. Often, the heads of governments or organizations that the negotiators were representing formally sign the agreement, frequently at a public event. This gives visibility to the agreement and further commits the signatories to honor the agreement; like a wedding ceremony, its public na-ture announces the new status of the relationship and serves to bind the par-ties who have jointly reached the agreement.

Frequently, the agreement also must be ratified by the constituency that the negotiators and those signing the agreement represent. For example, a treaty signed by the president of the United States must be ratified by two-thirds of the U.S. Senate for the treaty to be legally binding on the United States. A labor contract signed by a union president usually must be approved by a majority of the union's members for the agreement to commit the union.

The concessions made to significant constituency groups to gain ratifica-tion sometimes undermine the goals of an agreement. For example, during the cold war, after an arms control agreement was reached, promises of weap-ons modernization were often made to those whose support was important but who were reluctant to provide it. This was the case with the ratification of SALT I, and the result was a continuing increase in the number of nuclear warheads after the number of missile launchers was capped.

Implementing

Attention must also be given to the degree to which an agreement is ad-hered to and the extent the signatory parties believe it to be faithfully imple-mented. An agreement that is violated is a source of mistrust and renewed struggle. A sound agreement is one that is self-enforcing, giving both sides reason to comply with the agreement. In addition, committees and other mechanisms may be established to monitor compliance and to reconcile dis-crepant interpretations of the agreed-upon document. Implementation of agreements is increasingly recognized as a vital component in conflict resolu-tion, and is analyzed in chapter 10.

In summary, negotiations incorporate several interrelated stages. Further-more, various forms of negotiation tend to be suitable at different stages of negotiation. Being aware of these many possibilities helps those engaged in negotiations to conduct them more effectively. Experience and exchanging stories of past negotiations help expand negotiators' repertoires and so im-prove their skills. Similarly, research and training can supplement and specify such experience.

Shaping the Outcome

Having outlined the many ways in which a conflict comes to an end, we consider now the effects that different conflict-termination paths have on the nature of the outcome. The effects on three dimensions of outcome will be examined: (1) whether or not a negotiated agreement is reached, (2) the degree to which one side wins or both sides jointly win or jointly lose, and (3) the degree to which the adversaries subsequently become more engaged with each other or more separated. In order to consider the impact of different conflict-termination paths, however, two other sets of factors shaping the outcome should be considered: the conflict itself and factors external to the conflict.

The Conflict Itself

The character of a struggle greatly affects how it ends. Three particularly significant features of conflicts must be discussed: the goals of the adversaries, the means of struggle, and the balance of resources relevant to the struggle.

Adversary Goals

The magnitude and the content of the adversaries' goals profoundly affect whether or not there will be a negotiated ending of their struggle and the character of that outcome, negotiated or not. Consider, first, the magnitude of the goals. It might seem reasonable to expect that the more a conflict party seeks, the more it will get, even if it fails to get all that it wants. But it is also reasonable to expect that the more an adversary seeks, the more resistance it will face and therefore the greater the likelihood that it will fail to get what it sought. What is crucial here is the discrepancy between the goals held by the opposing sides, and hence the tenacity with which each will pursue its goals.

The magnitude of a goal is not inherent in a conflict party's stated objective, rather, its importance depends on how the opponent regards it—whether as a vital threat or as a trivial matter. To illustrate the ambiguity of magnitude, consider the issue of amnesty in resolving a conflict. In university student uprisings and in prison riots, some members of the groups protesting sometimes commit acts deemed illegal or violations of organizational rules. Then, as part of a settlement the protesters demand amnesty for those who committed the "illegal" acts. For those in authority, granting amnesty seems to be an admission of their guilt and may establish an impermissible precedent. The insistence upon punishing the leaders of a rebellion may be the basis for a new grievance and for the continuation of the struggle or even its escalation, as in the Columbia University student rebellion of 1968.[59] The challengers may insist on amnesty as a symbolic vindication of their actions. As a leader of the Columbia students, Mark Rudd, said, "We demanded an amnesty to all who participated in the demonstration. This would have forced the administration to say we were right."[60]

Various matters in contention can be accorded great significance, coming to symbolize vital concerns with profound emotional investment for the adversaries. When an issue takes on great symbolic significance, it becomes more difficult to fractionate, and more difficult to settle by negotiation. The significance accorded a matter varies considerably and may be considered arbitrary by observers: granting amnesty at the end of a struggle need not be weighted with great symbolic importance. It may be regarded as a necessary component in ending a protracted armed struggle, and treated as a practical measure. For example, for more than twelve years, an armed struggle was waged in El Salvador, costing more than seventy-five thousand lives. The government, dominated by military and economic elites, was controlled by ARENA (the Nationalist Republican Alliance); the FMLN (Farabundo Marti National Liberation Front) challenged this power. Neither side was able to impose a settlement, but the 1987 Esquipulos II Agreement, envisaging a comprehensive solution for the conflicts in Central America, provided a context for negotiations regarding El Salvador. Negotiators did not have to deal with amnesty as a matter of honor. Negotiations for a settlement in El Salvador were undertaken in 1989, aided by UN mediators, and a peace agreement between the government of El Salvador and the FMLN was signed in January 1992.[61] As part of the package, the armed forces would be reduced in numbers and reorganized, the FMLN would demobilize, and former combatants of both parties would be given preference to receive state-owned land for farming. Moreover, free elections would be held and institutions to protect human rights were to be established.

Another kind of amnesty may be granted by the successful challengers to a government. They may allow the head of government and a few others to leave the country, sometimes with the understanding that the return of large funds previously placed in secret bank accounts in other countries would not be sought. Finally, an agreement may be reached between those challenging a government and the government heads to hold free elections but to provide amnesty for military and police officials who committed or ordered grievous violations of human rights. Obviously these various options pose ethical dilemmas and have grave consequences for the future social order.

The magnitude of an issue does not whimsically depend on the perspectives of various parties. It may be said that goals have dispositions so that they tend to be viewed as deadly threatening, or as seriously threatening, or as requiring strong resistance, or as subject to easy compromise, or as easily yielded. Some attributes of goals with relatively strong dispositions to be viewed one way or another will be briefly noted. In general, the perceived magnitude of conflict goals is largely determined by the degree to which changes in the relations between the adversaries are sought. In some struggles, a conflict party may be seeking a radical restructuring of the relationship, while in others a modest reform is sought.

One indicator of the degree to which the changes sought are radical or reformist is whether the goals pertain to changing the rules under which interests and values are advanced or only to modifying apportionments within the existing understandings.[62] For example, in labor-management relations, a conflict over wages is generally regarded as of lesser magnitude than one about union recognition or worker control of investment and marketing policies.

Another indicator of the magnitude of goals is the relative emphasis on modifying the opponent's policies or on removing those making the policies. Challengers who seek to modify policies rather than remove those who make the policies will of course be seen by the defenders as easier to accommodate. Thus, a conflict party may aim to make the other side more responsive and grant certain requests, or it may seek to displace the persons deciding such matters, or even remove everyone implementing them. To illustrate, a women's citizen organization may ask city government officials (who are overwhelmingly male) to institute working conditions in government offices that are more consistent with women fulfilling parental as well as employee responsibilities, or the organization may seek to have more women elected and appointed to government offices. This difference in goals may also be seen in ethnic struggles, marked by one people's seeking the right to pursue certain cultural practices or seeking the removal of persons not of their ethnicity from positions with the authority to determine that right.

The demand for removal of personnel is likely to be regarded as of greater magnitude than is the demand for policy change. Moreover, the demand for removal will be perceived to be of greater or lesser magnitude depending upon the presumed permanence of the removal and the remaining opportunities available to those who are removed. One of the conflict-resolving advantages of democratic processes in a society with a widely shared high living standard is that removal from office is not likely to be totally resisted, since the alternatives are not impoverishment, or imprisonment, or death.

Conflicts involving issues of high magnitude do not tend to be settled by negotiation, except after protracted struggle. The claims of the party seeking radical change will be rejected and its defeat sought. Only if the group seeking radical change can sustain the struggle does a negotiated settlement become likely. At that time, the outcome is likely to entail concessions by the opposing sides and a compromise settlement; under certain conditions, the protracted struggle can generate changed conceptions so that an integrative solution becomes feasible. That may come about from mutual weariness and conversion to new shared image, as happened in Central America in the late 1980s. It also may come about by the defeat of a dominant segment of one side and the liberation or transformation of many members of that side, as happened in Eastern Europe as the cold war came to an end.

Whether or not ended by negotiation, challenging groups whose goals are relatively modest are more likely to achieve some gains, while those with goals of great magnitude are less likely to be successful in a distributive sense. This is supported by William Gamson's analysis of fifty-three challenging groups that arose in the United States between 1800 and 1945, and his review of challenging groups since 1945.[63] For example, he found that groups not seeking to displace their antagonists were much more likely than other challengers to gain acceptance and to gain new advantages. He also observes that framing issues broadly to engage larger shared solidarities is particularly important in the period since 1945 when the mass media have greatly increased in significance in disseminating information.

In addition to the magnitude of goals, various other features of goals are also important. For example, we previously noted that goals framed in terms of collectively shared attainments rather than aggregated-individual attainments are more likely to be seen as threatening to the opposition. The sense of threat is also affected by the opposition's tendency to frame thinking about intergroup relationships in a collectivist as against an individualistic fashion, since it is the discrepant quality of the framing that is important. In cultures with collectivist tendencies, goals articulated in terms of collectively shared attainments would tend to be less problematic than in cultures such as the American.

Several other qualities of the goals in a conflict are relevant for the way a struggle is ended. In general, when the conflicting goals are consensual, the outcomes tend to be distributive, with varying amounts of compromise. When the adversaries' goals have large dissensual elements, the outcome—if one is negotiated—tends to have integrative features. A mutually acceptable and even beneficial outcome follows because if a settlement is to be reached, a new formula must be found. That formula may include recognition of the other side's legitimacy as a negotiating partner, and that entails some tolerance, perhaps even appreciation of their values. Acceptance of the new formula may result from changed thinking, arising from persuasion and new experiences. For example, in Spain, the Fascist government headed by Francisco Franco imposed a centralized system of governance, suppressing any expressions of Basque, Catalan, or other communal identities except the Spanish nation. After Franco died in 1975, a constitutional monarchy and democratic institutions were established, and regional autonomy was made legitimate. The Constitution of 1978 enunciated the unity of Spain and the cultural and linguistic rights of the several communities of Spain. For example, Article 2 states: "The constitution is based on the indissoluble unity of the Spanish Nation, the common and indivisible fatherland of all the Spaniards. It acknowledges and guarantees the right to autonomy of the nationalities and regions which form it and the solidarity among them." Within the context of the constitution, statutes of autonomy were written and ratified by the several communities of Spain, including the Basque country, Catalonia, and Galicia.

When goals are not highly discrepant, negotiated solutions to conflicts become possible and even likely. Furthermore, the outcomes are more likely to be integrative than when the goals are highly discrepant, since significant conversion is not required to find the bases for shared interests.

Means of Struggle

The effects of various means of struggle on the nature of the outcome cannot be separated from the goals sought by the adversaries, the relationship between the adversaries, and the many aspects of their social environment. We can only indicate the impact that different conflict modes tend to have on particular aspects of the conflict outcomes, keeping in mind the many other factors affecting these results. We are particularly interested in discovering which means of struggle contribute to constructive outcomes. Although relatively little research has been designed to examine that relationship, two bodies of literature are relevant: the role of violence in waging struggles and studies of nonviolent action.

Violence is popularly viewed as the means of last resort in a struggle and can be countered or overcome only by even greater violence. The pain it inflicts is severe, and furthermore its use demonstrates deep commitment. Yet, as the analyses of earlier chapters indicated, violence can be counterproductive, stiffening resolve and resistance by the opponent, inviting retaliation, and often enabling the other side to mobilize support from bystanders. These consequences are particularly likely when the violence seems to threaten vital concerns of either side, while limited violence with a clear option of finding a mutual accommodation is less likely to have such consequences. Obviously much depends on the nature of the violence, the alternatives available, the capabilities of the adversaries, and the prevailing cultural and institutional patterns. Only a few empirically grounded tendencies will be noted for specific conditions.

Consider the situation of a relatively small group in a society, challenging the state authority and the dominant groups in the society. Such groups relying on violent means tend not to be effective in gaining redress; rather, they are most likely to be suppressed, covertly and/or overtly. Coercive action, even in the form of labor strikes has often been met with overwhelming force and their organizing efforts set back. This type of action and reaction has been the history of trade union efforts in the United States during the nineteenth century and even the beginning of the twentieth century.[64] Evidence from other countries also indicates that strikes involving violence were more likely to fail than were work stoppages without violence. For example, this was found in a study of labor strikes in Italy between 1878 and 1903, controlling for many other factors affecting success.[65]

Coercive action, if not violent, however, often contributes to the success of challenging groups. Thus, Gamson's research indicates that groups acting disruptively to gain attention and to exercise pressure against those they believe to be responsible for their plight, tend to be more successful than are those challengers who are not unruly.

Nonviolent action, when combined with reassurances to the other side, often can be effective in obtaining constructive outcomes. Reassurance may be expressed by not threatening the other side's vital interests and by acknowledging the propriety of their concerns. Furthermore, the use of nonviolence can reduce the dangers of dehumanizing the other side and of provoking retaliation that denies the humanity of those taking nonviolent action.

The use of violence by authorities to counter such nonviolent actions frequently is counterproductive for them. As noted earlier, widespread popular outrage at the use of violence against the nonviolent civil rights demonstrations in Selma, Alabama, in 1965 contributed greatly to the U.S. Congress's passing the Civil Rights Act of 1965. Gene Sharp uses the term *political jiu-jitsu* to refer to such processes, "By combining nonviolent discipline with solidarity and persistence in struggle, the nonviolent actionists cause the violence of the opponent's repression to be expressed in the worst possible light. This in turn may lead to shifts in opinion and then to shifts in power relationships favorable to the nonviolent group."[66]

On the basis of theoretical and empirical work regarding nonviolent action, Ackerman and Kruegler developed twelve principles to guide nonviolent action campaigns.[67] The applicability of the principles was assessed by analyzing the effectiveness of nonviolent action campaigns in six struggles: the 1904–6 Russian revolution, the 1923 resistance to the French and Belgian occupation of the Ruhr in Germany, the Indian independence struggle in 1930–31, the resistance to the German occupation of Denmark in 1940–45, the civic strike of 1944 in El Salvador, and the 1980–81 struggle between Solidarity and the Polish Communist Party. They concluded that the principles were generally operative in accounting for the successes and failures of the campaigns. One set of principles pertains to development: formulating concrete and specific objectives, developing organizational strength, securing access to critical material resources, cultivating external assistance, and expanding the repertoire of sanctions. Another set of principles pertains to engagement: attack the opponents' strategy for consolidating control, mute the impact of the opponents' violent weapons, and alienate the opponents from their expected bases of support. The third set of principles relates to the conception of the campaign: sustain continuity between the sanctions employed, the mechanisms, and the objectives, and adjust offensive and defensive operations according to the relative vulnerabilities of the adversaries.

One of the interesting patterns Ackerman and Kruegler noted was that the challenged authorities skillfully used partial or temporary concessions. If they retained the preponderance of control, they were later able to modify or even renounce the concessions with little negative effect.[68] Analyses of official responses to challenging social movement organizations in the United States indicate another pattern of control becoming important with the development of the national security state arising in the cold war. Local and national government agencies such as the Federal Bureau of Investigation engage in covert actions to disrupt and discredit the organizations. These covert actions have contributed to reducing the effectiveness and in some cases the dissolution of those organizations.[69]

Of course, the means of struggle do not vary only by the degree and kind of coercion used. Other kinds of inducements are also significant, including positive sanctions and persuasive arguments. Empirical research about the way noncoercive inducements affect the outcomes of struggles, however, has been relatively neglected. Consequently, only a few general observations are made here. Conflicts effectively waged with great reliance on noncoercive inducements tend to result in integrative outcomes, whether negotiated or not. For example, those engaged in the civil rights struggle in the American South in the 1950s and 1960s used such means effectively, and that helped produce outcomes that were regarded as mutually beneficial. These matters are discussed in chapter 10, in the context of examining the consequences of struggles.

Balance of Resources

A traditional view of conflicts is that the outcome is basically shaped by the balance of forces among the antagonists. The power differences, usually measured only in terms of the capability to use coercive sanctions, are often assumed to determine the outcome of a conflict—everything else having only marginal effects. That is not the view taken in this analysis. First, as discussed in chapter 1, power is understood here to include recourse to noncoercive inducements. To minimize possible confusion, I often use the term *balance of resources* rather than balance of power. Resources more readily refer not only to the capacity to use violence or other forms of coercion, but also to the use of positive sanctions and persuasive inducements.

Furthermore, power, particularly coercive power, tends to weaken and require more expenditures the more distantly from its origin it is applied. A group defending itself against a distant antagonist need not have equal overall forces to sustain itself against the antagonist. In addition, the effects of resource differences vary with the significance of the issue for each side in a conflict. Obviously, a party for whom an issue is vital will risk much more of its resources than will a party for whom the issue is peripheral. Significantly, too, the skill in mobilizing and applying the right mix of resources greatly affects the degree to which the level of power is effectively applied. Finally, many noncontentious aspects of the relationship between the adversaries affect the impact of resource differences; these include shared identities, mutual dependency, and common interests.

Despite these qualifications, differences in resources significantly affect the outcome of conflicts, but not in a mechanical, deterministic fashion. The qualifications suggest some of the ways relative power affects the outcome of a struggle, depending on the nature of the power differences and on the peculiarities of the struggle. If the resources are greatly asymmetrical, along many dimensions, that tends to shape the character of a struggle's outcome, making it possible for the more powerful party to dominate the relationship.

Negotiated settlements with mutual concessions tend to be made when the negotiating parties are relatively equal in regard to matters pertaining to the issues in contention. For example, when the United States held an overwhelming superiority in nuclear weapons, relative to the Soviet Union, no bilateral accord on nuclear disarmament or arms control was reached. When the Soviets nearly attained parity, and each side had the capability of destroying much of the other country's population, agreements to limit at least some arenas of nuclear weapons competition were concluded, for example, the 1972 antiballistic missile treaty (ABM).

Noncoercive resources also often are asymmetrically distributed, and that shapes the nature of the outcome. One side may have the better side of an argument, given the prevailing values and understandings shared by many of the members of the opposing sides. That helps in mobilizing support, but it also helps in shaping the terms of any outcome. For example, once a major category of American citizens made it clear that they found it unacceptable to be legally denied equal opportunities to use public facilities, the Jim Crow laws could no longer be justified in the United States as a whole.

External Forces

Every social conflict is embedded in a specific historical context, with its particular configuration of ongoing trends and new developments, and some conflict outcomes are consistent with the emerging conditions. Of course, the partisans of a conflict often claim that they are on the side of history and for a while the claim and the experience may make it seem true, but then it may cease to be so. Communist Parties throughout the world for over a hundred years effectively used the argument that they represented the future. When that general claim became less and less credible and collapsed at the end of the 1980s, the outcomes of particular struggles in many countries favored the opponents of communism.

Changes and trends in the sociopolitical context, in population, in economic conditions, and the prevailing ways of thinking all impact on the nature of each conflict outcome. These changes and trends and the beliefs about them should be considered in assessing the impact of termination processes on conflict outcomes.

Shifts in Social-Political Context

Changes in alliances and in the salience of other conflicts profoundly affect how each particular conflict ends. For example, the end of the cold war impacted on many conflicts everywhere in the world, as many cases examined in this book make evident. As that overall conflict declined in salience and then disappeared, other conflicts that coincided with the divisions of the cold war declined in importance and many became amenable to settlement. This happened, for example, in Central America and Southern Africa. Other conflicts that were subordinated to the cold war emerged as more salient when the dominant one disappeared. For example, ethno-nationalist tensions and disagreements within the former Soviet Union and elsewhere in the Soviet-led bloc began to surface.

Shifts in Population

Since numbers are an important resource for each side in every intergroup conflict, changes in population affect the character of the outcome. In the short term, the relative population size is affected by differences in the movement of members in and out of each party, whether by voluntary or forced moves. Some parties are more able than others to sustain membership, particularly of those directly conducting the struggle. For example, governments generally are able to keep their agents working in a struggle against a challenging social movement organization, while participation in the movement may rapidly surge, but then dissipate under pressure or lack of success.[70]

In the longer term, demographic shifts resulting from changes in relative birth and death rates and in immigration and emigration patterns profoundly affect the shape of a conflict outcome. In Lebanon, for example, the political structure established by the National Pact of 1943 reflected the relative numbers of Maronite Christians, Sunni Muslims, and Shiite Muslims. The president was to be a Maronite, the prime minister, a Sunni, and the speaker of the legislature, a Shiite. The seats in the legislature were apportioned so that a six-to-five ratio of Christians to Muslims would be maintained. Over the years, however, demographic changes produced a higher proportion of Muslims, particularly Shiites, and the civil wars of the 1970s were partially due to the unchanged character of the political system. When the civil war was finally ended and a new political system established in 1989–90, the new power-sharing system increased the role of the Muslims relative to the Christians.

Finally, population changes are a function of changes in the boundaries of the relevant social system. Territorial conquests and secessions, organizational mergers and separations, and other imposed or agreed-upon shifts in social boundaries change the relative proportions of people in terms of ethnicity, class, or ideology. Those changes can be the basis of a new kind of integrative relationship, as well as the basis for new conflicts.

Economic Conditions

The level of economic standards and particularly the trends in those levels greatly affect the likely outcomes of many struggles. During periods of stagnation or decline, struggles tend to be viewed as zero-sum and waged in by each side to maximize its share of a constant or shrinking pie. But during periods of expansion, struggles can be conducted as if no side must lose, and all sides will gain. Integrative outcomes are more readily anticipated and achieved in those conditions.

Thus, during the mid-1960s in the United States, the growing economy and resulting increase in federal revenues made many of the goals of the civil rights movement and the war on poverty seem attainable with little or no costs to anyone. Affirmative action policies could enable minority members to enter jobs from which they had been excluded, without denying entry to members of the majority groups, since schools and jobs were expanding.

The relationship between affirmative action and an expanding economy was also explicit in the plan for reducing ethnic inequalities in Malaysia. The Malays and the indigenous peoples, known as *Bumiputra*, tended to be poor, less educated, and more engaged in traditional occupations compared with the non-*Bumiputra*, such as the Chinese.[71] Ethnic riots in May 1969 resulted in negotiations among the leaders of the major ethnic communities to establish a plan to institute preferential ethnic policies in an expanding economy.

Under particular conditions, even improving economic conditions and expanding resources can undermine agreements. This tends to be the case when the increased benefits are very unequally distributed among the former adversaries, thus aggravating the previous inequities. The differences in relative gains become a new source of resentment and antagonism.

Prevailing Thinking

Widely shared views of the ways the world works and how it should work provide a context influencing the form of every conflict outcome. One adversary may benefit more than another due to its goals better matching the prevailing views. For example, in periods and places where racist ideas are prevalent, outcomes with one race or ethnic group being dominant and another being discriminated against are more likely than in societies or organizations where racist ideas are rejected. Similarly, widespread acceptance of nationalist ideology supports claims for political control over a territory in the name of a particular ethnic community, while ideologies of democracy or of individualism undermine such claims and so influence the shape of the conflict outcomes.

Termination Processes

In addition to external factors and the general course of the conflict, how a conflict is brought to an end, whether by one or another kind of negotiation or by a kind of imposition, also helps shape the outcome. Accusations of losing at the negotiation table what was won on the battlefield may reflect polemical argument more than analysis, but we need to consider the effects of the termination process on the conflict outcome. We will examine negotiation and nonnegotiation forms of termination processes separately, although they are not wholly independent of each other.

Nonnegotiation Processes

One or both sides in a struggle may resolutely refuse to negotiate. They do so because they think that they will do better by continuing the struggle. But one side, and sometimes both, is often wrong and loses, recognizing in retrospect that it would have been better off by negotiating a settlement earlier. Nonnegotiated settlements are very likely to result in one-sided impositions compared with negotiated ones, particularly if intermediaries are involved in the settlement process. This may be seen in an analysis of seventy-seven major international conflicts between 1919 and 1939 and between 1945 and 1965.[72] In the cases in which there were no settlement attempts, *all* were unilaterally imposed (64 percent of the outcomes were conquest or annexation and the other 36 percent ended in forced submission, withdrawal, or deterrence). But in cases with bilateral settlement attempts, such one-sided imposed outcomes occurred only two-thirds of the time (29 percent by conquest or annexation and 36 percent by forced submission, withdrawal, or deterrence), and in the other third of the instances, by passive settlement, withdrawal-avoidance, or compromise. In cases with third-party involvement, only one-third of the outcomes were imposed by one side; the other outcomes were compromises (23 percent), third-party awards (23 percent), withdrawal-avoidance (14 percent), or "frozen" conflicts (6 percent).

Nonnegotiated outcomes tend to reflect the balance of resources of the adversaries engaged in the struggle. Furthermore, they tend to satisfy the interests and needs of only one of the parties, while not meeting those of the opposing side. Under some circumstances, and when the power resources are greatly asymmetrical, the weaker party may be effectively destroyed or otherwise cease to exist. This may occur as a result of a successful revolution when the ruling family or group is killed or flees the country or as a result of a successful government campaign to suppress a militant challenging organization.

Negotiation Processes

On the whole, negotiated agreements, compared with nonnegotiated settlements are less likely to be dominated by one side. The terms are more likely to reflect at least some of the concerns of the opposing sides.

Relatively little research has been done on the effect of various negotiation approaches on the nature of a struggle's outcome, but a few observations can be ventured. A problem-solving approach is particularly important to achieve an agreement entailing a high measure of integration, and less important if separation is sought. The negotiations between the government of South Africa and the ANC were conducted in several settings and mixed traditional and problem-solving negotiation approaches. For example, in addition to bilateral negotiations, a multiparty setting was used, the Convention for a Democratic South Africa (CODESA). Arrangements were constructed to ensure that each party and its constituents would have many of their basic requirements met.

Multiple tracks are probably essential to reach stable transformative outcomes. To reach agreements that bring enemies closer together, many channels are needed. But they may be pursued sequentially as well as simultaneously. For example, in South Africa, official meetings were preceded by nonofficial ones.

Intermediaries, as discussed in the previous chapter, often perform valuable services in negotiations, not only in reaching an agreement but in affecting the character of the agreement. On the whole, they tend to produce agreements that are relatively fair, and they provide some representation for stakeholders who are not sitting at the table. This may include rank-and-file constituents of the presumed leaders and representatives, for example by including provisions for elections as a part of the settlement. To some extent, this can be seen in the mediating role that Costa Rica's President Oscar Arias provided in central America and that U.S. Assistant Secretary of State Chester A. Crocker provided in linking the withdrawal of Cuban military forces from Angola with implementation of UN Resolution 435 on Namibia.

Conclusions

Problem-solving negotiation and mediation are always conducted within the context of many other conflict-ending processes. They are also conducted with the awareness that one or more of the protagonists may resort to more coercive means. These relatively coercive means include recourse to the judicial process, to traditional one-sided maximization negotiations, and to the use of violence.

Nevertheless, a struggle's outcome is not shaped only by the threat of coercive and legal controls. Outcomes are not simply the result of immutable forces and coercive balance. The negotiation process itself alters the context in which the struggle is viewed. Enemies become persons with concerns that are recognized, and the conflict becomes a problem to be solved by joint action. The complexities of a conflict and the negotiation processes can be recognized as often providing opportunities to fashion a mutually acceptable settlement.

Notes

1. Aldon D. Morris, "Birmingham Confrontation Reconsidered: An Analysis of the Dynamics and Tactics of Mobilization," *American Sociological Review* 58 (October 1993): 621–36.

2. Richard E. Walton and Robert B. McKersie, *A Behavioral Theory of Labor Negotiations* (New York: McGraw Hill, 1965); Morton Deutsch, *The Resolution of Conflicts: Constructive and Destructive Processes* (New Haven, Conn.: Yale University Press, 1973).

3. Richard E. Walton and Robert B. McKersie, *A Behavioral Theory of Labor Negotiations* (New York: McGraw-Hill, 1965), 132.

4. See reports on the outcomes of revolutions in Jack A. Goldstone, ed., *Revolutions: Theoretical, Comparative, and Historical Studies* (San Diego: Harcourt Brace Jovanovich, 1986).

5. Howard Raiffa, *The Art and Science of Negotiation* (Cambridge, Mass.: Harvard University Press, 1982).

6. Diane Mauzy, "Malaysia: Malay Political Hegemony and 'Coercive Consociationalism,' " in *The Politics of Ethnic Conflict*, ed. John McGarry and Brendan O'Leary (London: Routledge, 1993).

7. The literature on the nature of justice is, of course, vast. I do not venture to consider the ways this discussion is similar and dissimilar to various writers on this subject. Obviously, however, the discussion is beholden to many commentators on this subject. See, for example, John Rawls, *A Theory of Justice* (Cambridge, Mass.: Harvard University Press, 1971) and John Burton, *Conflict: Resolution and Provention* (New York: St. Martin's Press, 1990).

8. Paul R. Pillar, *Negotiating Peace: War Termination as a Bargaining Process* (Princeton, N.J.: Princeton University Press, 1983).

9. For a detailed journalistic account of the changes within the Soviet Union in the 1980s, see David Remnick, *Lenin's Tomb: The Last Days of the Soviet Empire* (New York: Random House, 1993). For an analysis of public opinion in the Soviet Union in

the period of transformation, see Nikolai Popov, *The Russian People Speak: Democracy at the Crossroads* (Syracuse, N.Y.: Syracuse University Press, 1995).

10. I. William Zartman, *Elusive Peace: Negotiating an End to Civil Wars, 1995–1996* (Washington, D.C.: Brookings Institution, 1995).

11. Pillar combined data from several sources. Generally, a war was defined as a conflict involving at least one member of the interstate system and causing at least one thousand battle deaths among the belligerents that belonged to the interstate system. Percentages calculated from data in table 1 in Pillar, *Negotiating Peace*, 18–22.

12. Zartman, *Elusive Peace*.

13. Civil war refers to conflicts meeting all three of the following criteria: (1) "some influential leaders must be concerned about possibly having to live in the *same political unit* with their current enemies. (2) There must be *multiple sovereignty*. (3) [It] involves *large-scale violence*" (Roy Licklider, "The Consequences of Negotiated Settlements in Civil Wars, 1945–1993," *American Political Science Review* 89 [September 1995]: 682).

14. P. H. Gulliver, *Disputes and Negotiations: A Cross-Cultural Perspective* (New York: Academic Press, 1979).

15. For an analysis of informal negotiatons in many spheres of social life, see Anselm Strauss, *Negotiations: Varieties, Contexts, Processes, and Social Order* (San Francisco: Jossey-Bass, 1978). Reviews and analyses of formal negotiations include P. Terrence Hopmann, *The Negotiation Process and the Resolution of International Conflicts* (Columbia: University of South Carolina Press, 1996); Howard Raiffa, *The Art and Science of Negotiation* (Cambridge, Mass.: Harvard University Press, 1982); Thomas C. Schelling, *The Strategy of Conflict* (Cambridge, Mass.: Harvard University Press, 1960).

16. Schelling, *The Strategy of Conflict*.

17. Mosley reports how he used that technique in 1944 in negotiating with the Russians about the armistice terms for Bulgaria. The Soviets were opposed to the payment of reparations for Bulgaria, and Mosley informally explained to the Soviet representatives that if it were not included, a review by Congress might lead to an investigation and he might be punished. The next day the Russians agreed to include the disputed provision. See Philip E. Mosley, "Some Soviet Techniques of Negotiation," in *Negotiating with the Russians*, ed. Raymond Dennett and Joseph E. Johnson (Boston: World Peace Foundation, 1951), 288.

18. Some of these matters are being examined using data from India, China, Greece, Korea, the Netherlands, United States, and elsewhere. For example, using a scenario method, Peter Carnevale and Harry Triandis found that persons from collectivist cultures were more willing to lie than those from individualist cultures in situations where lying helps the ingroup or saves face. Findings reported at a symposium of the Illinois Studies of Culture and Negotiation, at the Ninth Annual Conference of the International Association for Conflict Management, Ithaca, N.Y., June 1996.

19. See Louis Kriesberg, "The Development of the Conflict Resolution Field," in *International Conflict Resolution*, ed. I. William Zartman and Lewis Rasmussen (Washington, D.C.: United States Institute of Peace Press, 1997); and Hopmann, *The Negotiation Process and the Resolution of International Conflicts*, 76.

20. I. William Zartman and Maureen Berman, *The Practical Negotiator* (New Haven, Conn.: Yale University Press, 1982).

21. Zartman and Berman, *The Practical Negotiator*, 66.

22. P. Terrence Hopmann, *The Negotiation Process and the Resolution of International Conflicts*, 80, and James K. Sebenius, *Negotiating the Law of the Sea* (Cambridge, Mass.: Harvard University Press, 1984).

23. Louis Kriesberg, *International Conflict Resolution* (New Haven, Conn.: Yale University Press, 1992).

24. Roger Fisher, "Fractioning Conflict," in *International Conflict and Behavioral Science*, ed. Roger Fisher (New York: Basic Books, 1964).

25. This is the basic premise of exchange theory. For example, see Peter M. Blau, *Exchange and Power in Social Life* (New York: Wiley, 1964). For applications to negotiations, see Raiffa, *The Art and Science of Negotiation*.

26. Kriesberg, *International Conflict Resolution*.

27. Jack P. Manno, "Advocacy and Diplomacy: NGOs and the Great Lakes Water Quality Agreement," in *Environmental NGOs in World Politics*, ed. Thomas Princen and Matthias Finger (London: Routlege, 1994).

28. Laura Nader, "Harmony Models and the Construction of Law," in *Conflict Resolution: Cross-Cultural Perspectives*, ed. Keven Avruch, Peter W. Black, and Joseph A. Scimecca (New York: Greenwood Press, 1991).

29. Roger Fisher and William Ury, *Getting to YES* (Boston: Houghton Mifflin Company, 1981).

30. Richard N. Haass, "Ripeness, De-Escalation, and Arms Control: The Case of the INF," in *Timing the De-Escalation of International Conflicts*, ed. Louis Kriesberg and Stuart J. Thorson (Syracuse, N.Y.: Syracuse University Press, 1991).

31. Louis Kriesberg, "Introduction: Timing Conditions, Strategies, and Errors," in *Timing the De-Escalation of International Conflicts*, ed. Louis Kriesberg and Stuart J. Thorson (Syracuse, N.Y.: Syracuse University Press, 1991).

32. For a discussion of the hurting stalemate and a settlment formula see Saadia Touval and I. William Zartman, eds., *International Mediation in Theory and Practice* (Boulder, Colo.: Westview, 1985).

33. See Louis Kriesberg, "On Advancing Truth and Morality in Conflict Resolution," in *Conflict Resolution and Social Justice*, ed. Richard E. Rubenstein and Frank Blechman (forthcoming).

34. Strobe Talbott, *Deadly Gambits* (New York: Knopf, 1984).

35. Alva Myrdal, *The Game of Disarmament: How the United States and Russia Run the Arms Race* (New York: Pantheon Books, 1982), originally published in 1976.

36. John Forester, "Lawrence Susskind: Activist Mediation," in Deborah M. Kolb and Associates, *When Talk Works: Profiles of Mediators* (San Francisco: Jossey-Bass, 1994).

37. Raymond Cohen, *Negotiating across Cultures* (Washington D.C.: United States Institute of Peace Press, 1991); and Edward T. Hall, *The Silent Language* (New York: Doubleday, 1959).

38. Hans Binnendijk, ed., *National Negotiating Styles* (Washington, D.C.: U.S. Government Printing Office, Department of State Publication, 1987).

39. Marie Provine, *Settlement Strategies for Federal District Judges* (Washington, D.C.: The Federal Judicial Center, 1986).

40. John Lofland, *Polite Protesters: The American Peace Movement of the 1980s* (Syra-

cuse, N.Y.: Syracuse University Press, 1993); and Sam Marullo and John Lofland, eds., *Peace Action in the Eighties* (New Brunswick: Rutgers University Press, 1990).

41. Sebenius, *Negotiating the Law of the Sea.*

42. Janie Leatherman, "Conflict Transformation in the CSCE: Learning and Institutionalization," *Cooperation and Conflict* 28, no. 4 (1993):403–31; Janie Leatherman, *Principles and Paradoxes of Peaceful Change* (Syracuse, N.Y.: Syracuse University Press, forthcoming).

43. See Henry Kissinger, *White House Years* (Boston: Little, Brown, 1979); also see Gerald Smith, *Double Talk: The Story of the First Strategic Arms Limitation Talks* (New York: Doubleday, 1960), and John Newhouse, *Cold Dawn: The Story of SALT* (New York: Holt, Rinehart and Winston, 1973).

44. See John W. McDonald, "Further Explorations in Track-Two Diplomacy," in *Timing the De-Escalation of International Conflicts*, ed. Louis Kriesberg and Stuart J. Thorson (Syracuse, N.Y.: Syracuse University Press 1991); and, Joseph V. Montville. "Transnationalism and the Role of Track-Two Diplomacy," in *Approaches to Peace: An Intellectual Map*, ed. W. Scott Thompson and Kenneth M. Jensen (Washington, D.C.: United States Institute of Peace Press, 1991).

45. The Rhodesian Prime Minister Ian Smith, led the opposition to Black political participation in the 1960s. His son, Alec, describes the regular meetings of White and Black Christian leaders, which became known as the Cabinet of Conscience. It began to meet in 1975 and continued until independence was achieved in 1980 for Zimbabwe. Alec Smith and Arthur Kanodereka, a Black resistance leader, traveled together and organized meetings attracting Blacks and Whites, until Kanodereka was assassinated in December 1978. See Alec Smith, *Now I Call Him Brother* (Basingstoke, U.K.: Marshalls Paperbacks, 1984). See note 27 in chapter 7.

46. During and after the First World War, secret diplomacy was widely viewed as bearing major responsibility for the war. President Woodrow Wilson, in the Fourteen Points, proclaimed the goal of "open covenants of peace, openly arived at, after which there shall be no private understandings of any kind, but diplomacy shall proceed always frankly and in the public view." Cited and discussed in Hans J. Morgenthau, *Politics among Nations* (New York: Alfred A. Knopf, 1950); 426–27.

47. See Jeffrey Z. Rubin and Bert R. Brown, *The Social Psychology of Bargaining and Negotiation* (New York: Academic Press, 1975).

48. For an account of the secret meetings, see Steve Posner, *Israel Undercover* (Syracuse, N.Y.: Syrcause University Press, 1987); and for an analysis of the managed relations between Israel and Jordan, see Yehuda Lukacs, *Israel, Jordan, and the Peace Process* (Syracuse, N.Y.: Syracuse University Press, 1997).

49. Terrell A. Northrup, "The Dynamic of Identity in Personal and Social Conflict," in *Intractable Conflicts and Their Transformation*, ed. Louis Kriesberg, Terrell A. Northrup, and Stuart J. Thorson (Syracuse, N.Y.: Syracuse University Press, 1989); Walker Conner, *Ethnonationalism: The Quest for Understanding* (Princeton, N.J.: Princeton University Press, 1994); and Anthony Smith, *National Identity* (Reno: University of Nevada Press, 1991).

50. According to the analysis developed here, the content of the identity is critical as well as its association with particular grievances and goals. Differences in ethnic identity do not necessarily result in severe conflicts but generally do if associated with

doctrines of ethnonationalism. See Charles Tilly, "States and Nationalism in Europe, 1492–1992," in *Perspectives on Nationalism and War*, ed. John L. Comaroff and Paul C. Stern (Amsterdam: Gordon and Breach, 1995).

51. Roy Licklider, "The Consequences of Negotiated Settlements in Civil Wars, 1945–1993," *American Political Science Review* 89 (September 1995): 686.

52. Louis Kriesberg and Stuart J. Thorson, eds., *Timing the De-Escalation of International Conflicts* (Syracuse, N.Y.: Syracuse University Press, 1991).

53. Kriesberg, *International Conflict Resolution*; Christopher R. Mitchell, "A Willingness to Talk," Working Paper 4, Center for Conflict Analysis and Resolution, George Mason University, Fairfax, Virginia, 1990; Chrisopher R. Mitchell, "Ending Conflicts and Wars: Judgment, Rationality and Entrapment," *International Social Science Journal* 127 (February 1991): 35–55; and Louis Kriesberg and Susan French, "Reactions to Soviet Initiatives," Presented at International Studies Association annual meeting, London, U.K., March 1989.

54. Moshe Dayan, *Breakthrough* (New York: Alfred A. Knopf, 1981), 38–54. Also, personal interview with Don Patir in Washington, D.C., 17 June 1982.

55. Kriesberg, *International Conflict Resolution*.

56. Roger Fisher, "Negotiating Inside Out: What Are the Best Ways to Relate Internal Negotiations with External Ones," *Negotiation Journal* 5 (January 1989): 33–41.

57. Raymond Cohen, *Negotiating across Cultures* (Washington, D.C.: United States Institute of Peace Press, 1991).

58. Huthwaite Research Group and Huthwaite, Inc., *The Behavior of Successful Negotiators* (Sheheld, Eng.: Huthwaite Research Group and Huthwaite, Inc., 1982).

59. Cox Commission, *The Crisis at Columbia: Report of the Fact-Finding Commission Appointed to Investigate the Disturbances at Columbia in April and May 1968* (New York: Vintage, 1968), 182–83.

60. Mark Rudd, "We Want Revolution," *Saturday Evening Post*, as reprinted in William Lutz and Harry Brent, eds., *On Revolution* (Cambridge, Mass.: Winthrop, 1968) 321.

61. For a summary account and analysis of the peace process, see Fen Osler Hampson, *Nurturing Peace: Why Peace Settlements Succeed or Fail* (Washington, D.C.: United States Institute of Peace Press, 1996), 129–70, and for documentation, see *El Salvador Agreements: The Path to Peace* (New York: United Nations Department of Public Information, DPI/1208—92614—July 1992—5M).

62. Tom Baumgartner, Tom R. Burns, and Philipe DeVille, "Conflict Resolution and Conflict Development," in *Research in Social Movements, Conflicts, and Change* vol. 1, ed. Louis Kriesberg (Greenwich, Conn.: JAI Press, 1978).

63. William A. Gamson, *The Strategy of Social Protest*, 2d Ed. (Belmont, Calif.: Wadsworth Publishing Co., 1990).

64. Phillip Taft and Phillip Ross, "American Labor Violence: Its Causes, Character, and Outcome," in *Violence in America*, ed. Hugh Davis Graham and Ted Robert Gurr (New York: Bantam, 1969).

65. David Snyder and William R. Kelly, "Industrial Violence in Italy, 1878–1903," *American Journal of Sociology* 82 (July 1976): 131–62.

66. Gene Sharp, *The Politics of Nonviolent Action* (Boston: Porter Sargent, 1973), 657.

67. Peter Ackerman and Christopher Kruegler, *Strategic Nonviolent Conflict* (Westport, Conn.: Praeger, 1994).

68. Ackerman and Kruegler, *Strategic Nonviolent Conflict*, 325.

69. Gamson, *The Strategy of Social Protest*, and Anthony Oberschall, "The Decline of the 1960s Social Movements," in *Research in Social Movements, Conflicts, and Change*, vol. 1, ed. Louis Kriesberg (Greenwich, Conn.: JAI Press, 1978).

70. Lofland, *Polite Protesters*.

71. Diane Mauzy, "Malaysia: Malay Political Hegemony and 'Coercive Consociationalism,' " in *The Politics of Ethnic Conflict*, ed. John McGarry and Brendan O'Leary (London: Routledge, 1993).

72. Louis Kriesberg, *Social Conflicts* (Englewood Cliffs, N.J.: Prentice-Hall, 1982), table 6.2, based on data from K. J. Holsti, "Resolving International Conflicts: A Taxonomy and Some Figures," *Journal of Conflict Resolution* 10 (September 1966): 272–96.

10

Consequences

The outcome of a struggle and how it was brought about have long-term consequences. They affect the lives of the members of each adversary and the social system of which the adversaries are constituent parts, contributing to equity and stability or to new cycles of injustice and conflict. They similarly affect the continuing relations between the former antagonists, to which we give particular attention. We draw especially on the expanding body of research and theorizing about the conditions and policies that foster constructive conflict transformations.[1]

Aspects of Consequences

One influential body of work on consequences, notably stimulated by Lewis Coser, has treated these effects as functions of social conflicts.[2] This treatment places them in an important theoretical context, functionalism, and provides many suggestive insights about the occurrence and persistence of social conflicts. In one version of this approach, a pattern of behavior may be understood as a mechanism serving to maintain the social system, even if unrecognized by the partisans themselves.[3] In another version of functionalism, a social pattern may be viewed as filling a function or need of the individual members of the social system.[4] Some functionalists, recognizing that certain patterns of conduct also damage the social system or parts of it, write of dysfunctional social conduct.[5]

The various functionalist perspectives provide useful insights for interpreting many aspects of social conflicts. For example, they suggest that waging conflict generally has long-term consequences, often unintended ones. Nevertheless, in this analysis, the more general term *consequences* will be used in preference to function for three reasons. First, it makes it necessary to be explicit about who experiences the consequences. Second, it does not carry any implication that particular patterns of conduct are explained by their consequences, that they are performed in order to fill some function.[6] Third, the analysis in this work takes into account the variety of social systems in which each person and group acts and the openness of the boundaries of many social systems. But this makes problematic what is assumed in some functionalist thought: that there is a single social system and that the maintenance of its boundaries is critical.

Who Experiences the Consequences

Conflicts have consequences not only for the social system of which the adversaries are a part and for the internal affairs of each adversarial group but also for the continuing relations between the adversaries. Therefore, the relevant qualities of each arena need to be identified, before examining how specific conflict characteristics affect them.

Relations between Adversaries

Given our focus on social conflicts, the relations between adversaries must retain center stage when we examine consequences related to avoiding future destructive conflicts and outcomes. A primary concern about the relationship between former adversaries, once the conflict has been settled, is whether or not the new relationship based on the outcome is equitable and enduring. The analysis made in chapter 3 indicates that a conflict will not reemerge if the four necessary factors for its emergence remain critically diminished for at least one of the adversary parties. The four factors identified are (1) forming a collective identity, (2) having a grievance that is believed to be reducible by changes in another party, (3) formulating a goal that would bring about the desired changes, and (4) believing that their struggle can achieve their goal.

In a sense, if those factors do not exist in a combination that is minimally significant, the conflict has been resolved. For example, if at the end of a struggle one of the adversaries has substantially lost its collective identity as an antagonist, the conflict is over. If the adversaries' grievances are significantly redressed or are perceived to be unattainable by their efforts against an opponent, then, too, the conflict may be regarded as resolved. Redressed or re-framed grievances may also indicate that a mutually acceptable outcome, based on some degree of mutually defined equity and justice, has been attained. The conflict has become transformed.

Some conflict outcomes greatly reduce the levels of one or more of these factors, making the reemergence of an overt struggle unlikely, even if justifiable. Often, the outcome of the struggle leaves one or more parties with heightened levels in some conflict-generating conditions and lowered levels in another. For example, a defeated party may feel high levels of grievance and hold goals that involve retaliation and revenge but believe itself to be unable to alter its antagonist in ways that would satisfy its grievances and reach its goals. Such resolutions, however, may not endure forever.

In considering changes in the relations between adversaries as a consequence of a terminated conflict, an important analytic issue should be taken into account. The adversaries in large-scale conflicts are not unitary or homogenous, and therefore the relations between some elements in each side may change constructively but not be so constructive for other elements. For example, the success of the American civil rights struggle of the 1960s opened up opportunities for many African Americans, particularly the relatively well educated, but the economic and social conditions of many others in the Black community had improved little and their standing relative to Whites had increased only in limited ways.

Members in Each Conflict Party

Members of an adversary party generally undergo changes in their internal relations and self-conceptions as a result of the way their struggle was waged and concluded. A frequently noted expectation is that internal solidarity and cohesion tend to increase when a collectivity is engaged in an external struggle, and that may further increase in the short term if it considers itself victorious.[7] In the long term, however, victory may lead to a falling out among the coalition partners who defeated the enemy.[8] This is often the case, for example, in postrevolutionary periods when the assorted victors disagree about which group should rule or which policy should be followed. Such disagreements sometimes result in bloody suppression of erstwhile allies, as in postrevolutionary France, Russia, Cuba, and Iran.

Members of each party tend to think of themselves differently as a result of the conflict in which they had engaged. For example, viewing themselves as victorious, they may believe victory resulted from their bravery or their ideology's correctness and therefore are more prone to fight again. Not only the content of adversary members' identities, but also the salience of their identities are likely to change after a destructively waged fight in ways that could then foster a renewed destructive struggle. Thus, shared identities with the adversary are likely to be weakened while those that embody antagonism would become more salient. Conversely, the transformation of a conflict partly with cooperative efforts, in joint problem solving, as allies against a common enemy, or by collaborating in economic development, may result in strengthening shared identities.

The adversary members' material conditions also tend to change as a result of struggle, often having deteriorated in the course of a destructive struggle and therefore handicapping future improvement. This can be the source of new grievances and a stimulus to search for groups to blame and fight against.

The members' propensity to use particular modes of conflict is likely to have altered as a result of using certain means and assessing their effectiveness, often making for continuities in conflict methods. Finally, internal differences and specialization, developing from the way the struggle had been waged, are likely to grow; these changes increase the likelihood that an internal struggle will be waged using those means, whether violent coercion or mediated negotiation.

Social Context

Entities not directly engaged in a conflict may still be impacted by it through various processes. Impacts occur as the adversaries' relations with third parties change as a result of the conflict's outcome. For example, revolutionary victors may seek to spread their ideology and use coercion to bring about similar changes in nearby countries or in similarly situated communities. Impacts may also occur through diffusion, as the methods and results of struggles in one place become the models for other possible adversaries in other settings. Finally, the social systems within which a conflict was waged often are modified as a result of a struggle or series of struggles. For example, after the First World War the League of Nations was founded, and after the Second World War the United Nations was founded, each to prevent the recurrence of such wars.

Dimensions of Consequences

Two dimensions of consequences are of primary concern in the present analysis. One dimension pertains to the conflict outcome's *stability* and the other to the degree of *equity* or justice resulting from the outcome. Stability refers to the duration and degree of order and the prevention of renewed struggle. Equity refers to the degree of mutual acceptance of the outcome, particularly acceptance based on fulfillment of fundamental preferences of the membership on each side.

An important analytic issue in interpreting such long-term consequences should be recognized. The nature of the changes can appear quite different, depending on the time frame used in assessing them. Analysts and partisans are likely to differ about what is the correct before-the-conflict base year, about when the conflict has ended, and about what length of time after the conflict's end is best used to assess consequences. For example, consider the Russian revolution of October 1917, when the Bolsheviks seized control of the state, ending the Russian Empire and creating the Soviet Union. To assess the economic achievements of the Soviet Union, should the base year be 1917, after three years of engagement in the First World War, or 1914, or 1910 before the war, or 1920, when the civil war was over and the Bolsheviks had established the Soviet borders? At the other end, measures of Soviet achievement looked quite different in the early 1960s, when growth rates were relatively high, than in the early 1970s, when economic stagnation had set in, or in the early 1980s, when a sense of crisis had begun to arise.

Another analytic issue must be noted. Not everything that happens after a struggle ends should be attributed to that struggle. Many other factors and changing conditions are undoubtedly operative. In examining consequences, then, we will be careful to discuss those connections that support such linkage to the conflict.

Consequences for Internal Features

Every struggle of great magnitude has wide-ranging, long-term effects on the internal life of each adversary. We examine, here, how the means used in waging a struggle and the outcome of that struggle affect the internal relations among members of each party.

Consequences of Conflict Modes

Conflict modes that vary in the use of violence, of nonviolent action, and of problem-solving approaches help set precedents, form preferences, and shape expectations about whether and how to engage in further struggles. We examine the effects particularly on equity and stability. These are considered in the light of the four matters that are critical to the emergence of overt struggle: collective identities, sense of grievance, contentious goals, and belief in the capability to achieve the contested goals. The conditions combine to affect the emergence of a renewed conflict, but if their combined level is below the threshold, a new conflict will not emerge. The partisans' sense of equity is particularly affected by their level of grievance and the content of their collective identity. Since equity tends to foster stability, equity will be discussed before examining stability.

Equity

Three noteworthy processes affect the sense of equity among members of a collectivity who have engaged in a struggle. First, they may come to feel more unity, so that the differences among them seem less critical than their commonalties and shared fate. Second, members tend to experience varying burdens and benefits from waging a struggle and from its outcome, and hence may have developed new grievances among themselves. Finally, policies may be pursued that enhance the sense of equity or inequity about the differential burdens carried and benefits gained.

The idea that external conflict fosters internal solidarity is one of the often-noted generalizations in conflict analysis. As Lewis Coser reformulated Georg Simmel, "Conflict with another group leads to the mobilization of the energies of group members and hence to increased cohesion of the group."[9] Another important proposition Coser adapts from Simmel is, "Conflict with other groups contributes to the establishment and reaffirmation of the identity of the group and maintains its boundaries against the surrounding social world." This phenomenon is evident in the tendency for people to "rally around the flag." There is evidence that American presidents gain approval for themselves and for their policies when they act in response to foreign conflicts.[10]

External struggle can reduce internal dissension through several processes. Feelings of loyalty are aroused and called upon by leaders, supported by group norms, and often fostered by interpersonal networks. Furthermore, the increased prominence of an external conflict tends to reduce the salience of internal fights, and striving for a shared purpose tends to subordinate internal discord. For example, during civil rights campaigns in the United States, aggressive crimes by Blacks decreased.[11] This decrease may have resulted from the civil rights struggle absorbing energy and attention or by appearing to provide alternative ways of attaining sought-for ends. The decrease can also result from placing internal divisions within the context of fighting a common enemy. When the major basis for solidarity is a common enemy, increased hostility toward that foe will tend to strengthen solidarity. Thus, military alliances tend to have less internal dissension when confrontations with an adversary intensify. This seems to have been the case during the cold war for NATO solidarity and for Soviet-Chinese solidarity.[12] But this internal solidarity may quickly dissolve once the external conflict loses salience. This phenomenon can be seen in the tendency for winning coalitions to fall apart and former allies to fight over the spoils after a victory has been won. The fights among coalition partners often are deadly and destructive, as frequently has been the case after successful revolutions.

Relatively constructive modes of conflict tend to produce a sense of group pride and solidarity, and may be more enduring. For example, after the negotiations in South Africa for a new constitution were completed, and the transition to a new, freely elected government was accomplished, White South Africans, as well as non-Whites, were generally proud of what they had accomplished. This helped the transition through very difficult challenges.

The African-Americans' struggle for their civil rights and their reliance on nonviolence in the 1950s and most of the 1960s was a source of pride and contributed to their feeling favorable about themselves. But the conflicts and the modes of struggle used by resisting Whites in the South were abhorrent to many Whites in the United States, even in the South. Consequently, when Blacks and Whites were asked in a 1964 national survey to say how favorably they felt about various groups, almost two-thirds of the Blacks answered that they felt favorable to Blacks, compared with only about half of the Whites who said they felt favorable to Whites.[13] Furthermore, in two later surveys, the proportion of Whites reporting that they felt favorable to Whites declined, to 39 percent in 1968 and only 30 percent in 1970. But the proportion of Blacks reporting that they felt favorable to Blacks did not significantly decline, remaining 65 percent in 1968 and slipping to 63 percent in 1970.

Many persons who committed atrocities during a struggle or were members of collectivities that did, later often regard those actions as wrong and blame their leaders, or assume responsibility and feel guilty, or try to deny what happened.[14] For example, in Bosnia and Herzegovina, after the brutal fighting marked by "ethnic cleansing" was ended and the peace agreement mediated by the U.S. government began to be implemented, many former Bosnian Serb combatants expressed shame and bewilderment about what they had done. As one young man in a small rural town in what had become a Serb republic within Bosnia and Herzogovina said in January 1996, "I don't remember what we were trying to do with this war, and now I don't care. I got out alive, and now I want to leave the Serbian republic. I'll go almost anywhere else."[15]

External conflict, then, often becomes a source of subsequent internal dissension and intense conflict. The externally induced internal cohesion that sometimes occurs tends to weaken as an external conflict persists, as the burdens of waging the struggle rise, and particularly as those costs are unevenly borne. In addition, the insistence on loyalty sometimes is experienced as repression and a reason for increasing opposition to those pursuing the struggle against an external enemy. The relative impact of processes making for increased and decreased internal cohesion depends on a variety of circumstances, as will be considered shortly.

The sense of equity is likely to be affected by the distribution of the costs of conducting a struggle and of its outcome. Given the internal differences in rank and power within any large-scale adversary group, it might seem reasonable to expect that the costs would be disproportionally borne by members of the low-ranking strata. There is abundant evidence supporting this generalization.

Where the fighting is intense and burdens great, often the relatively disadvantaged are further harmed. For example, during the First World War, the health of the working class on the European continent suffered.[16] The effects of poor health are long-lasting, particularly upon children. Furthermore, many people, especially those who have few resources, become desperate refugees as a result of international wars, civil wars, and severe state repression. The number of refugees has grown rapidly in the 1980s and 1990s.[17] The United Nations high commissioner for refugees (UNHCR) estimates that at the end of 1992, there were 18.2 million refugees around the world, and 24 million internally displaced persons.

Under certain circumstances, nevertheless, the waging of a struggle and the outcome achieved actually reduce the previous inequalities within an adversary party. Thus, in large-scale conflicts involving high levels of mobilization, the previously disadvantaged within an adversary party may win new gains. Consider what often happens in protracted interstate wars and civil wars. Minority groups, women, and other less-advantaged and previously underutilized persons gain new advantages and become more valuable. Thus, quantitative cross-national analyses indicate that countries with relatively high military participation ratios tend to have more income equality, holding other factors constant.[18] Erich Weede argues more generally that interstate conflict has tended to empower the middle and lower strata of the societies in Europe and contributed to the development of capitalism and freedom.[19] More particularly, research indicates that in the United States, in the Second World War and in the Korean and Vietnam Wars, wages increased relative to profits.[20] Other research finds that overall income inequality decreased in the United States in the Civil War and in the First and Second World Wars, but not during the U.S. engagement in wars in Korea and Vietnam.[21] The impact of war on societal inequality undoubtedly varies with the war's duration and the degree of mobilization associated with it. Furthermore, increased equality is not necessarily perceived as fair; the dominant groups may find this change wrong and threatening and seek to restore their relatively higher rank.[22]

Particular advantaged groups, in some circumstances, actually suffer disproportionate costs of a fight. By taking the lead, they sometimes expose themselves to greater risks. In the First World War, the British elite suffered heavy casualties—greater than the rest of the population.[23] The sons of the elite, graduates of Oxford and Cambridge, volunteered and served in military roles that had very high mortality rates. This contributed to the subsequent antimilitarist and pacifist sentiments in Great Britain in the 1920s and 1930s.

Finally, the way costs and benefits are distributed within an adversary party is not mechanically transferred to varying feelings of equity. What appears to be just depends on various standards of judgment and on how the benefits and costs are presented. Thus, the appearance of profiteering in wartime, of corruption by some greedy individuals personally benefiting by the way the struggle is waged or how it is settled, often arouse feelings of outrage. Public campaigns to control such behavior increase the sense of fairness among the members of a conflict party. On the other hand, if leaders and their families flaunt their personal gains from a struggle, they risk repudiation and the discrediting of the cause they claimed to lead, as illustrated by the opposition to some of the leaders, after the wars in the former Yugoslavia.

Clearly, in warfare, young men are particularly likely to bear the heaviest burden, but that is often viewed as just, or in any case inevitable, in war.

Frequently, too, class and ethnic differences are associated with making un-equal sacrifices, and that may be seen as unfair. For example, during the American Civil War, in the North, a draft was instituted in 1863, including the provision that a drafted man could hire a substitute or pay three hundred dollars and so escape service. Opposition was widespread, and riots broke out in many cities, most notably in New York City.

In the American engagement in the Vietnam War, Blacks suffered higher casualties than Whites. For example, while Blacks averaged about 9.3 percent of the total active duty personnel in 1965–70, they suffered 12.6 percent of the deaths, "35.5 percent in excess of their percentage in the U.S. armed forces and 30 percent in excess of their percentage in Indochina."[24] This contributed to Blacks' sense of injustice within American society even after the war was over. But the protests against the war, while it was being waged, were more evident among White college students, when they were subject to the draft.

Stability

The destructiveness with which a conflict is waged and ended affects the chances that the relations among the members of each adversary party will be destructively renewed. We have noted how variations in the mode of conflict affect the sense of equity among members of an adversary group. Insofar as equity is increased, or at least not damaged, the chances of nonhostile rela-tions among the members of an adversary party are increased. We now con-sider three other factors: first, changes in social and material conditions within a conflict party; second, the past use of particular conflict methods; and third, the degree of joint decision making in settling the conflict.

First, conflicts of great magnitude, involving large proportions of the mem-bers of an adversary party, are obviously disruptive of routine life. Such dis-ruptions create hardships for many persons, and if severe enough, produce social disorder resulting in widespread violence, famine, and flight. At a mod-erate level, however, the disruptions provide new opportunities for many per-sons, as they change roles and locations. The disruption may foster a spurt of growth, spurred by new ideas, combinations, and innovations arising from the experience of the struggle itself. The expansion may compensate for some of the losses of those who had suffered hardships. More generally, social sys-tems confronting recurrent threats of conflict develop internal discipline and organizational efficiencies that tend to enhance their productivity in many arenas.

The reliance on large-scale violence in waging wars or revolutions can im-pose heavy burdens and significant declines in the well-being of people. The declines can become self-perpetuating as the material and social bases for productive lives are destroyed. This occurred in Europe after the Second World War, and more recently in Somalia, Rwanda, Cambodia, and Lebanon.

It may take years or even decades to overcome those loses. The costs are not only economic, but also social, such as fostering official secrecy, reducing tolerance for dissent, and distracting attention from other social problems.

At more moderate levels of violence and threatened violence, however, there is evidence that such destructive effects are avoided and even have some effects that group members are likely to regard as beneficial. At the interstate level, even war may be related to economic expansion, if conducted elsewhere. For example, the U.S. economy's growth surged during World War II, the Korean War, and the Vietnam War.[25] Such economic expansion tends to mute internal dissension and instability.

The second important factor affecting internal stability is the support developed for particular modes of conflict. Each adversary party, as a struggle goes on, becomes increasingly differentiated in ways relevant to waging the struggle with the particular methods used in that struggle. The use of armed attacks, of covert actions, of nonviolent protests, of rent strikes, of diplomacy, or of persuasive appeals makes it likely that more human and other resources will be devoted to the chosen method. Even after the conflict is over, the resources devoted to the previously important mode tend to remain salient and be used again. Some of them are likely to result in instability.

A variety of evidence demonstrates how these effects occur. For governments that have waged a war, the resources devoted to the military may decline afterward, but generally not to the prewar levels. There is frequently an upward ratchet effect, based on the vested interests created by past usage and on the understandings about what is expected in the future.

Despite what was written earlier about the energizing and equalizing effects of mobilizing resources to conduct a struggle, the effects are quite different if the mobilization is at very high levels and is sustained for an extremely long time. In civil and in international wars, if large proportions of the youth are preparing for and engaging in violent struggle, they fail to learn the skills and knowledge needed for economically and politically productive participation in civil life. Even sustained mobilization to maintain readiness for armed struggle can drain and divert intellectual and material resources in ways that undermine the goals that the mobilization is supposed to serve. The collapse of the Soviet Union is an extreme example of this. For decades, the Soviet Union had devoted 12 to 15 percent of its GNP to military expenditures by CIA estimates; but Soviet and Russian sources after the cold war ended estimated even higher percentages, in the 25 to 30 percent range. This allocation of resources greatly contributed to the failure of the Soviet system to satisfy the basic needs of the Soviet peoples. Even in the United States, a much smaller percentage of a much larger GNP devoted to the military contributed to a slower growth than many other advanced industrialized countries devoting smaller proportions of their GNP to military expenditures.[26]

The use of nonviolent and noncoercive means of struggle, on the other hand, often enhances internal stability. For example, large-scale participation in nonviolent campaigns can be exhilarating and tends to build solidarity among the participants. Although difficult to sustain, it provides models and encourages approaches for settling internal disputes, which reduce the likelihood of destructive escalation of the conflict. Where use of nonviolent actions was widespread, popular engagement in political life was fostered, at least initially; this is illustrated in the independence and anticommunist struggles in the former Soviet Union and the countries it dominated.[27]

Third, problem-solving negotiated endings of conflicts tend to have their own problematic consequences for internal stability. If the ending is concluded secretly by the leadership, internal dissension may arise at a later time, particularly if a there is an internal opposition faction or leadership group. This tends to occur when the constituents have not participated in the transformative interactions among the persons engaging in the actual negotiations.[28] The way the meetings between PLO and Israeli representatives near Oslo were conducted, while effective in reaching an accord, provoked resistance among many Palestinians and Israeli Jews who were surprised by the agreement. The problem can be reduced by enabling more segments of the constituents to be informed and participate in the process of change, or having parallel processes at various levels. At a minimum, if the negotiations are publicly concluded and ratified, the chances of the agreement receiving continued support are increased.

In short, the particular conflict mode used in a struggle often has lasting impacts on the equity and stability for relations within the party using them, frequently unintended consequences. The effects of the means used may actually undermine the goals that they were intended to serve. Thus, struggles are often waged to improve the material conditions of the constituency in whose name the struggle is conducted or to gain more freedom and control for them. But even victory may bring about only a little of what was sought and in some ways lower attainments for years. This is particularly the case when the means of struggle create high levels of disorder and resentment and high degrees of centralization and control within the organization conducting the struggle. Such consequences have often been noted in regard to revolutions. As Martin Oppenheimer observed in the late 1960s, when romanticism about armed struggle and guerrilla warfare was relatively widespread, "the types of personalities, as well as the forms of organization that usually emerge in a violent revolutionary struggle . . . are those which undercut the humanistic hopes of such endeavors."[29]

The process of waging and ending a conflict has diverse consequences for relations within each of the adversary parties, in some ways enhancing internal equity and stability, but in other ways reducing them. The consequences are also shaped by the outcome of the struggle, in interaction with the way the struggle was conducted.

Consequences of Outcomes

Conflict outcomes have long-term as well as immediate effects on the internal relations of the members of each side. The effects on equity and stability are likely to differ for the adversaries since the outcomes of conflicts are usually not symmetrical. Thus, the side that believes it lost much of what it struggled for will experience quite different consequences than its adversary. But consequences of joint as well as distributive aspects of conflict outcomes also need to be considered.

Equity

Insofar as the distribution of losses in the outcome are unequal, the members of the side believing they have lost the most are likely to feel that they are suffering an injustice. They tend to feel disappointment, resentment, and anger, and those feelings may be directed at persons on their own side, the leadership being a likely target. Trade union leaders who fail to win benefits desired by their constituency, for example, are likely to face factional disputes and challenges to their leadership.[30] Leaders of the adversary party, foreseeing such consequences, may try to avoid framing the outcome as a defeat for the opponent so as to preserve the opponent's leadership and to preserve the outcome.

One internal faction is likely to accuse another of being responsible for the loss of a struggle, and the reason may vary from incompetence to treason. Such accusations may be well grounded, but frequently they are self-serving, explaining away the accusers' own responsibility or justifying the accusers' rise to power. A classical example of this phenomenon was the disagreement within Germany after its defeat by the allies in the First World War. Many of the former military leaders explained Germany's defeat by arguing that internal enemies had stabbed Germany in the back.

A defeat may result in severe loses that impose ongoing burdens. The burdens are the consequence of damaged assets, of reduced capacity to function effectively, and of increased demands arising from the inequities resulting from the different harms suffered by various segments of the population. Those burdens may contribute to harsh economic or social conditions, pitting subgroups against each other. That can contribute to scapegoating, blaming a relatively vulnerable person, group, or people who had little capacity to affect the outcome. The ability of Adolph Hitler to use hostility against Jews in mobilizing Germans to join and support the Nazi Party after the First World War and the inflation of the 1920s is an infamous example.[31] Policies, however, can be implemented that help limit the adverse consequences of severe losses. For example, after the Second World War, the West German state took many measures to incorporate the German refugees from Eastern Europe.[32]

The members of the winning side, on the other hand, more often feel content with each other. Insofar as the members share a common identity, the victory of their side is gratifying. Those who led in the struggle are likely to be honored and their cause in the struggle vindicated. But the gains of victory are rarely evenly distributed, and that can be the source of changes in the relative position of groups within the winning side and a source of internal dissension. Thus, a collective bargaining agreement that gives all workers a fixed-sum increase will improve the relative position of the lower-paid workers, while an across-the-board percentage increase will be of greater benefit to the higher-paid workers. Either strategy if pursued consistently for a long time is likely to arouse opposition from the disadvantaged members.

Outcomes, as stressed here, are not always simply zero-sum; conflict outcomes generally also have joint benefits and losses. The internal consequences of those outcomes vary greatly, depending on the characterization of the results by the members of each side. Outcomes that have been failures for both sides are likely to produce high levels of cynicism and resentment among the rank-and-file members of each side. On the other hand, mutually beneficial outcomes, particularly if they seem to have averted anticipated disaster, tend to foster a sense of shared triumph and pleasure. This was the case for many of the people in South Africa, as the transition to majority rule was made. Of course, many problems remain and new ones have arisen; the new harsh realities require new problem-solving negotiations.

Stability

External conflicts that result in one-sided defeats are often the basis for internal revolts against the leadership of the defeated party. As the discussion about the emergence of overt struggle in chapters 3 and 5 indicated, research on revolutions demonstrates the importance of severe and failed external conflicts in explaining revolutionary challenges and their success.

Victories too can be the source of internal dissension. Expectations may be raised by victories, and if the anticipated benefits are not forthcoming, the resulting disappointment may generate challenges against the leaders or the relatively advantaged groups within the same side. This is particularly likely when the previously disadvantaged had been mobilized to wage the struggle and therefore feel they have a special claim after the struggle has been won. They may also have more capability than they had earlier to make their claims effectively. These factors contributed to the rise of the civil rights movement in the United States, years after the Second World War ended.

Win or lose, the end of a fight allows people to turn their attention to previously submerged internal conflicts. The loss of an external enemy generally raises the salience of internal fights since the need for internal solidarity is reduced. For example, during the Second World War, the U.S. federal government induced the trade unions to make a no-strike pledge. Nevertheless, strikes increased each year of the war, except 1942, perhaps because the tight labor market increased the power of the workers relative to the managers and so presented an opportunity for them. However, some stifling of labor disputes probably did occur, as indicated by the wave of labor strikes immediately after the war ended. The increase in strikes may also have been driven by employers seeking to regain ground since their bargaining power was better and also by workers seeking to counter the inflation of the period.

Attention to internal enemies after threats from an external enemy have disappeared also arise from the tendency of some people to organize their lives around the fight with the enemy, and the loss of one produces a search for others. In the United States, after the end of the cold war, some groups gained support for their struggle against internal enemies, including the federal government, which some characterized as the Zionist Occupation Government (ZOG).[33]

Implications

The way a conflict is waged and the way it comes out have many interacting implications for the equity and stability within each adversary party. They are discussed in the context of the much-studied relationship between external and internal conflicts. Although the proposition that external conflict strengthens internal cohesion is often cited, the evidence is not generally supportive of it. Rather, the nature of the relationship depends on many factors, such as the previous condition of solidarity, the kinds of internal conflict, and the severity and duration of the external conflict.

Consider the responses in the United States to waging the Second World War, the Korean War, and the Vietnam War. Examinations of changing public attitudes, evasive draft behavior, and protests and repression indicate increasing disaffection and dissent during the Korean and Vietnam Wars, but not in the Second World War.[34] Several factors help account for these differences. First, the Second World War was a relatively total war, which tends to be more equally deprivational than a limited war. Thus, income inequality decreased during the Second World War, but not during the Korean War.[35] Second, the circumscribed goals of the limited wars were less likely to submerge internal differences than was the greater shared threat to the collectivity against which the Second World War was seen to be waged. Third, internal solidarity was already relatively low, prior to the escalation of the Vietnam War, as the emerging civil rights struggle and university student uprisings indicated. In addition, the Vietnam War was waged for a relatively long time. Finally, the results of the limited wars were not generally viewed as successful as were those of the Second World War. Failure is reason enough to punish leaders and withdraw support, as the Argentine military junta found after their 1982 attempt to unite the Malvina/Falkland Islands with Argentina by military force was defeated by Britian.[36] Moreover, leaders of failed endeavors are likely to be seen as less competent and therefore more readily challenged than are leaders of successful efforts. Whether dissatisfaction becomes expressed in overt struggles with the government or among different groups within the society depends upon additional factors.

A study of five major wars in which the United States was engaged between 1890 and 1970 indicated that the wars were associated with increases in domestic violence.[37] This was most evident following World War I, with violence by Whites against Blacks in race riots, attacks by National Guard units against striking workers, and federal government raids during the "Red Scare" in 1919 and 1920. Not only were the differences within American society exacerbated by the wars, but the resort to violence appeared to be more acceptable.

Considerable cross-national research has been conducted about the linkage between external and internal conflict. This evidence generally does not support the theoretical proposition that external conflict reduces internal conflict. Rummel's, Tanter's, and many other studies have found no overall relationship. Moreover, several studies have found a positive relationship between external conflict and internal conflict.[38] Another body of research has examined the relationship between internal and external conflict among different kinds of countries. For example, Wilkenfeld reanalyzed Tanter and Rummel's data on conflict behavior for eighty-three nations between 1955 and 1957.[39] He distinguished two dimensions of internal conflict: turmoil (riots, demonstrations, general strikes, assassinations, and government crises) and internal war (revolutions, purges, guerrilla warfare, and number killed in all domestic violence). He distinguished three dimensions of external conflict: diplomatic (number of ambassador or other officials expelled or recalled), belligerent (number of antiforeign demonstrations and number of countries with which diplomatic relations were severed), and war (military clashes, number of wars, mobilizations, and persons killed in foreign conflicts).

Wilkenfeld examined the relationship of external conflict in one year with internal conflict one and two years later, in countries with three kinds of regimes: personalist, centrist, and polyarchic. Personalist regimes were dictatorial but less centralized than the centrist regimes; they were primarily in Latin America. The centrist regimes were centralized dictatorships; half were socialist and some were Middle Eastern. The polyarchic regimes were in economically developed Western countries. He found that in countries with personalist regimes, diplomatic conflict behavior was somewhat correlated (.26) to internal turmoil a year later, and belligerency was correlated with internal war one and two years later (.37 and .29, respectively). War was somewhat correlated, two years later, to both turmoil and internal war (.17 and .15, respectively). Presumably personalist regimes tend to have difficulty in waging popularly supported external conflicts or in suppressing internal dissension.

In countries with centrist regimes, external conflict behavior was not related to subsequent domestic turmoil or with internal war.[40] Apparently centrist regimes were generally able to control whatever dissension external conflict evoked.

In polyarchic societies, there was a small positive relationship between diplomatic conflict behavior and internal turmoil one or two years later (.21 and .19, respectively). There were also positive correlations, although even smaller, between belligerency and war and subsequent internal turmoil. However, there was no significant relationship between external conflict and internal war. On the other hand, there was some evidence that nonviolent external conflict behavior was related to reduced internal violent conflict: diplomacy and belligerency were negatively related to internal war two years later ($-.15$ and $-.11$, respectively). It appears that polyarchic regimes allow the expression of dissent about external conflict and other issues, but this does not escalate to internal war. Indeed, for legitimate regimes engaging in nonviolent external conflict behavior appears to lessen the chances of internal war.

The general proposition that external conflict generates internal solidarity is certainly not universally valid; the relationship depends upon many specific circumstances. If external conflict is conducted by severe and protracted violence and waged by a leadership regarded as illegitimate by its constituents, internal dissension, not cohesion, is likely. Conflicts conducted for a short time and without recourse to violence seem to have different consequences, at least for countries with democratic regimes. For example, considering increased approval for the president of a country as an indicator of internal cohesion, there is evidence that becoming engaged in a foreign conflict produces a "rally-round-the-flag" effect and a surge of support for the president.[41] However, engagement in peacemaking efforts also tends to have the same effect.[42]

In short, the effects of external conflict spread out into many aspects of the lives of each adversary's members. They are not all likely to be foreseen or desired. Some probabilities, however, are discernible, and attending to them could helpfully influence the choices of ways to wage and end a conflict so as to reduce unwanted consequences. In general, moderate external challenges often foster internal equity and stability; on the other hand, destructive, protracted struggles result not only in heavy burdens at the time, but in internal changes perpetuating inequities and restrictions. As Erich Weede concludes from his analysis of the effect of interstate conflicts on revolutionary change and individual freedom, the "expansion of freedom seems best served by some modest amount of interstate conflict, by moderate threats to regime security rather than by extreme threats."[43]

Consequences for Adversary Relations

The outcome of a struggle and the mode used in ending it contribute to the perceived justness of the new relations between the former adversaries, the belief that their grievances have been redressed, and other conditions affecting the likelihood that the former antagonists will renew their overt struggle or will avoid future destructive conflict.

Consequences of Modes

The experience with past conflicts between adversaries engenders emotions, expectations, and capabilities regarding the means that they will use against each other in the future. In chapter 5, we cited evidence that the means used in the past are often perpetuated in the future, the victors believing themselves to be vindicated in the choice of means and sometimes even the losers believing they should have done more of what they had tried before. But sometimes, particular methods are judged to have failed or been too costly and are rejected for future struggles. We consider the several processes that help explain the continuities and discontinuities, focusing on means of struggle not only with high components of violence, but also those involving nonviolent action, and problem-solving methods.

Equity

The means used in waging and ending a conflict affect the sense of equity between the adversaries, after the fight has ended. It is likely that inflicting grave injuries and humiliations on an opponent, and unilaterally imposing a settlement, results in members of the opposing side feeling resentment and believing they have been wronged. On the other hand, problem-solving methods of waging and ending a conflict tend to give all parties in the struggle a sense of fairness in the outcome. Some evidence of this sense of satisfaction was discussed previously, particularly in chapter 9 and the research on alternative dispute resolution (ADR).

Even struggles waged with considerable coercion, if conducted so as to consistently acknowledge the opponents' humanness and their concerns, tend to foster a sense of justness in the outcome that is attained. This was part of the great achievement of the nonviolent civil rights struggle in the southern United States in the late 1950s and early 1960s and of the ultimately negotiated end to apartheid in South Africa in the early 1990s. The steadfastness and persuasive efforts contributed to the conviction among members of the dominant party that their previous relationship was oppressive and wrong.

Of course, the transformation of one side can be the basis for a fundamental change in the relationship between adversaries and the establishment of an equitable and enduring cooperative relationship. Such transformations sometimes result from a change in the ruling person, group, or class of one side and the emergence of new leadership reflecting the values and interests of a majority of the constituents or of a new coalition of constituents. Such changes sometimes occur as a result of a defeat and the victor's assistance in establishing a new internal order, as occurred in Germany and Japan after their defeat in the Second World War.

Stability

Suffering severe and widespread violence tends to evoke not only feelings of anger and resentment, but also the desire for revenge and retribution. This pattern is often culturally elaborated in notions of honor that require retribution to overcome the humiliation and shame of having been violated by the other family, clan, or nation.[44] This is the essence of feuds that go on for generations, with recurrent outbreaks of deadly fights. It might therefore be argued that a settlement that is relatively equitable, preserving honor and fundamental interests of the antagonists, would be stable.

An alternative consequence of a one-sided outcome compared with a mutual settlement also can occur.[45] One side may be so severely defeated that the chances of it renewing fighting are greatly reduced. In civil wars, for example, the defeated side may have its organizational structure destroyed and be unable to fight again. Furthermore, negotiated settlements may tend to create balance-of-power arrangements that make it difficult for the government to rule and give the challengers continuing capability of resorting to overt struggle.

The increase in civil wars after the end of the cold war has generated case studies and also quantitative analyses of how such struggles ended and the consequences of their modes of termination. For example, Roy Licklider analyzed all civil wars between 1945 and 1993, finding that of those that had ended, three-fourths had ended by military victory and only one-quarter by negotiation.[46] Most relevantly here, civil wars terminated by negotiation were *more* likely than those ended by military victory to be followed by a renewed war more than five years later (50 percent compared with only 15 percent). However, the analysis also suggests that civil wars ended by military victory may more likely be followed by genocide against the losing side than are civil wars ended by negotiation.

It is likely that for internal conflicts that have not escalated to the level of a civil war, a negotiated settlement would forestall an escalation into violence. A negotiated settlement at that early stage would also be stable, in the sense that a severe protracted struggle would not arise. The many ethnic and other civil conflicts that are conducted within the electoral process, sometimes combined with street protests and demonstrations, attests to this. Negotiated termination agreements, even in civil wars, are as likely to endure as not. Therefore, we must consider the characteristics of agreements that tend to endure without a renewed war.

First, it should be noted that any signed agreement has a binding quality that is lacking in a termination without such symbolic closure. A signed agreement, publicly announced and witnessed, imposes an expectation of being upheld, so that persons who disregard their signed agreements are widely viewed as dishonorable. Staging a signing ceremony, therefore, is often a device to heighten a sense of commitment to the agreement. Furthermore, involving intermediaries in the final negotiations and in the signing ceremony is another way of increasing the signatories' costs should they violate the agreement.

Finally, the process of reaching an agreement may provide for varying amounts of precision and specificity in the terms. In general, ambiguity in the terms eases the difficulty in reaching an agreement but leaves more room for problems arising from implementation afterward. No agreement can incorporate agreed-upon understandings for every future contingency. Indeed, agreements vary widely in their degree of open-endness and ambiguity. The parties doing the negotiation may differ in their concern about precision, due to cultural differences, their degree of confidence in their ability to impose their interpretation, and many other characteristics of the conflict and the nature of the agreement being sought.

Consequences of Outcomes

The nature of the outcome, as well as the process by which it has been reached, has implications for the equity and stability of the future relationship between adversaries. The possible consequences are often the basis for instituting policies to enhance justice and the survival of the agreement ending a conflict. The policies may include fostering vested interests in the newly established outcome and generating conditions that will build trust and mutual dependence.

Equity

An outcome resulting from the transformation of one side, producing a fundamental redefinition of itself, can provide the major adversaries with the sense that the outcome attained is just. To a significant degree, for example, the transformation of German society after Nazism, of Russia after the dissolution of the Soviet Union, and of the Whites of South Africa after apartheid was abolished, made the outcome in many senses a victory for their new selves.

Yet even without such transformation, problem-solving conflict resolution may still yield outcomes that are seen by the former adversaries as equitable. Each side may have achieved something very close to its aspirations, after a long, costly struggle. More often, in actual conflict settlements, the result is one step in an ongoing ameliorating relationship. Issues of contention remain, but they may be pursued in a less antagonistic relationship than previously.

This is illustrated in the relations between the Israeli and Egyptian governments, following the peace treaty they signed in 1979.

Most outcomes, however, are not regarded as equitable by the partisans of each side. Generally, one adversary suffers what it must, accepting what it can get. It may bide its time, waiting for more opportune circumstances to try to win what it seeks by engaging in a renewed struggle. Sometimes an adversary settles after gaining only some of what it sought while still aspiring to win more later. Even members of the triumphant side may seek new conquests, finding that the fruits of victory are not as sweet as they expected. Finally, as the glow of victory passes, the awareness of remaining injustices and unfulfilled expectations rise in salience. For example, the victory marked by ending legally enforced segregation in the American South left standing much defacto segregation and great inequalities in educational and occupational opportunities for African Americans.

Partisans of the side that has been largely defeated often may experience an increased sense of injustice. Relations and values they took for granted have become disrupted in painful ways. They feel that the other side has gone too far and try to mobilize support for a renewed struggle to regain what they consider lost ground. There is a backlash. For example, in the United States social changes resulting from several interrelated struggles in the 1960s and early 1970s constituted a kind of cultural revolution profoundly affecting social relations between men and women and between persons of different ethnicity, sexual orientation, and other social identities.[47] Many persons adhering to relatively traditional values and practices became deeply offended by these changes and they mobilized to restore what they regarded as dangerous losses. In the context of that social movement, some issues became matters of intense struggle, such as abortion, gun control, prayer in the schools, and affirmative action. Organizations arose seeking reversals or more radical changes and willing to use coercion, even violence, to implement their views. These proliferated in the 1980s and 1990s.

Stability

The inequities various parties experience as a result of the conflict outcome sketched above can be an important source of instability in the ongoing relations between former adversaries. Principally, the grievances related to the perceived injustices, if not resolved, fuel renewed struggles. But other specific characteristics of the outcome also affect the chances that it will endure without renewed struggle.

An agreement to end a protracted conflict often incorporates mechanisms to help sustain the agreement. This includes provisions to dismantle the structures that had perpetuated the struggle and provide alternatives for the people who had a vested interest in continuing it. Structures may also be created to generate new vested interests that help sustain the agreements reached. Finally, practices and institutions may be established to manage the disagreements that arise about the terms of the agreement.

Dismantling the structures that had perpetuated the struggle is often critical in maintaining a de-escalatory agreement or in raising the chances that it will be a step toward a full peace and mutual accommodation.[48] In any protracted struggle, particularly between large-scale adversaries, a significant problem is the redeployment of those who made a career of waging the struggle. In the aftermath of civil wars, for example, the disarming of the militias and large military forces and finding employment for the former combatants is a severe challenge. Consequently, procedures and institutional safeguards for reducing the weapons of war have been incorporated in the settlement package ending the civil wars in Namibia and in El Salvador, including a land-for-arms exchange to former combatants.[49]

Creating vested interests for a new accommodation between former adversaries is also important to sustain a de-escalatory agreement. This may take the form of creating organizations with paid staffs whose job it is to implement and monitor the provisions of an agreement, as was done in the United States to fulfill legislation barring discrimination. It may also take the form of establishing institutions bringing representatives of the former adversaries to work in a common enterprise. A particularly notable example of this is the European Coal and Steel Community (ECSC).[50] Established in 1952, by France, West Germany, Italy, Belgium, the Netherlands, and Luxembourg, it was a supranational institution with authority over the production of coal and steel in the six countries. In accord with the logic of functional integration, transnational organizations and actions followed. Slowly and with interruptions, integration among the six European countries grew and then expanded into a wider European Union.[51]

Ensuring compliance to an agreement ending a conflict obviously is critical to the survival of the agreement and constructive relations between the former adversaries. Compliance and full implementation can be made more certain by several mechanisms and conditions. Thus, the signatories to an agreement may establish an ongoing agency to consider differing interpretations of the agreement, receive charges of violations, and discuss possible revisions under changing circumstances. For example, as part of the 1972 agreement to limit the number of strategic nuclear weapons, the Standing Consultative Commission was established by the Memorandum of Understanding between the Government of the United States of America and the Government of the Union of Soviet Socialist Republics on Certain Measures with Respect to the Limitation of Strategic Offensive Arms (SALT I).[52]

Intermediaries often play critical roles in the implementation of an agreement. They sometimes monitor an agreement, and if violations occur, impose sanctions or provide compensation to the disadvantaged side. They may provide the resources needed to ensure that particular terms of the agreement are implemented, for example, by observing elections to help ensure that they are fair and regarded as legitimate. Following protracted civil strife, demobilization of armed forces is generally needed, and intermediaries have filled important roles in this process, as in Namibia and El Salvador.[53]

In short, the nature of an outcome and how it is reached contribute to the equity and stability of the relationship between former adversaries, but these qualities are not determined solely by what has gone before. Subsequent policies also are crucial. Destructive consequences can be averted or attenuated by well considered policies, and a constructive future may be undermined by poor follow-up policies. Adherence to an agreement is a basic condition for developing a future based on cooperative relations. The general violation of an agreement may unleash a bitter, prolonged, and destructive struggle. For example, in the Sudan a power sharing agreement ended the seven-year-long civil war between the northern Muslim region and the non-Muslim southern region. But in 1983, the northern-dominated government violated key elements of the agreement, and a second civil war erupted that has lasted for more than a decade.[54]

Consequences for the Social Context

The outcome of a conflict and the mode of reaching it affect not only the parties directly engaged in the struggle, but also the larger social systems of which they are a part. In addition, they often affect many other parties in the social environment who themselves might not have been adversaries in the previous struggle, but who are likely to become partisans in new fights. We examine some effects that are direct and profound and many others that are indirect.

Consequence of Modes

The constructiveness of a conflict's ending creates new conditions for many people, even if they had not been engaged directly in the struggle. A destructive conflict tends to create a variety of problems, as a result of the disruptions, dislocations, and traumas experienced not only by the combatants but also by those associated with them. Thus, civil strife in one society may disrupt trade relations or generate mass movements of people, imposing severe burdens on members of nearby societies. For example, beginning in the late 1970s, the number of refugees in the world has sharply and immensely increased. A time-series analysis of refugees between 1971 and 1990 indicates that generalized violence such as genocides/politicides, ethnic rebellion, and civil war with foreign military intervention are the best predictors of refugee flows.[55] Other factors such as human rights violations, ethnic conflict, and poverty or underdevelopment did not generate the large numbers of refugees that generalized violence did.

The means used in a past struggle affect not only how the former adversaries wage other conflicts, but also how other parties do so, based on what they learned from the previous struggle. Thus, an analysis of selected countries that became independent since the Second World War examined the consequences of varying amounts of violent and nonviolent actions preceding independence.[56] A relatively strong positive relationship between violence before independence and later external violent behavior was found. In addition, the means an adversary used in its struggle, particularly if it gains much of what it sought, often is adapted by other parties in their own struggles. Thus, in the 1960s, nonelectoral methods of protest in the United States such as street demonstrations and nonviolent action spread among civil rights groups in different cities, to student groups on different campuses, to women's groups, and subsequently to many other identity and interest groups.

Equity

Means of struggle that are extremely severe affect persons who were not directly engaged in the primary conflict and often create new injustices and long-lasting injuries. Violence in which people are driven from their homes, killed, tortured, raped, and otherwise brutalized inflicts enduring emotional impairments upon the surviving victims of such trauma and their family members. Consequently, they may act with desperation to find security and protect themselves, individually and collectively. To take an extraordinary case, the largely successful Nazi effort to destroy European Jewry contributed immensely to the drive among the survivors to get to Palestine and to fight to establish a Jewish state there. That in turn resulted in a disaster for Palestinians, which reverberated throughout the Arab world.

Certain conflict modes affect the sense of equity among parties in the social environment who had not been engaged in the previous struggle. Thus, modes of action used by one group may promise the chance for other groups to redress grievances that previously had not seemed available. Those other groups then seek greater equity for themselves, now that greater justice seems attainable. Conditions that may have seemed inevitable and therefore tolerable may come to be seen as alterable and therefore regarded as intolerable. This rise of claims for justice by groups who had endured discrimination and disadvantages may improve their condition, as happened in the 1960s and 1970s in the United States. But the gains may be sought by some antagonistically, and the absence of problem-solving methods result in too little consideration of the adverse effects on the opponents. That may then contribute to still other groups feeling that satisfaction of those claims puts *them* at a new disadvantage, and they try to counter those gains, raising their own cries for justice. The fight against affirmative action for minorities and women in the 1980s and 1990s in the United States is illustrative.

Stability

The way a conflict was conducted tends to have enduring consequences for those who engaged in the struggle; usually, the mode tends to be perpetuated. Only under particular circumstances, such as great losses, will the mode be rejected in future struggles. Continuities are evident in the analyses of persons who had been activists in social struggles when they were students in colleges and universities. They continue to be relatively active in advocating political and social change in later years.[57]

Major conflicts often have strong and enduring impacts upon those reaching political maturity while they are under way. Through processes examined in the work on political generations by Mannheim and Heberle and others, certain identities and ways of thinking may be enduringly strengthened.[58] For example, the Americans who became politically mature in the great economic depression of the 1930s became relatively more class conscious than other American generations.[59] Similarly, certain issues and ways of managing them become salient as a result of a generation's experience. Thus, the age cohorts becoming politically mature around the First and Second World Wars, according to this hypothesis, would each tend to have particular enduring orientations regarding foreign affairs. This is borne out by the evidence that persons who became eighteen years old between 1914 and 1918 and between 1934 and 1938 accord relatively high salience to foreign policy matters.[60] Furthermore, advocacy of war in dealing with international crises is relatively high for persons who turned eighteen in either of the wars.

The Vietnam generation is expected to exhibit different consequences. Indeed, studies indicate that in 1973 and 1975, the Vietnam generation was disproportionally likely to say that the United States was spending too much on arms, while the Second World War generation were likely to say that too little was being spent.[61] By 1978, however, the generational effects were no longer significant. The lack of consensus about the meaning of the Vietnam War probably reduced any generationwide enduring consequence of the experience.

If the struggle has brought severe and widespread destructive effects, attempts at developing a social system solution to avoid its recurrence are likely to be made and generally supported. For example, the devastating effects of the Second World War had many profound consequences for the global system, on Europe, and on each of the countries of Europe. Thus, at the global level, the United Nations organization and many associated international governmental organizations were established to avert future wars. The presumed defects in the earlier structures, including the League of Nations, were to be avoided.

The devastating impact of the Second World War on the peoples in Europe followed many previous European wars and the failure of policies to prevent and control them. One consequence of these terribly destructive experiences, particularly on the continent, was the increased salience of a pan-European identity and support for binding the peoples of Europe together. These widespread sentiments nourished the European movement and the support given, for example, to the establishment in 1952 of the European Coal and Steel Community and then the later steps toward a European Union. The results were remarkably successful in ending the long-enduring enmity among countries in western Europe, most notably between France and Germany.

Within European societies, too, attempts were made to contain and reduce extreme ethnonationalism that might threaten the rights of minority communal groups or might result in threats against neighboring countries. This was especially the case in West Germany where policies of de-Nazification were implemented, laws banning Nazi activities were passed, and the major political parties pursued policies to absorb German refugees and contain irredentist appeals.

The application of a problem-solving approach in a struggle contributes to the chances of sustaining stable relations in the larger system. Thus, we may consider alternative ways of conducting struggles regarding discrimination against ethnic and other minorities and against women in the labor market. If framed and waged as a struggle in which increased opportunities for some are won at the expense of reduced opportunities for others, the struggle takes on zero-sum qualities, and contention between winners and losers will result. The matter in many circumstances, however, can be viewed differently, stressing common values and interests. Thus, it is argued that cultural diversity within occupations will provide better service and production than hiring policies that sustain traditional homogeneity. For example, the ethnic makeup of the police force will better protect the citizens if it reflects the ethnic diversity of the citizenry. In addition, if the labor pool decreasingly consists of White males, a labor policy that does not prepare people of diverse identities to work together collaboratively reduces productivity and damages the collective standard of living. Discriminatory practice then is a problem that needs to be solved to satisfy the shared interest in improving productivity and the quality of service. In the 1990s, this kind of reasoning influences much social policy and private practice.

Consequence of Outcomes

The outcome of every struggle affects many other parties in the former adversaries' social environment and the social systems of which they are a part. Consequences affecting the sense of equity and the stability of the adversaries' other relationships and of the social system as a whole are especially relevant here.

Equity

The outcome of a struggle often creates new injustices for people who had not been directly involved in the conflict itself. This is particularly likely for destructively waged and disastrously terminated conflicts. For example, persons whose lives are endangered by widespread violence and disorder resulting from civil strife or wars are likely to flee to other places, but the areas to which they flee may then endure burdens for which the people there are ill-prepared. Precarious demographic, cultural, and economic balances may be upset, causing severe conflicts to erupt.

Conflicts are generally waged by organizations and groups who claim large constituencies. But that wider constituency often does not share the intense convictions of those active in leading and conducting the fighting. The peripherally engaged, even if the struggle is victorious, may find that the revolution and its outcome inflicts a heavy burden on their lives. This continues to be an issue in assessing the consequences of historic revolutions.[62] Most research has focused on the economic consequences, and three views of the effects have been distinguished: conservative, Thermidorian, and Marxist.[63] According to the conservative view, revolutions disrupt productive forces and so inflict enduring harm on a country's capacity to produce.[64] The Thermidorian view is that "normalcy" returns after the fall in production immediately following a revolution. Finally, according to the Marxist view, initial dislocation results in short-term losses, but these are more than offset by the improved capacity for greater production.

Research indicates that long-lasting violent revolutionary turmoil generally produces significant and relatively long periods of reduced production. For example, France did not regain its prerevolutionary (1789) levels of foreign trade until well after 1815.[65] The relative gains and losses of different segments of the population, however, even more directly affect their sense of justice. A comparative analysis of revolutions in Mexico, Bolivia, Cuba, and Peru indicated that low-income groups made relative gains in each country during the new regime's consolidation of power, and land reform in each country generally improved the position of the rural groups.[66] Nevertheless, in subsequent years, the interests of the lower-income groups suffered relative to the middle- and upper-income groups. In these developing countries, the global economy seemed to limit labor's gains by fostering government policies primarily aimed at attracting foreign investment and financial assistance rather than policies that more directly targeted social inequities.

The long-term consequences of revolution for society members vary not only with the country's place in the world economy, but also with the degree of destructiveness with which it is brought about and the character of the revolutionary change. Palace-guard revolutions, in which a ruling family or small faction is turned out and replaced by a similar small group, are not likely to have profound consequences. Such top-down revolutions may seem liberating at times, as when they are made in the name of national liberation, but their effects are likely to be disappointing and stultifying rather than economically and socially satisfying for the general population—perhaps partly because they were attained without popular involvement. For example, the countries that had been part of the USSR or controlled by it became free of Soviet control with varying degrees of popular engagement. For most of the republics of the former USSR, the union was dissolved by decisions made among a small group of officials. In a few countries, such as Lithuania, nonviolent demonstrations and other actions propelled the movement toward independence.

When a struggle is not destructive, it can be a catalyst for increased diffuse benefits, as indicated in the earlier analysis of external conflicts that are not very severe. This is also indicated by studies of the effects of trade union struggles. Labor leaders and some economists provide evidence that if workers increase labor costs to the employer, workers will be used more efficiently and the employer will also have more incentive to replace workers by machinery. The general economy will be improved by pressures on management to be more efficient, introduce technical improvements, and increase capital investments.[67]

Stability

Theoretical approaches stressing the centrality of power or of ideology raise the expectation that victors in one conflict tend to pursue additional conflicts. The victors would feel confident in their ability to wage conflicts, have heightened conviction in the justness of their cause, and have greater resources to use in a fight, as a result of their victory. For example, triumphant revolutionary regimes often try to spread the doctrines that provided the presumed ideological basis for their coming to power, as illustrated by the French, Russian, Cuban, and Iranian revolutions.

Attention should also be given to the consequences of what one side regards as its defeat for its social environment. As discussed earlier, a humiliating destructive loss may lead to renewed struggle against the victor to recover what was lost or to gain revenge. But if that path is effectively blocked by superior force, more vulnerable targets may be sought out. Even losses perceived as less damaging may lead to hidden efforts to subvert and undermine the gains of the apparent victor, as has occurred after relative gains by previously subordinated groups such as minorities and women.

The consequences are likely to be different insofar as members of a defeated group interpret their failure as indicating that their goals and their means were unrealistic or ethically wrong. To the extent that they have become persuaded about the erroneous nature of their past struggle, a new course of action will be chosen that makes possible constructive struggle or even a fundamental reconciliation, as discussed in chapter 11.[68]

Conflicts that end with negotiated outcomes, or otherwise incorporate the concerns of all or many of the previously struggling parties have reduced likelihood of the former adversaries aggressively pressing their views or interests against new adversaries. Rather, the need and the possibility for continuing work among the former adversaries tend to absorb their attention and energy.

In addition, accommodative solutions may serve as models for members of other societies, organizations, and relationships. In social systems challenged by divisions along ethnic lines, for example, many kinds of arrangements have averted or mitigated destructive struggles, such as provisions for cultural autonomy, structures of confederation, and norms of tolerance. In societies torn by ethnic-related struggles, successes elsewhere have been held up as exemplary ways out of their troubles. For example, the achievements of the civil rights struggle in the United States, the establishment of a system of regional autonomy in Spain, and the ending of apartheid in South Africa have been so used.

Implications

Conflicts may be expected to foster an ever-widening circle of additional conflicts, but they may also inhibit additional conflicts. The research on the relationship between internal and external conflicts can help assess which is more likely. There are several reasons to expect that internal conflicts will generate external ones. Thus, it may be argued that domestic turmoil encourages leaders to engage in an external conflict as a distraction and a way to create solidarity. It may also be argued that when one domestic party triumphs over an internal enemy, it will believe itself able to defeat other groups who are holding the wrong ideas or exercising unjust domination. In addition, internal disorder may harm or endanger groups who have external ethnic, ideological, or economic ties with external groups who intervene to counter the threats. Finally, domestic conflict may weaken the party so much that it becomes an inviting target for aggressive action by external parties.

However, there are also reasons to expect that internal conflicts make external conflicts less likely. Thus, internal disorder can so weaken a party that it tries to avoid engagement in external conflicts, believing it will be defeated. Furthermore, posing little threat to external adversaries, the potential adversaries would not engage in threatening actions themselves and would pursue cooperative relations.

Evidence based on analyzing countries can be cited in support of each line of argument, depending on specific conditions, such as the nature of the countries' regimes and the kind of conflict behavior being considered. Thus, for countries with personalist regimes, but not with centrist or polyarchic regimes, internal warfare was found to be inversely correlated to external war one and two years later, to a small degree: $-.15$ and $-.30$, respectively.[69] Internal war, however, was *positively* correlated to belligerence (antiforeign demonstrations and severance of diplomatic relations) one and two years later, .28 and .29, respectively. These findings suggest that leaders of personalist regimes, facing internal disorder, may act belligerently against other countries, but not so far as to enter military clashes and wars.

In countries with polyarchic regimes, internal war is related neither to subsequent belligerence nor to external war. An internal war may sometimes stimulate an external conflict, or sometimes inhibit it, depending on the circumstances. Internal *turmoil*, however, is *positively* correlated to belligerence one year later (.19) and to war two years later (.32). Possibly, leaders of polyarchic regimes, facing moderate internal conflict, resort to external conflict behavior to divert internal dissension.

Finally, in countries with centrist regimes, internal turmoil is positively correlated to belligerence a year later (.28), and internal war is positively correlated to external war one and two years later (.32 and .43, respectively). Perhaps leaders in centrist regimes are particularly prone to resort to external conflict as a way of diverting attention from domestic difficulties. It may also be that internal wars in such societies are particularly likely to invite external intervention. Another possible explanation of the relationship is that the victors of internal wars, especially if they are ideologically driven, tend to promote their beliefs by advancing them aggressively in other countries.

Conclusions

Struggles generally have long-lasting consequences, not only for the relationship between the adversaries, but also for each side in the struggle and for other parties in their social environment. Some of the consequences may have been intended by elements within one of the adversaries, but they are often unintended, unanticipated, and unwanted. The reverberating results are not under any one's control. That loss of control adds to the risk of engaging in a conflict, and particularly of doing so destructively. Furthermore, the resulting burdens are often borne by persons who were not parties to the fight, which, of course, is a reason for them to have been constructively engaged. Attention to the collateral diffuse consequences of conflicts is worthwhile because it can be the basis for conducting and ending conflicts so as to maximize the desired consequences and minimize the undesirable.

Adverse long-term consequences can be minimized by particular policies, undertaken by the partisans of a fight and by intermediaries. For example, partisans of each side can avoid imposing outcomes that are humiliating to the other side and that deny its rank-and-file members' critical needs. Insofar as the adversaries use elements of a problem-solving approach, mutually acceptable outcomes that contribute to stable and equitable future relations are enhanced. In addition, constructing agreements that are self-enforcing increases the likelihood that the agreement will become a building block for equitable and stable relations between former adversaries.

We have also seen that conflicts often do have constructive benefits for one or more sides in a struggle, and sometimes even for the relationship between the adversaries, and other groups who were not directly engaged in the struggle. Conflicts waged in ways that recognize the humanity of the other side increase that likelihood. Furthermore, avoiding the tendency to overreach and impose unilateral settlements also helps forestall continuing animosity and promotes enduring mutual accommodations.

The nature of a struggle's consequences depends significantly on how the former adversaries and others interpret the way the conflict ended. Thus, the consequences vary with the degree to which protagonists regard the outcome as fair and reached through a joint process. Consequently, interpretations of the past have implications for the future, and competing interpretations are set forth. For example, differing American views of how the Cuban missile crisis was settled or how the cold war ended have different implications for subsequent U.S. foreign policy.[70] Recognizing the elements of problem solving and mutuality in the way the struggles ended, as well as the unilateral and coercive elements, can contribute to more constructive future relations.

Thus, American-Soviet relations became somewhat more accommodating after the Cuban missile crisis, and not simply because both sides were frightened by getting so close to the brink of a nuclear war. The crisis was resolved in negotiations between President John F. Kennedy and Chairman Nikita Krushchev. The U.S. official policy carefully avoided appearing to gloat or to humiliate the Soviet Union for withdrawing its missiles from Cuba. The Soviets were able to claim they had achieved what was essential: the assurance that the United States would not try to overthrow the Cuban government. Furthermore, the U.S. missile base near the Soviet border in Turkey would be closed, although this was confidential at the time.

The cold war did not end because of its intensification in the early 1980s by the administration of Ronald Reagan. It was a result of fundamental problems within the Soviet Union, but the course of action chosen to manage those problems was greatly influenced by the preceding years of growing U.S.-Soviet accommodation. The years of cultural exchange, economic transactions, and other kinds of communication and interdependence made Western solutions seem increasingly attractive. At the same time, the fundamental interests of the Soviet Union seemed to be assured by previous agreements accepting the permanence of the borders established at the end of World War II.

In short, conflicts waged and terminated destructively tend to perpetuate destructive relations. Such persisting cycles, however, can be broken. To interrupt and alter these tendencies requires wise transforming policies, resolutely pursued. Intermediaries based outside of the primary adversaries can be crucial in undertaking and carrying out such policies. In addition, individuals and groups within one or more of the antagonistic sides can initiate and help implement such policies. Of course, conducting a struggle constructively in the first place makes the task easier and can contribute afterward to stronger cooperative relations between former adversaries. Elements of constructive struggle are often present, although sometimes not fully recognized, in the settlement of conflicts so that the likelihood of stable and equitable relations is increased.

Notes

1. Louis Kriesberg, Terrell A. Northrup, and Stuart J. Thorson, eds., *Intractable Conflicts and Their Transformation* (Syracuse, N.Y.: Syracuse University Press, 1989); Raimo Vayrynen, ed., *New Directions in Conflict Theory: Conflict Resolution and Conflict Transformation* (London: Sage, 1991); Kumar Rupesinghe, ed., *Conflict Transformation* (New York: St. Martin's, 1995); and John Paul Lederach, *Building Peace: Sustainable Reconciliation in Divided Societies* (Tokyo: United Nations University Press, 1995).

2. Lewis A. Coser, *Functions of Social Conflict* (New York: Free Press of Glencoe, 1956).

3. Analogously, the function of the heart in an animal is to pump blood to circulate throughout the body. See A. R. Radcliffe-Brown, *Structure and Function in Primitive Society* (Glencoe, Ill.: The Free Press, 1952); Talcott Parsons, *The Social System* (New York: The Free Press, 1951); and Robert K. Merton, *Social Theory and Social Structure* (New York: The Free Press, 1949; rev. and enl. ed., 1957; 3d ed., enl., 1968).

4. Bronislaw Malinowski, *Argonauts of the Western Pacific* (London: Routledge and Kegan Paul, 1922).

5. Merton, *Social Theory and Social Structure*.

6. See the critique regarding the teleological fallacy of such reasoning in George Caspar Homans, *Social Behavior: Its Elementary Forms*, rev. ed. (New York: Harcourt Brace Jovanovich, 1974).

7. See Coser, *Functions of Social Conflict*; William G. Sumner, *Folkways* (New York: Ginn & Co., 1906), 12; and Georg Simmel, *Conflict*, trans. Kurt H. Wolff (Glencoe, Ill.: The Free Press, 1955).

8. Charles Tilly, *From Mobilization to Revolution* (Reading, Mass.: Addison-Wesley, 1978), 218–19.

9. See Coser, *Functions of Social Conflict,* first quotation is from p. 95 and second quotation from p. 38; also see Sumner, *Folkways,* and Simmel, *Conflict.*

10. John E. Mueller, *War, Presidents and Public Opinion* (New York: John Wiley, 1973).

11. F. Solomon and others, "Civil Rights Activity and Reduction in Crime Among Negroes,"*Archives of General Psychiatry* 12 (March 1965): 227–36.

12. See P. T. Hopmann, "International Conflict and Cohesion in the Communist System," *Internatiional Studies Quarterly* 11 (September 1967): 212–36; Ole R. Holsti, "External Conflict and Internal Cohesion: The Sino-Soviet Case," in *Communist Party-States,* ed. Jan Triska (Indianapolis, Ind.: Bobbs-Merrill, 1969); and Tom Allen Travis, "A Theoretical and Empirical Study of Communication Relations in the NATO and Warsaw Interbloc and Intrabloc International Sub-Systems," unpublished Ph.D. dissertation, Department of Political Science, Syracuse University, 1975.

13. Angus Campbell, *White Attitudes toward Black People* (Ann Arbor: Institute for Social Research, University of Michigan, 1971), 141.

14. This struck me in many conversations with Germans while I was living in Germany in the summer of 1950 and the academic year, 1956–1957. Many spoke of what went on under the Nazis as insane and sought to understand how it could have happened that the Germans became caught up in that insanity. They wondered what it was about them that made it possible and felt they could not trust themselves. Others denied awareness of the Holocaust at the time, and some even denied that it had happened on the scale revealed.

15. *New York Times,* 18 January 1996, "Serbs in Bosnia . . . Are Angry at Leaders and Themselves."

16. The health of the British working class, however, improved during the war. See J. M. Winter, "The Impact of the First World War on Civilian Health in Britain," *Economic History Review* 30 (August 1977): 487–507.

17. J. Craig Jenkins and Susanne Schmeidl, "Flight from Violence: The Origins and Implications of the World Refugee Crisis," *Sociological Focus* 28 (February 1995): 63–82.

18. See Stanislaw Andrzejewski, *Military Organization and Society* (London: Routledge and Kegan Paul, 1954); Phillips Cutright, "Inequality: A Cross-National Analysis," *American Sociological Review* 32 (August 1967): 562–78; Maurice A. Garnier and Larry Hazelrigg, "Military Organization and Distributional Inequality: An Examination of Andreski's Thesis," *Journal of Political and Military Sociology* 5 (Spring 1977): 17–33; Louis Kriesberg, *Social Inequality* (Englewood Cliffs, N.J.: Prentice-Hall, 1979), 379; and Erich Weede, "Military Participation, Economic Growth and Income Equality," in *Defense, Welfare and Growth,* ed. Steve Chan and Alex Mintz (London: Routledge, 1992), 211–30.

19. Erich Weede, "The Impact of Interstate Conflict on Revolutionary Change and Individual Freedom," *Kyklos* 46, no. 4 (1993): 473–95.

20. Miroslav Nincic, "Capital Labor and the Spoils of War," *Journal of Peace Research* 17, no. 2 (1980): 103–17.

21. Kriesberg, *Social Inequality,* 58–65.

22. Michael Stohl, *War and Domestic Political Violence: The American Capacity for Repression and Reaction* (Beverly Hills, Calif.: Sage, 1976).

23. J. M. Winter, "Britain's Lost Generation of the World War," *Population* 31(November 1977): 449–66.

24. Dean K. Phillips, "The Case for Veteran Preferences," in *Strangers at Home: Vietnam Veterans Since the War*, ed. Charles R. Figley and Seymour Leventman (New York: Praeger, 1980), 348. Charles Moskos (in a personal communication) has pointed out various bases for calculating the relative death rate in combat of African Americans, yielding different implications. Indeed, in military operations since Vietnam, 1975–1995, Blacks comprised 15 percent of those killed in action, but blacks averaged 19 percent of active-duty military personnel during that same period. See Charles Moskos and John Sibley Butler, "Overcoming Race: Army Lessons for American Society," presented at the Symposium honoring Robin M. Williams, Jr., in Ithaca, New York, October 1996.

25. Nincic, "Capital Labor and the Spoils of War."

26. Seymour Melman, *The Permanent War Economy: American Capitalism in Decline* (New York: Simon & Schuster, 1974); and Robert W. DeGrasse, Jr., *Military Expansion Economic Decline*, exp. ed. (Armonk, N.Y.: M. E. Sharpe, 1983).

27. I was in Moscow in December 1988 and was impressed by the emphasis on nonviolence among the people engaging in the early demonstrations. In a conversation with some young people handing out literature on the steps of Lenin's library, when I asked how the West might help them, they said they wanted training in nonviolent action.

28. Larry Dunn made this observation in a personal communication, noting that this sometimes occurs in labor-management negotiations "where the rank-and-file accuse the leadership of caving in or selling out and they are left with two choices: not supporting a contract or blindly supporting it without understanding how that's the best they can get."

29. Martin Oppenheimer, *The Urban Guerrilla* (New York: Quadrangle/The New York Times, 1969), 71.

30. Stanley Weir, "U.S.A.: The Labor Revolt," in *American Society, Inc.*, ed. Maurice Zeitlin (Chicago: Markham, 1970).

31. See the characterizations of the great subversive power of Jews articulated in the book Adolph Hitler wrote in 1924, *Mein Kampf* (New York: Reynal & Hitchcock, 1941).

32. Louis Kriesberg, "Transforming Conflicts in the Middle East and Central Europe," in *Intractable Conflicts and their Transformation*, ed. L. Kriesberg, T. A. Northrup, and S. J. Thorson (Syracuse, N.Y.: Syracuse University Press, 1989).

33. Betty A. Dobratz and Stephanie L. Shanks-Meile, *"White Power, White Pride!" The White Separatist Movement in the United States* (New York: Twayne, 1997). Also see David H. Bennett, *The Party of Fear*, 2d ed. (New York: Vintage, 1995); Michael Barkun, *Religion and the Racist Right: The Origins of the Christian Identity Movement* (Chapel Hill: The University of North Carolina Press, 1994).

34. During and after the Korean War, dissatisfaction and loss of legitimacy contributed to the support of McCarthyism and repression of alleged Communist dissent. During the Vietnam War, the dissatisfaction lent support to nonviolent and violent

opposition to the war. See Robert B. Smith, "Some Effects of Limited War," unpublished manuscript, 1971.

35. Edward C. Budd, "An Introduction to a Current Issue of Public Policy," in *Inequality and Poverty*, ed. Edward C. Budd (New York: W.W. Norton & Co., 1967).

36. Nora A. Femenia, *National Identity in Times of Crises: The Scripts of the Falklands-Malvina War* (New York: Nova Science, 1996).

37. Michael Stohl, *War and Domestic Political Violence* (Beverly Hills, Calif.: Sage, 1976).

38. For example, see Rudy J. Rummel, "The Dimensions of Conflict Behavior within and between Nations," *General Systems Yearbook* 8 (1963):1–50; and Raymond Tanter, "Dimensions of Conflict Behavior within and between Nations, 1958–1960," *Journal of Conflict Resolution* 10 (March 1966), 41–64. For a review and interpretation of the studies, see Michael Stohl, "The Nexus of Civil and International Conflict," in *Handbook of Political Conflict*, ed. Ted Robert Gurr (New York: The Free Press, 1980).

39. Jonathan Wilkenfeld, "Some Further Findings Regarding the Domestic and Foreign Conflict Behavior of Nations," *Journal of Peace Research* 2 (1969): 147–56.

40. Jonathan Wilkenfeld and Dina A. Zinnes, "A Linkage Model of Domestic Conflict Behavior," in *Conflict Behavior and Linkage Politics*, ed. Jonathan Wilkenfeld (New York: D. McKay, 1973).

41. Mueller, *War, Presidents, and Public Opinion*.

42. Susan Borker, Louis Kriesberg, and Abu Abdul Quader, "Conciliation, Confrontation, and Approval of the President," *Peace and Change Journal* 11 (Spring 1985): 31–48.

43. Erich Weede, "The Impact of Interstate Conflict on Revolutionary Change and Individual Freedom," *Kyklos* 46, no. 4 (1993): 473–95.

44. Thomas J. Scheff, *Bloody Revenge* (Boulder, Colo.: Westview, 1994).

45. Robert Harrison Wagner, "The Causes of Peace," in *Stopping the Killing*, ed. Roy Licklider (New York: New York University Press, 1993).

46. Roy Licklider, "The Consequences of Negotiated Settlements in Civil Wars, 1945–1993, *American Political Science Review* 89 (September 1995): 681–90.

47. This has contributed to what some people have called the "culture wars." See, for example, James Davison Hunter, *Culture Wars* (New York: Basic Books, 1991).

48. Gavan Duffy and Nathalie Frensley, "Community Conflict Processes: Mobilization in Northern Ireland," in James W. Lamare, ed., *International Crisis and Domestic Politics* (New York: Praeger, 1991).

49. Fen Osler Hampson, *Nurturing Peace: Why Peace Settlements Succeed or Fail* (Washington, D.C.: United States Institute of Peace Press, 1996).

50. Ernst B. Haas, *The Uniting of Europe* (Stanford, Calif.: Stanford University Press, 1958); and Louis Kriesberg, "German Businessmen and Union Leaders and the Schuman Plan," *Social Science* 35 (April 1960): 114–21.

51. David Mitrany, *A Working Peace System* (Chicago: Quadrangle Books, 1966), esp. "The Functional Approach to World Organization," 149–166, originally published in *International Affairs*, July 1948.

52. SALT I refers to the strategic arms limitation talks resulting in the 1972 Memorandum of Understanding, and SALT II refers to the talks resulting in the treaty signed in 1979 on the limitation of strategic offensive arms. Article XVII of the SALT II

treaty provides for the continuing role of the Standing Consultative Commission. The provisions of the commission can be found in Strobe Talbott, *Endgame: The Inside Story of SALT II* (New York: Harper & Row, 1979), 286–87.

53. For example, see the discussion in Hampson, *Nurturing Peace: Why Peace Settlements Succeed or Fail.*

54. Ted Robert Gurr, "Transforming Ethno-Politcal Conflicts: Exit, Autonomy, or Access," in *Conflict Transformation,* ed. Kumar Rupesinghe (New York: St. Martin's, 1995), 15.

55. Susanne Schmeidl, "Exploring the Causes of Forced Migration: A Pooled Time-Series Analysis, 1971–1990," *Social Science Quarterly* 78 (June 1997): 284–308.

56. Maire A. Dugan, "The Relationship between Pre-Independence Internal Violence and Nonviolence and Post-Independence Violence, External Belligerency, and Internal Governmental Repressiveness," unpublished Ph.D. dissertation, Syracuse University, 1979.

57. For example, see James M. Fendrich and Ellis S. Krauss, "Student Activism and Adult Left-wing Politics: A Causal Model of Political Socialization for Black, White, and Japanese Students of the 1960s Generation," in *Research in Social Movements Conflicts, and Change,* vol. 1, ed. Louis Kriesberg (Greenwich, Conn.: JAI, 1978); and Beyong-chul Park, "Motivational Dynamics of Student Movement Participation in Contemporary South Korea," unpublished Ph.D. dissertation, Syracuse University, 1995.

58. See, for example, Karl Mannheim, "The Sociological Problem of Generations," in Paul Kecskemeti, ed., *Essays on the Sociology of Knowledge* (New York: Oxford University Press, 1952), originally published in 1928; Rudolf Heberle, *Social Movements* (New York: Appleton-Century-Crofts, 1951); Richard Braungart and Margaret M. Braungart, eds., *Life Course and Generational Politics* (Lanham, Md.: University Press of America, 1993).

59. John C. Leggett, *Class, Race, and Labor* (New York: Oxford University Press, 1968), 90–91.

60. Neal E. Cutler, "Generational Success as a Source of Foreign Policy Attitudes," *Journal of Peace Research* 1 (1970): 33–47.

61. Louis Kriesberg and Ross Klein, "Changes in Public Support for U.S. Military Spending," *Journal of Conflict Resolution* 24 (March 1980): 79–111.

62. Jack A. Goldstone, ed., *Revolutions: Theoretical, Comparative, and Historical Studies* (San Diego: Harcourt Brace Jovanovich, 1986).

63. Michael S. Lewis-Beck, "Some Effects of Revolution: Models, Measurement, and the Cuban Evidence," *American Journal of Sociology* 84 (March 1979): 1127–49. Thermidorian, deriving from the French Revolution, refers to the period following the extremists' reign of terror as tyranny is turned against the extremists and elements of the old order are restored.

64. Samuel P. Huntington, *Political Order in Changing Societies* (New Haven, Conn.: Yale University Press, 1968).

65. Theda Skocpol, *States and Social Revolutions: A Comparative Analysis of France, Russia, and China* (Cambridge: Cambridge University Press, 1979), 176.

66. Susan Eckstein, "The Impact of Revolution on Social Welfare in Latin America," in Goldstone, *Revolutions;* also see Beck, "Some Effects of Revolution."

67. Lewis Coser, *Continuities in the Study of Social Conflict* (New York: The Free Press, 1967); Sidney C. Sufrin, *Union Wages and Labor's Earnings* (Syracuse, N.Y.: Syracuse University Press, 1951); Seymour Melman, *Dynamic Factors in Industrial Productivity* (Oxford, U.K.: Blackwell, 1956); and Rhonda Levine and James A. Gewschwender, "Class Struggle, State Policy, and the Rationalization of Production: The Organization of Agriculture in Hawaii," in *Research in Social Movements, Conflicts and Change*, vol. 4, ed. Louis Kriesberg (Greenwich, Conn.: JAI Press, 1981).

68. Many members of the various social movements in the United States concluded in the early 1970s that earlier direct challenging of the dominant groups and policies in the country had failed, and they turned to local community improvement actions and to engagement in self-help groups instead.

69. Jonathan Wilkenfeld, "Some Further Findings Regarding the Domestic and Foreign Conflict Behavior of Nations," *Journal of Peace Research* 2 (1969): 147–56. Also see Tom Broch and Johan Galtung, "Belligerence among the Primitives," *Journal of Peace Research*, 1 (1966): 33–45; and Robert A. LeVine, "Socialization, Social Structure, and Intersocietal Images," in *International Behavior*, ed. Herbert C. Kelman (New York: Holt, Rinehart & Winston, 1965).

70. There is a large literature on these topics. See Richard Ned Lebow and Janice Gross Stein, *We All Lost the Cold War* (Princeton, N.J.: Princeton University Press, 1994); Raymond L. Garthoff, "Cuban Missile Crisis: The Soviet Story," *Foreign Policy* 72 (Fall 1988): 61–80; and Kriesberg, *International Conflict Resolution*.

11

Synthesis, Specification,
and Implications

T hree matters pertinent to waging constructive conflicts remain to be
discussed. First, the conflict model presented in chapter 1, and developed throughout this book, needs to be reexamined and elaborated,
integrating the analyses presented. Second, the findings should be specified for
different kinds of conflicts. Third, we should discuss the policy applications of
the approach taken and the interpretations made.

Synthesis

The analysis presented here offers a comprehensive approach to explaining
the course of a variety of social conflicts. It posits a series of stages through
which struggles tend to move and the processes and conditions affecting the
constructive or destructive way that antagonists traverse the course of the
struggle. In presenting the approach, we have considered alternative perspectives and drawn specific propositions, hypotheses, and generalizations from a
wide range of materials. The approach is necessarily general, given the variety
of conflicts and stages examined; but as discussed in subsequent sections, it
can be specified and there are policy implications for particular struggles.

Conflict Stages

The idea that conflicts move through a series of stages is useful, so long as
these are not treated as rigidly bounded and sequenced. We have considered
the stages as broad phases through which struggles tend to move, varying

greatly in how long each stage lasts, in the nature of the transition from one to the other, and in the reversals of their sequence. The designation of each stage also depends on the characterization of the parameters of the conflict being considered, since fights are generally embedded in larger and more enduring struggles, and encompass smaller and briefer disputes.

Underlying Conditions

We began the analysis by considering the underlying conditions that can become the source for an overt struggle. The bases for the emergence of a conflict include factors within one or more of the adversaries driving their members to contend with others, as well as aspects of the relationship between possible adversaries that tend to produce a sense of grievance and the formulation of antagonistic goals. In a sense, then, a conflict may arise not only from what an analyst is likely to regard as objective conflict relations, but also from what the analyst would regard as mistaken understandings of the relationship by the antagonists, or a combination of both.

Differences in rankings in terms of class, status, or power, as well as differences in values or cultural markers between categories of people, are the bases of struggles. They generally are waged about a combination of consensual and dissensual issues of contention. Interdependence between possible adversaries makes it difficult for them to escape these differences, but such integration may also inhibit the emergence of a conflict.

The social context of the adversaries is another important set of conditions. Changes in those conditions often generate shifts in the relations between various categories of people, thus creating the bases for a manifest struggle. Thus, economic and demographic changes in the social system, by affecting migration patterns, may intensify the interactions between people of different classes and cultures in ways that they come to view as competitive and even antagonistic.

The conditions for an infinite number of conflicts are always present; yet relatively few conflicts become manifest, and even fewer become destructive. This is the case partly because there are also many integrating processes and conditions within which possible conflicts are embedded and there are many nonconflictful ways to remedy the conditions that are the bases of a struggle. Such factors inhibit the emergence of a struggle.

Manifestation

In the initial conflict stage, a struggle becomes manifest. Four components must be minimally present for that to occur. First, at least one protagonist has a sense of its identity, distinguishing itself from other parties. Second, members of one or more of the adversary parties believe they have a grievance, some aspect of their situation being unsatisfactory and unjustified. Third, members of one or more sides, believing that their grievance would be reduced by a change wrought by another person or group, formulate a goal to bring about the changes in the other side so that their grievance will be reduced. Fourth, those asserting the goal must believe that they can act to help attain it.

The conflict has become manifest as one or both sides express these beliefs by mobilizing supporters or by directly trying to affect the opposing side so as to achieve their goal. Each of these component beliefs need not be explicitly articulated by all the adversaries. If one side acts in these terms, the other side will likely see itself as engaged in a struggle. Indeed, the other side's denial that there is any conflict is often experienced as provocative.

As illustrated in figure 11.1, the underlying conditions provide the bases for these four elements to emerge. A conflict arises as those underlying conditions change and become more conducive to the eruption of a struggle. The arrow from outside the primary sequence indicates that factors and actors external to the underlying conditions also affect the likelihood that a conflict becomes manifest. Thus, external actors not considered to be the potential adversaries in the analysis of underlying conditions may intrude and provoke a struggle. New ideologies or standards of evaluation may enter the system, and they may provide support for particular adversaries.

Many strategies can be pursued to prevent a conflict from becoming manifest. They include efforts to intimidate those who seek to force a change they desire, to deprive or reduce their resources for effecting change, and to convince them that they cannot achieve the alteration they seek. Other strategies entail trying to convince those who feel aggrieved that their condition is fair or is the result of their own actions. Later the actual amelioration of injurious conditions can reduce the likelihood of a struggle arising to correct those conditions. Another strategy is to promote an identity shared by the potential adversaries, for example, as members of the same nation, country, or organization.

Escalation

The next stage of a conflict, escalation, is often of long duration. In this phase, opposition becomes manifest and each side attempts to attain its goal, increasing its efforts by intensifying the means used and rallying support for its cause. The early efforts may rely on attempts at persuasion and perhaps promise future benefits for yielding what is sought. In addition, relatively mild kinds of coercion may be employed or threatened. Reliance on coercion, and especially on violent coercion, is likely to occur only if the conflict escalates greatly. There may be conventional understandings that act as barriers

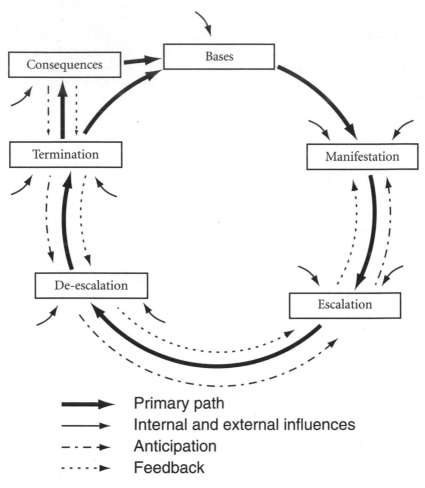

Primary path
Internal and external influences
Anticipation
Feedback

Figure 11.1   Conflict Cycle

to escalation; but once crossed, a much higher level of antagonism may be reached and sustained.

We have focused on why conflicts sometimes become destructive and seemingly intractable as they escalate. The explanations are to be found in the interactions between the adversaries, in processes internal to one or more sides, and in developments in the adversaries' social context. The interactions between the adversaries and the adversaries' view of those interactions are primary sources of escalation and destructiveness. Insofar as antagonists view themselves as struggling within a clearly bounded system that they constitute, they are likely to see themselves involved in a zero-sum conflict. This enhances the profoundly incompatible nature of their goals.

An important dimension of the relations between adversaries that contributes to the destructiveness of their struggle is their treatment of each other in waging the fight. Inhumane treatment deepens the antagonism and the desire to continue the struggle and even to seek revenge. The callous and indiscriminate use of violence, intended to intimidate and suppress the enemy, is frequently counterproductive, prolonging a struggle and making an enduring peace more difficult to attain.

Another important policy affecting the increasing destructiveness of a conflict is the rejection by one or more side of the other's claims regarding fundamental human rights, social recognition, and minimal living conditions. Related to this, another fundamental policy affecting a conflict's destructiveness is the refusal by one side to recognize the other as a legitimate collectivity and the consequent refusal by one side to directly communicate with the other.

A severe risk leading to destructiveness arises when a party believes it is winning and overreaches itself. Its goals become more extreme, and it gives little attention to the interests and concerns of the opposing sides. This tends to stiffen the resistance of the opponents and increase their sense of desperation. The struggle is then likely to be prolonged and intensified.

A variety of developments within one or more of the adversary parties can also contribute to escalation and destructiveness. For example, in the case of ethnic conflicts, widespread adoption of an ethnonationalist ideology by members of one or more adversaries is a likely source of intractability. Some political leaders, intellectuals, and mass media producers at times promote such ideologies, often through the manipulation of culturally significant symbols and myths, seeking to arouse emotions of fear and hatred toward ostensible enemies.[1] They may not only extol particular qualities claimed by members of their own community, but also condemn qualities attributed to an enemy.

For some members of a contending side, the sense of belonging to a larger entity engaged in a struggle provides meaning and significance to their lives. For others, it provides a livelihood as well as a sense of identity, and for still others, it provides a vehicle for power and influence. Thus, the struggle itself creates a vested interest for some people to continue the fight. Furthermore, the process of entrapment tends to lock some people into persisting in a course of action. Fighting on seems to justify what has already been expended in money, honor, or blood.

In addition, some organizational developments contribute to a conflict escalating destructively. For example, members of small groups, including elite decision-making circles, tend to pressure each other to conform to the prevailing views of the group. Dissenters within those groups are likely to withdraw or be excluded; consequently, dissenting voices are silenced and alternatives to continuing on the chosen path are not considered.

Every conflict is embedded in a larger social system and interlocked with other conflicts. Consequently, the nature of that larger social system and the interlocking conflicts also contributes greatly to a conflict's escalation and destructiveness. In some cases, the larger social system fosters the resort to destructive means of struggle, either by creating a high sense of mistrust and lack of security or by upholding norms of honor and revenge that tend to perpetuate fights. On the other hand, legitimate institutions for managing conflicts provide alternatives to destructive coercion, and norms of tolerance and restraints on violence constrain a conflict from escalating destructively.

A struggle also tends to destructively escalate as one conflict becomes superimposed upon other conflicts. Thus, insofar as class, ethnic, religious, ideological, and other cleavages coincide rather than crosscut each other, the more intense and the more difficult it is to resolve any one of the struggles. For example, the cold war was superimposed on many conflicts in the Middle East, Central America, Africa, and Asia. The U.S. and Soviet governments each justified its support of contending local parties as necessary to counter the actions of the other. Consequently, a governmental or nongovernmental actor may presume to act provocatively to gain regional goals, anticipating support from one of the superpowers. Once engaged in struggle, local adversaries were able to continue fighting, sometimes using powerful weapons, as each side gained support from an opposing superpower. The resulting local struggles were then made more intense, and a final agreement was difficult to reach and to sustain.

De-escalation

After varying duration, a transition to de-escalation does occur in every struggle. De-escalation arises from changes in the relationship between adversaries, from changes within one of the major adversaries, and from changes in the external context.[2] Often elements from two or three of these sources converge and contribute together to open passages out of a struggle. The processes that bring about de-escalation may entail the interaction between a set of changing conditions and of new policies, both long term and short.

Certain changes in adversarial relationships are important sources of de-escalation and movement away from destructiveness. One such change is the weakening of resolve or the inability to sustain resistance by one side against the other; consequently, the more vulnerable party yields and the victorious side largely imposes its terms of settlement. A precursor to such changes may be an intensification of the struggle by the challenging party, raising the cost for the dominant group until a settlement seems attractive. This is often the rationale used by the challenging party for resorting to violence, even terrorism. Nonviolent coercive means may also be employed, including demonstrations, noncooperation, and boycotts. In addition, the challenger may seek assistance from external supporters, thus shifting the balance of power and increasing coercive threats or experiences against the dominant party.

In addition to such coercive means, or in conjunction with them, noncoercive methods also help de-escalate conflicts. These include new ways of thinking about the relationship, developed from mutual interchange, growing interdependency, or confidence-building measures, as illustrated by the steps taken in de-escalating the cold war. Change within one of the parties is also an important source of shifts toward de-escalation. The change may include new political leaders, new thinking, or realignments in domestic forces, as occurred among the French regarding France's role in colonial Algeria, and among the South African Whites about their dominant position in South Africa. Changes in the social context of the focal conflict provide another set of possible factors fostering de-escalation. Such changes include according new salience to common enemies and external intervention by governments or other intermediaries.

In short, adversaries do not turn away from escalation along a single path; there are many possible paths away from a destructive struggle. The one actually taken is affected by many factors. First, it depends on where the antagonists start from—whether from the defeat of one side, a protracted cold war, or a violent stalemate. Second, it is affected by where the adversaries want to go. Thus, movement may be toward the utter defeat of one side, or it may be toward mutual acceptance. Unlikely as it seems, the defeat of one side may sometimes result in reconciliation, as in Franco-German relations after World War II.

Finally, an assessment of the way taken depends on the time frame that is used. The same path, when viewed for a short distance, may appear quite different when seen as part of a much longer road. For example, even an intensification of a conflict may appear as a step toward reconciliation when considered over a fifty- or hundred-year span.

Different parties with a stake in a struggle pursue varying strategies to achieve de-escalation. Some of these efforts are planned, and others may be considered strategic only in hindsight, by outside analysts. The strategies involve selecting parties for the de-escalating efforts, choosing the issues to be emphasized, and selecting the combination of inducements to be used. The strategies may be undertaken over the span of months or of years, and by various combinations of actors.

Two of the relative successes in transforming protracted destructive conflicts, discussed in chapter 7, are illustrative of various paths toward conflict de-escalation and transformation. The struggles in South Africa over apartheid were certainly long and often violent. Yet between the mid-1980s and mid-1990s, they underwent a surprisingly peaceful transformation.[3] Similarly, the long struggle between the United States and the Soviet Union did not become transformed by a military defeat or militarily imposed settlement.

Rather, it resulted from a convergence of domestic Soviet developments, but also from a series of prior conflict resolution efforts and achievements.[4]

A frequent element in a de-escalating process involves the growing sense by the adversaries that the old strategies are not working and will not succeed. The parties come to believe, or changed conditions make evident, that they cannot succeed with their current strategy and the efforts are increasingly injurious. The parties have reached a hurting stalemate.[5] The failure of the old policy encourages the search for a new one, and the new one therefore seems attractive.

Fresh thinking about possible options and new combinations helps the construction of new formulas for possible settlements. Ideas by outsiders, new players, or dissidents sometimes help provide the new thinking. The formulation of possible agreements, in conjunction with a hurting stalemate, often presents a mutually acceptable outcome. For example, South Africa's apartheid policy was not sustainable. Instead, there was increasing integration and a growing Black middle class.[6] Furthermore, although the ANC demanded the transfer of power to a government chosen by a majority of the people, it did not deny the equal right of Whites to South Africa as their native land and did not threaten their economic well-being.[7]

In the course of a long struggle, changes inevitably occur within each party engaged in struggle, and some of those changes foster de-escalation. Under certain circumstances, people weary of the struggle and the burdens it imposes, so the goals seem less and less worth the effort. Changes within the Soviet Union and among the Whites of South Africa certainly contributed significantly to the transformation of the protracted conflicts in which they were engaged.

The Soviet economy, beginning in the mid-1970s, was stagnating, and living conditions were deteriorating.[8] Improving relations with the West would help limit the immense and burdensome military expenditures and gain access to Western technological developments and improve consumer goods. Mikhail Gorbachev was chosen by the Communist Party, in 1985, to lead the Soviet Union into an accommodation with the West needed for domestic reforms. Some members of the elite strata had begun to lose their convictions about communist ideas, and many had begun to admire the rule of law and freedoms of the West.

Finally, external intermediaries can contribute to the de-escalation of even destructive and seemingly intractable conflicts. Their contributions include (1) arranging package deals to end the conflict, (2) expanding the pie to be divided by adding resources, (3) giving legitimacy to possible new options, and (4) helping implement and sustain the agreement that is reached. The availability of such intermediaries facilitates a transformation, when other conditions are favorable. The intermediaries can also help produce more propitious circumstances, for example, by lending support to one party or cutting off assistance to another or by helping to reframe the conflict and fashion the vision of mutually acceptable options for the adversaries.

Since every conflict is intertwined with many others, a shift in the salience of one of those other conflicts can help change a conflict's destructiveness and intractability. The reduced salience of an old superimposed conflict is likely to allow others that had been superimposed to become tractable and even resolved. Thus, the end of the cold war helped settle conflicts in the Middle East, Southern Africa, and Central America.

Changed conditions also affect one or more of the adversaries and the relations between them. This includes changes in economic, demographic, and social conditions. In addition, informational, normative, and ideological changes affect the sense of what alternatives are possible. For example, in the post–World War II era, many Whites in the United States increasingly lost their conviction regarding the inherent inferiority of Blacks, as racist beliefs decreased in legitimacy and credibility.

Conciliatory elements of old strategies can become more easily recognized as such when conditions become more supportive of those interpretations. Thus, the ANC goals had been nonracist, the Whites being regarded as another African people in South Africa, and ANC leaders did not seek to expropriate and redistribute the wealth of the country so concentrated in the Whites' hands. Such assurances became far more believable after the dissolution of the Soviet Union, and the accusation that the ANC was communist lost credibility.

Short-term policies include initiating conciliatory gestures to the other side. These range widely in word and deed and include offering concessions, acknowledging the legitimacy of the other side's concerns, and accepting responsibility for having inflicted injury.[9] Making gestures that are credible to the opposing side without exposing oneself to appear foolish and weak if rebuffed is a challenging task. To overcome the difficulties, intermediaries may be used to test possible responses, or secret overtures may be ventured. It is also important to mobilize constituency support for conciliatory moves and to develop strategies for dealing with constituency opposition, whether by suppression, co-optation, or persuasion.

Intermediaries can contribute to the de-escalation and even transformation of destructive conflicts in several ways. Intermediaries include officials from national governments and from international governmental organizations and also persons based in nongovernmental organizations.[10] They can foster new options by suggesting fresh options and by giving them support. Intermediaries can also provide critical assistance in monitoring and implementing the provisions reached by the adversaries.

Termination

Every conflict ends, but each one has a different ending. Sometimes the challenging party abandons its efforts to change its relationship with the adversary. Sometimes one party is able unilaterally to impose the resolution it wants. More often, none of the contending sides obtains all that it sought, but each comes to accept a compromise yielding some of what it wanted. In some cases, a creative mutually beneficial outcome is reached. The outcomes, however, are rarely symmetrical, and disagreements about assessing the relative gains are likely to persist. These outcomes are frequently tacitly reached, and only gradually become evident.

Of course, conflicts are often terminated through explicit processes, generally involving negotiations between the adversaries. Certainly, the outcome of negotiations is greatly dependent on the way a struggle has been waged and the resulting relative standing of the adversaries when the negotiations are undertaken. Nevertheless, negotiations have their own dynamics and can be conducted more or less effectively to produce mutually acceptable and enduring agreements.

Intermediaries also may play important roles in helping adversaries negotiate to settle or resolve their conflicts. They can provide critical services at each stage of negotiations: exploring the possibility of initiating negotiations, setting the agenda and selecting the negotiating partners, exchanging information about positions and underlying concerns, formulating trade-offs, winning support for the agreements reached, and implementing the agreements. These services can be provided by persons playing an official mediator role and also by quasi mediators. In negotiating endings of large-scale conflicts, a wide variety of agents are likely to perform intermediary activities.

The movement from de-escalation to termination is rarely a smooth, uninterrupted passage. Among the many reasons for the likely difficulties, only a few will be noted. The changed conditions supporting de-escalation and termination may change again and undermine the movement, the terms of the conflict's settlement may appear unacceptable upon closer inspection, and parties to the fight who are excluded from the termination proceedings may obstruct and sabotage the process. The difficulties in making peace between the Israeli government and the PLO, even after the transforming Declaration of Principles of 13 September 1993, is illustrative. Rejectionists on each side committed actions to derail the process, including the assassination by an Israeli Jew of the Israeli Prime Minister Yitzhak Rabin and the suicide bombings of Israeli buses by Hamas supporters. This resulted in a new Israeli government, which in the name of security and ethnonationalist claims acted in ways that countered PLO and Palestinian expectations about the ultimate terms of a peace agreement with the Israeli government. Unlike the leaders of the ANC and the Nationalist Party in South Africa, the leaders of the Israeli government and of the PLO were not seeking a common political union, but separation. Therefore, the leaders had less immediate interest in appealing to the constituency on the other side and building a cooperative relationship.

Outcome and Spirals

What seems at first the end of a conflict may become the basis for a renewed struggle in a short time; but sometimes, as discussed in chapter 10, it is enduring. Whatever the temporary end, the conflict never returns to the circumstances before the struggle began; surges and pauses in the struggle have their indelible consequences. In this sense, the metaphor of a conflict going through a cycle is misleading, insofar as it suggests coming back to the starting place. A spiral is a more apt image, as shown in figure 11.2, with each linked sweep varying in the degree of escalation and occurring in a different historical setting.

Certain kinds of outcomes and changes from one conflict to another over time warrant special attention. Here we emphasize mutually acceptable transformations and their sources in changes within one or more of the adversaries, in their relationship to each other, and in their social context.

Internal Changes

Some struggles result in the demise of one of the adversaries. This may occur by the destruction of one of the parties as a physical entity, an identifiable collectivity, or as a functioning social organization. Thus, a social movement organization may cease to exist when it is broken up, its members incapacitated, dispersed, or converted by rival organizations or by government repression. For example, the Black Panther Party erupted onto the American scene in 1966, proclaiming in its platform that it sought power to determine the destiny of the Black community, restitution for slavery, freedom for all Black men held in prisons and jails, and several other goals.[11] After a few years of militant multifaceted struggle, the organization, beset by dissension, was suppressed by government actions.

An adversary may also cease to be antagonistic because its internal structure is radically transformed. Thus, the leaders may change and the character of the collectivity proclaimed by the former leaders is rejected. This can occur as a result of a revolution and the replacement of the old leadership by a new ruling group. Sometimes, even when the leadership has been overthrown by an external enemy, the former supporters of the fallen leaders respond as if they too had been victims and were now liberated, as happened to a large degree in Germany after the defeat of Nazism. On occasion, the election of a new leadership marks a transformation that enables a resolution and reconciliation of an intractable conflict to be reached. This was the case in the ending of British colonial rule in India. In 1945, as the Second World War was coming to an end, the British electorate voted against the governing Conservative Party, led by Winston Churchill, choosing the Labor Party, led by Clement Attlee. The Labor government quickly moved to offer independence to India.

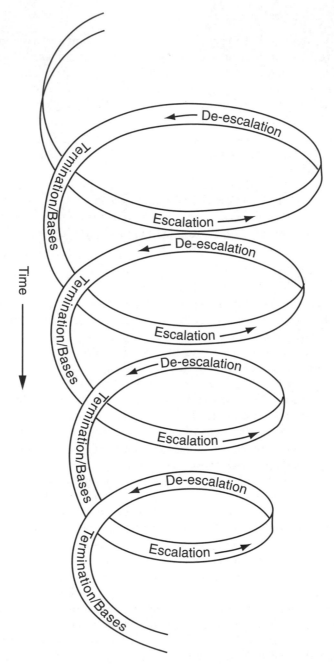

Figure 11.2   Conflict Spiral

Spain provides another example: after the death of Francisco Franco in 1975, the authoritarian centralized regime he led was replaced by a liberal democratic system that allowed for regional autonomy, thus helping to resolve the conflicts arising from Catalan, Basque, and other regional demands.

In addition, significant members of one of the partisan sides, in the course of a struggle, may become convinced of the correctness of specific previously contested views of their former antagonists. Such a change certainly would greatly contribute to resolving their conflict, as happened for many Whites in the United States during the civil rights struggle of the 1960s.

A change in the character of an adversary takes many forms. It may be marked by an ideological transformation, by a reorientation of alliances, by a shift from one political economy to another, or by a shift in the ethnicity of the dominant faction. Such changes often mark a definitive end of the previous conflict, but may also be the basis for the emergence of new ones.

The demise of a collectivity and of a shared identity is rarely complete, at least in the short term. Even with the physical disappearance of one entity, a significant constituent group is likely to retain a sense of continuity with its past identity. For example, the Soviet Union ceased to exist in 1991. Given the improbability of restoring the Soviet Union, the conflict between it and the United States is forever ended. Nevertheless, many citizens of the Russian Federation, the core of the former Soviet Union, although not viewing themselves as ideological enemies of the United States and believing they now share many common interests with the United States, also hold some opposing goals. The conditions for overt struggles are present, but are subordinated to other matters, and are waged in a relatively problem-solving manner.

Grievous Relationship Transformed and Reconciliation Achieved

The outcome of a conflict may embody a change in relations between former adversaries so that the grievance is greatly reduced. This transformation may result from the attainment of greater equity. One aspect of a changed relationship is given special attention in these conclusions: reconciliation between former enemies.[12]

In the post–cold war era, with its surge of often brutal struggles related to communal identities, the possibility of reaching an equitable and enduring reconciliation between enemies is a matter of intense and widespread concern. This is indicated by the creative efforts that have been undertaken in every region of the world to promote reconciliation between enemies.

The term *reconciliation* generally refers to the process of developing a mutual conciliatory accommodation between formerly antagonistic groups. It often refers to a relatively amicable relationship, typically established after a rupture in relations involving one-sided or mutual infliction of extreme injury. Reconciliation, however, has more than one meaning and includes contradictory elements. One meaning is to bring people back into concord with each other; but, another meaning is for people to acquiesce or submit to existing circumstances. The two meanings are not inconsistent. To bring people into accord often means that one or more parties accepts losses that cannot be recovered. Furthermore, coming into concord does not mean equal gains and losses for the former adversaries. One side may have more to atone for and the other more to forgive. Reconciliation may refer to members of one side accepting the painful reality of their circumstances after a struggle in which they experienced devastating losses.

Reconciliation refers here to accommodative ways adversaries come to regard each other after having engaged in intense, and often destructive, struggle. Many, but not all, members of opposing sides put aside their feelings of hate, fear, and loathing toward the other, put aside their views of the other as dangerous and subhuman, and put aside their desire for revenge and retribution. To "put aside" does not necessarily mean such feelings, perceptions, and goals disappear, rather they may be subordinated to other identities and goals. Some people, even those who have been victims of horrible deeds, are able to forgive members of the groups who committed those acts; they are relieved to feel released from the hatred they have felt.

Many instances of such conduct are reported at conferences held at Mountain House, established in 1946 in Caux, Switzerland.[13] It has served as a place where persons from countries and peoples who had warred against each other could meet for unofficial dialogue and to become open to reconciliation. In the first years of its operation, many participants came from France and Germany, and in many personal encounters and public statements, requests for forgiveness were reciprocated. For example, Irene Laure, executive member of the French Socialist Party, whose son had been tortured by the Gestapo, and who fought in the Resistance against the Nazis, when she met Germans at Caux wanted to leave, but as she said, "a miracle happened." Later, she spoke publicly, saying, "I have so hated Germany that I wanted to see her erased from the map of Europe. But I have seen here that my hatred is wrong. I am sorry and I wish to ask the forgiveness of all Germans present."[14] Her story and the response of the Germans has been used as an exemplar in later acts of reconciliation in other conflicts.

To achieve a comprehensive mutual accommodative relationship requires that significant members of the antagonistic parties combine a minimal level of four kinds of views.[15] First, they acknowledge the reality of the terrible acts that were perpetrated. Second, they accept with compassion those who committed injurious conduct as well as acknowledge each other's suffering. Third, they believe that their injustices are being redressed. Fourth, they anticipate mutual security and well-being. The coming together of these elements and the resolution of paradoxes arising from that encounter are crucial in the process of reconciliation. Reconciliation, however, is never complete in all these regards and is not the same for all members of each former adversary party. Therefore, we should consider further the variations in reconciliation as well as the commonalties.

A fundamental aspect of reconciliation is the open and shared recognition of the injuries suffered and the losses experienced. Official investigations, judicial proceedings, and literary and mass media reporting are all ways to openly face abuses that had been hidden or denied. Recognition ideally includes acknowledgment by those who had inflicted the harm that they accept responsibility for what happened. This may mean offering apologies and expressing regrets, and is part of discovering and facing the truth. This is difficult to achieve, particularly for the members of the relatively victorious and dominant groups.

In addition, many persons who have suffered oppression and atrocities in the course of an intense struggle seek redress for the injustices they endured. Redress may be made in the form of tangible restitution or compensation for what was lost; it may take the form of punishment for those who committed injustices; or it may be exhibited in policies that offer protection against future discrimination or harm. Many actions of the Federal Republic of Germany illustrate these methods.[16] For example, compensation has included payments to Jewish survivors of the Holocaust and assistance to the State of Israel. Trials have been held of persons charged with crimes against Jews and other victims of Nazism, and laws were enacted against organizations advocating racism and to provide asylum for victims of political repression.

A third important element in reconciliation involves expressions, by those who have suffered the harms, that acknowledge the humanity of those who committed the injuries. Most extremely, the acknowledgment may convey mercy and forgiveness. The forgiveness factor is greatly stressed by some advocates of reconciliation. It is given support by widespread religious beliefs regarding the value of every human being before God.

Frequently, recognition of the other side's humanity entails only expressing the thought that many members of the adversary community did not personally and directly carry out harmful actions and the next generation is not responsible for the acts of previous generations. Even less directly, persons from communities who had suffered injury may engage cooperatively in projects relating to past harms with members of the community that had inflicted the harm, but not express any apology or forgiveness.[17]

Finally, the adversaries look forward to living together without threatening each other, with mutual respect and security, perhaps even in harmony and unity. This may be in the context of high levels of integration or in the context of separation and little regular interaction. The nature of the anticipated peaceful relations varies, but the realization of the mutual preferences is what is critical.

Clearly, all these aspects of reconciliation are not fully realized and are even contradictory at times. Thus, mercy and justice often cannot be satisfied at the same time, although they may be compatible if pursued sequentially or even simultaneously, or if done so by different members of the previously antagonistic sides. Indeed, in some ways these various elements are interdependent. If members of one party acknowledge that another community has suffered great injury by their actions, forgiveness or at least acceptance of their humanity becomes easier to be felt and expressed.

This discussion indicates that there are many kinds and degrees of reconciliation, with different mixes of elements. In large-scale conflicts, full reconciliation among all members of the former adversaries is improbable. Even centuries after a struggle has ended, reconciliation is not likely to be complete. Thus, in the French celebration of the bicentennial of the 1789 French Revolution, commentators suggested that the revolution was finally over because nearly all French had accepted the legacy of the revolution, but disputes about the meaning and consequences of the revolution erupted again.[18] Five hundred years after the Europeans began settling in what came to be called Latin America, the peoples of many Latin countries regard themselves as a product of the melding of the indigenous peoples and their Spanish conquerors. They refer to the initial coming together as the encounter.[19] But this hardly precludes struggles over the consequences of that encounter.

The failure to carry out any measures of reconciliation endangers the stability in the relationship between former enemies. For example, the atrocities committed during the Second World War in Yugoslavia, particularly by the Croat Ustasha forces against Serbs, were not explicitly and openly adjudicated or investigated by the Yugoslavian government headed by Tito. The government leaders, partly on ideological grounds and concerned about stirring up ethnic animosities, treated the internal struggles among Yugoslavs in terms of class and ideological differences. The unreconciled ethnic hostilities were available to be aroused later and contributed to the breakup of Yugoslavia in bloody wars.

Actions that foster reconciliation need not await the ending of a conflict. Even when a conflict is being waged and escalated, attention to future coexistence and ultimate reconciliation can affect the way a struggle is conducted. For example, if the opposing ethnic group is not treated as a single unit and all its members are not dehumanized, reconciliation will be more readily attainable when the fighting ceases.

In de-escalating and ending a struggle, reassurances about seeking an equitable relationship can hasten a settlement and even a resolution of the conflict. Ethnic and other communal conflicts often are protracted and seem intractable because one or sometimes both sides feel that their very existence is at stake if they are defeated. Convincing assurances that their survival as individuals and as a people are not threatened becomes an important step toward settlement.

Efforts to attain certain aspects of reconciliation, however, sometimes hamper ending a conflict and establishing a stable relationship. For example, demands for justice by the aggrieved party may seem to pose unacceptable demands to the dominant party. Thus, insistence upon judicial trials of the leaders of the dominant collectivity charged with human rights violations are likely to be rejected by those leaders. This obviously was a complicating factor in efforts to end the war in Bosnia in 1996. But without some measure of justice, the resulting outcome may be the imposition of injustice and a relationship that is far from equitable and also is prone to renewed destructive struggle.

The earlier analyses of the course of struggles and their outcomes indicate that reconciliation is not an inevitable stage in every conflict. The obstacles to reconciliation often are so great that it is not achieved to a significant degree. Furthermore, the reconciliation that does occur may be fundamentally one-sided, incorporating only a few elements of a full and mutual reconciliation.

Restructuring of Social Context

The social system within which adversaries have struggled frequently is affected, sometimes profoundly, by the conflict or series of conflicts taking place within it. The resulting restructuring of the social system or more diffuse social environment then changes the character of subsequent struggles. Many conflicts are destabilizing for the larger social order as weakened institutions and normative controls foster conflicts and the use of violence. As a consequence, in societies disrupted by protracted civil strife, rebuilding a political order often takes a very long time.

Struggles sometimes result in strengthening the institutions for managing conflicts. Some evidence for this can be seen in the growth of international governmental and nongovernmental organizations after the First and the Second World Wars. It also can be seen in the development in the United States of laws and institutions relating to collective bargaining between unions and management. Later, in the United States, the civil rights struggle led to the establishment of legal procedures and institutions for dealing with issues about discrimination in employment, in schooling, and in other spheres of social life.

More specifically, major conflicts also affect the social environment so as to shape future contentious issues as well as how the struggles about them are waged. Thus, in the United States, the various struggles of the 1960s about political participation and civil rights for women and minorities often relied on using nonelectoral means of struggle. In later decades, persons waging other fights relied more on direct action and less on electoral or judicial procedures, and recourse to nonelectoral methods gained more legitimacy. This contributed to the weakening of the political party system, and that opened space for political struggles to be waged in terms of narrow identity concerns, rather than within broad coalitions constituting each major party.

Feedback and Anticipation Affecting Earlier Stages

Thus far we have usually discussed how partisans move from one stage to the next in the course of their struggle with each other as if that movement were unidirectional. In some ways, however, the future stages may be said to affect the earlier ones. This occurs through feedback and anticipation. These processes are indicated in figure 11.1, by arrows pointing from later to earlier conflict stages.

Feedback

Every conflict is usually interlocked with other conflicts, and the various conflicts are often at different stages. Consequently, partisans in one fight may experience the adversary's response to their actions in one dispute, and that response may be generalized and thus affect the likely manifestation or escalation of a related fight. The experience is a kind of feedback about the impact of their own actions, as people monitor the consequences of their past conduct. It allows for corrective measures to be taken to modify a course of action in order to get a better response.

Even within the same struggle, the stages are often so broad that experience within one stage affects ongoing conduct in the same and later stages. Thus, partisans waging protest demonstrations derive information about the difficulties of mobilizing large numbers of supporters, and that affects their decision to attempt expanding the demonstrations or settle for whatever can be gotten by the actions already taken.

In addition, conduct taken at one stage provides information for reframing earlier decisions. That is, earlier decisions and actions are reinterpreted in the light of new experiences, and these new interpretations impact on future conduct. For example, goals are set in part on the basis of what members of a contending party believe is attainable. Once a conflict has begun to escalate and the partisans are experiencing the costs of trying to attain their goals against the opposition of the other side, they tend to modify their former goals.

Another way of treating this phenomenon is to regard it as a kind of retroactive construction of consistency. Much of the analysis presented in the previous chapters assumed subjective consistency, as partisans moved through the course of a struggle, doing what seemed reasonable to them at each stage. What seems reasonable at any point is shaped largely by the existing circumstances as the partisans view them. Later experience may cast doubts on earlier understandings. Consequently, the previous actions and decisions are reinterpreted. For example, if the opposition treats the partisans more humanely than they anticipated, they may reinterpret their previous identity and the relationship they had with the opposition.

Anticipation

To some degree, partisans make choices at each stage of the conflict in terms of what they expect will happen at the next stage. They choose certain methods of escalation, anticipating that the opponents will respond in ways they must prepare to counter. These anticipations are matters of conjecture, and each adversary certainly tries to influence the other's views about what will happen if the other side takes particular steps. This is what deterrence is about: threatening dire consequences if the other side undertakes certain actions.

Expectation that a particular course of action will likely result in a protracted and destructive conflict is a reason to change that course. Antagonists may tend to reject evidence supporting such expectations, but intermediaries as well as factions within one or more of the antagonistic parties may be able to warn the leaders and other members of each side that the risk of escalating into a destructive struggle is great and that preventive action is needed.

Specification

Given that conflicts vary in many regards, it is not reasonable to expect that specific processes operate the same among all kinds of conflicts. We need to spell out how particular processes and policies actually are manifested for different kinds of conflicts. As discussed in the first chapter, no consensus about any typology of conflicts exists. Therefore, we differentiate conflicts in terms of several dimensions by which they vary: the issues in contention, the characteristics of the adversaries, the relations between the adversaries, and the social context. The discussion focuses on the implications of those dimensions for the destructive and constructive ways that struggles are conducted.

Protracted and seemingly intractable conflicts often become destructive. Such conflicts are also sometimes regarded as deep-rooted. The terms *intractable, protracted,* and *deep-rooted* are sometimes used interchangeably to characterize a class of large-scale conflicts that are usually destructive. Each term has its own connotations and limitations. Deep-rooted often refers to conflicts based on strife regarding the satisfaction of human needs between peoples with communal collective identities.[20] Protracted connotes long-lasting, but is often linked to ethnic and other identity-associated conflict.[21] Intractable suggests never-ending. The kind of conflicts considered here to be intractable are those that are particularly resistant to settlement. They persist despite efforts to resolve them, although they do eventually end or become transformed.[22]

Issues in Contention

With the end of the cold war, considerable attention has been given to ethnic, religious, or other intercommunal conflicts. They are often regarded as especially prone to being waged destructively. Indeed, some struggles for ethnic dominance have resulted in genocidal conduct, as in the struggle over control in Rwanda and in parts of the former Yugoslavia. Not all communally associated struggles, however, become destructive. Many are conducted and settled through legitimate institutionalized means.[23] For example, this has generally been true in Malaysia, Canada, Belgium, and India.

Furthermore, conflicts not associated with communal differences, but with differences in political ideology, class position, or relative power have also been destructive and protracted. For example, this was the case for the cold war between the Soviet Union and the United States, the struggle waged by the Khmer Rouge in Cambodia, the repression by the government of Guatemala, and the fighting among the major clans in Somalia.[24]

Some analysts have argued that conflicts based on value or identity differences or more generally dissensual conflicts are particularly difficult to resolve or to settle. However, this does not seem to be inherently the case. Much depends on many other aspects of the conflict, related to the adversaries, their relationship, and their social context.

Adversary Characteristics

Many qualities of each adversary in a conflict affect the course of any struggle they wage against each other. Thus, the degree to which an adversary is clearly bounded impacts on the course of a conflict, but in different ways at each conflict stage. For example, the likelihood of a conflict becoming manifest is reduced when one or more of the adversaries is not clearly bounded, due to the difficulties in mobilizing partisans. Once the conflict has escalated, however, the absence of clear boundaries can increase the chances of de-escalation since partisans may more readily drift away when the burdens of the struggle become very great. Subsequently, however, negotiating an explicit ending of a conflict is often more difficult when the membership of one or more sides is not clear and frequently shifts. The surges of confrontation in the United States during the late 1960s are illustrative.

The effects of the degree of internal differentiation also have paradoxical effects at different stages of a conflict. Thus, conflicts are prone to become manifest if one or more of the adversaries is highly differentiated, particularly with subgroups that have obligations to contend against external adversaries. On the other hand, highly differentiated parties tend to be hierarchically organized. Consequently, although leaders are often able to make decisions that result in a rapid escalation, they can lead moves toward de-escalation and a decisive settlement of a conflict.[25]

The relationship between constituents and representatives within each side is a particularly significant aspect of internal differentiation. Thus, the leaders or representatives may be varyingly constrained or guided by their constituents. In democracies or other systems in which the followers shape policy decisions, the leaders try to stay attuned to their presumed followers. Where leaders control many resources and are not subject to selection by their constituents, they can be autocratic in their decisions. Of course, these particular polar differences are imbedded in complex situations and vary in different cultures, about different issues, and at different times.

The implications of constituency considerations for the course of a struggle are important but quite varied. Those in authority are not always more bellicose or more conciliatory than are their constituents, since various mechanisms favor each direction. Thus, leaders dealing with an external adversary have reasons to be restrained and even accommodative in their conduct. These include interdependence with their counterparts (each can help or hurt the other) and mutual understanding that occurs from recurrent interactions. Their constituents are less likely to have such interests or experiences. On the other hand, leaders dealing with an external adversary have reasons to be more antagonistic than are their constituents for other reasons. These include an interest in rallying support for themselves by attacking outsiders and seeking gains for their constituents at the expense of outsiders. Strategies fostering the former mechanisms rather than the latter would contribute to waging a struggle constructively.

More consistently, leaders or representatives who tend to be independent of their constituents also tend to be capable of making relatively sudden moves, whether to escalate or to de-escalate a conflict. For example, Adolph Hitler and the Nazi leadership of Germany and Joseph Stalin and the Communist Party leadership of the Soviet Union had commanding control of their constituents in the summer of 1939. As a central tenet of their ideologies and policies, each had mobilized constituent support against the other. But their foreign ministers signed a nonaggression pact in August 1939, and Nazi Germany and Soviet Russia quickly occupied and divided Poland between themselves, initiating World War II.[26] The German-Soviet conflict, as far as public utterances were concerned, was suddenly ended, but it was revived with ferocious intensity when Nazi military forces suddenly invaded the Soviet Union in 1941.

Extremely destructive struggles are not likely to be sustained without the leadership of those in authority. Destructive episodes may erupt at the local level, executed by low-ranking persons within a group or organization or community. But even then, someone in authority is likely to provide leadership for the outbreak.[27] Conversely, to stop, reduce, or prevent destructive aspects of a struggle, initiatives from the grass roots and local leadership often pressure the higher levels of authority to move toward de-escalation, settlement, and reconciliation. Of course, de-escalating initiatives are also undertaken by persons with high-level authority in a country or organization, and by persons at the middle or subelite levels of an adversarial entity. Cooperation, or at least acquiescence, among different levels is generally necessary for major transitions from one stage of conflict to another.[28]

Finally, each adversary's self-conception significantly impacts on the course of a social conflict and the likelihood that it will be waged with relative constructiveness. One aspect of a person or group's self-conception that is particularly relevant to how destructively a fight is waged is their sense of specialness. On the grounds of religious faith, ideological beliefs, myths about the past, or presumptions about race differences, some persons or groups sometimes claim that they are inherently superior to their adversaries. They may believe they are chosen by God, History, or Nature to lead, convert, civilize, subdue, or destroy others. They may consider this to be true universally or only within a particular domain such as a particular territory. When an adversary is armed with such beliefs, genocidal acts may be committed with a sense of self righteousness.[29] For example, the racist views of Nazis were a reason and justification for the killing of six million Jews in Europe and the treatment of many other peoples as inferior humans.[30]

Not surprisingly, the interpretation of the meaning of such self-conceptions is often contested. For example, many Americans have celebrated that they are a chosen people in a promised land, with a manifest destiny. Some observers, however, regard such self-conceptions as justifications for domination and the denial of rights for other peoples in North America and throughout the world.[31] It is when pride in family, group, or nation, incorporates the belief that one's claims take complete precedence over those of other humans that manifest destiny becomes destructive. Those beliefs, for example, may justify claims for exclusive rights in particular territories, even places regarded as sacred by others, for example by indigenous American populations in the United States. Denying the legitimacy of the claims made by others prepares the ground for destructive treatment of the adversary.

Adversary Relations

Throughout this analysis, the relations between the adversaries have been found to be crucial for the way a conflict is conducted and ended. We might therefore expect that variations in the nature of the adversarial relationship are the most important ways to differentiate kinds of conflicts relevant for their course of development. Among the many variations in relationships, we return to the three discussed in the first chapter: numbers, integration, and dominance.

Numbers

We usually think of every conflict as having two sides, but there are always more than two parties in a struggle. This follows from the likelihood that each party has internal diversity in addition to allies and enemies who have a stake in the struggle and are varyingly engaged in it with their own concerns and interests. Moreover, each party may act and be reacted to as if it were part of a larger party or itself consisted of several actors, and so each fight may be regarded as interlocked in many others. Related to the likelihood that each fight is embedded in many others, the issues in contention are numerous and they shift in salience in the course of a struggle.

Given these many possibilities, agreement among analysts about how many adversaries are engaged in any particular conflict is not likely. In considering the numbers engaged in a struggle, therefore, we give priority to the way the adversaries themselves view their struggle. Some parties try to dominate these views, seeking to rally parties to their side and trying to simplify the fight so that it is regarded as being waged between only two sides.

Recognizing the involvement of many parties provides opportunities to explore possible solutions to the conflict before it escalates. Some parties may serve as quasi mediators, helping to discover possible mutually acceptable formulas. Or, the more moderate parties may find a satisfactory arrangement and conclude an agreement, shutting out the more extreme groups who would hold out for better terms. For example, in many public policy disputes relating to environmental issues, the number of affected parties is often large. Some of those with relatively radical positions may raise demands and opponents reject them, but others with a stake in the problem and desiring to find a solution without an escalated struggle can also impose a compromise.

Once escalation has gone far, however, having many parties directly engaged in a struggle can increase the difficulty of settling it. Each party has somewhat different interests and concerns, and a formula acceptable to all the parties on each side may be difficult to construct. For example, in the Second World War, the allied governments waging war against Germany and Japan insisted on unconditional surrender, partly because they understandably feared that trying to set surrender terms might break up the anti-Fascist alliance. This probably prolonged the war, but also resulted in a more unilateral victory than would otherwise have been the case.

Degree of Integration

The degree of mutual interaction and interdependence between actors generally tends to limit the emergence of conflicts and their escalation into severe struggles.[32] Integration between possible adversaries mitigates against a conflict between them becoming manifest because issues that might be in dispute are viewed in a relatively cooperative context. Increased mutual understanding and shared norms tend to limit conflict escalation, even when it becomes manifest.

The absence of shared understandings and norms is related to the degree of cultural differences between peoples, organizations, classes, and groups. Such differences contribute to the emergence and escalation of conflicts in two major ways. First, they may be the basis of denigrating the persons with a different culture and result in efforts to correct them or reject them. Recognizing the oneness of the human species and the values of diversity can help mitigate the destructive implications of cultural differences. Second, cultural differences may be the basis for misunderstandings and miscommunications helping to generate and perpetuate conflicts. Knowledge about each other's cultures, gained through training, experience, or the work of intermediaries, can help overcome these difficulties. Recognizing that no civilization, society, organization, social class, or group is culturally homogenous reduces the dangers of stereotyping and increases the possibilities of finding common bonds across cultural cleavages.

Higher levels of integration increase the alternative ways of conducting a struggle. Inducements of persuasion and possible rewards and of nonviolent coercion are more available because of the mutual dependency resulting from integration. Furthermore, the costs of disrupting the mutual dependency tend to inhibit escalating the means of struggle. There is strong evidence supporting these generalizations in the realm of international trade.[33]

The counterarguments that greater integration generates more issues of possible contention and grievances that result in struggles cannot be dismissed. There is case-study evidence indicating that asymmetry in dyadic relationships, for example in trade, is the source of conflicts and that those sometimes escalate.[34]

Dominance

Inequalities in resources, making it possible for one side to dominate the other, greatly affect the emergence and course of every conflict. Inequality between adversaries in controlling resources is an important source of grievance and therefore a basis for an underlying conflict becoming manifest, but this is not a linear relationship. Low levels of inequality tend to reduce a sense of grievance and extremely high levels of inequality tend to result in domination by one side that inhibits those who might have a grievance from believing they can correct the situation by struggling against it. The domination may be exercised in hegemonic ways, so that the subordinates internalize the legitimacy of their position.[35] Furthermore, great power differences permit great abuses of power. As Rummel has observed, "Power kills; absolute power kills absolutely."[36] If a conflict becomes manifest, the power concentration contributes greatly to the kind of escalation that occurs. Thus, genocides and politicides tend to occur when the target group is weak and vulnerable.

In general, mutually perceived symmetry in the ability to act and to be free of the other side's domination increases the likelihood that the struggle to right inequities will be conducted in a less-destructive manner, and under many conditions, even constructively.

The degree of resource asymmetry between groups, it should be recognized, is not always clear and unchanging. Adversaries in a protracted struggle tend to see themselves as beleaguered and threatened by the powerful other, and feel they must fight hard to defend themselves. In addition to the examples, cited in the first chapter, in Sri Lanka and Northern Ireland, others are worth noting: during the years of apartheid, South African Whites generally saw themselves as threatened by the much more numerous Blacks, while the South African Blacks regarded themselves as militarily, economically, and politically dominated and exploited by the Whites. Israeli Jews generally see themselves as surrounded by a vast Arab world, while Arabs generally see themselves as threatened by the militarily mighty Israel, backed by Western imperialism. Similar patterns of perceived insecurity can be noted for the Greeks and Turks in Cyprus, and for the Serbs and Muslims in Bosnia.

Such different views of power and vulnerability help explain the protracted nature of many conflicts. They can also suggest ways out of intractable conflicts, if the context and the parties to a conflict are altered. For example, in the 1980s, several Central American countries were wracked by long-lasting and interlocked conflicts, making it difficult to settle any one of them in isolation. A large step toward resolution was made by the accord reached among the presidents of the five Central American countries, meeting in Esquipulas, Guatemala.[37] The accord is often called the "Arias Plan" to recognize the great mediating contributions of the president of Costa Rica, Oscar Arias. The accords included three components to be implemented simultaneously in the countries devastated by civil wars, and according to a fixed time schedule. The components provided for ending the violent conflicts, promoting democracy, and fostering economic integration.

System Context

The particular social system within which a conflict is waged provides a conventional way to distinguish among different kinds of conflicts. Families, large-scale formal organizations, residential neighborhoods, countries, and regions of the world each have their own peculiarities that are relevant for the course of struggles within them.[38] Although the setting is a way of characterizing typical combinations of variations along several dimensions, consideration of the dimensions themselves help in comparing different conflicts. For example, resource differences tend to be greater within countries than within neighborhoods, but countries and neighborhoods also vary greatly in the degree to which control of resources is concentrated. We will consider the course of a conflict in the light of four aspects of social systems: culture and institutions, scarcity, resource distribution, and consistency and stability.

Culture and Institutions

It would seem obvious that shared cultural understandings and common institutions tend to inhibit the emergence of conflicts and their destructive escalation. They tend to reduce misunderstandings, foster mutual regard, and provide a basis for a shared identity.[39] They also increase the likelihood of intervention to mitigate the destructive course of a conflict.

Nevertheless, the content of the conflict-relevant rules of the shared culture and institutions is most important in affecting the course of conflicts. For example, the shared values may be conducive to competitiveness, individualism, and machismo. They may encourage revenge-seeking, feuds, and other practices tending to perpetuate conflicts. On the other hand, culturally prescribed procedures may be elaborated to provide for problem-solving ways to manage conflicts.

Scarcity

Conflicts are often viewed as contests over scarce resources. If there were enough to go around, common sense suggests, people would not fight each other. Indeed, families, organizations, and societies vary in the general level of material endowments and in trends of their growth and decline. Higher and increasing levels of such resources tend to reduce the manifestation of conflicts and facilitate the waging of constructive struggles, as indicated by the cross-national research on income distribution and violent conflicts.[40] To some extent, however, material goods and social attributes such as prestige or power are valued relatively, compared with how much others have. In so far as that is true, the ameliorating effects of abundance and its growth are reduced.

In one regard, scarcity is not inherent in the circumstances. It depends on the social boundaries within which abundance or scarcity is considered. Clearly, the experience of scarcity depends on the parameters of the social system being considered. Even prestige, which is relative, can be accorded to many people at the same time in different arenas. Consequently, even in apparent conditions of scarcity, the conditions underlying a struggle may be reconfigured.

Resource Distribution

The adversaries, whatever the symmetry of their resources, exist in a larger social context, characterized by differing kinds of resource distributions, with varying implications for how the conflict is conducted. Within a hierarchical system in which the adversaries are relatively low ranked, the way they conduct a struggle will be greatly affected by the rules and interventions of the superordinate group. On the other hand, in a system of numerous, relatively equal, autonomous parties, the rules are more likely to reflect all the parties in the system, but the rules are less likely to be precise and to be enforced.

Consistency and Stability

Inconsistencies among different aspects of a social system and the lack of stability tend to generate conflicts and to foster their escalation, particularly in combination. For example, research on genocide and politicide indicates that they occur when the political opportunity structure permits.[41] Already occurring disorder and violence frees some people to engage in other struggles destructively. Thus, in the shadow of military operations, a ruling group is more able to implement policies of suppression and destruction, as was true for the genocide of Armenians in Turkey during the First World War.[42]

This discussion of the many ways conflicts differ indicates too that they vary in their predispositions to escalate destructively or constructively. Such predispositions affect the consequences of pursuing policies to foster constructive struggle. For some conflicts, the challenge of finding ways to conduct a conflict constructively is relatively easily met; but for others, the challenge may be insurmountable, at least in the short run.

Implications

Perhaps the primary reason that people study how social conflicts are waged is in order to mitigate their destructive effects. It is widely presumed that knowledge about specific struggles and general understandings about the bases of conflicts and their destructive escalation can be useful. Such knowledge could be effectively applied to avoid conflicts, to conduct struggles constructively, to resolve them cooperatively, or to advance good causes, such as freedom, equity, or peace. Applying knowledge to advance such values, however, is difficult. We will consider two major problems and how to overcome them: first, how general knowledge can be applied to particular conflicts, and second, how moral choices can be made.

The Clinical Approach

Persons doing applied conflict resolution work are usually concerned about specific conflicts and what to do in each case. Medical practice offers a useful metaphor. Physicians generally value their clinical skills: the ability to diagnose what is happening to a particular patient at a specific time and to decide on the most effective therapy to treat that particular patient. In doing so, they draw on general theories of physiology, pharmacology, and many other disciplines. But it is the peculiar and unique interactions of many general processes that account for the particular condition of each patient. On the other hand, scientists studying a specific process, try to isolate and hold constant other variables that affect that process. Their knowledge is generally presented in probabilities, the likelihood that particular consequences will result from a set of conditions, everything else being equal. Furthermore, theorists often emphasize relatively immutable conditions and processes and not the readily manipulable factors affecting individual cases that are of greater interest to practitioners.

In the practice of conflict resolution, the clinical approach is preeminent. Conflict resolvers use their moral standards and draw from their general knowledge about relevant conflicts to prescribe actions for the adversaries and for themselves in particular struggles.[43] Analysts of conflict resolution sometimes also indulge in prescribing policies, applying their understandings of general truths and morality to specific cases. But they usually seek general patterns of effective mediation, negotiation, and constructive struggle and so may provide general prescriptions for classes of conflicts.

There is no single conflict resolution formula for ameliorating every conflict and preventing each from becoming more destructive; however, being able to select from a large repertoire of methods increases the chances of choosing an appropriate method. Thinking about each case as freshly as possible, and not assuming it is just like another struggle, is a good general rule.

In order to apply general knowledge about conflicts to specific struggles, researchers and practitioners generally analyze the struggle carefully, considering how it is like and unlike others. But there is no agreed-upon comprehensive theory of conflicts that can specify the consequences of every act any partisan might take. The knowledge is often quite general and abstract and valid only in a probabilistic sense, if that.

General knowledge can be applied more readily to large sets of similar conflicts than to a single case. This is like using a public-health rather than a clinical-medical model. Using a public-health approach, the systemic causes of a disease are treated in order to reduce the incidence of that disease. For example, this may include improving sanitation, although that is not a cure for someone already sick.

Conflict resolvers increasingly are concerned with designing systems to prevent conflicts from becoming manifest or from escalating destructively. They seek to fashion constructive ways to manage conflicts in particular settings such as corporations, churches, schools, or factories.[44] This may include developing procedures for introducing changes and for handling grievances; and it includes training members of such organizations in ways to settle their own disputes nonviolently or train a few members to mediate conflicts before they escalate.

In applying theoretical understanding to ameliorating conflicts, whether individual struggles or recurrent fights, it is useful to recognize the stages and types of conflicts, and consider the various methods that tend to be effective at each stage of different kinds of conflict.[45] Certainly, increasing attention is being given to preventing destructive conflicts, to interrupting them, to getting adversaries to the negotiating table, to negotiating agreements, and to building cooperative relations. More attention is needed to learn which problem-solving conflict resolution methods are appropriate for different kinds of conflicts.[46] In addition, we need to specify what methods can be used by different kinds of people, since actors, whether partisans or intermediaries, vary in their skills and resources to apply different methods.

Issues of Morality

Acting to resolve or even to mitigate conflicts necessarily involves issues of morality and value preferences. Choices must be made about which course of action is the right one to pursue, and the choices generally pose moral dilemmas for three major reasons.[47] First, we each hold a variety of values, and maximizing one is often done at the expense of another. Thus, we generally believe that preserving life, maintaining order, advancing justice, and promoting freedom are good, but we are uncertain about how much of each should be sacrificed for the other in a particular historical circumstance. For would-be conflict resolvers, a frequent moral dilemma is whether they should seek a settlement under existing conditions or support continuing the struggle in the hope that future conditions will yield a more equitable agreement.

Another source of dilemmas is that we each have many identities, and they offer different vantage points, providing different priorities and meaning to the values we hold. For example, we may share identities with an oppressed minority struggling for greater equality, with all the citizens of the country in which the minority lives, with others who believe all humans are equally children of God, and with adherents of a political ideology extolling individual liberty. Thus, the priority and interpretation of the many values we hold are likely to differ depending on the salience of the various identities we assume.

Third, moral dilemmas arise from the multiplicity of struggles. Conflicts are often intertwined so that resolving one may hamper resolving another. For example, in the United States after the long, destructive Civil War, the

Whites of the former Confederacy were reincorporated into the Union against which they had rebelled.[48] That reconciliation was made partly at the expense of the Blacks of the South, the former slaves. The Whites of the South were allowed to dominate the former slaves after the reconstruction policy slackened and ended.

Resolving these dilemmas might seem to be a matter of personal taste or of social conventions about values. One view of morals and values is that they are relative, deriving from culture and personal experience. Admittedly, there is no universal consensus about any absolute standards that provide a ranking of values to be honored. Morality is traditionally based on value preferences, and according to an important social science tradition, value preferences cannot be derived from beliefs about reality. Morality is articulated in the form of "should" statements, not factual statements.[49] It is given authority by shared understandings, for example about God or human nature. For many social scientists, this has meant that morality is a matter of faith and convictions that are socially constructed. It follows that morality is variable; it is culturally relative and not to be judged by absolute standards.

Also, however, according to a related social science tradition, there is an objective reality that can be approached by empirical methods of research. Full and accurate understanding of the objective reality may never be attained, but by seeking it, more and more can be learned about it. That is the goal of the social as well as the natural sciences.

These conceptions of beliefs and values have been subjected to severe criticisms and newer views warrant consideration here, because they help lessen the dilemmas about acting morally in resolving a conflict.[50] The existence of a reality separable from the observation of it is now widely questioned. The argument is that what we know must derive from observations and those must be filtered through our senses, however they are augmented by instruments.[51] It follows that reality can be known only under specific conditions of observation, and therefore reality varies under different conditions and from differently situated perspectives. This does not mean that we can construct reality any way we like. Matters vary in the strength of their predispositions to be perceived one way rather than another. Some matters are generally viewed similarly, regardless of the bases of observations.

Our understanding of morality has also been affected by recent social experience and thought. One development has been the growing sense that certain kinds of conduct are almost universally deplored. Even those persons who perpetrate the condemned acts often hide or deny that they or members of their group committed them, or they construct them as other kinds of acts. But sometimes they even come to acknowledge that their group was wrong or that they themselves did wrong. The extension of shared norms may be seen in the growing acceptance of the existence of universal human rights and the condemnation of genocidal acts.[52] The study of normative regimes in international affairs also reveals the existence of moral standards that influence the conduct of governments sharing those standards.[53]

The attention to shared normative standards provides a broad basis for moral imperatives. This is exemplified by the argument for conventionalism as the basis for ethics in international relations and other domains. Ethics is based on principles that people use to justify and win acceptance from others for their actions. The principles must be shared by the concerned parties to be effective. Rather than promulgating any particular ethical tradition as the foundation for moral theory, as David A. Welch writes, moral obligation can be and is based upon agreement to regard "certain rules as authoritative, and certain practices as legitimate. . . . Whatever the parties concerned agree to regard as just or legitimate *is* just or legitimate," according to this view.[54] The present discussion is based on this conventionalist approach. Accordingly, I neither assert that there is a universally agreed-upon moral code nor assume that a particular moral code is supreme. But the argument does not assert that every conventional moral code is equally supportable.

In addition to developments in intellectual thought, new insights have emerged from the application of social policies to promote human welfare. The frequent ineffectiveness of public and private policies to improve human conduct and the frequent unintentional and undesired repercussions of such policies have also long been recognized. In recent decades, increased use has been made of social science knowledge to help formulate social policies; but that has not ensured that the policies have the desired effects and avoid undesired ones. We are too often reminded that good intentions do not guarantee good results. One response may be skepticism about trying to implement any public policies, but another is to examine even more carefully the consequences of alternative policies. The concern with the consequences of policies grounds morality in empirical and practical considerations.

Work in problem-solving conflict resolution, in particular, has stimulated practitioners and analysts to reflect upon the nature of knowledge and morality. Such conflict resolution compels attention to the varying interpretations of the past and the present that adversaries construct, even about the same events. Moreover, the insight of many practitioners of nonviolence and conflict resolution is that through mutual probing all parties can gain a more-complete truth.[55] The probing takes many forms, as diverse, for example, as those in the context of interactive workshops or confrontations in a nonviolent campaign.

Experience with problem-solving conflict resolution efforts requires attention to moral issues.[56] For example, mediators and other kinds of intervenors face choices about the propriety of intervening and just how to intervene. Moreover, the partisans waging a struggle endeavor to morally justify their actions to their constituents and allies and also to their adversaries. If they take a problem-solving conflict resolution approach, the moral issues are particularly salient. One stance taken by some persons concerned about the morality of various kinds of conflict resolution methods is to declare particular basic values or moral principles that should guide conflict resolution work. Laue and Cormick, for example, argued that conflict resolution ethics rest on "the basic premise . . . that persons are inherently valuable, and to be treated as ends-in-themselves."[57] They derive three core values from this premise: proportional empowerment, justice, and freedom; and on the bases of those values, they derive several ethical principles for intervenors. Helpful as such directives may be, they may not be accepted by the parties in a conflict, or different priorities are given to these values and principles by various partisans and intervenors.

The study of conflicts makes evident that no means of struggle and no settlement has unmixed good or bad consequences. Every course of action embodies a mixture of moral characteristics. Thus, people may be struggling for a future with greater social justice, but in doing so they reduce freedom for many, engage in killing, and suffer severe losses; or a settlement may end the killing, but only briefly and in a way that engenders new injustices. Indeed, to insist upon the primacy of one's own value-ordering and moral principles seems to contradict some aspects of the problem-solving conflict resolution perspective.

Conclusions

The world is in flux and in transition to a still unclear future. Many of our old paradigms are no longer valid. For example, a world divided up among sovereign states with people largely interacting with each other within each country is less and less the kind of world in which many people actually live. Conflicts based on universal ideologies or narrow economic interests seem less salient than they had been, as struggles related to identity issues seem to have become more urgent.

Furthermore, globalization links people all over the world. This is manifested in the growth of international trade, the expansion of investments from several countries to much of the world, and the movement of people from one region to another as laborers, technicians, professionals, and even refugees from war and disorder. It is also manifested in people's exposure to the same information and entertainment generated by the mass media. In addition, the newer technologies of communication enable people to quickly communicate with each other, forming new networks and sustaining old ones over long distances. Finally, changes in the environment and populations constitute growing problems threatening everyone. We face common problems in our neighborhoods, countries, and planet.

In addition, the changes in weapons technologies also increase the possibility that struggles will be waged with even greater destructive consequences. Weapons capable of inflicting immense harm are increasingly accessible to more and more people.

These developments are the source of many old and new kinds of conflicts, and they implicate each of us in each other's affairs, giving each of us a stake in the way others behave. They therefore provide an impetus to find and pursue constructive ways of waging struggles. They encourage us to recognize that no person or group is in sole possession of truth or morality. Increased reliance on constructive conflict strategies can enhance benefits for all.

Another consequence of these developments is that intermediaries have become more important than ever before in managing conflicts. More parties than before have a stake in a conflict and therefore have incentives to intervene and try to avert its destructive escalation. Furthermore, intervention is increasingly expected and considered proper. There is less tolerance for conduct, even in large-scale conflicts, that violate increasingly shared understandings of human rights.

The analysis presented here indicates that everyone can contribute something to the amelioration of struggles of any magnitude. This is true whether we are working at the grassroots level, the middle range, or as system leaders. This is the case partly because of the interconnectedness of many conflicts. Certainly, large-scale conflicts are manifested in numerous localities between particular sets of adversaries. Appendix B lists many organizations engaged in intermediary and partisan activities seeking to foster the productive waging of struggles.

We humans are not doomed to endless and all-pervasive destructive struggles. We may not escape them all, but we can certainly reduce them and limit them. Awareness that conflicts can be waged constructively is increasing. We need more and better knowledge about how that occurs because such knowledge will help replace destructive conflicts with ones that are constructively waged.

Notes

1. David I. Kertzer, *Ritual, Politics, and Power* (New Haven, Conn.: Yale University Press, 1988).

2. Louis Kriesberg, "De-escalation of International Conflicts," in *World Encyclopedia of Peace*, (Oxford, U.K.: Pergamon, 1998).

3. Allister Sparks, *Tomorrow Is Another Country* (New York: Hill and Wang, 1995); also Hendrik W. van der Merwe, *Pursuing Justice and Peace in South Africa* (London: Routledge, 1989).

4. Louis Kriesberg, *International Conflict Resolution* (New Haven, Conn.: Yale University Press, 1992).

5. Saadia Touval and I. William Zartman, eds., *International Mediation in Theory and Practice* (Boulder, Colo.: Westview, 1985).

6. John Kane-Berman, *South Africa's Silent Revolution* (Johannesburg: South African Institute of Race Relations, 1990).

7. Benyamin Neuberger, "Nationalisms Compared: ANC, IRA, and PLO," in *The Elusive Search for Peace: South Africa and Northern Ireland*, ed. Hermann Giliome and Jannie Gagiano (Cape Town: Oxford University of Press, 1990).

8. Christopher Davis and Murray Feshback, *Rising Infant Mortality in the USSR in the 1970's*, U.S. Department of Commerce, Bureau of the Census (Washington, D.C.: U.S. Government Printing Office, 1980); and John Dutton, Jr., "Changes in Soviet Mortality Patterns, 1959–77," *Population and Development Review*, no. 5 (June 1979): 267–91.

9. Kriesberg, *International Conflict Resolution*; Christopher R. Mitchell, "A Willingness to Talk," Working Paper 4, Center for Conflict Analysis and Resolution, George Mason University, Fairfax, Va., 1990; and Christopher R. Mitchell, "Ending Conflicts and Wars: Judgment, Rationality, and Entrapment," *International Social Science Journal* 127 (February 1991): 35–55.

10. Larry Dunn and Louis Kriesberg, "Mediating Intermediaries: Expanding Roles of Transnational Organizations," in *Studies in International Mediation: Essays in Honour of Jeffrey Z. Rubin*, ed. Jacob Bercovitch (London: Macmillan, and New York: St. Martin's, forthcoming).

11. For accounts of the Black Panther Party, see Reginald Major, *A Panther Is a Black Cat* (New York: William Morrow, 1971) and William Foner, ed. *The Black Panthers Speak* (Philadelphia: J. B. Lippincott, 1970). For an analysis of the decline of the 1960s' social movements, see Anthony Oberschall, "The Decline of the 1960s Social Movements," in *Research in Social Movements, Conflicts, and Change*, vol. 1, ed. Louis Kriesberg (Greenwich, Conn.: JAI, 1978).

12. See Louis Kriesberg, "Coexistence and Reconciliation of Communal Conflicts," in *Handbook on Coexistence*, ed. Eugene Weiner (New York: Continuum Press, 1998).

13. Mountain House was established by the Swiss government, inspired by the American, Frank Buchman, the initiator of Moral Re-Armament (MRA). See Michael Henderson, *The Forgiveness Factor* (London: Grosvenor Books, 1996), 3–5.

14. Henderson, *The Forgiveness Factor*, 26.

15. John Paul Lederach, *Building Peace: Sustainable Reconciliation in Divided Societies* (Tokyo: United Nations University Press, 1995).

16. For excerpts by several authors about aspects of these policies, see, "Germany (after Nazism)," in *Transitional Justice*, vol. 2, ed. Neil J. Kritz (Washington, D.C.: United States Institute of Peace Press, 1995).

17. For example, a southern plantation from the time before the American Civil War is being restored in the 1990s, and the work is being overseen by a group including a descendent of the family that owned the plantation and a descendent of one of the family of slaves from that plantation.

18. Lynn Hunt, "It's Not Over Till It's Over, and It's Not Over," *New York Times Book Review*, 10 September 1989, 12, reviewing Francois Furet and Mona Ozouf, eds., *A Critical Dictionary of the French Revolution*, trans. Arthur Goldhammer (Cambridge, Mass.: Belknap Press/Harvard University Press, 1989).

19. Miguel Leon-Portilla, "The New World, 1492–1992: An Endless Debate?" *Diogenes* 157 (Spring 1992): 1–21.

20. John Burton, *Conflict: Resolution and Provention* (New York: St. Martin's Press, 1990).

21. Edward A. Azar, Paul Jureidini, and Ronald McLaurin, "Protracted Social Conflict, Theory and Practice in the Middle East," *Journal of Palestine Studies* 29 (Fall, 1978): 41–60.

22. Louis Kriesberg, Terrell A. Northrup, and Stuart J. Thorson, eds., *Intractable Conflicts and Their Transformation* (Syracuse, N.Y.: Syracuse University Press, 1989).

23. See Roy Licklider, "The Consequences of Negotiated Settlements in Civil Wars, 1945–1993," *American Political Science Review* 89 (September 1995): 682.

24. Under the leadership of Pol Pot, the Khmer Rouge ruled Cambodia from 1975 to 1979. During their regime, an estimated 1.7 million Cambodians were killed or starved to death—21 percent of the population. Although the Khmer Rouge claimed to be advancing communism, the killing was directed at ridding the society of imperialist influences, but the death rates also varied by ethnicity. See Ben Kiernan, *The Pol Pot Regime: Race, Power, and Genocide in Cambodia under the Khmer Rouge, 1975–1979* (New Haven, Conn., and London: Yale University Press, 1996). The great inequalities in Guatemala were brutally sustained for decades by military governments, following the U.S.-backed military coup of 1954. See Robert M. Karmic, ed., *The Harvest of Violence: The Maya Indians and the Guatemalan Crisis* (Norman: University of Oklahoma Press, 1988). After Siad Barre's dictatorship in Somalia was overthrown and he fled the capital in January 1991, the fighting among the many clan-families in Somali escalated, producing large-scale killing and extensive famine.

25. These moves may be made quickly and the closely held preparations conducted in secrecy. See Michael I. Handel, *The Dictionary of Surprise: Hitler, Nixon, Sadat* (Cambridge, Mass.: Center for International Affairs, Harvard University, 1981).

26. Handel, *The Diplomacy of Surprise*, 97–175.

27. This can be seen in the case of pogroms against Jews in Tsarist Russia and elsewhere and in intimidating violence directed against African Americans in the reign of Jim Crow laws in the American South. Also see the account of a communal riot between Hindus and Muslims in a Pakistani village, examined in Beth Roy, *Some Trouble with Cows* (Berkeley: University of California Press, 1994).

28. Even in the great transforming breakthroughs, seemingly led by top leaders such as Anwar Sadat of Egypt, Mikhail Gorbachev of the Soviet Union, or Frederik Willem deKlerk of South Africa, we can see persons formulating responses to constituency concerns. Their responses were creative and constructive toward an outside adversary as part of the solution for their immediate constituency concerns. See Kriesberg, *International Conflict Resolution*.

29. There is a large and growing literature on genocide; see for example, Leo Kuper, *Genocide: Its Political Use in the Twentieth Century* (New York: Penguin, 1981); Michael Dobkowski and Isador Walliman, *Genocide in Our Time: An Annotated Bibliography with Analytical Introductions* (Ann Arbor, Mich.: The Pierian Press, 1992); Samuel Totten, William S. Parsons, and Israel W. Charney, eds., *Century of Genocide: Eyewitness Accounts and Critical Views* (New York & London: Garland, 1997); and Barbara Harff and Ted Robert Gurr, "Toward an Empirical Theory of Genocides and Politic-

ides: Identification and Measurement of Cases since 1945," *International Studies Quarterly* 32 (1988): 357–71.

30. For studies of the Holocaust, see for example, Helen Fein, *Accounting for Genocide: National Responses and Jewish Victimization during the Holocaust* (New York: The Free Press, 1979) and Raul Hilberg, *The Destruction of the European Jews* (New York: Holmes and Meier, 1985).

31. Johan Galtung, "Global Projections of Deep-Rooted U.S. Pathologies," Occasional Paper 11, Institute for Conflict Analysis and Resolution, George Mason University, Fairfax, Va., 1996.

32. Integration is discussed here as a characteristic of the relationship between possible adversaries, but it can also be viewed as a characteristic of a single actor or of the system within which the adversaries are acting. See Arthur R. Stein, "Governments, Economic Interdependence, and Cooperation," in *Behavior, Society, and International Conflict*, vol. 3, ed. Philip Tetlock, Jo L. Husbands, Robert Jervis, P. C. Stern, and Charles Tilly (New York: Oxford University Press, 1993).

33. John R. Oneal and Bruce Russett, *International Studies Quarterly* 41 (June 1997): 267–94.

34. For a review of the literature pertaining to international trade and conflict, see Susan M. McMillan, "Interdependence and Conflict," *Mershon International Studies Review* 41 (May 1997): 33–58.

35. See discussion on "internalized ideology" in Roy, *Some Trouble with Cows*, 149–50.

36. Rudy J. Rummel, *Death by Government* (New Brunswick, N.J.: Transaction Books, 1994), 1.

37. P. T. Hopmann, "Negotiating Peace in Central America," *Negotiation Journal* 4 (1988): 361–80; and Paul Wehr and John Paul Lederach, "Mediating Conflict in Central America," *Journal of Peace Research* 28 (1991): 85–98.

38. Kriesberg, *Social Conflicts*.

39. See the discussion of mediation of the conflict in Nicaragua between the Miskitos and the Sandinistas in Dunn and Kriesberg, "Mediating Intermediaries: Expanding Roles of Transnational Organizations."

40. Erich Weede, "Some New Evidence on Correlates of Political Violence: Income Inequality, Regime Repressiveness, and Economic Development, *European Sociological Review* 3 (September 1987): 97–108; E. N. Muller, "Income Inequality and Political Violence: The Effect of Influential Cases," *American Sociological Review* 51 (1986): 441–45.

41. Matthew Krain, "State-Sponsored Mass Murder," *The Journal of Conflict Resolution* 41 (June 1997): 331–60.

42. For accounts of the Armenian genocide of 1915–23, see Vahakn N. Dadrian, "The Secret Young-Turk Ittihadist Conference and the Decisions for the World War I Genocide of the Armenians," *Holocaust and Genocide Studies* 7 (1993): 173–201.

43. I am adapting the use of the term *prescription* from the comments of Allan T. Griffith.

44. Of course, attention to designing such systems has been a part of all human history, as systems to control warfare, communal strife, class conflict, and family relations have been created and modified. Recent work in conflict resolution has fostered

ways of decision making and rule making that engage stakeholders at an early stage to prevent conflicts from arising.

45. See Loraleigh Keashly and Ronald J. Fisher, "Complementarity and Coordination of Conflict Interventions: Taking a Contingency Perspective," in *Resolving International Conflicts,* ed. Jacob Bercovitch (Boulder, Colo.: Lynne Rienner, 1996); Cristopher Mitchell, "The Process and Stages of Mediation," in *Making War and Waging Peace: Foreign Intervention in Africa,* ed. David R. Smock (Washington, D.C.: United States Institute of Peace Press, 1993); and Louis Kriesberg, "The Phases of Destructive Communal Conflicts and Proactive Solutions," in *The International Politics of Ethnic Conflict: Prevention and Peacekeeping,* ed. David Carment and Patrick James (Columbia: University of South Carolina Press, forthcoming).

46. Louis Kriesberg, "Applications and Misapplications of Conflict Resolution Ideas among Conflict Domain," in *Beyond Confrontation: Learning Conflict Resolution in the Post–Cold War Era,* ed. John Vasquez, James T. Johnson, Sanford Jaffe, and Linda Stamato (Ann Arbor: University of Michigan Press, 1995).

47. Louis Kriesberg, "Dilemmas in Nonviolently Settling International Conflicts," in *Forum,* vol. 13, ed. C. Dandeker and J. Kuhlman (Munich: Sozialwissenschaftliches Institut der Budenswehr, 1991), 77–91.

48. The abandonment of the policy of reconstruction was due to many other factors including the resistance of White southerners, the waning of northern enthusiasm to overcome slavery, and increasing economic problems. See John Higham, "America's Three Reconstructions," *New York Review of Books* 17 (6 November 1997): 52–56; and Eric Foner, *Reconstruction: America's Unfinished Revolution, 1863–1877* (New York: Harper and Row, 1988).

49. This important distinction was expounded influentially by Max Weber. See his essays "Politics as a Vocation" and "Science as a Vocation," in H. H. Gerth and C. Wright Mills, trans., *From Max Weber: Essays in Sociology* (New York: Oxford University Press, 1946).

50. Louis Kriesberg, "On Advancing Truth and Morality in Conflict Resolution," in *Conflict Resolution and Social Justice,* ed. Richard Rubenstein and Frank Blechman (forthcoming).

51. Hillary Putnam, *The Many Faces of Realism* (LaSalle, Ill.: Open Court, 1987). Also see the distinction between operational environment and cognized environment, as discussed in R. A. Rubinstein, C. D. Laughlin, and J. McManus, *Science as Cognitive Process: Toward an Empirical Philosophy of Science* (Philadelphia: University of Pennsylvania Press, 1984).

52. John Mueller, *The Retreat from Doomsday: The Obsolescence of Major Wars* (New York: Basic Books, 1983).

53. Stephen D. Krasner, ed., *International Regimes* (Ithaca, N.Y.: Cornell University Press, 1983).

54. David A. Welch, "Can We Think Systematically about Ethics and Statecraft?" *Ethics & International Affairs* 8 (1994): 33.

55. Erik H. Erikson, *Gandhi's Truth* (New York: W. W. Norton, 1969).

56. Some critics of the problem-solving approach to conflict resolution argue that its advocates and practitioners too often try to submerge and ignore moral issues. See for example, Laura Nader, "Harmony Models and the Construction of Law" in *Con-*

flict Resolution: Cross-Cultural Perspectives, ed. Kevin Aruch, Peter W. Black, and Joseph A. Scimeca (New York: Greenwood Press, 1991).

57. James Laue, "Ethical Considerations in Choosing Intervention Roles," *Peace and Change* 8 (Summer 1982): 34; also see James Laue and Gerald Cormick, "The Ethics of Intervention in Community Disputes," in *The Ethics of Social Intervention,* ed. Gordon Bermant, Herbert C. Kelman, and Donald P. Warwick (Washington, D.C.: Halstead Press, 1978). The basic human needs approach as formulated by John Burton also posits a standard by which to judge intervenor and other conflict resolution efforts to satisfy those needs. See Burton, *Conflict: Resolution and Provention.*

Appendix A

Acronyms

ABM	antiballistic missile
ADR	alternative dispute resolution
ANC	African National Congress
ARENA	National Republican Alliance
BATNA	best alternative to a negotiated agreement
CBM	confidence building measure
CDR	complementary dispute resolution
CODESA	Convention for a Democratic South Africa
CORE	Congress of Racial Equality
CPRS	Center for Palestine Research and Studies
CSCE	Conference on Security and Cooperation in Europe
DOD	Department of Defense
DOP	declaration of principles
ESSC	European Coal and Steel Community
FLQ	Front de Liberation du Quebec
FMCS	Federal Mediation and Conciliation Service
FMLN	Farabundo Marti National Liberation Front
GNP	gross national product
GRIT	graduated reciprocation in tension-reduction
IGO	international governmental organization
INF	intermediate-range nuclear forces
LTTE	Liberation Tigers of Tamil Eaalam
MRA	Moral Re-Armament
NAACP	National Association of Colored People
NATO	North Atlantic Treaty Organization
NFWA	National Farm Workers Association
NGO	nongovernmental organization

OPEC	Organization of Petroleum Exporting Countries
OSCE	Organization on Security and Cooperation in Europe
PARC	Program on the Analysis and Resolution of Conflicts
PD	Prisoners' Dilemma
PDFLP	Popular Democratic Front for the Liberation of Palestine
PIP	Partido Independentista Puertorriqueno
PLO	Palestine Liberation Organization
PRC	People's Republic of China
SALT	Strategic Arms Limitation Treaty
SAMED	Syracuse Area Middle-East Dialogue
SCLC	Southern Christian Leadership Conference
TFT	tit for tat
UNESCO	United Nations Educational, Scientific, and Cultural Organization
UNHCR	United Nations High commissioner for refugees
UNPROFOR	United Nations Protection Force
ZOG	Zionist Occupation Government

Appendix B

Selected Organizations
in the Field of Constructive Conflicts

The following list suggests the diversity of organizations contributing to the general process of constructively waging conflicts. The list provides a sampling of centers, associations, and institutions, based in the United States, engaging in relevant activities including:
- degree-granting education (EDU) related to constructive struggle
- intermediary services (INT), including mediation, facilitation, and consultation
- research and theory-building (RTB)
- training (TRA) in conflict resolution and related practices

American Arbitration Association (INT)
140 W. 51st St., New York, N.Y. 10020
Tel: 212/484-4000 Fax: 212/765-4874
Web: www.adr.org

The Carter Center of Emory University (INT, RTB)
One Copenhill, Atlanta, Ga. 30307
Tel: 404/420-5151 Fax: 404/420-5196

CDR Associates (INT, TRA)
100 Arapahoe Ave., Suite 12, Boulder, Colo. 80302
Tel: 303/442-7367

Conflict Research Consortium (EDU, RTB)
University of Colorado, Campus Box 327, Boulder, Colo. 80309
Tel: 303/492-1635 Fax: 303/492-2154
Web: http://www.colorado.edu/conflict

Department of Dispute Resolution (EDU, RTB, TRA)
Nova Southeastern University, 3301 College Ave., Ft. Lauderdale, FL 33314
Web: www.nova.edu/CWIS/centers/ssss/index.html

Educators for Social Responsibility (TRA)
22 Garden St., Cambridge, Mass. 02138
Tel: 617/492-1764

Fellowship of Reconciliation (TRA, INT)
Box 271, Nyack, N.Y. 10960
Tel: 914/358-4601 Fax: 914/358-4924
Web: http://www.nonviolence.org/~nvweb/for

Institute for Conflict Analysis and Resolution (EDU, INT, RTB, TRA)
George Mason University, 4400 University Dr., Fairfax, Va. 22030-4444
Tel: 703/993-1300 Fax: 703/993-1302

Kroc Institute for International Peace Studies (EDU, RTB)
University of Notre Dame, P.O. Box 639, Notre Dame, Ind. 46556-0639
Tel: 219/631-6970

Mennonite Conciliation Service (INT, TRA)
21 South 12th Street, P.O. Box 500, Akron, Penn. 17501-0500
Tel: 717/859-3889

Ohio Commission on Dispute Resolution and Conflict Management (INT, TRA)
77 S. High St., Columbus, Ohio 43266-0124
Tel: 614/752-9595

Program on Conflict Resolution (EDU, INT, RTB, TRA)
University of Hawaii at Manoa, 2424 Maile Way, Honolulu, Hawaii 96822
Tel: 808/956-7792 Fax: 808/956-921

Program on Negotiation at Harvard Law School (EDU, INT, TRA, RTB)
500 Pound Hall, Cambridge, Mass. 02138
Tel: 617/495-1684 Fax: 617/495-7818

Program on the Analysis and Resolution of Conflicts (EDU, INT, RTB, TRA)
Syracuse University, Syracuse, N.Y. 13244
Tel: 315/443-2367 Fax: 315/443-3818
Web: http://www.maxwell.syr.edu/parcmain.htm

Search for Common Ground (INT, TRA)
1601 Connecticut Ave., NW, Washington, D.C. 20009
Tel: 202/265-4300 Fax: 202/232-6718
email: searchcg@igc.apc.org

United States Institute of Peace (RTB, TRA)
1550 M Street, NW, Washington, D.C. 20005-1708
Tel: 202/457-1700 Fax: 202/429-6063
Web: www.usip.org

Index

About the Author

Louis Kriesberg (Ph.D. 1953, University of Chicago) is Professor Emeritus of Sociology and Maxwell Professor Emeritus of Social Conflict Studies at Syracuse University. He was founding director of the Program on the Analysis and Resolution of Conflicts (1986–1994) and continues as an affiliate of PARC. In addition to over 80 book chapters and articles, his published books include: *Social Processes in International Relations* (ed., 1968), *Social Conflicts* (1973, 1982), *Intractable Conflicts and Their Transformation* (co-ed., 1989), *Timing the De-Escalation of International Conflicts* (co-ed., 1991), and *International Conflict Resolution* (1992). He was President of the Society for Social Problems (1983–1984), and he provides consultation and training regarding conflict resolution.